Life on the Autism Spectrum

Matthew Bennett · Amanda A. Webster
Emma Goodall · Susannah Rowland

Life on the Autism Spectrum

Translating Myths and Misconceptions into Positive Futures

Springer

Matthew Bennett
University of Wollongong
Wollongong, NSW, Australia

Amanda A. Webster
University of Wollongong
Wollongong, NSW, Australia

Emma Goodall
University of Wollongong
Wollongong, NSW, Australia

Susannah Rowland
University of Wollongong
Wollongong, NSW, Australia

ISBN 978-981-13-3358-3 ISBN 978-981-13-3359-0 (eBook)
https://doi.org/10.1007/978-981-13-3359-0

Library of Congress Control Number: 2018962125

Illustrations by: India C. Webster

This Springer imprint is published by the registered company Springer Nature Singapore Pte Ltd.
The registered company address is: 152 Beach Road, #21-01/04 Gateway East, Singapore 189721, Singapore

Preface

In 1980, autism was included for the first time as a distinct diagnosis in the third edition of the *Diagnostic and Statistical Manual of Mental Disorders (DSM-III).* This sparked a flurry of speculation, media attention and research, which has only increased in the ensuing decades as more people have attempted to understand the phenomenon of autism. Along with the growing public awareness of autism has come an increasing number of myths and misconceptions about the condition as well as of autistic people. Not only has this created a plethora of inaccurate conceptions about what it means to be "autistic", but many of these myths are centred on the perceived deficits and limitations of autism and autistic individuals. More importantly, it could be argued that this has created a "culture of apprehension and fear" of autism and, by association, of autistic people. Certainly, it has created a public perception that people on the autism spectrum are limited by their autism and are not capable of achieving the same outcomes as their non-autistic peers.

The initial impetus for this book was a desire to analyse and debunk the foremost myths about autism. Upon closer examination, however, we quickly realised that this would involve much more than just presenting the current research and facts. If we wished to truly change the public's attitudes and assumptions about autism, we had to unpack the factors that have created these myths as well as look at the continuing deficit-based beliefs that underlie and maintain them. We would also need to create an alternative perspective of autism and autistic individuals, viewing them not as "disabled" but as unique and capable individuals whose primary need is a support to navigate the complex expectations of their environments and to manage their own innate challenges and anxieties. In this book, we have attempted to create a discourse regarding the myths and mythologies of autism in order to discover the current ways in which these myths are promoting a deficit-based model of autism and negatively impacting and limiting autistic individuals. While we acknowledge that there are a number of autistic individuals who experience ongoing challenges that have a significant impact on their lives, we believe that a dialogue based solely on these individuals' "disabilities" is counterproductive to creating the environments and supports required to enable them to build their knowledge, skills and competencies as adults. Rather, it is our intention to offer an alternative perspective whereby all autistic individuals are viewed as possessing individual strengths and potential competence if they are provided with the opportunities to build on their unique ways of thinking, working and engaging with the world around them. It is our contention that this involves not just enabling autistic individuals to develop the skills needed to engage more effectively with a non-autistic world, it also means that the non-autistic community needs to spend the time and effort to learn the perspectives of autistic individuals so that they can also adjust their ways of working. More than anything, this will necessitate new ways of interaction in which autistic individuals and their non-autistic counterparts listen to each other in order to modify their own personal styles and create new and more effective means of communicating with each other.

This point was illustrated to us as we began to work as a group to complete this text. As a group of autistic and non-autistic individuals, we discovered that to effectively work together, we needed to explore our assumptions both about ourselves and about each other in order to actively listen to each other and recognise that each of us had our own unique ways of looking at the world, and that we could not presume the intentions of the others. To work together, we needed to be open to expressing our individual needs and working through how we could accommodate the needs of each other. We also recognised that we each brought individual skill sets, which although different, added additional elements to provide a comprehensive understanding of the phenomenon of autism. Thus, by working together to write this book, we also developed key learnings we wished to convey through the book.

This book begins, in the first chapter, by exploring the reasons that myths develop and autism myths have become so prevalent in our society. In the subsequent chapters, eleven myths are presented. In each chapter, the origins of each myth are explored, followed by a presentation of the current research and facts relevant to the myth. This is followed by an analysis of the ways in which the myth is continuing to impact autistic individuals. In the final section, we provide an alternative view of the myth and suggest the means required to create a more positive future that empowers autistic individuals rather than focuses on remediating their perceived deficits. Throughout this book, we have utilised identity-first language to reflect the current preference of the autistic community, and to convey a message of empowerment in supporting autistic individuals to claim their identity, rather than be limited by the labels placed on them by others.

In today's society, increasing tensions have developed between the various groups of people involved in the lives of autistic individuals. These include parents and family members, service providers and professionals, researchers, policy-makers and, of course, autistic individuals. It is our hope that through this book, we can stimulate a valuable discussion which can bring these people together so that they can identify their shared goals and create more effective ways of collaboratively working to create opportunities and supports to achieve these goals. Most importantly, we hope that this book offers both a paradigm shift in thinking about the autism spectrum as well as a vision for an alternative and positive future, which supports the competence of all autistic individuals, as well as a pathway for creating that future.

Wollongong, Australia

Amanda A. Webster
On behalf of the authors

Acknowledgements

A book like this takes more than just the effort of the authors. It reflects the experiences and encouragement of a number of people. We would like to acknowledge our families and friends for the tremendous emotional support and understanding they provided as we worked to put this book together. We want to thank them for all the times they listened when the stress threatened to overtake us, and for putting up with all the late nights and weekends we had to spend at our computers.

We would acknowledge the efforts of Katrina Williams who agreed to edit our work and exercised real patience as we rushed to work through very short time frames. We would also like to extend a special thanks to India Webster for bringing our words to life with her wonderful illustrations.

Finally, this book would not be possible without the years of efforts of the many autistic individuals and families who have continued to raise their voice to challenge the prevalent perceptions and expectations of others. It is our wish that this book serves to change these perceptions and give strength to your voice.

Contents

1 Translating Autism Myths into Positive Futures 1
1.1 What Are Myths and How Do They Develop? 2
1.2 Myths About Autism 7
1.3 The Impact of Myths 10
1.4 Transforming Myths 11
1.5 Conclusion 13
References 13

2 Exploring the Identity of Autistic Individuals: Reconstructing the Autism Epidemic Myth 17
2.1 The Origins 18
2.2 The Research 21
2.3 The Impact 26
2.4 The Future 28
2.5 Conclusion 31
References 32

3 Challenging the Public's Perception of Life on Autism Spectrum: The Impact of the Vaccination Myth 37
3.1 The Origins 38
3.2 The Research 44
3.3 The Impact 47
3.4 The Future 50
3.5 Conclusion 53
References 53

4 Establishing Contexts for Support: Undoing the Legacy of the "Refrigerator Mother" Myth 61
4.1 The Origin 62
4.2 The Research 65
4.3 The Impact 68

4.4 The Future 72
4.5 Conclusion 75
References 76

5 Creating Inclusive Societies for Autistic Individuals: Negating the Impact of the "Autism Can Be Cured" Myth 81
5.1 The Origin 82
5.2 The Research 85
5.3 The Impact 88
5.4 The Future 93
5.5 Conclusion 96
References 97

6 Understanding the "True" Potential of Autistic People: Debunking the Savant Syndrome Myth 103
6.1 The Origins 104
6.2 The Research 108
6.3 The Impact 112
6.4 The Future 115
6.5 Conclusion 120
References 120

7 Creating Contexts for Interaction in a Neurotypical World: Confronting Myths of Social Communication and Empathy 125
7.1 The Origins 126
7.2 The Research 130
7.3 The Impact 136
7.4 The Future 139
7.5 Conclusion 143
References 143

8 Constructing Contexts for Success in a Social Society: Undoing the Impact of the Behaviour/Mental Disorder Myth 149
8.1 The Origin 150
8.2 The Research 154
8.3 The Impact 158
8.4 The Future 163
8.5 Conclusion 165
References 165

9 Establishing Social Inclusion the Autism Way: Denying the "They Don't Want Friends" Myth 173
9.1 The Origins 174
9.2 The Research 177

9.3 The Impact 182
9.4 The Future 186
9.5 Conclusion 188
References 189

10 Intimacy and Romance Across the Autism Spectrum: Unpacking the "Not Interested in Sex" Myth 195
10.1 The Origins 196
10.2 The Research 199
10.3 The Impact 202
10.4 The Future 205
10.5 Conclusion 208
References 208

11 Supporting Self-efficacy and Self-determination on the Autism Spectrum: Refuting the "Autism Can Be Outgrown" Myth 213
11.1 The Origins 214
11.2 The Research 217
11.3 The Impact 222
11.4 The Future 223
11.5 Conclusion 226
References 226

Chapter 1
Translating Autism Myths into Positive Futures

Abstract Since *Early Infantile Autism* was first described by Leo Kanner in 1943, myths and misperceptions about the nature of what is now known as autism spectrum disorder (ASD) have proliferated. These myths have played a role in shaping autism research and clinical practice and have impacted the way in which autistic individuals are viewed by others in society. This book will explore popular myths, beliefs and misconceptions about ASD and autistic people. Each chapter explores a different myth and begins by investigating the origins of the myth. The current research and impacts related to each myth will be examined and the underlying themes relevant to the lives of autistic children and adults will be discussed. At the end of each chapter, the authors will discuss the ways in which the myth can be reconstructed, in the light of current knowledge and research, and will provide recommendations for current and future practice. This book will start by reconstructing myths that relate to the ways that autism has been viewed by society. Next, the myths that reflect the public's perception of autistic individuals will be critiqued. Finally, this book will examine myths about the traits and abilities of autistic children and adults and will present an alternative view in which contexts are created and autistic individuals are presumed to be competent and capable of constructing their own futures.

Keywords Autism · Misconceptions · Myths · Pseudoscience

Myths often develop and are used by society to explain less tangible aspects of the world around them (Massey, 2002). Often what starts as an explanation of a tangible phenomenon develops over time to become a persistent and pervasive belief that no longer has any basis in reality. Although some may dismiss the enduring influence that myths and misperceptions can have on people's perceptions and beliefs, many current societal myths have significantly overshadowed scientific findings and resulted in individual actions that defy common sense. For example, the myth that "*you can't*

The use of identity-first language is the preference of many individuals in the autism community (see Kenny et al., 2016). As the voice of the autistic community is integral to the focus of this book, the use of identity-first terms such as autistic individuals, autistic children, and autistic advocates will be used throughout this book.

M. Bennett et al., *Life on the Autism Spectrum*,
https://doi.org/10.1007/978-981-13-3359-0_1

get pregnant if you are breastfeeding" is generally accepted as untrue. However, some young women still cite it as a reason for not using birth control.

Autism is associated with a number of the most persistently sustained myths. These myths have had a significant impact on the lives of autistic individuals and their families as well as on the way that society views and supports them. To be able to understand and negate the impact of these myths, it is important to first look at the nature of myths and how they develop.

1.1 What Are Myths and How Do They Develop?

The *Oxford English* Dictionary defines a myth as a widely held, but false belief or idea. Myths are stories or customs that inform and give meaning to a person, community or culture and are important to help people make sense of their lives (Morris, 1997). However, myths need to be examined to determine if they are having a positive or negative impact on individuals or society, and if negative, how and whether they can be altered.

One of the areas that is most susceptible to myths and misperceptions is the field of psychology. Myths in this area are so common that researchers (Lilienfeld et al., 2009) have coined the term *psychomythology* to describe the misconceptions and urban legends that have permeated the public's understanding of many psychological constructs. In their examination of common psychological myths, Lilienfeld et al. (2009) liken many popular psychological myths to cognitive illusions, which fool the mind rather than the eyes. They argue that these myths become widespread because they align with the first impression or intuition of an individual or group. Mocarski (2014) adds that "myths are stories that speak of meaning and purpose and speak truth to those who take it seriously" (p. 2), while personal, family and cultural mythologies provide a foundation for more deeply embedded beliefs and myths. Mocarski also suggests that the study of myths is really the study of the communities' beliefs and values and the ways that they are passed from one person to the next. Furthermore, myths are not fixed, but are constantly evolving and changing, as society tries to assimilate and reconcile new information with intrinsically held beliefs. It can be argued that all myths contain both elements of truth and misinformation (Csiernik, Forchuk, Speechley, & Ward-Griffin, 2007). It is this combination of fact and misinformation that can have the most negative consequences for individuals.

In many ways, myths are theories that have taken on the illusion of fact in the collective consciousness, without being proven. They are an attempt to provide an explanation for a phenomenon that is observed repeatedly (Hayden, 2014). Myths develop over time and in a variety of ways. Many come from personal experiences, or from stories and beliefs related to culture or religion (Mocarski, 2014). At the foundation of many myths is fear. Many cultures have oral or written stories, or myths, that represent an attempt to explain unusual phenomenon that when not understood, made people afraid. Creating a myth that provides an explanation for the phenomenon can enable people to decrease their fear of the phenomenon.

Myths, particularly those related to health or psychology, often result from the gap between scientific inquiry, which is often highly specialised and difficult to access, and the public's need to make sense of an unexplained but problematic issue. For example, Mocarski (2014) argues that the myth that vaccinations cause autism has grown because there is a gap between the public's understanding and researchers' knowledge about the causes of autism. This example also highlights the intractability of many commonly held myths. Once they become enmeshed in the belief system of a group of individuals, challenging these myths becomes even more difficult, even when scientific research proves the myth has no basis in fact. Complexity of scientific theory can present additional challenges in refuting myths. As scientists have offered complex theories rather than simple explanations about the cause(s) of autism, concerned parents and professionals have often resorted to drawing their own conclusions.

The vaccine-autism myth also meets Mocarski's (2014) criteria of stickiness, which he defines as the lasting appeal that a myth has. To be long-lasting, a myth must have stickiness at all levels, including its origin, the ways it is enacted and the way it is remembered. The vaccine-autism myth has all of these. Pseudoscientists and the media have continued to produce stories that add to the seeming validity of the claim that vaccines are dangerous and may cause autism. Some health practitioners and anti-vaccine groups continue to support parents' refusal of vaccines for their children and continue to discredit scientific claims that vaccines are safe. Because this is such an emotional issue for parents, and autism is often characterised as a condition with harmful consequences, some parents have chosen not to vaccinate their children, deciding that the risk of their child contracting a vaccine-preventable disease is preferable to them developing autism.

Lilienfeld et al. (2009) identify errors in thinking that have led to the development of common psychological myths. These errors in thinking not only create misperceptions and myths, but help to sustain them by spreading them widely. By communicating these myths to more people who view them as plausible, they become so widespread that they become perceived as fact. In other words, they must be true, because everyone knows them and believes them to be so. Each of Lilienfeld et al.'s errors in thinking are commonly found in society and can be used to unpack many of the most widely believed myths.

Lilienfeld et al.'s (2009) first error in thinking is *word of mouth*. This is a particularly effective source of spreading a myth across a community or society. Verbal communication can convey simple, appealing and easily remembered, but fictional statements, which sound true but which are actually false. Word of mouth often relies on short, catchy phrases, which people readily remember. For example, the phrase *"an apple a day keeps the doctor away"* uses rhyme and rhythm to convey the myth that eating an apple every day will make you healthy. Of course, this is a gross oversimplification of the fact. Apples, while a healthy food, do not necessarily keep you healthy. However, the phrase is appealing and easy to remember, so people retain it and start to believe it. More importantly, when they repeat this myth to others, even if they do not believe it consciously, they are conveying their support for this myth. Although none of the myths about autism can be distilled into short, catchy phrases, word of mouth has certainly played a role in their rapid dissemination. One myth that is particularly easy to remember is the myth that autism can be cured. This myth also has the allure of offering a seemingly desirable outcome, which relates to another error of thinking.

A *desire for easy answers and quick fixes* (Lilienfeld et al., 2009), another error of thinking, is particularly likely in situations where individuals encounter problems that are complex and difficult to solve. This creates a tension for people who are motivated to believe that something can easily fix their problem as well as helping to perpetuate their belief that a solution works because they desperately need it to work. For example, for many people who either want or need to lose weight, the idea of exercise and eating healthily on a long-term basis is a daunting and not particularly pleasant prospect. As a result, they may choose instead to believe claims that taking supplements or going on fad diets will help them to lose weight quickly and effortlessly. Of course, this is not a long-term solution and often creates further problems as they may eliminate essential nutrients from their diet. Even if they later recognise that the diet did not work, they may be just as susceptible to the next claim of a miracle cure if it is still viewed as the more palatable option. It is the emotional investment and willingness to believe that create and sustain these types of myths. A similar idea is the belief of many people that special diets such as a gluten–casein-free diet can help to treat or even cure autism. Despite any lack of evidence for its effectiveness (Whitehouse, 2013), the relative simplicity of this approach has made it attractive to many parents.

Selective perception and memory is a third source of myths described by Lilienfeld et al. (2009). This error of thinking is linked to the brain's ability to selectively filter or focus on specific aspects of the environment if they relate to other things the person is already thinking about. For instance, when an individual meets someone who has a unique car, they start to remember other times when they have seen this type of car, or they might notice similar cars throughout the day. Likewise, once an individual has heard a claim or myth that relates to something in their life, they start to see evidence that appears to support the myth. For example, once an individual has heard a claim that a particular herb or oil will "treat" autism, they might perceive many ways in which the autistic individual has improved after they have been "treated". Unfortunately, while the individual is becoming aware of supporting examples, their brain is also filtering out other information which does not support the myth. In the example above, the parent or professional may be so focused on seeing improvement, that they may unconsciously dismiss evidence that shows the treatment is not effective. Since the brain is focused on seeing a certain detail, it tends to be more alert to its occurrence. It is this selective memory that supports the placebo effect that is sometimes noticed when people believe something is working.

Lilienfeld et al.'s (2009) next two errors of thinking are related to a tendency to see a relationship between two factors, which does not exist. The first of these, *inferring causation from correlation,* occurs when individuals assume that because two things are related, one must cause the other. The second, *post hoc, ergo propter hoc reasoning* relates to the belief that just because one thing occurs before another, it must cause that event or action. Both of these are common to psychological and health-related myths, but fail to consider the relevance of additional factors, which may actually be the cause of both the first and second elements. For example, many people have speculated that gut bacteria causes autism or autistic symptomology due to the fact that a person reports having pain before they exhibit other behaviours such as non-compliance or tantrums. It is possible, however, that sensory sensitivity to certain foods may result in poor nutrition and eventual gut problems. Alternatively, anxiety associated with autism may contribute to gut problems rather than vice versa. In addition, a new field of research (Mulle, Sharp, & Cubells, 2013) is investigating whether genetic differences that may cause autism also cause gut problems. In other words, both autism and gut problems could be attributed to a third physiological factor such as genetic anomalies.

The next error of thinking leading to myths is *exposure to a biased sample* (Lilienfeld et al., 2009). This happens when people make generalisations and judgments about a wider group of people based on their experience with a specific group. Basically, people form conclusions based on their subjective perception rather than the evidence. For example, a teacher who works with students with intellectual disabilities in an inner-city school where many students come from homes that are impacted by violence and drugs might conclude that most individuals with intellectual disabilities come from violent and drug-addicted parents. Of course, this is patently untrue and illustrates the natural human tendency to overgeneralise from personal experience. In another example, a person who has met a group of non-verbal autistic children may assume that all autistics cannot talk. This is why scientific inquiry and collection of objective evidence are so important.

Reasoning by representation is another source of myths in which individuals demonstrate a tendency to see relationships that do not exist (Lilienfeld et al., 2009). This error in thinking occurs when people assume that two things, which appear similar, are connected. For instance, a person may meet someone from a specific location and assume that this individual has a connection to another person from the same location. Another example is assuming that all people diagnosed with autism spectrum disorder will display similar behaviours or needs.

In today's society, *misleading film and media portrayals* have played a significant role in shaping people's beliefs, including creating false beliefs that eventually become myths (Lilienfeld et al., 2009). To get ratings, the media may dramatise phenomena in an effort to create a story or to make mundane facts more interesting and appealing to their audience (Beins, 2008). For instance, it is much more interesting to present stories about individuals with autism who have savant skills such as Raymond Babbitt from the movie *Rain Man* than it is to portray the average autistic person who does not have these skills. This overrepresentation of individuals with savant abilities has contributed to the myth that autism is synonymous with savant syndrome. Another of Lilienfeld et al.'s errors of thinking, *exaggeration of a kernel of truth,* is similar as it involves an exaggeration of claims that are based, at least in part, on fact. Since they have some basis in truth, these errors in thinking may be perceived as having a particular claim to legitimacy. An example of this is the common myth that autism is synonymous with behaviour disorders. Although it is true that some individuals, particularly children, diagnosed with autism spectrum disorder do exhibit challenging behaviours, these behaviours can be the product of a variety of individual and/or environmental factors. Certainly, it would be a gross exaggeration to suggest that all autistic children have behaviour disorders.

The last error of thinking is particularly common in scientific fields, such as psychology and social sciences. *Terminological confusion* results when people make the wrong assumptions about scientific or medical terms and vocabulary (Lilienfeld et al., 2009). Terminological confusion may arise from an incomplete understanding of specific terms or from the changing meanings given to terms over time. For example, the terms aural and oral are often confused as they are homonyms, and both relate to communication. Aural relates to the ear and the sense of hearing, whereas oral is linked to the operations of the mouth. In another example, the term dichotomy is often misused as a reference to a difference between two things when it actually means two mutually exclusive alternatives, like black or white. The term autism has undergone several changes since it was first used in 1911 (Greydanus & Toledo-Pereyra, 2012). Originally used to denote a form of schizophrenia, research over the past 30 years has significantly advanced the understanding of autism as a distinct neurodevelopmental condition. Despite this, there are still many who question the overlap between these two conditions (Fitzgerald, 2013).

The errors of thinking identified by Lilienfeld et al. (2009) provide a starting point for understanding many of the notable myths about child development and psychology. A number of these have become indistinguishable from fact in the public perception. In their book, *Great Myths of Child Development,* Hupp and Jewell (2015) describe a set of criteria for what they call the "great myths". These are myths that have taken hold in the public consciousness, are held as fact by a large number of people and have had a wide-reaching impact. Hupp and Jewell's criteria include:

- A lot of people have heard the myth;
- A lot of people currently believe the myth;
- The myth sounds true and is believable;

- The myth is supported by some professionals (or pseudoscientists);
- There is a great deal of scientific evidence to contradict the myth;
- People's belief in the myth can cause harm; and
- The myth discourages the use of another scientifically supported practice.

Hupp and Jewell (2015) and Lilienfeld et al. (2009) have explored some of the most widely held myths in the fields of psychology and child development. These include common myths such as *"you can learn languages in your sleep"*, *"handwriting reveals personality traits"* and *"dolphin therapy helps children with disabilities"*. All of these myths carry a degree of credibility with at least some individuals, but are not supported by evidence. All meet Hupp and Jewell's criteria for great myths. As one of these criteria is that myths cause harm, it is important that great myths be examined to ascertain their origins, to understand how to change the public's perception into a more accurate and scientific view, and to prevent further harm from occurring.

1.2 Myths About Autism

Autism is a field, which has been particularly susceptible to myths. Both Lilienfeld et al. (2009) and Hupp and Jewell (2015) include myths about autism in their discussion of great myths. Given autism's complicated history, and the diverse spectrum of characteristics and behaviours exhibited by autistic individuals, it is not surprising that a number of myths have developed in this area (Mocarski, 2014). Many of these can be linked to Lilienfeld et al.'s errors in thinking. For instance, assuming the relationship between autism symptomology and an external factor means that this factor must in some way cause autism is an example of *inferring causation from correlation.*

The media has also played a significant role in the spread of autism myths by presenting speculations about autistic individuals and airing debates about the causes and treatments for autism, without providing research or scientific evidence to support these stories. Some myths, such as the belief that vaccines cause autism, have been particularly sensationalised in the media, which is further compounded by statements of support from a number of celebrities such as Jenny McCarthy and Robert Kennedy Jr. (Offit, 2008). Vyse (2005) argues that celebrities possess a significant amount of power and can influence the public's attitudes and beliefs. When they promote misperceptions about autism, they help to build the public's perception that these beliefs have credibility (Nyhan, 2016).

Although autism myths have developed in different ways, the need for explanations and solutions to pressing problems, particularly from parents seeking answers and information to help their children, lies at the core of most myths about autism. Since autism was first identified in the 1940s, scientists and researchers have worked to gain an understanding of the nature of autism and the common characteristics demonstrated by autistic individuals. Unfortunately, much of the knowledge and research generated is not easily accessible to the public or has been very slowly disseminated (Pellicano & Stears, 2011).

More importantly, scientific research is often written in complex and difficult terminology, containing statistics and findings that are not easily interpreted by lay people who are not researchers or scientists. As Mocarski (2014) explains, the gap between scientific knowledge and public knowledge creates a climate for myths to develop. It could be argued that this is especially true in situations where people are dealing with highly emotional and stressful situations, and in which they face challenges for which they feel they have few answers or support. This is the case for a number of parents and professionals working with autistic children.

Two other reasons that myths about autism have become so widespread are the proliferation of popular psychology (Lilienfeld, Lynn, Ruscio, & Beyerstein, 2011) and a distrust of research and scientific inquiry (Camargo & Grant, 2015). In the twenty-first century, lay psychology has become common. This is evidenced by the number of self-help books and other types of sources promoting solutions for a variety of issues experienced by families and autistic individuals, such as dealing with anxiety and stress, curing children and eliminating challenging behaviours. It could be argued that the increased proliferation of self-help material has at least partly resulted from an increased public awareness of the link between mental health and emotional well-being and physiological health and positive outcomes and success.

This awareness has helped generate an increase in funding for psychological issues, which may have also contributed to the number of people offering services and treatments, many of whom may not have adequate training in scientific inquiry or evidence-based practices. This is evident in the number of individuals who have begun offering applied behaviour analysis (ABA) services and therapy as the market and money available for these services has increased. Keenan, Dillenburger, Moderato, and Rottgers (2010) contend that this has damaged the public's perception of the benefits of ABA, as practitioners who may be primarily interested in monetary gain have employed poor strategies under the guise of ABA. Unfortunately, these individuals and other popular psychology sources are readily available via the Internet and other media. Although these sources can provide high-quality information about human behaviour or topics such as autism, they often contain an equal, if not greater amount, of misinformation. Lilienfeld et al. (2009) term this body of misinformation *psychomythology* because it perpetuates myths and misunderstandings about topics related to the field of psychology.

Pseudoscience involves the use of scientific-sounding terminology and statistics to persuade people that an approach is backed by science. Unlike real science, which may take years or decades to research a hypothesis or practice, pseudoscience often offers quick and easy cures, meeting people's need for a rapid solution. As mentioned earlier, people tend to believe information they believe is likely to be true (Schwarz, Sanna, Skurnik, & Yoon, 2007) or that appeals to, or fits with, their beliefs and worldview (Nyhan, 2016). To counteract pseudoscience and psychomythology, the public needs access to accurate information that provides them with answers and helps them to adjust their faulty predispositions. Unfortunately, researchers have found a growing gap between scientists and the public (Mocarski, 2014). This gap can be attributed to an unavailability of research information, which may be either physically or technically inaccessible for most people. Unlike psychomythology and pseudoscientific claims, which are readily available via the Internet and news media, scientific studies are generally only published in technical journals and are only accessible through a subscription. As the majority of the public would lack knowledge of scientific inquiry, research methods, statistics or research-specific vocabulary, they may find research studies perplexing, intimidating or even threatening (Nyhan & Reifler, 2015). These barriers mean that much of the public, including parents, are unable to easily access understandable and credible research which has a high level of evidence. In contrast, popular psychology is presented in language designed to be easily understood and persuasive and is more readily available and more easily accessible. Furthermore, popular psychology gives parents searching for ways to help their children answers which sound appealing while offering them hope. These claims may also refute scientific knowledge, giving individuals even more reason to rely on and trust information they access via the Internet rather than accessing scientific research.

The inaccessibility of scientific research has meant that the majority of research information is disseminated through individuals or organisations who act as translators for the general public (Mocarski, 2014). Translators of autism research can include professionals such as physicians or psychologists, academic staff and autism organisations, who may also create distrust among individuals seeking information. Researchers have found that both parents and autistic individuals have expressed their distrust of researchers because of past experiences (Pellicano, Dinsmore, & Charman, 2014a). Harrington, Patrick, Edwards, and Brand (2006) found that parents of autistic children were distrustful of medical professionals who they felt had not listened to them or who had been slow in providing a diagnosis for their child and helping them to access appropriate support. In addition, parents have reported that they do not trust education staff who do not acknowledge the parents' knowledge about their children (Webster, Cumming, & Rowland, 2017). Another example of public distrust of autism research is the continued belief that vaccinations cause autism, despite the overwhelming amount of research disproving this claim. Not only has research not changed the view of many people about vaccinations, but it may have actually increased anti-vaccine resistance (Nyhan, Reifler, Richey, & Freed, 2014) due to the insistence of some individuals who have interpreted research information as continuing evidence of the motivation of pharmaceutical companies to sell their vaccines (Yaqub, Castle-Clarke, Sevdalis, & Chataway, 2014).

Researchers have also highlighted a division between the research and autistic communities. Milton (2014) cites several reasons why autistic adults have developed a mistrust of researchers. These include a failure to consider their views in research, research priorities that do not align with the priorities of the autistic community, and a lack of engagement between researchers and the autistic community. Milton recommends that the expertise of autistic individuals needs to be acknowledged by researchers and funding bodies. Pellicano et al. (2014a) conducted a study to ascertain the views of researchers, parents and autistic adults regarding researchers' engagement of autistic individuals and their families. Pellicano et al. found that researchers believed they were engaged with the autistic community, whereas parents and autistic adults did not share this view. Researchers were sceptical about the ability of non-researchers to engage in the research process, while parents and autistic adults spoke about the difficulties they encountered in being included and having a voice in research processes. Pellicano et al. recommended that researches utilise a more participatory and "user-friendly" approach, so that research is not seen as the purview of Ph.D.'s and scientists, but as a process of working together to solve problems that directly impact the autistic community. Not only would this help parents and autistic individuals to have a more ongoing investment and belief in autism research, but it would also make this more accessible and meaningful to professionals working with autistic individuals.

1.3 The Impact of Myths

To better understand some of the myths and misconceptions about autism, John, Knott, and Harvey (2018) conducted focus groups with a community sample of non-autistic students and community members. They found that participants disclosed seven beliefs and misperceptions about individuals diagnosed with autism. The first four beliefs were related to social interactions and included the beliefs that autistic individuals: (1) do not want social relationships; (2) do not like being touched; (3) are all introverts; and (4) are unable to notice rejection. The fifth misperception was that autistic people have special talents, and the last two were that they are dangerous or mad. The researchers concluded that inaccurate beliefs about autism were common and probably had an impact on the ways that most people treat or even stigmatise autistic individuals. They also suggested that providing people with accurate information and positive contact with autistic children and adults may help reduce their anxiety about social contact with these autistic persons and dispel some of their misconceptions about these individuals. Although the myths identified by John et al. are just some of the myths that people hold about autism, they do indicate how widespread these beliefs may be and the impact they may have on the ways in which people view and engage with autistic people.

By definition, great myths cause harm, but they can also impact individuals in other ways, both directly and indirectly (Hupp & Jewell, 2015). Lilienfeld et al. (2009) have identified three reasons why myths need to be examined. First, myths can cause direct physical or emotional harm. For example, the myth that vaccines cause autism has resulted in lower vaccination rates and higher rates of vaccine-preventable diseases, like measles and whooping cough. Lower vaccination rates have resulted in more deaths (Flaherty, 2011). Similarly, autistic people have suffered physical harm and some have died when subjected to holding therapy, a therapy based on the myth that autism is caused by limited bonding between parents and their child in the early months of life (Mercer, 2013).

Secondly, myths can cause indirect damage. An example of indirect damage is seen when parents and professionals spend time and money on interventions and strategies that are ineffective or even harmful. Not only does this deplete their resources, but it delays access to supports, which might be effective. For example, believing that autism can be cured, parents, organisations and even governments have devoted a great deal of money to finding a cure. This has consequently decreased the money that is available for supports and services and has led many individuals and families to protest that they need resources to support them now, and not at some point in the future that may or may not ever eventuate (Pellicano, Dinsmore, & Charman, 2014b). Furthermore, the mistaken belief that autistic children and adults do not want social relationships may cause indirect harm by way of excluding them unnecessarily from opportunities for social interaction. Additionally, beliefs that autistic individuals are dangerous or mad may influence the behavioural intentions that people have towards these individuals and may result in them avoiding or excluding them from environments and groups (Csiernik, Forchuk, Speechley, & Ward-Griffin, 2007).

Third, acceptance of myths may impede the ability of individuals to exercise critical thinking and judgement (Lilienfeld et al., 2009). As an example, Matson, Adams, Williams, and Rieske (2013) found that parents with higher levels of education are just as susceptible as less-educated parents to try fad treatments. Myths may result in confusion, feelings of disempowerment and helplessness for parents and service providers about the strategies that will most effectively support their child or client, and may distract them from utilising more scientifically proven approaches (Lilienfeld et al., 2009). Moreover, myths represent beliefs that motivate people to act in ways they view as positive, preventing them from seeing the negative consequences of their actions. Mocarski (2014) contends that with time, these myths and actions become viewed as normal, resulting in long-term detrimental impacts for both individuals and the community.

1.4 Transforming Myths

If myths about autism are pervasive, and have a widespread impact, it is critical that these myths be explored to expose the reasons that continue to resonate with people's beliefs and values. To counteract the current negative impact of autism myths, misperceptions and false beliefs must be transformed into new and positive understandings that enable people to gain new insight into current issues and to engage in new ways of thinking about these issues that offer a more positive perception of future possibilities for autistic individuals, their families and support networks. To do this, it is important to examine both the false beliefs regarding autism as well as the origins of these beliefs. This will facilitate a better understanding of how and why different myths align with people's perceptions and needs as well as help prevent future autism myths from arising (Scudellari, 2015). One of the best ways to correct a myth is to link a misconception with the truth. To correct misconceptions about autism, parents and professionals need ready access to accurate, trustworthy research that addresses their beliefs and needs. This information should be presented in easily understandable language, using terms that will help the public make sense of technical information that is often confusing and frightening and enables them to make more informed choices and decisions.

Lilienfeld et al. (2009) caution that debunking myths can backfire, as memory is often selective. Thus, people may forget the new information they have gathered about the myth, creating a misplaced, but increased belief in the myth itself. For example, attempting to correct the vaccine-autism myth may strengthen a person's belief that autism is caused by vaccines as they may not remember the complex science indicating that vaccines do not cause autism, but simply remember vaccines cause autism. In this example, it is important that a wide range of accurate and easily accessible information is made available to the public about vaccinations and autism. This information also needs to challenge the views that make them hold onto current beliefs about autism and vaccinations in order to enable them to trust and be open to incorporating new knowledge. This will allow the facts about vaccinations and autism to be more widely understood giving the myth less authority and credibility.

In a recent study, Gillespie-Lynch et al. (2015) found that by providing college students with clear information about autistic individuals, and accurate information about common autism myths, their misperceptions about autism were successfully changed and their positive attitudes, acceptance and desire to interact with their autistic peers increased. Educating the public is essential if meaningful alternatives are to be explored that will support autistic children and adults. Increasing public knowledge and decreasing misconceptions will also reduce the stigma associated with autism and will facilitate more productive discussions of how to create environments and practices that support and empower autistic people.

Mocarski (2014) argues that reducing the negative impacts of myths involves uncovering the tensions and voices of the people whom the myth silences, as well as the tensions and voices of the people whom the myth supports. To address the needs of both groups necessitates communicating information in ways that enable both groups to find common ground and to develop a shared understanding and alternative perception of the phenomena. It is hoped that examining the origins, research and impact of common autism myths will facilitate a shared understanding between the autistic and non-autistic communities about the true capabilities of autistic people, decreasing the fear that is at the core of many autism myths and creating an alternative perception of the potential of autistic people. Instead of focusing on the ways in which autism is perceived as limiting the lives of individuals and their families, transforming these myths will offer an alternate outlook in which autistic individuals are regarded as valuable community members who are capable of having a voice in constructing supports and services that better enable them to succeed. It is only through constructing new ways of thinking that the myths of autism will be truly discredited, paving the way for the public to not just envision a more positive future for autistic people, but to actively create a more inclusive society in which both autistic and non-autistic individuals are empowered as equal partners.

1.5 Conclusion

In conclusion, people use myths to make sense of phenomenon, which they have observed, but do not understand. Myths may have some basis in fact, but contain more inaccurate than accurate information, misleading people into beliefs or actions that have a range of negative and long-term impacts for everyone involved. In the twenty-first century, many myths have developed because of a gap between science and common knowledge, resulting in psychomythology and pseudoscience. One area that has been particularly susceptible to the development of myths is the field of autism. Currently, there are many myths both about autism and about autistic people. These myths often have their source in the emotions of confusion, anxiety and fear as parents and members of the community have tried to understand and support autistic children and adults whom they see struggling to meet challenges in everyday life. This has led to widespread misperceptions in the community about autism and has contributed to stigma and barriers to the enactment of positive strategies for autistic people. To counter these negative perceptions, accurate and accessible information and positive alternatives of thinking are needed.

In the remainder of this book, we will examine the origins of some of the most common myths about autism to understand how and why these beliefs have developed. We will then present the most current research and information to address the beliefs, emotions and tensions behind these myths and will analyse the impact of these myths for the autistic community, their families and the wider community. Finally, we will offer an alternative way of thinking to provide more positive and supportive environments in which autistic individuals can contribute fully and equally as members in a diverse society.

References

Beins, B. C. (2008). Why we believe: Fostering critical thought and scientific literacy in research methods. In *Teaching critical thinking in psychology: A handbook of best practices* (pp. 199–210). Wiley-Blackwell: Malden, MA.

Camargo, K., Jr., & Grant, R. (2015). Public health, science, and policy debate: Being right is not enough. *American Journal of Public Health, 105*(2), 232–235. https://doi.org/10.2105/AJPH.2014.302241.

Csiernik, R., Forchuk, C., Speechley, M., & Ward-Griffin, C. (2007). De" myth" ifying mental health—Findings from a Community University Research Alliance (CURA). *Critical Social Work, 8*(1).

Fitzgerald, M. (2013). Overlap between autism and schizophrenia: History and current status. *Advances in Mental Health and Intellectual Disabilities, 8*(1), 15–23. https://doi.org/10.1108/amhid-09-2013-0058.

Flaherty, D. K. (2011). The vaccine-autism connection: A public health crises caused by unethical medical practices and fraudulent science. *Annals of Pharmacotherapy, 45*(10), 1302–1304. https://doi.org/10.1345/aph.1Q318.

Gillespie-Lynch, K., Brooks, P. J., Someki, F., Obeid, R., Shane-Simpson, C., Kapp, S. K., … Smith, D. S. (2015). Changing college students' conceptions of autism: An online training to

increase knowledge and decrease stigma. *Journal of Autism and Developmental Disorders, 45*(8), 2553–2566. https://doi.org/10.1007/s10803-015-2422-9.
Greydanus, D. E., & Toledo-Pereyra, L. H. (2012). Historical perspectives on autism: Its past record of discovery and its present state of solipsism, skepticism, and sorrowful suspicion. *Pediatric Clinics of North America, 59*(1), 1–11. https://doi.org/10.1016/j.pcl.2011.10.004.
Harrington, J. W., Patrick, P. A., Edwards, K. S., & Brand, D. A. (2006). Parental beliefs about autism: Implications for the treating physician. *Autism, 10*(5), 452–462. https://doi.org/10.1177/1362361306066609.
Hayden, J. A. (2014). *Introduction to health behavior theory* (2nd ed.). Burlington, MA: Jones & Bartlett Publishers.
Hupp, S., & Jewell, J. (2015). *Great myths of child development* (1st ed.). Malden, MA; Chichester, West Sussex, Wiley-Blackwell.
John, R., Knott, F. J., & Harvey, K. N. (2018). Myths about autism: An exploratory study using focus groups. *Autism, 22*(7), 845–854. https://doi.org/10.1177/1362361317714990.
Keenan, M., Dillenburger, K., Moderato, P., & Rottgers, H.-R. (2010). Science for sale in a free market economy: But at what price? ABA and the treatment of autism in europe. *Behavior and Social Issues, 19,* 126–143.
Kenny, L., Hattersley, C., Molins, B., Buckley, C., Povey, C., & Pellicano, E. (2016). Which terms should be used to describe autism? Perspectives from the UK autism community. *Autism, 20*(4), 442–462. https://doi.org/10.1177/1362361315588200.
Lilienfeld, S. O., Lynn, S. J., Ruscio, J., & Beyerstein, B. L. (2009). *50 great myths of popular psychology: Shattering widespread misconceptions about human behavior*, Hoboken, NJ: John Wiley & Sons.
Lilienfeld, S. O., Lynn, S. J., Ruscio, J., & Beyerstein, B. L. (2011). *50 great myths of popular psychology: Shattering widespread misconceptions about human behavior*. Hoboken, NJ: Wiley.
Massey, D. S. (2002). A brief history of human society: The origin and role of emotion in social life. *American Sociological Review, 67*(1), 1.
Matson, J. L., Adams, H. L., Williams, L. W., & Rieske, R. D. (2013). Why are there so many unsubstantiated treatments in autism? *Research in Autism Spectrum Disorders, 7*(3), 466–474. https://doi.org/10.1016/j.rasd.2012.11.006.
Mercer, J. (2013). Holding therapy in Britain: Historical background, recent events, and ethical concerns. *Adoption & Fostering, 37*(2), 144–156. https://doi.org/10.1177/0308575913490498.
Milton, D. E. (2014). Autistic expertise: A critical reflection on the production of knowledge in autism studies. *Autism, 18*(7), 794–802. https://doi.org/10.1177/1362361314525281.
Mocarski, R. (2014). *Health mythologies: Developing an understanding of health myths and how they stick and spread through the vaccines cause autism myth*i. Doctoral thesis, The University of Alabama. Retrieved from https://search-proquest-com.libraryproxy.griffith.edu.au/docview/1620540756?pq-origsite=summon.
Morris, R. (1997). Myths of sexuality education. *Journal of Moral Education, 26*(3), 353–361. https://doi.org/10.1080/0305724970260309.
Mulle, J. G., Sharp, W. G., & Cubells, J. F. (2013). The gut microbiome: A new frontier in autism research. *Current Psychiatry Reports, 15*(2), 337. https://doi.org/10.1007/s11920-012-0337-0.
Nyhan, B. (2016). *The challenge of false beliefs*. Paper presented at the how we can improve health Science communication, University of MIchigan, Ann Arbor. https://www.isr.umich.edu/cps/events/Nyhan_20160613.pdf.
Nyhan, B., & Reifler, J. (2015). The roles of information deficits and identity threat in the prevalence of misperceptions. *Journal of Elections, Public Opinion and Parties* (Manuscript submitted for publication).
Nyhan, B., Reifler, J., Richey, S., & Freed, G. L. (2014). Effective messages in vaccine promotion: A randomized trial. *Pediatrics, 133*(4), e835–3842. https://doi.org/10.1542/peds.2013-2365.
Offit, P. A. (2008). *Autism's false prophets: Bad science, risky medicine, and the search for a cure*. New York: Columbia University Press.

Pellicano, E., Dinsmore, A., & Charman, T. (2014a). Views on researcher-community engagement in autism research in the United Kingdom: A mixed-methods study. *PLoS ONE, 9*(10), e109946. https://doi.org/10.1371/journal.pone.0109946.

Pellicano, E., Dinsmore, A., & Charman, T. (2014b). What should autism research focus upon? Community views and priorities from the United Kingdom. *Autism, 18*(7), 756–770. https://doi.org/10.1177/1362361314529627.

Pellicano, E., & Stears, M. (2011). Bridging autism, science and society: Moving toward an ethically informed approach to autism research. *Autism Research, 4*(4), 271–282. https://doi.org/10.1002/aur.201.

Schwarz, N., Sanna, L. J., Skurnik, I., & Yoon, C. (2007). Metacognitive experiences and the intricacies of setting people straight: Implications for debiasing and public information campaigns. *Advances in Experimental Social Psychology, 39,* 127–161. https://doi.org/10.1016/S0065-2601(06)39003-X.

Scudellari, M. (2015). The science of myths that will not die. *Nature, 528,* 322–325.

Vyse, S. (2005). Where do fads come from? In J. Jacobson, R. Foxx, & J. A. Mulick (Eds.), *Controversial therapies for developmental disabilities: Fad, fashion, and science in professional practice* (pp. 3–18). Mahwah, NJ: Erlbaum.

Webster, A. A., Cumming, J., & Rowland, S. (2017). *Empowering parents of children with autism spectrum disorder: Critical decision-making for quality outcomes*. Singapore: Springer.

Whitehouse, A. J. (2013). Complementary and alternative medicine for autism spectrum disorders: Rationale, safety and efficacy. *Journal of Paediatrics and Child Health, 49,* E438–E442. https://doi.org/10.1111/jpc.12242.

Wing, L. (1997). The history of ideas on autism: Legends, myths and reality. *Autism, 1*(1), 13–23. https://doi.org/10.1177/1362361397011004.

Yaqub, O., Castle-Clarke, S., Sevdalis, N., & Chataway, J. (2014). Attitudes to vaccination: A critical review. *Social Science and Medicine, 112,* 1–11. https://doi.org/10.1016/j.socscimed.2014.04.018.

Chapter 2
Exploring the Identity of Autistic Individuals: Reconstructing the Autism Epidemic Myth

Abstract Currently, there is much discussion in print, online and television media across the world about the "autism epidemic". Although the rates of diagnoses of autism spectrum disorder (ASD) have increased, it could not accurately be described as an "epidemic". This chapter begins with an examination of the origins of this myth and an overview of studies, which have measured the prevalence of autism spectrum diagnoses. It then explores current theories surrounding the increasing numbers of individuals who have received a diagnosis of ASD, with specific attention to the changing diagnostic criteria and greater awareness of the autism spectrum among parents, teachers and healthcare professionals including paediatricians and psychologists. The impact of this myth for the autistic community will be explored, and the implications of a neurodiversity paradigm on revising perceptions around the autism epidemic myth will be discussed. The chapter will conclude with an exploration of the benefits of shifting current thinking from viewing the increasing prevalence of autism as an "epidemic" to be stopped, to developing a consciousness of autistic individuals as comprising part of the natural variation of society who encompass a range of strengths and needs.

Keywords History and diagnosis of ASD · Prevalence · Incidence
Public awareness · Neurodiversity theory

M. Bennett et al., *Life on the Autism Spectrum*,
https://doi.org/10.1007/978-981-13-3359-0_2

Before autism was included as a diagnostic category in 1980, the condition was unfamiliar to many people including medical professionals and the general public. Following its inclusion in the third edition of the *Diagnostic and Statistical Manual of Mental Disorders* (*DSM-III*) and the addition of Asperger's syndrome in the *DSM-IV* in 1994, the visibility and recognition of autism among the public increased rapidly. The changes in diagnosis and the increased public awareness led to an increased incidence of autism and other pervasive developmental disorders. This created the myth of an "autism epidemic" and established a belief that an external factor must be causing this "disorder" to spread rapidly.

2.1 The Origins

The "autism epidemic" myth is one of the more recent myths about autism and arguably one of the most publicised. In the decades following the publication of Kanner's (1943) original study of autistic individuals, autism was considered to be a rare condition, affecting approximately two to four children per 10,000. Since the late 1990s, researchers have reported a steady annual increase in the reported incidence and prevalence rates of autism (Centers for Disease Control and Prevention, 2018; Özerk, 2016). In the USA, the Autism and Developmental Disabilities Monitoring (ADDM) network is funded by the Centre for Disease Control and Prevention (CDC) to collect data and publish detailed prevalence estimates on the number of children who are 8-years-old and have a diagnosis of autism spectrum disorder (ASD) (Özerk, 2016; Sheldrick & Carter, 2018). In 2000 and 2002, estimates from the ADDM network indicated that 1 in 150 American children had a diagnosis of ASD. This number has progressively risen, with 1 in 125 children having a diagnosis of ASD in 2004, 1 in 110 in 2006, 1 in 88 in 2008, 1 in 68 in 2010 and 2012, and 1 in 59 in 2014 (Centers for Disease Control and Prevention, 2018). Furthermore, a review of over 50 empirical studies published between 2000 and 2016 across 21 countries, revealed that this trend has been reflected worldwide as prevalence rates have risen in a number of countries (Özerk, 2016).

As prevalence (i.e. number of diagnosed individuals in the total population) and incidence (i.e. number of new diagnoses per year) rates have climbed, media coverage of the rates of autism diagnoses has also increased. This has created both a heightened public awareness of autism and a growing concern about the expanding incidence of autism. While there is little doubt that both the incidence and prevalence of autism have increased (Nassar et al., 2009), rising statistics alone do not constitute a cause for alarm, as a number of simple factors could have contributed to these statistics. These include changes to the way in which public health authorities measure the incidence and prevalence of autism (Nassar et al., 2009), changes in the criteria used to diagnose autism (Beighley & Matson, 2014), and increased awareness and knowledge of autism among health professionals and parents (Elsabbagh et al., 2012). Unfortunately, the rising numbers have often been interpreted to mean that some new factor is at work that is suddenly making people more at risk of developing autism.

The news media plays a significant role in shaping public opinions (Jones & Harwood, 2009). The proliferation of news stories has been instrumental in promoting public awareness and alarm around the growing incidence and prevalence rates for autism. As these rates have increased (Centers for Disease Control and Prevention, 2018; Sheldrick & Carter, 2018), the media's attention on autism has grown as well (McKeever, 2013; Zhai, Sun, Wang, & Ding, 2017). In an analysis of more than 3,500 health stories across 48 different US news services, autism was one of the top five stories included in health news (Pew Research Center, 2008). Between 1996 and 2005, there were a total of 1,515 articles about autism published in Australian newspapers. These articles have increased exponentially each year, with nine articles published in 1996, 26 in 1998, 68 in 2000, 247 in 2002, 380 in 2004 and 310 in 2005 (Jones & Harwood, 2009). Likewise, both *The New York Times* and *The Washington Post* increased their coverage of autism-related statistics and stories exponentially in the period between 1996 and 2006.

The media's focus on autism has also increased public awareness of both the nature of autism and of the rising rates of autism incidence and prevalence. Ebben (2018) suggests that many of these news items and articles include metaphors of danger and contagion, which encourage the public to take action to stop the spread of something that is perceived as a threat or harmful to the general public. These stories convey a sense of urgency, implying that only prompt action will stop an impending disaster and restore a state of normalcy. Ebben argues that frequent discussions of environmental or biological causes and potential cures imply that underlying contagious elements are to blame, for the spread of autism. Even when these stories do not use the word "epidemic", metaphors of contagion, disease and cure help to instil a public perception and belief that increasing prevalence and incidence rates constitute an epidemic.

The growing media attention on autism has also increased the public's interest in autistic people. This is evident in the growing number of fictional characters displaying autistic traits that have been increasingly featured in television programs (e.g. *Parenthood*, *The Good Doctor*) and movies (e.g. *Rain Man*, *Salmon Fishing in the Yemen*) (Belcher & Maich, 2014). Additionally, autism awareness campaigns such as *Light It Up Blue* and autism funding organisation such as *Autism Speaks* have helped to increase the visibility of autism within society (Dillenburger, Jordan, McKerr, Devine, & Keenan, 2013). Similar to the news media, in an effort to raise money, these organisations often use language and images that liken autism to a dangerous disease that has harmed potentially "normal" children (Broderick, 2009).

The popularity of public forums and social media has allowed a number of autistic individuals to share their thoughts and experiences with the public. For instance, on the internet portal, *Aspies for Freedom*, autistic individuals from a number of countries have generated more than half a million posts since 2004 (Owren, 2013). Similarly, the number of autistic individuals, both children and adults, posting YouTube clips continues to rise each year. In 2018, a Google search using the keywords "autism and YouTube" yielded a result of 1.25 million clips. Other autistic adults, such as Daniel Tammet, Temple Grandin and John Elder Robison, have published autobiographies. Although these stories and videos have certainly promoted a more positive view of autistic people, they have also increased the public's awareness of autistic individuals. Moreover, the dramatic increase in self-narratives over the past few years may have led people to believe that there are now many more autistic people than in the past.

Ironically, increased public awareness and understanding of autism may also have contributed to rising diagnosis rates, as learning more about the characteristics of autistic individuals may prompt some to recognise these characteristics in themselves and subsequently seek out a diagnostic assessment for ASD. For example, in a study conducted by Webster and Garvis (2017), 10 women who had all received their diagnosis as adults, related the factors that led them to seek a diagnosis. A number had been influenced by viewing a story or reading about an autistic individual, while the rest had sought diagnosis after a family member, such as their child, received a diagnosis of ASD. These women also discussed their need to share their stories and experiences so that other girls could be diagnosed earlier and avoid the difficulties, which they had experienced while growing up. This example illustrates the cyclical effect of public attention, public awareness and increased diagnosis, all of which contribute to the "autism epidemic" myth.

Increased public awareness and media attention have also increased the awareness of psychologists and physicians who provide autism diagnoses. When autism was first recognised, only a handful of clinicians knew of its existence. However, its inclusion as a distinct diagnosis in the *DSM-III* led more psychologists and physicians to focus on autism. This in turn led to more diagnoses and to rising incidence rates for autism (Nassar et al., 2009). Furthermore, the expanding of the diagnostic criteria to include Asperger's syndrome and Pervasive Developmental Disorder-Not Otherwise Specified (PDD-NOS) in 1994 resulted in a greater awareness and understanding of the varying ways in which individuals across the autism spectrum could present. No longer was autism primarily a condition associated with non-verbal and highly stereotypical behaviours. The new criteria meant that people formerly un-identified were able to seek a diagnosis and support.

Growing public awareness of the autism spectrum contributed to an increase in the number of people being diagnosed with autism or a related condition for several reasons. Firstly, this led many who had previously struggled in social situations and other areas to recognise the characteristics in themselves. Additionally, the widening definition of autism-related conditions led others, including medical professionals, to re-evaluate other diagnoses. For example, an individual presenting with the same set of symptoms may have been given a different diagnosis, such as intellectual disability, schizophrenia or emotional disturbance (Mitka, 2010). With the growing understanding of autism, individuals and professionals realised that some of these individuals more accurately met the criteria for autism, and diagnoses were revised.

In short, a deepened awareness of autism among clinicians, coupled with changing diagnostic criteria, has resulted in a dramatic rise in the number of individuals identifying as autistic. This has created an increased demand for services and supports as well as a greater public awareness of autism and autistic individuals. Confronted with public campaigns about the growing threat of autism (Broderick & Ne'eman, 2008; McGuire, 2012), combined with a lack of information about influencing factors, many have concluded that there is an autism epidemic (Gernsbacher, Dawson, & Hill Goldsmith, 2005).

2.2 The Research

Research has shown that over the past few decades, there has been an increase in the prevalence and incidence of ASD within societies throughout the world (Centers for Disease Control and Prevention, 2018; Özerk, 2016; Russell, Collishaw, Golding, Kelly & Ford, 2015; Saracino, Noseworthy, Steiman, Reisinger, & Fombonne, 2010). To better understand these statistics, it is important to first examine the difference between incidence and prevalence rates. Incidence is defined as the number of new cases of ASD in a given population within a specific time frame (Özerk, 2016). For example, reports on the incidence of autism in Australia for the past three years provide statistics on the number of new diagnoses across Australia between 2015 and 2018. Prevalence, on the other hand, is defined as the number of people in a population who have a specific diagnosis relative to the entire population. This is sometimes stated as a ratio. For example, the prevalence of autism in Australia for the year 2012 was 115,400 in the total population or 1:200 (0.5%) (Australian Bureau of Statistics, 2012).

In addition, it is necessary to delineate the nature of an epidemic. Green et al. (2002) defined an epidemic as "the occurrence in a community or region of cases of an illness, specified health behaviour, or other health-related events clearly in excess of normal expectancy" (p. 3). This can also be referred to as an "outbreak". This definition provides a number of key factors in determining whether something constitutes an epidemic. First, it clearly specifies that an epidemic involves an illness or health-related event. Second, prevalence and incidence rates must exceed those that would normally be expected in a given population. Green et al. also added that an epidemic usually involves a sudden increase in an illness, which peaks and then eventually wanes, as the factor that caused the epidemic is eradicated either naturally or through specific intervention. For autism to be considered an epidemic, the numbers would have to dramatically increase beyond that which would normally be expected and be attributable to a specific factor. However, current research indicates that a number of factors, rather than one specific factor, have contributed to increased incidence of autism over time (Gernsbacher et al., 2005). Moreover, as autism prevalence statistics have only been reported in the last 20–30 years, little baseline data is available meaning that it cannot be ascertained if the current incidence of autism diagnoses is above the rate that would be normally expected over a period of time (Leonard et al., 2010).

Researchers have suggested several factors, which have contributed to rising incidence and prevalence rates of autism (Gernsbacher et al., 2005). Firstly, as mentioned earlier in the chapter, as the understanding of autism has developed, the diagnostic criteria have expanded resulting in greater eligibility for diagnosis (Leonard et al., 2010). To understand the ways that changing criteria can shape prevalence or incidence data, Coplan (2016) provides an analogy in which a survey is conducted to determine the incidence and prevalence of people in Australia who are considered to have tall stature. If tall stature is defined as anyone who is greater than 200 cm, incidence and prevalence statistics are likely to be extremely low as people of this height are very unusual in the overall population. However, if the criterion for tall stature is revised to include anyone who is taller than 160 cm, then the prevalence and incidence of tall stature within the Australian population will increase fairly quickly, because a much larger number will meet the criteria. The increased prevalence and incidence rates of tall stature do not mean that suddenly a number of people have gotten taller, only that they are now formally acknowledged as being tall.

The same phenomenon can be applied to understand how the change in diagnostic criteria for autism has contributed to increased prevalence and incidence rates. From the *DSM-III* until the release of the *DSM-V*, the diagnostic criteria have expanded to encompass wider criteria for autism (Bennett & Goodall, 2016). The most significant change occurred with the release of the *DSM-IV* in 1994 in which a single diagnosis of autism was amended to include five diagnoses under the broad category of pervasive developmental disorders (American Psychiatric Association, 1994), often referred to as autism spectrum disorders. Most noticeably, this included the diagnoses of Asperger's syndrome and Pervasive Developmental Disorder-Not Otherwise Specified (PDD-NOS), which meant that a number of people with higher language and cognitive skills, but who met other criteria, were suddenly eligible for an autism spectrum diagnosis (Gernsbacher et al., 2005; Grandin, 2013).

Since the diagnostic criteria for autism-related conditions have changed multiple times since 1980, it is not possible to accurately determine if or how much the prevalence and incidence of autism have actually changed over time. To accurately determine whether incidence and prevalence have increased substantially would entail applying the same diagnostic criteria to a set population over time. Taylor, Jick and Maclaughlin (2013) conducted an analysis of medical records of autism diagnoses in the UK over a 20-year period. They found that prevalence and incidence rates rose in the first few years, but that incidence rates stabilised and decreased from around

1998. They concluded that the initial increase was a result of the introduction of the expanded diagnoses in the *DSM-IV*, but that once initial diagnoses were made, the rate of new diagnoses within the total population did not increase. These findings illustrate how changes to diagnostic criteria have influenced the incidence and prevalence of autism (Beighley & Matson, 2014; Beighley et al., 2013).

Other researchers have also examined the influence of changing diagnostic criteria on the incidence and prevalence rates of autism. Utilising case records of 7003 patients born before 1987, King and Bearman (2009) determined that the odds of a patient acquiring an autism-related diagnosis were elevated in periods in which diagnostic criteria had changed. They concluded that changes to diagnostic criteria and practices accounted for one-quarter of the increase in prevalence in California between 1992 and 2005. In another study, Bishop, Whitehouse, Watt and Line (2008) found that when current diagnostic criteria for autism was applied to 38 adults who had been previously diagnosed with a developmental language disorder under the *DSM-III*, 12 of these adults (32%) met the criteria for an autism spectrum disorder. Similarly, Croen, Grether, Hoogstrate and Selvin (2002) examined how improvements in detection and changes in diagnosis have contributed to the increased prevalence of autism and concluded that changes in diagnostic criteria may have accounted for at least one-third of the increased prevalence of autism in California.

With the release of the *DSM-V* in May 2013, researchers (Bennett & Goodall, 2016; Maenner et al., 2014) measured the impact that the new diagnostic criteria could potentially have on the incidence of autism. Specifically, they sought to determine whether the revised criteria and reduction of diagnostic categories in the *DSM-V* could affect the proportion of people who were eligible for an autism diagnosis compared to those who were eligible under the *DSM-IV* or *DSM-IV-TR* (Volkmar & McPartland, 2014). Bennett and Goodall (2016) collected and summarised studies, which compared the percentage of people with an existing *DSM-IV* or *DSM-IV-TR* ASD diagnosis, who would be diagnosed with ASD under the more recent *DSM-V*. They found that a small percentage of people with an existing autism diagnosis would no longer meet the diagnostic criteria under the *DSM-V*.

Gibbs, Aldridge, Chandler, Witzlsperger and Smith (2012) examined the records of children who were referred to an autism-specific assessment service against both the *DSM-IV-TR* and *DSM-V* ASD diagnostic criteria. Of the 132 children who were referred, 111 were eligible for a diagnosis under the *DSM-IV-TR* (i.e. 59 autistic disorder, 18 Asperger's disorder and 34 PDD-NOS), while only 84 met the criteria for a diagnosis of ASD under the *DSM-V*. This reflected a reduction of 24.3%. Other studies have had similar findings (Maenner et al., 2014; McPartland, Reichow, & Volkmar, 2012). These studies all determined that it is likely that some individuals will no longer meet the criteria for the new diagnosis of ASD and concluded that incidence rates would possibly decrease following the implementation of the *DSM-V*. Although these studies certainly indicate that diagnostic criteria can potentially decrease or increase incidence and prevalence rates, it should be noted that all of these studies were only able to speculate about the potential impact as the *DSM-V* had not yet been implemented. Currently, no study has yet been published to determine if incidence rates have decreased following the implementation of the *DSM-V*.

In addition to changing diagnostic criteria, researchers have shown that the prevalence and incidence of autism can change when public health authorities alter the processes, they use to measure its prevalence and incidence (Nassar et al., 2009). Isaksen, Diseth, Schjølberg and Skjeldal (2013) illustrate this point, "It would be controversial to say that the prevalence of ASD has increased internationally over the past 10 years. There is considerable variation in the way data are collected, processed statistically and presented" (p. 331). A number of studies (Hansen, Schendel, & Parner, 2015; Hinkka-Yli-Salomäki et al., 2014; Nassar et al., 2009; Parner et al., 2011) have investigated how changing reporting processes have affected the incidence and prevalence of ASD. Hansen et al. (2015) examined whether the prevalence of autism in Denmark was influenced by changes made in the identification of medical and psychiatric conditions in the Danish Psychiatric Register (DPR). From 1995 onwards, the DPR began to record psychiatric conditions exhibited by patients who were exiting the healthcare system. Prior to this time, the DPR only recorded patient's psychiatric conditions during their admission. Hansen et al. measured autism prevalence before, during and after the change and found that a 42% increase in the prevalence of autism was attributable to the introduction of outpatient reporting and examination practices.

Similarly, Hinkka-Yli-Salomäki et al. (2014) measured the incidence of autism, Asperger's syndrome and PDD-NOS among children born in Finland between 1987 and 1998. They found that changes to diagnostic procedures had resulted in increased incidence of autism across the country. Based on inpatient register information, there had been an eightfold increase in the incidence rates of autism, Asperger's syndrome and PDD-NOS between 1987 and 1992. Hinkka-Yli-Salomäki et al. concluded that increased awareness of ASD among clinicians, and more precisely changes to diagnostic criteria and practices for identifying autistic symptomology had likely contributed to the increased incidence rate.

Parner et al. (2011) compared the trends in reporting of autism prevalence rates in Denmark and Western Australia. These jurisdictions were selected for comparison as both used population-based registers and similar diagnostic systems. Parner et al. found that the reported prevalence of autism in children born between 1994 and 1999 was greater in Denmark (68.5 per 10,000 children) than Western Australia (51.0 per 10,000 children). They concluded that this variation was most likely a result of differing policies and methods for detecting autism. For example, Western Australia, unlike Denmark, does not provide assessments free of charge, which may have impact the number of families who are able to access diagnostic assessment for their children. In addition, reporting of ASD diagnoses is not required in Western Australia, while in Denmark, all suspected cases are referred through a common pathway. This may mean that Denmark has a better system of tracking autism diagnoses than Western Australia.

Nassar et al. (2009) examined the ways in which a variety of factors including changes to diagnostic criteria, eligibility for services, changes in diagnostic practices and age contributed to trends in autism diagnoses (including autistic disorder, Asperger's syndrome and PDD-NOS) between the years of 1983 and 1999. From 1985 until 1994, the average incidence of autism was less than 1 per 10,000 individuals. However, between the years of 1994–2002, the incidence of autism diagnoses increased by 11.9% per annum to 46 cases per 10,000 births in 1999. This was the same time period in which a new cross-disciplinary assessment and reporting processes were introduced to coincide with the changes in diagnostic criteria reflected in the *DSM-IV*. The statistics on incidence rates for Asperger's syndrome and PDD-NOS were particularly revealing. As neither was a diagnosis prior to the introduction of the *DSM-IV*, incidence rates before 1994 were 0. However, in the period 1994 until 2000 the incidence of Asperger's syndrome in Western Australia increased quickly to 0.5 per 10,000 individuals before stabilising. These figures indicate that a number of new cases could be directly attributed to the new diagnostic classification and criteria. A similar statistic was determined for the incidence of PDD-NOS. Interestingly, during the same years (i.e. 1983–1999) diagnoses of severe intellectual disabilities decreased, while an increase in diagnoses of individuals exhibiting a mild to moderate intellectual disability was noted. These individuals would have shared some of the same traits as those with Asperger's syndrome or PDD-NOS. This led Nassar et al. to conclude that changing assessment practices had resulted in greater awareness of children who exhibited delays, which consequently influenced incidence rates for autism and other mild to moderate developmental disabilities.

Monitoring and reporting practices used by public health authorities have also been attributed to changing prevalence and incidence rates of autism or ASD (Hansen et al., 2015; Nassar et al., 2009; Parner et al., 2011). For example, the incidence of a medical or psychiatric condition can increase or decrease when the eligibility criteria for access to a government program changes. During 1991, the US Department of Education expanded the eligibility criteria for special education services to include students with autism. Yeargin-Allsopp et al. (2003) found that this change most likely contributed to an increase in the incidence of autism diagnoses in American school-aged children in the following years. In a later study, Shattuck (2006) found that between 1994 and 2003 the administrative prevalence of ASD among American students increased from 0.6 to 1 per 1,000. At the same time, the prevalence of both learning disabilities and mental retardation diagnoses among students decreased substantially. Shattuck concluded that these two changes were most likely related and linked to the inclusion of autism as an eligibility category for school-based special education services. For instance, prior to the revision of the eligibility criteria, a number of autistic individuals may have received diagnoses of learning disabilities or mental retardation in order to ensure that they would receive support. Now that autism was recognised as an eligible diagnosis, the number of students reported to exhibit this condition had steadily increased. In Australia, Bent, Dissanayake and Barbaro (2015) similarly concluded that the introduction of specific funding for children diagnosed with ASD under the age of 7 had resulted in an increasing number of children who were diagnosed with ASD between the ages of 5 and 6.

Research clearly shows that while the incidence and prevalence of autism have increased, there may be a variety of plausible explanations that do support the "autism epidemic" myth. Changes to diagnostic criteria, administrative practices used to identify new cases of ASD and changing eligibility for services have led individuals, who would previously have been ineligible or received a different diagnosis, to either seek or be eligible for autism diagnoses and services. Correspondingly, this has resulted in an increase in the number of individuals in the population with an autism diagnosis. For an epidemic to occur, these increases would need to be caused by one specific agent, rather than from multiple influences. Moreover, researchers (Shattuck, 2006) have specified that even if these factors had not influenced rates of autism incidence and prevalence, these rates have not increased to the level that would be considered an epidemic. Incidence rates have not increased as dramatically or suddenly as would be expected if a new and unexplained factor was the cause. Rather, these rates have steadily increased in association with the introduction of factors, which were predicted to alter the rates of autism diagnoses. Although environmental or biological factors cannot be definitively excluded, it is likely that the majority of new cases are highly predictable and reasonable. Unfortunately, linking increasing prevalence and incidence numbers with an epidemic has created a sense that increasing diagnosis rates are indicative of a growing risk that is cause for alarm and needs to be halted.

2.3 The Impact

It can be argued that the primary impact of the "autism epidemic" myth is that it has generated a public anxiety or fear of autism, and by association, of autistic people. Epidemics, such as the Black Plague during the 1330s, the Spanish flu outbreak of 1918, the acquired immunodeficiency syndrome (AIDS) epidemic of the 1980s and 1990s, and the 2014 Ebola epidemic, are generally associated with contagions, tragedy and panic. Epidemics instil much fear in society, as their causes are often mysterious, their spread is unpredictable, and many people are concerned that they are susceptible (Ebben, 2018). Epidemics are emotionally charged and are perceived as having dire consequences for the individuals involved. This provokes general alarm as people work to gather information in order to avoid being infected or eliminate the disease altogether. Information sources, such as government agencies and news services, can both shape the public's perception of the existence of an epidemic and contribute to the sense of panic regarding the epidemic. For example, the news media was instrumental in informing the public about the spread of a mysterious new disease, which was later identified as AIDS (Lupton, 2013). Subsequent coverage of the AIDS epidemic helped to promote people's belief that AIDS only affected certain groups. The media also played a key role in both promoting and decreasing stigma of AIDS-affected patients (Mahajan et al., 2008).

In 1990, the American writer, Susan Sontag published an essay in which she discussed the ways that common diseases, such as cancer, tuberculosis and AIDS, had captured the public's imagination. Similarly, Broderick and Ne'eman (2008) argue that the current dialogue around autism as an epidemic and "global health crisis" has positioned autism as a disease, while comparisons with cancer or other diseases have helped to promote the perception of autism as a terrible affliction that harms children and devastates families. Grinker (2008) a father of an autistic daughter, and an anthropologist who has studied the views of different cultures about autism, discusses the ways in which the epidemic analogy has heighted public unrest about growing prevalence rates stating:

> [Epidemic] implies danger and incites fear, calling up associations with plagues that can sweep through the streets, something contagious in the air that you breathe or in the food you eat, threatening the ones you love. With autism, the label of "epidemic" sounds both frightening and tragic. (p. 5)

An epidemic usually occurs when an external pathogen, such as a virus or bacteria, spreads quickly throughout a population before it subsides. In other words, there is a sudden increase in its incidence over a short period of time, and then a more gradual decrease once a treatment or cure is found (Green et al., 2002). This has not been the case with autism. Although incidence rates have risen quickly after new diagnostic criteria were introduced, they have generally increased more slowly or even remained steady for periods of time. The initial recognition that an epidemic is occurring is also generally associated with a sense of urgency to find a cure. Sontag (1990) explains this reaction, "Disease is regularly described as invading the society, and efforts to reduce mortality from a given disease are called a fight, a struggle a war" (p. 98). Likewise, autism is portrayed as a disease that has invaded potentially healthy, normal children, and calls are made to fight a war on autism (McGuire, 2012). This has resulted in a disproportionate level of funding that has been, and continues to be, spent on finding treatments, preventions and cures for autism, rather than on developing services or supports to better support autistic individuals.

Researchers have investigated the priorities that have been targeted through research funding in Canada (Krahn & Fenton, 2012) and the UK (Pellicano, Dinsmore, & Charman, 2014a, b). They found that the vast majority of public research funds have been spent on understanding causes of autism and on finding a treatment or cure for the condition. In contrast, only a small percentage of funds have been spent on creating services and supports for autistic people. Krahn and Fenton found that between 2000 and 2010, the *Canadian Institutes of Health Research* allocated most of its financial resources towards biomedical (44%) and clinical research (42%), whereas only 5% of funds were allocated towards studying the ways that social, cultural, environmental and economic factors affect the lives of autistic individuals. Even more concerning was the finding that only 3% of funds were spent on identifying and improving services and supports for autistic individuals and their families.

The results of these studies indicate two additional impacts of the "autism epidemic" myth. Firstly, the myth and discourse of epidemic and disease have supported a medical perspective of autism and autistic people. The medical model of disability focuses on the individual's deficits or limitations and views disability as a problem to be fixed or cured (Krcek, 2013). The medical view of autism perceives autism as a problem to be treated or managed and, by association, identifies autistic people as suffering, unhealthy and problematic. The worth of these individuals is measured in terms of what they can become if their autistic symptomology is eliminated (Bagatell, 2010). In a recent study, only 7% of a sample of 111 autistic adults stated they felt that society accepted them as an autistic person, while 43% stated they were not accepted and 48% said they were sometimes accepted (Cage, Di Monaco, & Newell, 2018).

These findings indicate that autistic adults do not feel they have value in society as they are, but only if they can act or become "normal".

Additionally, it can be argued that the medicalisation of autism derived from the "autism epidemic" myth has resulted in the de-humanisation of autistic people. In essence, the focus on the disease of autism has taken away the attention from autistic people. This has meant that the lived experiences, perspectives and support needs of autistic people have been largely overlooked (Gillespie-Lynch, Kapp, Brooks, Pickens, & Schwartzman, 2017; Milton, 2014; Pellicano et al., 2014a, b). Pellicano et al. (2014a, b) found that many autistic adults (61%) and family members (61%) felt that the majority of research funds were spent on things that would have no benefit for them. Instead, they believed that public funds should be spent on examining how public services could be used to better meet the needs of autistic people and improve their lives. Pellicano et al. (2014a, b, p. 768) concluded that: "research activity should be broadened to reflect the priorities of the U.K. [United Kingdom] autism community, focusing in particular on research that helps people live with autism".

In contrast to the medical model of autism, the social model takes the view that it is not autistic individuals themselves that are limited, but that it is society which places limitations on them (Krcek, 2013). Proponents of the social model argue that to succeed, autistic individuals need to be perceived as capable if they are provided with the right supports. Rather than focusing on curing the perceived disease of autism in order to rescue normal and healthy children, it is necessary to perceive autism as an aspect of human diversity rather than as a deficit, and autistic people as exhibiting strengths and abilities rather than limitations and problems. Neurodiversity theory provides a foundation for challenging this perception and for shifting the current discourse and fear associated with the "autism epidemic" myth.

2.4 The Future

Over the last century, autistic people have been portrayed as broken individuals who need to be fixed to allow them to function normally in their communities (Robertson, 2010). This viewpoint is illustrated in a 1962 article published in a London newspaper, entitled *Children in Chains*, which states:

> A newly-formed Society for Autistic Children has set to work to awaken the nation to the claims of these sad, lost little souls… It is easy to feel pity for the child physically crippled… Can't we feel pity too for the baby whose mind is locked? And urge, by weight of public opinion, that the nation should provide the keys that will, in the light of today's knowledge, unlock it? (Frame, 1962)

Despite the advances in autism research and knowledge in the intervening years, autism is still predominately viewed as a medical disorder and the source of fear and anxiety (Baron-Cohen, 2017). This deficit-focused view of autism often ignores the diversity that autistic people offer to society, encompassing a unique way of being, as well as individual strengths, interests and talents. To mitigate and transform the negative impact of the "autism epidemic" myth, a shift is needed from a medical view of the deficit and disease of autism to creating a society which values and supports the abilities and needs of autistic people.

In contrast to a medical and deficit-based model, neurodiversity theory encourages a perception of autism as an alternative way of behaving and thinking, rather than a disorder to be cured (Romoser & Baker, 2012). Viewed through a neurodiversity lens, autism is perceived as an integral aspect of the individual's makeup and identity, much like gender, hair colour, nationality, sexual orientation, religion or ethnicity (Jaarsma & Welin, 2012; Robertson, 2010). Proponents of neurodiversity theory suggest that autism be regarded, not as a disorder, but as a natural variation from the "typical" (Lorenz, Reznik, & Heinitz, 2017), which should be welcomed rather than feared.

Over the past two decades, the neurodiversity movement has steadily gained momentum, aided by the support of autism support groups and organisations. Autistic self-advocates and parents have lobbied for autistic differences to be recognised, accepted and respected, rather than normalised or "cured" (Langan, 2011; Silberman, 2010). These groups have theorised that autism is a neurological difference and different way of thinking and being, rather than an impairment (Owren, 2013). Additionally, proponents of neurodiversity theory state that autism is not something they have, but something that is integral to who they are (Grinker, 2008). These individuals express their view that attempting to cure them of autism is essentially saying that they need to change into someone else. Jim Sinclair, an autistic adult and one of the founders of the neurodiversity movement, explains this perspective:

> Autism is a way of being. It is not possible to separate the autism from the person – and if it were possible, the person you would have left would not be the same person you started with. Only when someone had decided that the characteristic being referred to is negative, would they want to separate it from the person. (Sinclair, 1993)

Baron-Cohen (2017) explains neurodiversity theory through a comparison with historical attempts to force left-handed people to use their right hand. People who are left-handed can be viewed as a minority in a predominately right-handed world. In the past, being left-handed was seen as a condition to be corrected. Today, it is acceptable to use either the left or right hand as society has recognised that doing things differently does not mean less able. In the same way, autistic individuals can be viewed as a minority group in a society comprised of a non-autistic majority. Traditionally, autistic individuals have been "treated" in an attempt to normalise them and enable them to fit in with the non-autistic majority (Broderick, 2009). Proponents of neurodiversity theory challenge this thinking offering an alternative vision for a society, which welcomes individuals with different types of thinking, both autistic and non-autistic, work together to form a diverse community.

The neurodiversity movement could be seen as analogous with other civil rights movements in which activities and supporters have successfully advocated for recognition, acceptance and equality of opportunity for various minority groups (Baron-Cohen, 2017). Similarly, the neurodiversity movement aims to end discrimination and prejudice against autistic people and to improve the dignity and rights of this group within society. At its foundation, the neurodiversity movement aims to help autistic people to be successful, while still retaining their uniqueness and individual identity, and challenges the societal barriers, which have marginalised and excluded them (Jaarsma & Welin, 2012). Ari Ne'eman, autistic self-advocate and president and co-founder of the *Autistic Self Advocacy Network* (ASAN), suggests that for autistic people to achieve, society needs to be better at adapting its communities and expectations to support the strengths and accommodate the needs of its autistic citizens (Owren, 2013; Silberman, 2010).

In a large-scale study conducted in the UK, autistic adults, professionals and family members noted the role that society plays in disabling autistic people, citing a lack of awareness of autism and common needs and accommodations identified by autistic people and their families (Kenny et al., 2015). This finding suggests a need for greater public awareness of the positive aspects of autism as well as the strengths of autistic people. This will facilitate greater recognition and acceptance of the unique skills exhibited by autistic people and to promote understanding about ways that different environments may impact the participation of autistic individuals.

According to the social model of disability, autistic individuals may demonstrate strengths in some environments and impairments in others (Baron-Cohen, 2017). Borrowing an idea from Einstein, a fish will appear to have a disability if required to climb a tree, but if placed in water, the fish's innate characteristics will allow them to thrive. Similarly, a person in a wheelchair does not experience disability if the necessary structural accommodations are made to allow them to independently access all aspects of the environment (Kenny et al., 2015). Providing necessary accommodations or "autism-friendly environments" to allow autistic individuals to build on their strengths and adjust for their needs will limit their "disability" and maximise their participation and engagement with their communities (Baron-Cohen, 2017). For instance, in Australia, selected supermarkets have launched "quiet hours" in which lights are dimmed, and unnecessary noises are avoided, to accommodate the sensory challenges of autistic customers. Similarly, local government bodies have created sensory-friendly playgrounds, which are designed to help autistic children to remain calm and safe while playing alongside their peers (McGhee, 2017).

Autistic people face a number of contextual difficulties, sensory demands, social ambiguities and information complexities in their day-to-day lives (Robertson, 2010). To create supportive environments, it is necessary to gather the perspectives of autistic individuals about the difficulties and challenges they experience when living and participating in communities, which have been designed for non-autistic ways of being. This can be likened to the way in which increased public knowledge and understanding of the needs of visually impaired individuals has led to the development of audible road crossing signals, level footpaths and greater acceptance of guide dogs in public spaces. A similar approach could be taken to empower autistic children and adults. Unfortunately, the majority of society still views autistic individuals as disabled by autism, rather than by the expectations and inflexibility of their environments to meet their needs (Grinker, 2008).

While there is mounting support for neurodiversity theory, particularly by autistic self-advocates (Sinclair, 1993) and parents (Langan, 2011), not everyone in the autism community is a proponent of this perspective. Sue Rubin, a person with minimal verbal skills who uses technology to communicate, rejects the proposition that finding a cure is no longer needed saying:

> As a person who lives with autism daily and will not live a normal life, I find people who are high functioning and saying society should not look for a cure offensive. They have no idea what our lives are like. Killing autism lets me enjoy a life with great friends and allows me to go to college. (Ortega, 2009, p. 430)

Like Sue Rubin, other community members and advocacy organisations emphasise the profound challenges they or their children face and consequently advocate for treatments for autism symptomology, or in some cases, for a cure (Humphrey & Lewis, 2008).

Regardless of their personal views on neurodiversity theory, all agree that more relevant services and supports are needed. In addition, the opinions and participation of the autistic community including parents of autistic children are essential in determining future directions for research and practice (Milton, 2014; Pellicano et al., 2014a, b). Given that the autism spectrum includes individuals with a wide variety of needs and abilities, a range of supports, strategies and adaptations are needed to ensure all autistic individuals are able to pursue their own particular interests and goals. More importantly, flexibility is needed to support the opinions and values of all members of the autistic community including families that play an essential role in supporting and advocating for autistic children in their early years of life. Rather than focusing on differences, finding common ground and establishing shared goals among all individuals and their family members will provide better avenues to empower the voice of each autistic individual. It is only through portraying autism through the voices of the autistic community that will decrease the fear and anxiety sustaining the "autism epidemic" myth, by promoting a view of autism "difference" rather than "disorder".

2.5 Conclusion

The prevalence and incidence of autism have risen over the past decades, largely due to greater public awareness and understanding of the condition, in addition to changes to diagnostic criteria, the monitoring of disease by public health authorities and changes to eligibility criteria for government programs. As prevalence and incidence rates have risen, so too has the visibility and attention on autism in the media and general public. All of these factors have created the myth that there is an autism epidemic. This myth has generated a discourse, which has prompted growing alarm and instigated an urgency to find a cure or successful treatments. At the same time, the medicalisation of autism has diminished autistic people who feel they must conform to notions of normalcy if they are to have value in society. Neurodiversity theory provides an important development in promoting the equality and recognition of unique strengths of autistic individuals, and the contributions these individuals can make to society if their communities are able to adapt to meet their particular ways of thinking and working. To translate this theory into action will require a transformation from the current medical to a more social view of autism. Empowering the voice of autistic individuals will be critical to realise the goal of creating truly inclusive communities in which difference and diversity are celebrated rather than feared.

References

American Psychiatric Association. (1994). *Diagnostic and statistical manual of mental disorders—-Fourth edition*. Washington, DC: American Psychiatric Publishing. Retrieved from http://www.terapiacognitiva.eu/dwl/dsm5/DSM-IV.pdf.

Australian Bureau of Statistics. (2012). *Autism in Australia*. Canberra, Australia Retrieved from http://www.abs.gov.au/AUSSTATS/abs@.nsf/Lookup/4428.0Main+Features12012?OpenDocument.

Bagatell, N. (2010). From cure to community: Transforming notions of autism. *Ethos, 38*(1), 33–55. https://doi.org/10.1111/j.1548-1352.2009.01080.x.

Baron-Cohen, S. (2017). Editorial perspective: Neurodiversity—A revolutionary concept for autism and psychiatry. *Journal of Child Psychology and Psychiatry, 58*(6), 744–747. https://doi.org/10.1111/jcpp.12703.

Beighley, J., & Matson, J. (2014). Comparing social skills in children diagnosed with autism spectrum disorder according to the DSM-IV-TR and the DSM-5. *Journal of Developmental & Physical Disabilities, 26*(6), 689–701. https://doi.org/10.1007/s10882-014-9382-4.

Beighley, J., Matson, J., Rieske, R. D., Jang, J., Cervantes, P. E., & Goldin, R. L. (2013). Comparing challenging behavior in children diagnosed with autism spectrum disorders according to the DSM-IV-TR and the proposed DSM-5. *Developmental Neurorehabilitation, 16*(6), 375–381. https://doi.org/10.3109/17518423.2012.760119.

Belcher, C., & Maich, K. (2014). Autism spectrum disorder in popular media: Storied reflections of societal views. *Brock Education: A Journal of Educational Research and Practice, 23*(2), 97–115.

Bennett, M., & Goodall, E. (2016). A meta-analysis of DSM-5 autism diagnoses in relation to DSM-IV and DSM-IV-TR. *Review Journal of Autism and Developmental Disorders, 3*(2), 119–124. https://doi.org/10.1007/s40489-016-0070-4.

Bent, C. A., Dissanayake, C., & Barbaro, J. (2015). Mapping the diagnosis of autism spectrum disorders in children aged under 7 years in Australia, 2010-2012. *The Medical Journal of Australia, 2015, 202*(6), 317–320. https://doi.org/10.5694/mja14.00328.

Bishop, D. V. M., Whitehouse, A. J. O., Watt, H. J., & Line, E. A. (2008). Autism and diagnostic substitution: Evidence from a study of adults with a history of developmental language sisorder. *Developmental Medicine and Child Neurology, 50*(5), 341–345.

Broderick, A. A. (2009). Autism, "recovery (to normalcy)", and the politics of hope. *Journal of Intellectual and Developmental Disability, 47*(4), 263–281. https://doi.org/10.1352/1934-9556-47.4.263.

Broderick, A. A., & Ne'eman, A. (2008). Autism as metaphor: Narrative and counter-narrative. *International Journal of Inclusive Education, 12*(5–6), 459–476. https://doi.org/10.1080/13603110802377490.

Cage, E., Di Monaco, J., & Newell, V. (2018). Experiences of autism acceptance and mental health in autistic adults. *Journal or Autism and Developmental Disorders, 48*(2), 473–484. https://doi.org/10.1007/s10803-017-3342-7.

Centers for Disease Control and Prevention. (2018). *Data & statistics*. Retrieved from https://www.cdc.gov/ncbddd/autism/data.html.

Coplan, J. (2016). *Autism epidemic or explosion? (And why it matters)*. Retrieved from https://www.psychologytoday.com/blog/making-sense-autistic-spectrum-disorders/201607/autism-epidemic-or-explosion-and-why-it-matters.

Croen, L. A., Grether, J. K., Hoogstrate, J., & Selvin, S. (2002). The changing prevalence of autism in California. *Journal of Autism and Developmental Disorders, 32*(3), 207–215. https://doi.org/10.1023/a:1015453830880.

Dillenburger, K., Jordan, J. A., McKerr, L., Devine, P., & Keenan, M. (2013). Awareness and knowledge of autism and autism interventions: A general population survey. *Research in Autism Spectrum Disorders, 7*(12), 1558–1567. https://doi.org/10.1016/j.rasd.2013.09.004.

Ebben, H. (2018). The desire to recognize the undesirable: De/Constructing the autism epidemic metaphor and contagion in autism as a discourse. *Feminist Formations, 30*(1), 141–163.

Elsabbagh, M., Divan, G., Koh, Y. J., Kim, Y. S., Kauchali, S., Marcín, C., ... Fombonne, E. (2012). Global prevalence of autism and other pervasive developmental disorders. *Autism Research, 5*(3), 160–179. https://doi.org/10.1002/aur.239.

Frame, C. (1962). Children in chains. *The Evening News*.

Gernsbacher, M. A., Dawson, M., & Hill Goldsmith, H. (2005). Three reasons not to believe in an autism epidemic. *Current Directions in Psychological Science, 14*(2), 55–58.

Gibbs, V., Aldridge, F., Chandler, F., Witzlsperger, E., & Smith, K. (2012). Brief report: An exploratory study comparing diagnostic outcomes for autism spectrum disorders under DSM-IV-TR with the proposed DSM-5 revision. *Journal of Autism and Developmental Disorders, 42*(8), 1750–1756. https://doi.org/10.1007/s10803-012-1560-6.

Gillespie-Lynch, K., Kapp, S. K., Brooks, P. J., Pickens, J., & Schwartzman, B. (2017). Whose expertise is it? Evidence for autistic adults as critical autism experts. *Front Psychology, 8,* 438. https://doi.org/10.3389/fpsyg.2017.00438.

Grandin, T. (2013). *The autistic brain*. New York: Houghton Mifflin Harcourt.

Green, M. S., Swartz, T., Mayshar, E., Lev, B., Leventhal, A., Slater, P. E., et al. (2002). When is an epidemic an epidemic? *The Israel Medical Association Journal, 4*(1), 3–6.

Grinker, R. R. (2008). *Unstrange minds: Remapping the world of autism*. New York: Basic Books.

Hansen, S. N., Schendel, D. E., & Parner, E. T. (2015). Explaining the increase in the prevalence of autism spectrum disorders: The proportion attributable to changes in reporting practices. *JAMA Pediatrics, 169*(1), 56–62. https://doi.org/10.1001/jamapediatrics.2014.1893.

Hinkka-Yli-Salomäki, S., Banerjee, P. N., Gissler, M., Lampi, K. M., Vanhala, R., Brown, A. S., et al. (2014). The incidence of diagnosed autism spectrum disorders in Finland. *Nordic Journal of Psychiatry, 68*(7), 472–480. https://doi.org/10.3109/08039488.2013.861017.

Humphrey, N., & Lewis, S. (2008). Make me normal: The views and experiences of pupils on the autistic spectrum in mainstream secondary schools. *Autism, 12*(1), 23–46. https://doi.org/10.1177/1362361307085267.

Isaksen, J., Diseth, T. H., Schjølberg, S., & Skjeldal, O. H. (2013). Autism spectrum disorders—Are they really epidemic? *European Journal of Paediatric Neurology, 17*(4), 327–333. https://doi.org/10.1016/j.ejpn.2013.03.003.

Jaarsma, P., & Welin, S. (2012). Autism as a natural human variation: Reflections on the claims of the neurodiversity movement. *Health Care Analysis, 20*(1), 20–30. https://doi.org/10.1007/s10728-011-0169-9.

Jones, S. C., & Harwood, V. (2009). Representations of autism in Australian print media. *Disability & Society, 24*(1), 5–18. https://doi.org/10.1080/09687590802535345.

Kanner, L. (1943). Autistic disturbances of affective contact. *Nervous Child, 2*(3), 217–250.

Kenny, L., Pellicano, E., Hattersley, C., Molins, B., Povey, C., & Buckley, C. (2015). Which terms should be used to describe autism? Perspectives from the UK autism community. *Autism, 20*(4), 442–462. https://doi.org/10.1177/1362361315588200.

King, M., & Bearman, P. (2009). Diagnostic change and the increased prevalence of autism. *International Journal of Epidemiology, 38*(5), 1224–1234. https://doi.org/10.1093/ije/dyp261.

Krahn, T. M., & Fenton, A. (2012). Funding priorities: Autism and the need for a more balanced research agenda in Canada. *Public Health Ethics, 5*(3), 296–310. https://doi.org/10.1093/phe/phs027.

Krcek, T. E. (2013). Deconstructing disability and neurodiversity: Controversial issues for autism and implications for social work. *Journal of Progressive Human Services, 24*(1), 4–22. https://doi.org/10.1080/10428232.2013.740406.

Langan, M. (2011). Parental voices and controversies in autism. *Disability & Society, 26*(2), 193–205. https://doi.org/10.1080/09687599.2011.544059.

Leonard, H., Dixon, G., Whitehouse, A. J. O., Bourke, J., Aiberti, K., Nassar, N., … Glasson, E. J. (2010). Unpacking the complex nature of the autism epidemic. *Research in Autism Spectrum Disorders, 4*(4), 548–554. https://doi.org/10.1016/j.rasd.2010.01.003.

Lorenz, T., Reznik, N., & Heinitz, K. (2017). A different point of view: The neurodiversity approach to autism and work. In M. Fitzgerald & J. Yip (Eds.), *Autism: Paradigms, recent research and clinical applications*. InTech: Open Access.

Lupton, D. (2013). *Moral threats and dangerous desires: AIDS in the news media*. Routledge.

Maenner, M. J., Rice, C. E., Arneson, C. L., Cunniff, C., Schieve, L. A., Carpenter, L. A., … Durkin, M. S. (2014). Potential impact of DSM-5 criteria on autism spectrum disorder prevalence estimates. *JAMA Psychiatry, 71*(3), 292–300. https://doi.org/10.1001/jamapsychiatry.2013.3893.

Mahajan, A. P., Sayles, J. N., Patel, V. A., Remien, R. H., Ortiz, D., Szekeres, G., et al. (2008). Stigma in the HIV/AIDS epidemic: A review of the literature and recommendations for the way forward. *AIDS (London, England), 22*(Suppl 2), S67.

McGhee, R. (2017). *Sensory-friendly playground helping people with autism to feel safe and calm*. Retrieved from http://www.abc.net.au/news/2017-12-29/sensory-friendly-playground-helping-people-with-autism-qld/9292498.

McGuire, A. (2012). Representing autism: A sociological examination of autism advocacy. *Atlantis: Critical Studies in Gender, Culture & Social Justice, 35*(2), 62–71.

McKeever, B. W. (2013). News framing of Autism: Understanding media advocacy and the combating autism act. *Science Communication, 35*(2), 213–240. https://doi.org/10.1177/1075547012450951.

McPartland, J. C., Reichow, B., & Volkmar, F. R. (2012). Sensitivity and specificity of proposed DSM-5 diagnostic criteria for autism spectrum disorder. *Journal of the American Academy of Child and Adolescent Psychiatry, 51*(4), 368–383. https://doi.org/10.1016/j.jaac.2012.01.007.

Milton, D. E. (2014). Autistic expertise: A critical reflection on the production of knowledge in autism studies. *Autism, 18*(7), 794–802. https://doi.org/10.1177/1362361314525281.

Mitka, M. (2010). Rising autism rates still pose a mystery. *JAMA, 303*(7), 602. https://doi.org/10.1001/jama.2010.113.

Nassar, N., Dixon, G., Bourke, J., Bower, C., Glasson, E., De Klerk, N., et al. (2009). Autism spectrum disorders in young children: Effect of changes in diagnostic practices. *International Journal of Epidemiology, 38*(5), 1245–1254. https://doi.org/10.1093/ije/dyp260.

Ortega, F. (2009). The cerebral subject and the challenge of neurodiversity. *BioSocieties, 4*(4), 425–445.

Owren, T. (2013). Neurodiversity: Accepting autistic difference. *Learning Disability Practice, 16*(4), 32–37.

Özerk, K. (2016). The issue of prevalence of autism/ASD. *International Electronic Journal of Elementary Education, 9*(2), 263–306.

Parner, E., Thorsen, P., Dixon, G., Klerk, N., Leonard, H., Nassar, N., … Glasson, E. (2011). A comparison of autism prevalence trends in Denmark and Western Australia. *Journal of Autism & Developmental Disorders, 41*(12), 1601–1608. https://doi.org/10.1007/s10803-011-1186-0.

Pellicano, E., Dinsmore, A., & Charman, T. (2014a). Views on researcher-community engagement in autism research in the United Kingdom: A mixed-methods study. *PLoS ONE, 9*(10), e109946. https://doi.org/10.1371/journal.pone.0109946.

Pellicano, E., Dinsmore, A., & Charman, T. (2014b). What should autism research focus upon? Community views and priorities from the United Kingdom. *Autism, 18*(7), 756–770. https://doi.org/10.1177/1362361314529627.

Pew Research Center. (2008). *Health news coverage in the U.S. media*. Retrieved from http://assets.pewresearch.org/wp-content/uploads/sites/13/legacy/HealthNewsReportFinal.pdf.

Robertson, S. M. (2010). Neurodiversity, quality of life, and autistic adults: Shifting research and professional focuses onto real-life challenges. *Disability Studies Quarterly, 30*(1), 27.

Romoser, M. F., & Baker, D. L. (2012). The politics of neurodiversity: Why public policy matters. *Review of Disability Studies: An International Journal, 8*(1), 78.

Russell, G., Collishaw, S., Golding, J., Kelly, S. E., & Ford, T. (2015). Changes in diagnosis rates and behavioural traits of autism spectrum disorder over time. *British Journal of Psychiatry Open, 1*(2), 110–115. https://doi.org/10.1192/bjpo.bp.115.000976.

Saracino, J., Noseworthy, J., Steiman, M., Reisinger, L., & Fombonne, E. (2010). Diagnostic and assessment issues in autism surveillance and prevalence. *Journal of Developmental & Physical Disabilities, 22*(4), 317–330. https://doi.org/10.1007/s10882-010-9205-1.

Shattuck, P. T. (2006). The contribution of diagnostic substitution to the growing administrative prevalence of autism in US special education. *Pediatrics, 117*(4), 1028–1037. https://doi.org/10.1542/peds.2005-1516.

Sheldrick, R. C., & Carter, A. S. (2018). State-level trends in the prevalence of autism spectrum disorder (ASD) from 2000 to 2012: A reanalysis of findings from the Autism and Developmental Disabilities Network. *Journal of Autism and Developmental Disorders*. https://doi.org/10.1007/s10803-018-3568-z.

Silberman, S. (2010). *Exclusive: First autistic presidential appointee speaks out*. Retrieved from https://www.wired.com/2010/10/exclusive-ari-neeman-qa/.

Sinclair, J. (1993). *Don't mourn for us*. Retrieved from http://www.autreat.com/dont_mourn.html.

Sontag. (1990). *Illness as metaphor and AIDS and its metahpors*. New York: Anchor.

Taylor, B., Jick, H., & Maclaughlin, D. (2013). Prevalence and incidence rates of autism in the UK: Time trend from 2004-2010 in children aged 8 years. *British Medical Journal Open, 3*(10), e003219. https://doi.org/10.1136/bmjopen-2013-003219.

Volkmar, F. R., & McPartland, J. C. (2014). From Kanner to DSM-5: Autism as an evolving diagnostic concept. *Annual Review of Clinical Psychology, 10*(1), 193–212. https://doi.org/10.1146/annurev-clinpsy-032813-153710.

Webster, A. A., & Garvis, S. (2017). The importance of critical life moments: An explorative study of successful women with autism spectrum disorder. *Autism, 21*(6), 670–677. https://doi.org/10.1177/1362361316677719.

Yeargin-Allsopp, M., Rice, C., Karapurkar, T., Doernberg, N., Boyle, C., & Murphy, C. (2003). Prevalence of autism in a US metropolitan area. *JAMA: Journal of the American Medical Association, 289*(1), 49–55. https://doi.org/10.1001/jama.289.1.49.

Zhai, Y., Sun, S., Wang, F., & Ding, Y. (2017). Multiplicity and uncertainty: Media coverage of autism causation. *Journal of Informetrics, 11*(3), 873–887. https://doi.org/10.1016/j.joi.2017.07.005.

Chapter 3
Challenging the Public's Perception of Life on Autism Spectrum: The Impact of the Vaccination Myth

Abstract A popular myth about autism is the belief that vaccinations administered during childhood contribute to the development of autism spectrum disorder. This chapter will unpack the origins of this myth, beginning with a discussion of Wakefield and colleagues' controversial 1998 study, which received widespread media attention. The media's portrayal of the vaccination–autism controversy will then be examined, followed by a review of the research on known contributors or causes of autism spectrum disorder. The impact of this myth on creating a culture of fear will be discussed, and the ways this has resulted in the devaluing of autistic people and their potential contributions to society will be explored. A future perspective will be offered, which challenges the belief held by some that autistic children have limited potential because of their autistic differences and allows them to view autistic differences in a positive light. Finally, suggestions will be made for reworking this myth in the light of current research on the impact that autistic individuals have made in today's world and the positive and negative aspects of life on the autism spectrum.

Keywords Vaccination · Causes · Outcomes · Public perception · Presentation

Many myths develop from a need to find an explanation for phenomena, particularly those that cause concern (Mocarski, 2014). Ever since autism was identified, psychologists, physicians and parents have speculated about its aetiology. As a result, there have been a number of theories over the years about the causes of autism. Although most of these theories have since been disproven, a few have developed into myths. Certainly, the most widely known and controversial is the myth that autism is caused by vaccinations. Despite significant scientific evidence demonstrating that autism is not linked to vaccinations, there are still many individuals, including parents and celebrities, who continue to expound this belief (Gross, 2009) and blame vaccines for causing their child's autism.

M. Bennett et al., *Life on the Autism Spectrum*,
https://doi.org/10.1007/978-981-13-3359-0_3

3.1 The Origins

Unlike some of the other autism myths, the "vaccination causes autism" myth can be specifically linked to a few distinct sources. One of the earliest claims that vaccinations contributed to the development of autism was made in 1985 by Coulter and Fisher in their book, *A Shot in the Dark*. Barbara Loe Fisher argued that her son had suffered significant disabilities following his fourth Diphtheria, Pertussis and Tetanus (DPT) vaccination. Fisher, along with several other parents, founded the National Vaccine Information Center (NVIC), which has become one of the largest anti-vaccination organisations in the USA (Boom & Cunningham, 2014). In 1991, Coulter and Fisher updated their book linking the DPT vaccine with a host of neurological disorders including autism writing, "with the increasing number of vaccinations American babies have been required to use has come increasing number of reports of chronic immune and neurologic disorder... including... autism" (Chatterjee, 2013, p. 187). Barbara Coulter has continued her anti-vaccination campaign appearing on television and generating written features through her organisation's website. In these, she offers pseudoscientific "evidence" to support her belief that children are being poisoned and subsequently damaged by vaccines, which she contends have caused these children to suffer disabilities, such as autism. Fisher's book and subsequent efforts to link vaccines with autism have influenced many parents to decline vaccinations for their child and have encouraged others to take legal action against vaccine companies (Boom & Cunningham, 2014).

Although Fisher's book has certainly had a significant impact on parents, it did not receive as much media attention as a study published in 1998 by a team of scientists working at the Royal Free Hospital and School of Medicine in London (Boom & Cunningham, 2014; Chatterjee, 2013). This group, which was led by Dr. Andrew Wakefield, published a case study of 12 children who exhibited regressive disabilities and delays and offered evidence to support their theory that the Measles, Mumps and Rubella (MMR) vaccination had caused these children to develop a new autistic phenotype which they called "*regressive autism enterocolitis syndrome*" (Wakefield et al. 1998). Wakefield et al. claimed that there were associations between the MMR vaccination, regressive autism and bowel disorders, which he later termed *autistic enterocolitis*. The researcher's hypothesised that *autistic enterocolitis* is an emergent irritable bowel disorder phenotype in which children who are seemingly developing normally, suddenly experience a loss of skills or regression in their development (Fombonne & Cook, 2003). Wakefield and colleagues concluded that this regression of skills was the result of the child's exposure to the MMR vaccination at a time when their immune system was rapidly developing. Wakefield et al. proposed that when a child received their MMR vaccine, they were exposed to the measles virus, which caused them to develop intestinal inflammation. Subsequently, this inflammation released harmful proteins that contaminated the recipient's brain and resulted in autism (Chatterjee, 2013).

Unlike Coulter and Fisher's book which initially received little public attention (Coulter & Fisher, 1991), Wakefield et al.'s (1998) study was published in *The Lancet*, a well-respected scientific journal. This article came to the attention of a leading medical charity who invited Wakefield to present his findings at a televised press conference (Flaherty, 2011). The study quickly gained national and international attention, prompting a health crisis in the UK as parents began to refuse to have their children vaccinated. Subsequently, a sharp decline in vaccination rates was noted in the UK, as well as a significant increase in the cases of measles and mumps. Parents in the USA also began to question the safety of vaccines, while anti-vaccine advocates, such as Barbara Fisher, were quick to cite Wakefield's findings as support for their own theories about the role that vaccines played in the rising rates of autism and other developmental disabilities (Fisher, N.D.).

Wakefield et al.'s (1998) study prompted a number of researchers (Dales, Hammer, & Smith, 2001; Kaye, del Mar Melero-Montes, & Jick, 2001; Madsen et al., 2002; Mäkelä, Nuorti, & Peltola, 2002; Taylor et al., 1999) to investigate the possibility of a causal relationship between vaccines and autism. None found any link, concluding that autism rates were just as high for non-vaccinated children as for those who had been vaccinated (Boom & Cunningham, 2014) leading the CDC (Hinman, O'renstein, Schuchat, & CDC, 2011) and the Institute of Medicine (Institute of Medicine (IOM), 2012) to conclude that there was no evidence to support the theory that the MMR or other vaccinations cause autism.

As researchers began to question the results of Wakefield et al.'s (1998) research, facts indicated that Wakefield et al.'s findings were invalid and that the study itself was fraudulent. Brian Deer, an investigative journalist, examined Wakefield's professional conduct and found that he had failed to disclose a financial conflict of interest, as he was listed on a patent for a new vaccine, which would net him royalty payments (Deer, 2011; Flaherty, 2011). The UK's General Medical Council (GMC) conducted a subsequent investigation concluding that Wakefield and two of his co-investigators were guilty of professional misconduct and ethical infractions (General Medical Council (GMC), 2010) as they had falsified information about their participants' medical histories in an effort to support their findings (Deer, 2011). It was discovered that three of the nine children in Wakefield et al.'s study did not have a diagnosis of autism, while the onset of autistic symptomology in the remaining six children occurred not days after they received the MMR vaccine, as Wakefield et al. stated, but had appeared months later. In addition, the study was funded by a personal injury lawyer whose clients were pursuing a case against the manufacturers of the vaccine (Deer, 2011; Offit, 2011). As a consequence of these findings, Wakefield was stripped of his medical licence (Deer, 2011; Offit, 2011) by the GMC who found that he had demonstrated "callous disregard" by exposing the children to unnecessary and invasive medical procedures (Boom & Cunningham, 2014).

On 6 March 2004, 10 of the 12 co-authors of Wakefield et al.'s (1998) study issued a formal retraction, declaring that their research findings were compromised, and that they had found no causal link between the MMR vaccine and autism (Murch et al., 2004). They stated:

> We wish to make it clear that in this paper (Wakefield et al. 1998) no causal link was established between MMR vaccine and autism as the data were insufficient. However, the possibility of such a link was raised and consequent events have had major implications for public health. In view of this, we consider now is the appropriate time that we should together formally retract the interpretation placed upon these findings in the paper, according to precedent. (p. 750)

Despite this retraction, Wakefield has continued to maintain that the findings of his original study are still valid (Wakefield, 1999, 2017; Wakefield, Harvey, & Linnell, 2004; Wakefield, Stott, & Limb, 2006). Moreover, anti-vaccine advocates such as Barbara Loe Fisher and the NVIC have continued to support Wakefield and his findings claiming that he has been "relentlessly persecuted by vaccine bullies" (Fisher, 2009). Together these individuals have significantly contributed to the ongoing myth, and belief of many, that "vaccinations cause autism".

Even after Wakefield et al.'s findings were discredited, many anti-vaccine advocates began to claim that vaccines containing mercury in the form of thimerosal, caused autism (Bernard, Enayati, Redwood, Roger, & Binstock, 2001; Bernard, Enayati, Roger, Binstock, & Redwood, 2002; Boom & Cunningham, 2014). Thimerosal is a compound containing ethylmercury, which was introduced in the 1940s as a preservative in some vaccines (Stehr-Green, Tull, Stellfeld, Mortenson, & Simpson, 2003). Anti-vaccine proponents offer two theories regarding a link between vaccines containing ethylmercury or thimerosal and autism. The first theory is based on the perception that autistic individuals demonstrate symptoms resembling mercury poisoning (Healy & Pickering, 2011) even though the two present dissimilarly. More importantly, while mercury poisoning can be quite serious, ethylmercury has been found to be safe (Offit, 2007; Parker, Schwartz, Todd, & Pickering, 2004; Verstraeten et al., 2003). The second theory is that exposure to thimerosal results in a weakened immune system. This enables the live virus in the vaccine to damage the gut and brain (Autism Spectrum Australia, 2015; Office of Special Masters, 2009) resulting in autism symptomology. To date, there has been no evidence to support either of these theories. However, many individuals continue to believe and publicly state that thimerosal in vaccines is a contributor to autism (Offit, 2008).

Despite no research to indicate that it was harmful, public concern about its safety resulted in the removal of thimerosal from all vaccinations by 2001, with the exception of the Hepatitis B vaccine in Australia and one influenza vaccine in the USA (National Centre for Immunisation Research and Surveillance of Vaccine Preventable Diseases (NCIRS), 2009). Even before thimerosal was removed from the MMR vaccine, researchers determined that there was no evidence to suggest that the small quantities of ethylmercury contained in vaccines contributed to the development of autism (Parker et al., 2004). As evidence of this, prevalence rates of autism continued to rise even after thimerosal was removed from childhood vaccines (Matson & Kozlowski, 2011).

The observation of some parents that their child displayed obvious differences in their behaviour after receiving their MMR vaccination has been cited as proof by anti-vaccine proponents that the vaccination must have caused these differences (Richler et al., 2006). However, this reasoning is flawed, as it assumes that correlation and causation are synonymous. Researchers caution that the coexistence or correlation of two events does not necessarily mean that one event is responsible for causing the other (DeStefano, Bhasin, Thompson, Yeargin-Allsopp, & Boyle, 2004). Instead, both events may be linked to a third factor, in this instance the age of the child, which correlates with both administration of the initial MMR vaccination and the recognition of autism symptomology. Autism is classified as a neurodevelopmental disorder. The neurological or brain differences associated with autism may manifest at the same age as the administration of the MMR vaccination, making the relationship coincidental. As Rao and Andrade (2011) point out, both vaccinations and autism occur in early childhood, so at least a temporal link is predestined, but this does not imply a causal relationship between the two.

Some parents have suggested that it is the combination of multiple vaccines given at one time, which overwhelms their child's immune system and contributes to them developing autism (Hilton, Petticrew, & Hunt, 2006). Gerber and Offit (2009) argue that this theory is not valid for several reasons. Firstly, there is no evidence that vaccines overwhelm the immune system and contribute to the development of neurological conditions, such as autism. In fact, the immunological reaction caused by vaccines is much weaker than that encountered by a person's immune system in a regular environment, such as at a shopping centre or school (Hilton et al., 2006). Secondly, studies have shown that multiple vaccinations given at one time do not weaken the body's immune system (Miller, Andrews, Waight, & Taylor, 2003). Most importantly, Gerber and Offit stress that autistic individuals demonstrate no signs, such as inflammatory lesions in their central nervous system or activation of immune systems, that would indicate that autism is an immune disease. In contrast, the available evidence strongly suggests that in the majority of cases, autism is more likely linked to genetic variations or predispositions that are impacted in no way by the administration of vaccines (O'Roak & State, 2008).

Walsh, Thomas, Mason and Evans (2015) explored the factors in the UK, which have influenced parents' decision about whether they should have their child receive the MMR vaccine. They found that newspapers, news programs, and websites appeared to have the most influence on parents. Despite the lack of evidence to support the myth that vaccines cause autism, the news media has continued to publish stories, which question the safety of vaccinations (Ackermann, Chapman, & Leask, 2004; Hussain et al., 2011). Hussain and colleagues (2011) explored the ways in which American newspaper stories portrayed the issue of vaccine safety. They analysed 1,147 stories, published between 1995 and 2015 and discovered that 46% of them reported concerns about vaccine safety, while only 20% reported the safety of vaccinations. More recently, Holton, Weberling, Clarke and Smith (2012) examined 281 newspaper articles published in ten different countries between 1998 and 2011 in order to determine how information was presented in regard to the MMR–autism controversy. These researchers discovered that the media's reporting tended to assign blame primarily to Wakefield, emphasising his role in the controversy rather than multiple parties. They also found that media sources often provided opinions rather than facts, with some still defending Wakefield. Holton et al. questioned the validity of taking a balanced approach on an issue that had a definitive side, concluding that offering competing views on the MMR controversy was not providing parents with the facts and perpetuated uncertainty about the link between vaccines and autism.

Dannetun, Tegnell, Hermansson and Giesecke (2005) examined Swedish parents' reasons for postponing or declining the MMR vaccine for their child. They found that parents were primarily concerned about adverse effects, and that their primary source of information was the news. Offit and Coffin (2003) suggested that many news reports have played on the public's emotions by presenting emotional and dramatic accounts of parents relating their concerns about the harmful effects of the MMR vaccine. For example, in a *60 Minutes* report broadcast on 12 November 2000, a mother and father were shown struggling to control their tears as they told their story saying, "Nicholas appeared perfectly normal until just after his first birthday, when he received the MMR vaccine…. I should never have let him have that vaccine" (Offit & Coffin, 2003, p. 3). In the same story, reporters interviewed Andrew Wakefield who discussed his concern about vaccine safety expressing his belief that the MMR vaccine caused autism. The report did not include any interviews with researchers who had completed studies refuting the link between the MMR vaccine and autism. Since this story aired, other reports have continued to provide either biased or "balanced" views of the vaccine–autism controversy, further substantiating a possible link for many parents (Offit, 2008). Further compounding this is Brown et al.'s (2010) finding that parents tend to trust media reports about vaccines more than scientific research or government reports.

Celebrities are another source of misinformation and influence on the public's perception regarding the link between vaccines and autism (Holton et al., 2012). Researchers (Poland, 2011; Vyse, 2005) have stressed the influence that celebrities have on public opinion, with many people confusing celebrity status with authority.

One celebrity who has been a very vocal proponent of the link between vaccines and autism is Jenny McCarthy (Boom & Cunningham, 2014; Gross, 2009). McCarthy has consistently blamed vaccines for her son's diagnosis of autism, even when confronted with a lack of evidence to support her beliefs. McCarthy and her former partner, celebrity Jim Carrey, have vocally encouraged parents to question vaccine safety. In 2008, they led a march and rally in Washington, D.C., calling for health authorities to eliminate toxins and "green our vaccines" (Offit, 2011). McCarthy has published two books (McCarthy, 2007, 2008) and appeared on television on multiple occasions (Boom & Cunningham, 2014) to present her theories and condemn the medical community for continuing to push vaccinations. Many researchers have cited the influence that she has had on the perception of the public, and parents in particular, that vaccines cause autism (Boom & Cunningham, 2014; Gross, 2009; Langan, 2011; Larson, Cooper, Eskola, Katz, & Ratzan, 2011). Unfortunately, McCarthy is not the only celebrity to support the "vaccine causes autism" myth. Recently, public figures such as Robert F. Kennedy, Jr. and actor Robert De Niro have also questioned the link between vaccines and autism (Sharfstein, 2017).

A final source of the "vaccination causes autism" myth comes from the Internet and social media. Scullard, Peacock and Davies (2010) explored the reliability of medical advice offered when five common paediatric questions were entered into the Google search engine. Of the 500 sites they examined, 39% gave accurate information, 11% gave inaccurate information and advice, and 49% failed to answer the question. Government websites provided accurate information about vaccines 100% of the time, and education websites offered accurate information 80% of the time. In contrast, the information presented on news websites was only accurate 50% of the time, while sponsored websites were found to give little accurate information or advice. In addition, many sponsored websites were found to have conflicts of interest. The researchers found this to be a particularly troublesome finding, given that sponsored websites pay a premium to be visible and often appear across multiple pages.

Kata (2010) examined anti-vaccination websites and found they often presented arguments about a parent's right to refuse vaccinating their child. Additionally, many questioned the safety of vaccines, claiming that they were poisonous and caused a range of illnesses, including autism. These websites used emotional appeals in the form of personal testimonials from parents who credited vaccines with harming their children. Kata also found that some anti-vax websites portrayed Wakefield as a martyr and applauded doctors who spoke out against vaccinations. These sites often contained misinformation and incorrect statistics about vaccination research, including studies of the MMR vaccination, and provided an extremely one-sided view about childhood vaccination.

Social media has also contributed to the public debate regarding a vaccination–autism link. Larson et al. (2011) and Venkatraman, Garg and Kumar (2015) highlighted that freedom of speech on the Internet has led to a dominance of opinions by anti-vaccination groups, whereas scientists and researchers are a little more circumspect in their contributions to the Internet, tending to rely on peer-reviewed sources to disseminate their findings. Anti-vaccination messages are prominent on

YouTube, while parents and anti-vaccination groups use Facebook and other sites to debate vaccine safety and links with autism. Correspondingly, the findings of scientific research are rarely presented in such public forums and require individuals to actively seek them out.

Although the origins of the "vaccination causes autism" myth can be originally traced to a couple of key sources, the growth of sources such as news media, the Internet, and public support of celebrities has contributed to its longevity. To contradict this myth, scientists and researchers have continued to explore research that sheds light not just on the correlation between autism and vaccines, but on other possible causes of autism. This has resulted in a fairly significant amount of knowledge amassed over the past decade about the aetiology and incidence of autism in both vaccinated and unvaccinated populations.

3.2 The Research

For a scientific study to be credible, other studies must be able to use the same methodological procedures and replicate its findings (Chatterjee, 2013). To date, researchers have failed to find any correlation between either the MMR vaccine and autism (Dales et al., 2001; Fombonne & Cook, 2003; Kaye et al., 2001; Klein & Diehl, 2004; Madsen et al., 2002; Mäkelä et al., 2002; Taylor et al., 1999) or between autism and other vaccines such as the DPT (Gerber & Offit, 2009; Taylor, Swerdfeger, & Eslick, 2014). Moreover, researchers have consistently found that the prevalence rates of autism in samples of vaccinated children are similar to the rates of autism in unvaccinated children (Honda, Shimizu, & Rutter, 2005; Madsen et al., 2002; Taylor et al., 2014; Uchiyama, Kurosawa, & Inaba, 2007; Uno, Uchiyama, Kurosawa, Aleksic, & Ozaki, 2015).

Researchers have examined whether vaccination rates are correlated with incidence rates of autism and have found no link between the two (Kaye et al., 2001; Taylor et al., 1999). Dales et al. (2001) conducted a retrospective analysis of MMR immunisation rates among children born between 1980 and 1994 who were attending Californian kindergartens. They found that the proportion of children who were administered the MMR vaccine remained relatively consistent, while the proportion of autism diagnoses increased dramatically. These results were replicated in a large-scale study conducted in Denmark by Madsen et al. (2002). After reviewing government health records of 537,303 children, of which 440,655 (82%) had received the MMR vaccine, Madsen et al. found that the percentage of children diagnosed with autism was comparable in the two groups. The researchers concluded that there was no correlation between the MMR vaccine and autism diagnoses. Japan has presented a unique opportunity to explore the possibility of a link between the MMR vaccine and autism. Japan removed the MMR vaccine from their country's national immunization program in 1993 due to concerns over aseptic meningitis. Honda et al. (2005) measured the cumulative incidence of autism in Japanese children up to seven years of age, born between 1988 and 1996. Their study showed that despite a decrease in the proportion of children receiving an MMR vaccination, the rate of autism diagnoses within this population continued to increase.

Studies have also compared autism rates among children who have received vaccines with thimerosal and those who either received vaccines without thimerosal or who received no vaccines. Hviid, Stellfeld, Wohlfahrt and Melbye (2003) examined the health records of 467,450 children and compared the prevalence of autism among those who had received a vaccine containing thimerosal to those who had received a thimerosal-free version of the same vaccine. They found no evidence of an increased risk for a later diagnosis of autism or a related disorder for children who had received the vaccine with thimerosal. Similarly, they found no evidence of a dose–response relationship. In another study, Madsen et al. (2003) investigated whether the rates of autism diagnoses in Denmark decreased after thimerosal-containing vaccines were discontinued. They found there was actually an increase in diagnoses rates after thimerosal was removed. Madsen et al. concluded, "Our ecological data do not support a correlation between thimerosal-containing vaccines and the incidence of autism" (p. 604). Similarly, Parker et al. (2004) conducted an extensive review of 12 studies to examine the link between thimerosal in vaccines and autism. They found that although studies varied in design, most had found no evidence that thimerosal in vaccines contributed to the development of autism. The three studies (Geier & Geier, 2003a, 2003b, 2004) that did support the thimerosal hypothesis were all conducted by the same researchers, were of poor quality and had many design flaws that invalidated their conclusions. They concluded that not only has past research not demonstrated a link between thimerosal or ethylmercury in vaccines and autism, but that the pharmacokinetics of ethylmercury made any association highly unlikely. Since this review was published, other studies have consistently found no link between rates of autism and vaccines, either with or without thimerosal and ethylmercury (Andrews et al., 2004; Price et al., 2010; Stehr-Green et al., 2003; Uno et al., 2015; Verstraeten et al., 2003). Given that health organisations have taken the further precaution of removing thimerosal from vaccines, it is even more unlikely that any such link will be found.

In summary, research does not support the hypothesis that vaccines contribute to the development of autism in children. While a very few published studies have suggested that there is a link (Geier & Geier, 2003a, 2003b, 2004), a closer inspection reveals that these studies incorporate methodologies which are problematic and/or are conducted by individuals who have a specific conflict of interest or anti-vaccine bias. This lack of evidence, however, does little to alleviate the concerns about parents who notice their young children experiencing difficulties and challenging behaviours associated with autism. For these parents, recent research offers some insight into the aetiology of autism.

The exact aetiology of autism is still unknown. This void in the knowledge base has led to a number of theories, such as the refrigerator mother theory (Langan, 2011), as people grappled for answers and understanding around the cause or causes of autism. As a more sophisticated understanding of autism has developed, many of these theories have been discredited. Researchers now acknowledge that autism is a complex neurodevelopmental condition, which involves differences in cognitive, emotional and sensory processing (Chamak, Bonniau, Jaunay, & Cohen, 2008; Frith,

1997; O'Connor & Kirk, 2008; Rajendran & Mitchell, 2007; Vermeulen, 2015). Researchers have also speculated that these differences indicate that autism may have several, rather than one definitive aetiology (Happé & Ronald, 2008). Current research indicates that autism has a biological and genetic derivation, which may also be influenced by environmental factors (Frith, 2003).

Over the past decade, scientists and researchers have learnt more about the role of genetics in the development of autism. Twin and family studies have demonstrated that autism is highly inheritable (Freitag, 2007; Hallmayer et al., 2011). Colvert et al. (2015) assessed sets of twins, who were born in either England or Wales between January 1994 and December 1996. They found that the chance of identical twins both receiving a diagnosis of autism was significantly higher (range, 0.77–0.99) than that of fraternal twins (range, 0.22–0.65). These results were confirmed by Tick, Bolton, Happé, Rutter and Rijsdijk (2016) who conducted a meta-analysis of twin studies and found that identical twins had a greater probability of both being diagnosed with autism, than did fraternal twins.

Happé and Ronald (2008) have developed a theory, known as the *Fractionable Triad theory*, as a result of their research on the ways in which autism symptomology is related or independent in nature. This theory suggests that autism is not caused by one gene, but by multiple genetic variations and combinations, which contribute to the differing profiles of skills and needs in individuals diagnosed with autism. Presenting data from twin studies, Happé and Ronald argue that no single gene can account for the symptoms typically associated with autism and that different genes may contribute to the individual characteristics exhibited across the autism symptomology of social, communication and restricted and repetitive behaviours. This thinking is corroborated by Verhoeff (2012) who suggests that no single gene can possibly account for the amount of diversity seen among autistic individuals. Robinson et al. (2012) conducted further examination of twins, confirming the fractionation of genetic and environmental influences across autistic traits. Happé and Ronald (2008) contend that scientists need to stop trying to find a single gene responsible for the development of autism. Rather, they should look at a variety of genes, that when combined or influenced by environmental factors, result in the behavioural characteristics needed to meet the diagnostic criteria for autism spectrum disorder.

Other researchers have explored neurological characteristics of autistic children (Courchesne, Campbell, & Solso, 2011; Wolff et al., 2012) in an attempt to understand the way that autism symptomology develops. These researchers reveal evidence that brain differences may develop in early infancy, well before the emergence of behavioural manifestations of autism. More importantly these brain differences occur before the child has received their first vaccinations. Dr. Temple Grandin and other autistic individuals, including Gunilla Gerland and Dr. Stephen Shore, (Chamak et al., 2008) have contributed to our understanding of the ways in which the physiological structure of the brain as well as the cognitive processing of autistic individuals may differ from their neurotypical peers (Grandin, 2013). Grandin, as well as with other researchers (Happé & Frith, 2006), stresses that these differences do not necessarily equate to deficits in thinking, but may contribute to the unique strengths exhibited by autistic individuals. For example, Grandin contends that an acute focus on detail and specialised interests, commonly exhibited by autistic individuals, is a particular asset of autistic individuals.

Studies have suggested that some environmental influences, either in isolation or in combination with genetic factors, may also be contributors in the aetiology of autism (Hallmayer et al., 2011; Landrigan, 2010). Most of these factors have also been linked to other developmental disabilities (Frith, 2003). These include environmental contributors that affect the mother and foetus during pregnancy such as maternal smoking (Rosen, Lee, Lee, Yang, and Burstyn, 2015), maternal disease (Xu, Jing, Bowers, Liu, & Bao, 2014) and complications during pregnancy (Goldin & Matson, 2016). Prenatal exposure of mothers to high-stress situations (Varcin, Alvares, Uljarević, & Whitehouse, 2017), anti-depressants (Boukhris, Sheehy, Mottron, & Bérard, 2016) and alcohol (Singer et al., 2017) are other environmental factors that have been linked to higher rates of autism. Maternal exposure during pregnancy to infections, such as cytomegalovirus (Sakamoto, Moriuchi, Matsuzaki, Motoyama, & Moriuchi, 2014) and bacterial infections (Zerbo et al., 2015), has also been cited as possible risk factors for autism. Ironically, diseases such as rubella or meningitis, which are preventable by vaccines, have been linked to several developmental disorders in infants, including autism (Hutton, 2016).

Although studies do indicate that maternal exposure may place babies at a slightly higher risk for autism, no evidence has been found that vaccines contribute to autism (Landrigan, 2010). Despite this, many public figures and parents have continued to insist that their children are evidence that vaccines are harmful (Boom & Cunningham, 2014; Fischbach, Harris, Ballan, Fischbach, & Link, 2016; Langan, 2011), while others express concern about vaccine safety (Chow, Danchin, Willaby, Pemberton, & Leask, 2017; Freed, Clark, Butchart, Singer, & Davis, 2010) and some elect to forego having their child vaccinated (Brown et al., 2010, 2012; Dannetun et al., 2005). Until these concerns are adequately addressed, the "vaccination causes autism" myth will continue to have an impact not just on families, but on the public welfare, as well as the public perception of autistic individuals.

3.3 The Impact

It could be argued that the "vaccine causes autism" myth has had the most significant impact of all the autism myths, as it has significantly affected public perception of vaccines and autism on an international scale (Flaherty, 2011; Larson et al., 2011; Yaqub, Castle-Clarke, Sevdalis, & Chataway, 2014). In particular, the "vaccine causes autism" myth has contributed to a decline in childhood vaccination rates, particularly in the UK and the USA (Leask, Booy, & McIntyre, 2010). Smith, Ellenberg, Bell and Rubin (2008) found that the number of unvaccinated children more than doubled in the USA, following the publication of Wakefield et al.'s (1998) study. They attributed this decline to parent's concern about vaccination safety and autism as a result of the media's coverage of Wakefield et al.'s study.

The decline in vaccination rates has resulted in increased incidences of vaccine-preventable diseases, such as measles and whooping cough (Phadke, Bednarczyk, Salmon, & Omer, 2016). Phadke et al. (2016) found that within the USA there has been a resurgence of pertussis because of waning immunity and the proliferation of vaccine refusal behaviours. Cases of measles have also risen significantly in England during the 10-year period from 1998 to 2008 (Flaherty, 2011), and outbreaks of measles and whooping cough have been reported in Australia and Europe (Andrews et al., 2008; Chiappini, Stival, Galli, & De Martino, 2013). Flaherty (2011) contends that the vaccine–autism controversy has created a public health crisis calling it the "most damaging medical hoax of the last 100 years" (p. 1302). He also expressed his theory that the "vaccine causes autism" myth has endured as it provides a simple explanation for a complex problem. He cautions that scientific evidence is unlikely to be sufficient to sway public opinion regarding vaccines and autism.

Freed et al. (2010) conducted surveys to examine parents' beliefs and concerns about vaccine safety. They found that 11.5% of the parents had refused at least one vaccination for their children, and many parents had concerns about side effects including the possibility of autism. The researchers concluded that vaccine safety information was not effective in changing parents' opinion. In a more recent study, Chow et al. (2017) surveyed parents regarding their attitudes, beliefs, behaviours and concerns about vaccinations in Australia. They found that 21% of respondents either strongly agreed or agreed with the statement "I am concerned that vaccines can cause autism in healthy children". Young, Elliston and Ruble (2015) also surveyed parents of autistic children about their attitudes and beliefs about vaccines. They found the majority of parents believed that vaccines were effective and necessary. Regardless, 56% of parents surveyed believed that vaccines contributed, at least in part, to autism, and 16% said they would discourage other parents from having their child vaccinated. In another study, Fischbach et al. (2016) compared the attitudes of parents of autistic children with scientists. They found that the parents were much more likely to blame vaccines for their child's diagnosis, while scientists rarely communicated directly with parents. Fischbach et al. recommended that to combat misperceptions about vaccinations, scientists needed to communicate their findings and implications more readily to the public including parents.

Other researchers have explored the reasons that anti-vaccine messages are not effective in mitigating the "vaccine causes autism" myth. Yaqub et al. (2014) found that lack of awareness and misinformation played only a partial role in parent's attitudes and decisions about vaccines. More important was the degree to which they trusted health institutions or providers. Larson et al. (2011) also stressed that public trust plays a role in parents' perception of vaccine safety, as does assessment of risk. Similarly, Leask, Chapman, Hawe and Burgess (2006) found that parents used a risk–benefit equation to help them decide whether to vaccinate their child, weighing the risk of their child getting the disease with perceived side effects of receiving the vaccine. This included their perceptions about the risk of autism and the harm associated with autism.

While some parents may decide that diseases such as measles and pertussis pose a greater risk than autism, others may decide that autism has the potential to cause their child greater harm. Senier (2008) explored the ways in which parents assessed vaccine risks and benefits. Parents' considered factors such as their family's medical history and their child's susceptibility to adverse events in deciding whether autism was the greater risk. A few parents stated that autism was their "worst case". These individuals highlighted that they did not want to be responsible, through vaccines, for their child not being able to become a fully functioning member of society. Burgess, Burgess and Leask (2006) provide a more detailed analysis of parents' considerations when weighing the possible risks associated with autism and vaccines. Using Sandman's model of public risk perception, Burgess et al. explained that perception of risk involves parents constructing a summation of the hazards involved in combination with their sense of outrage about the factors that make them worried, frightened or upset. They conclude that the possibility of their child being "afflicted" with a lifelong and debilitating condition presented parents with a low hazard, high outrage situation in which autism is perceived as a dreaded and frightening condition. Burgess et al. suggested that acknowledging this fear is important in supporting parents and in changing parents' perceptions about vaccines and autism.

Burgess et al.'s (2006) findings highlight another key impact of the "vaccine causes autism myth". By continuing to focus attention and debate on the "dreaded outcome" of autism, the media and professionals are promoting a negative stigma of autism and of autistic individuals. This is evident in the finding of Fischbach et al. (2016) that although scientists and parents of autistic children disagree about the causes of autism, they agree about the negative stigma attached to public discussions of autism and autistic individuals. Anti-vaccine advocates often rely on overdramatised accounts of children who have "been lost to autism" (Gross, 2009) to promote their message that vaccines are dangerous. The influence of these messages on the public perception of autism was highlighted by one parent in a recent study describes her assessment of the risk of her child contracting autism as a result of vaccines:

> But, you know, having children who just don't respond and who are not affectionate and who have a really hard time learning and really can't...grow up and participate in life... is just so sad... and to fear that somehow, some decision you made, made them that way is really frightening. (Senier, 2008, p. 221)

This statement indicates the extremely negative view the parent had of autism, feeling it would significantly limit her child. It also conveys the significant level of hazard and harm she feels that autism would have for both her child and her potential relationship with her child.

Media coverage of anti-vaccine advocates frequently depicts these individuals discussing the ways that their child has been damaged by autism (Pellicano & Stears, 2011). For example, McCarthy described her observations of her son following his MMR immunisation saying, "Soon thereafter I noticed a change. The soul was gone from his eyes" (Boom & Cunningham, 2014, p. 8). These comments reinforce the image of the autistic child as a normal child who has been permanently damaged and who has vanished in some way. Another example can be found in the book, *Evidence of harm: Mercury in vaccines and the autism epidemic*, which was written by David Kirby with the support of anti-vaccine parent groups (Langan, 2011). These messages have contributed to the devaluing of autistic people, with both members of the public and families, perceiving autistic individuals as having limited potential. Unfortunately, pro-vaccine scientists have done little to contradict this image. Instead, they have focused on arguing that vaccines do not cause autism, and thus there is little risk of children becoming autistic. It could be argued that this does little to alleviate parents' fears of autism, only their fears that vaccines will cause autism. As researchers have demonstrated, this approach has not been successful in mitigating the impact of the "vaccine causes autism" myth (Chatterjee, 2013; Kata, 2010; Yaqub et al., 2014).

3.4 The Future

Mocarski (2014) suggests that many myths originate from fear as individuals seek out explanations to decrease their anxiety about things they do not understand or which cannot be explained. Fear is derived from phenomena that are seemingly unexplained, random and have the potential to cause people harm. Autism is a condition, which up until recently was relatively mysterious in its aetiology and associated with challenging behaviours and barriers in adaptive functioning. Moreover, autism has been portrayed as a disease or disorder that has the potential to cause serious harm, which damages the "normal child" and traps them behind the barrier of autism (Sarrett, 2011). It can be argued that the core belief underlying the "vaccinations cause autism" myth is a fear of autism, or in the case of parents, anxiety that their child will become autistic and consequently be limited in what they can achieve in life. To transform this myth, the public's perception of what it means to be autistic must be challenged enabling parents and the wider community to alter their image of the autistic individual as capable rather than as deficient. This will mean transforming the view of what constitutes a quality life and developing an understanding of autistic difference rather than disability.

Milton (2014) and other advocates (Broderick, 2009) contend that the disability of autism is not innate, but created by the social environment and perceptions and expectations of others. Grinker (2008) adds that autism is constructed as much by societal culture as it is by medical science. In contrast, autism research and practice are often dominated by a medical model, which focuses on the deficits and disability of autistic individuals (Bagatell, 2010; Broderick, 2009; Grinker, 2015). In recent years, parents and autistic advocates have begun to resist these ways of thinking, particularly challenging the prevalent discourse of autism as a destructive condition that significantly affects both the lives of the individual and their family (Langan, 2011). These individuals argue for an alternative and expanded concept of autism in which autistic individuals are viewed as contributors rather than burdens on society and valued rather than stigmatised for their differences. For these individuals, the vaccination debate centres not just on tensions between scientists and parents, but on the value society places on them as autistic individuals (Grinker, 2010). For example, the statements of both parents and scientists have often focused on the limited ability of autistic individuals to engage socially with others. Advocates argue that this notion is based on a "neurotypical" version of sociability and does not mean that they do not want or are unable to interact with others, but that they do so in a different way.

In recent years, researchers have begun to engage with autistic children and adults, as well as some parents, to develop a more detailed understanding of the autistic identity (Lester, Karim, & O'Reilly, 2015). For many individuals, this means finding a community in which they can relax and be themselves, rather than having to conform to societal expectations, which are often based on neurotypical norms (Bagatell, 2012). This body of research has revealed that autistic individuals view their differences or "atypicalities" as both strengths and weaknesses. These include talents in areas such as visuospatial tasks as well as challenges in managing anxiety and sensory input. Also, apparent is the variation that exists within the autistic community. While some individuals eschew any notion of a cure, others state that they would welcome treatments or interventions that would help them to decrease some of their more significant challenges (Pellicano & Stears, 2011). This view is more common for individuals who have higher support needs as well as a higher degree of physical and sensory needs. Almost all individuals agree, however, that being autistic means they have a different style of thinking and interacting with their world (Chamak et al., 2008), and that they require societal understanding, acceptance and support for them to achieve.

Recent years have also seen a shift in perspectives and advocacy of some parents of autistic children (Langan, 2011). Although the vaccine–autism debate has provided a forum to showcase the disaffection of parents who are looking to place blame for their child's difficulties, a few parents have begun to express the positive impact of autism for their child and family (Myers, Mackintosh, & Goin-Kochel, 2009). These parents consistently highlight the benefits of their child's unique qualities and talents and resist the efforts of medical communities to subject their children to stressful interventions with the aim of helping them to lead "normal" lives (Langan, 2011). One of these parents, Dr. Richard Grinker, used his background and expertise as an anthropologist to investigate the ways in which parents across the world have adapted to their child's "unstrange" worldviews (Grinker, 2008). Another example is Ron Suskind, whose book, *Life Animated*, journeys his family's use of his son's special interest to connect with him after he stopped talking (Suskind, 2016). Now translated into a documentary film, this story is indicative of the ways in which an autistic adult can experience success and engage with the wider world if they are supported to do so in their own way.

Grinker and Suskind's stories provide an illustration of one way of transforming the public's perception of autism by showcasing their child's individuality and adaptability. To change the public view of autism, it is important that parents who have found ways to embrace their child's autism share their stories so that other parents can see the positive aspects of autism for their children and families. Moreover, these examples need to be showcased as much, if not more, in the media as the negative stories of parents who are distressed, frustrated, and only able to view autism in a negative light. It should also be noted that even parents that have espoused the positive aspects of autism have expressed their concern about their child's future, particularly in the light of limited supports for autistic adults (Myers et al., 2009). It is this fear, more than any other, that may have sustained the vaccine–autism debate, as it provides hope for parents who view autism as synonymous with a limited future.

To truly alter the "vaccine causes autism" myth, parents, scientists and community members must be able to envision a positive future for autistic individuals. This can be accomplished in several ways. Firstly, showcasing stories of successful autistic adults will help to illustrate the future possibilities for autistic children. Many autistics have published their own life stories indicating the challenges they have faced and the factors that have enabled them to succeed. More importantly, these stories indicate the unique ways that these individuals have achieved success in their own ways. A number of these stories can be found in Grandin's book, *Different Not Less* (Grandin, 2012). In this book, 14 autistic adults relate their stories illustrating how they have built on their special interests and dealt with their difficulties to succeed in different areas of their life. Showcasing such stories is critical if public perceptions of autistic individuals are to change.

Recently, the television and film industries have taken some positive steps, by incorporating autistic characters in shows such as *The Good Doctor, Atypical, The A Word* and even *Sesame Street.* Too often, however, these portraits have focused on the eccentric and exceptional abilities of autistic characters, or on the challenges faced by their parents. Additionally, some autistic advocates have criticised these shows for only presenting a limited depiction of the autism spectrum, which does not encompass the full range of skills and needs exhibited by autistic children and adults. More importantly, these shows have almost never illustrated the autistic individual's perspective. Rather, they have positioned the autistic individual as the one who is different and struggling to cope. Changing the public's perception will necessitate allowing them to see the world through the autistic perspective. A few television shows, such as *Atypical*, have employed consultants to try to get an accurate portrait of individuals with autism, but almost none have employed a consultant who is themselves autistic. Giving the public a truly insider perspective can only come from someone who lives and sees this perspective everyday. A transformed future will see autistic individuals being consulted, or better yet, sharing their own stories and the voices of autistic characters being a key element of these shows.

Pellicano and Stears (2011) stressed that researchers and scientists need to engage with the autistic community to ensure that their research and practice align with autistic priorities and are conducted in a way that is relevant and meaningful to autistic persons. Similarly, reconstructing the public's perception of autism will necessitate closer collaboration between researchers, medical practitioners, parents and the autistic community. This will enable not just parents, but scientists and researchers to see these individuals as capable and to help them to view a positive future for autistic individuals. Caution should be taken, however, to ensure that the collaboration is an equal one in which autistic individuals are valued for the knowledge and skills they bring (Milton, 2014), rather than seen only as recipients of strategies and as participants and not collaborators in research. In addition, strategies are needed to ensure that all autistic individuals, including those with lower levels of spoken language, are able to participate and communicate their experiences and perspectives.

This will also help to ensure that the range of autistic perspectives is considered, rather than just those of individuals who are able to negotiate typical contexts (Pellicano & Stears, 2011). Instead of focusing on fixing these individuals, it is hoped that future researchers will concentrate on finding ways to facilitate the participation of all autistic individuals in their communities and families.

3.5 Conclusion

The myth that vaccinations cause autism is arguably one of the most enduring and impactful of all the autism myths. Despite overwhelming research indicating vaccines are not linked to autism, many parents and members of the public continue to maintain their support for this myth and advocate for better vaccine safety. As a result, vaccination rates have declined in some parts of the world, with corresponding outbreaks in vaccine-preventable diseases, such as whooping cough and measles. The continuing vaccine–autism debate has also resulted in the further stigmatisation of autistic individuals as they are described and portrayed as damaged and limited. Current strategies to rectify the beliefs of anti-vaccine supporters and anxious parents have not been successful in discrediting this myth as it has not addressed the central issue, which is parents' concern that autism poses a greater risk to their child than the possibility of them contracting a vaccine-preventable disease. It is only through presenting a positive view that enables parents and researchers to see them as different, but able with unique talents and needs, that the "vaccines cause autism" myth can be truly transformed. Supporting autistic individuals to depict their own worldview will not only reduce the deficit perspective, which sustains the medical model and the "vaccine causes autism" myth, it will also enable the public to envision a positive future in which autistic individuals engage and contribute to their communities in their own ways.

References

Ackermann, D., Chapman, S., & Leask, J. (2004). Media coverage of anthrax vaccination refusal by Australian Defence Force personnel. *Vaccine, 23*(3), 411–417. https://doi.org/10.1016/j.vaccine.2004.03.068.

Andrews, N., Miller, E., Grant, A., Stowe, J., Osborne, V., & Taylor, B. (2004). Thimerosal exposure in infants and developmental disorders: A retrospective cohort study in the United Kingdom does not support a causal association. *Pediatrics, 114*(3), 584–591. https://doi.org/10.1542/peds.2003-1177-L.

Andrews, N., Tischer, A., Siedler, A., Pebody, R. G., Barbara, C., Cotter, S. … Johansen, K. (2008). Towards elimination: Measles susceptibility in Australia and 17 European countries. *Bulletin of the World Health Organization, 86*(3), 197–204.

Autism Spectrum Australia. (2015). *Fact sheet 5: Vaccinations and autism*. Retrieved from http://www.positivepartnerships.com.au/sites/default/files/images/fact-sheet/fact_sheet_5_vaccinations_and_autism_feb2017.pdf.

Bagatell, N. (2010). From cure to community: Transforming notions of autism. *Ethos, 38*(1), 33–55. https://doi.org/10.1111/j.1548-1352.2009.01080.x.

Bagatell, N. (2012). Engaged moments: Mediated action and children with autism in the classroom setting. *OTJR: Occupation, Participation and Health, 32*(1), 258–265. https://doi.org/10.3928/15394492-20110722-01.

Bernard, S., Enayati, A., Redwood, L., Roger, H., & Binstock, T. (2001). Autism: A novel form of mercury poisoning. *Medical Hypotheses, 56*(4), 462–471. https://doi.org/10.1054/mehy.2000.1281.

Bernard, S., Enayati, A., Roger, H., Binstock, T., & Redwood, L. (2002). The role of mercury in the pathogenesis of autism. *Molecular Psychiatry, 7*(S2), S42–S43.

Boom, J. A., & Cunningham, R. M. (2014). *Understanding and managing vaccine concerns*. New York: Springer Cham.

Boukhris, T., Sheehy, O., Mottron, L., & Bérard, A. (2016). Antidepressant use during pregnancy and the risk of autism spectrum disorder in children. *JAMA Pediatrics, 170*(2), 117–124. https://doi.org/10.1001/jamapediatrics.2015.3356.

Broderick, A. A. (2009). Autism, "recovery (to normalcy)", and the politics of hope. *Journal of Intellectual and Developmental Disability, 47*(4), 263–281. https://doi.org/10.1352/1934-9556-47.4.263.

Brown, K. F., Kroll, J. S., Hudson, M. J., Ramsay, M., Green, J., Long, S. J., … Sevdalis, N. (2010). Factors underlying parental decisions about combination childhood vaccinations including MMR: A systematic review. *Vaccine, 28*(26), 4235–4248. https://doi.org/10.1016/j.vaccine.2010.04.052.

Brown, K. F., Long, S. J., Ramsay, M., Hudson, M. J., Green, J., Vincent, C. A., … Sevdalis, N. (2012). U.K. parents' decision-making about measles-mumps-rubella (MMR) vaccine 10 years after the MMR-autism controversy: A qualitative analysis. *Vaccine, 30*(10), 1855–1864. https://doi.org/10.1016/j.vaccine.2011.12.127.

Burgess, D. C., Burgess, M. A., & Leask, J. (2006). The MMR vaccination and autism controversy in United Kingdom 1998-2005: Inevitable community outrage or a failure of risk communication? *Vaccine, 24*(18), 3921–3928. https://doi.org/10.1016/j.vaccine.2006.02.033.

Chamak, B., Bonniau, B., Jaunay, E., & Cohen, D. (2008). What can we learn about autism from autistic persons? *Psychotherapy and Psychosomatics, 77,* 271–279. https://doi.org/10.1159/000140086.

Chatterjee, A. (2013). The controversy that will not go away: Vaccines and autism. In A. Chatterjee (Ed.), *Vaccinophobia and vaccine controversies of the 21st century* (pp. 181–211). New York, NY: Springer. https://doi.org/10.1007/978-1-4614-7438-8_10.

Chiappini, E., Stival, A., Galli, L., & De Martino, M. (2013). Pertussis re-emergence in the post-vaccination era. *BMC Infectious Diseases, 13*(1), 151. https://doi.org/10.1186/1471-2334-13-151.

Chow, M. Y. K., Danchin, M., Willaby, H. W., Pemberton, S., & Leask, J. (2017). Parental attitudes, beliefs, behaviours and concerns towards childhood vaccinations in Australia: A national online survey. *Australian Family Physician, 46*(3), 145–151.

Colvert, E., Tick, B., McEwen, F., Stewart, C., Curran, S. R., Woodhouse, E., … Bolton, P. (2015). Heritability of autism spectrum disorder in a UK population-based twin sample. *JAMA Psychiatry, 72*(5), 415–423. https://doi.org/10.1001/jamapsychiatry.2014.3028.

Coulter, H. L., & Fisher, B. L. (1985). *DPT, a shot in the dark*. San Diego, CA: Harcourt Brace Jovanovich.

Coulter, H. L., & Fisher, B. L. (1991). *A shot in the dark: Why the P in the DPT vaccination may be hazardous to your child's health*. New York: Avery.

Courchesne, E., Campbell, K., & Solso, S. (2011). Brain growth across the life span in autism: Age-specific changes in anatomical pathology. *Brain Research, 1380,* 138–145. https://doi.org/10.1016/j.brainres.2010.09.101.

Dales, L., Hammer, S. J., & Smith, N. J. (2001). Time trends in autism and in MMR immunization coverage in California. *Year Book of Psychiatry and Applied Mental Health, 2001*(1), 47–48.

Dannetun, E., Tegnell, A., Hermansson, G., & Giesecke, J. (2005). Parents' reported reasons for avoiding MMR vaccination. A telephone survey. *Scandinavian Journal of Primary Health Care, 23*(3), 149–153. https://doi.org/10.1080/02813430510031306.

Deer, B. (2011). How the case against the MMR vaccine was fixed. *BMJ, 342,* c5347. https://doi.org/10.1136/bmj.c5347.

DeStefano, F., Bhasin, T. K., Thompson, W. W., Yeargin-Allsopp, M., & Boyle, C. (2004). Age at first measles-mumps-rubella vaccination in children with autism and school-matched control subjects: A population-based study in metropolitan Atlanta. *Pedatrics, 113*(2), 259–266.

Fischbach, R. L., Harris, M. J., Ballan, M. S., Fischbach, G. D., & Link, B. G. (2016). Is there concordance in attitudes and beliefs between parents and scientists about autism spectrum disorder? *Autism, 20*(3), 353–363. https://doi.org/10.1177/1362361315585310.

Fisher, B. L. (2009). Vaccine bullies and fighting back. *NVIC Vaccine News*. Retrieved from https://www.nvic.org/NVIC-Vaccine-News/March/Vaccine-Bullies-And-Fighting-Back.aspx.

Fisher, B. L. (N.D.). Dr. Wakefield and his compelling courage. Retrieved from http://www.naturalhealthstrategies.com/andrew-wakefield.html.

Flaherty, D. K. (2011). The vaccine-autism connection: A public health crisis caused by unethical medical practices and fraudulent science. *Annals of Pharmacotherapy, 45*(10), 1302–1304. https://doi.org/10.1345/aph.1Q318.

Fombonne, E., & Cook, E. H. (2003). MMR and autistic enterocolitis: Consistent epidemiological failure to find an association. *Molecular Psychiatry, 8*(2), 133–134. https://doi.org/10.1038/sj.mp.4001266.

Freed, G. L., Clark, S. J., Butchart, A. T., Singer, D. C., & Davis, M. M. (2010). Parental vaccine safety concerns in 2009. *Pediatrics, 125*(4), 654–659. https://doi.org/10.1542/peds.2009-1962.

Freitag, C. M. (2007). The genetics of autistic disorders and its clinical relevance: A review of the literature. *Molecular Psychiatry, 12*(1), 2–22. https://doi.org/10.1038/sj.mp.4001896.

Frith, U. (1997). The neurocognitive basis of autism. *Trends in Cognitive Sciences, 1*(2), 73–77. https://doi.org/10.1016/S1364-6613(97)01010-3.

Frith, U. (2003). *Autism: Explaining the enigma* (2nd ed.). Malden, MA; Oxford: Blackwell Pub.

Geier, D. A., & Geier, M. R. (2003a). An assessment of the impact of thimerosal on childhood neurodevelopmental disorders. *Pediatric Rehabilitation, 6*(2), 97–102. https://doi.org/10.1080/1363849031000139315.

Geier, D. A., & Geier, M. R. (2004). A comparative evaluation of the effects of MMR immunization and mercury doses from thimerosal-containing childhood vaccines on the population prevalence of autism. *Medical Science Monitor, 10*(3), P133–P139.

Geier, M. R., & Geier, D. A. (2003b). Thimerosal in childhood vaccines, neurodevelopment disorders, and heart disease in the United States. *Journal of the American Physicians and Surgeons, 8*(1), 6–11.

General Medical Council (GMC). (2010). *Dr Andrew Jeremy Wakefield: Determination on serious professional misconduct (SPM) and sanction*. Retrieved from www.gmc-uk.org/Wakefield_SPM_and_SANCTION.pdf_32595267.pdf.

Gerber, J. S., & Offit, P. A. (2009). Vaccines and autism: A tale of shifting hypotheses. *Clinical Infectious Diseases, 48*(4), 456–461. https://doi.org/10.1086/596476.

Goldin, R. L., & Matson, J. L. (2016). Premature birth as a risk factor for autism spectrum disorder. *Developmental Neurorehabilitation, 19*(3), 203–206. https://doi.org/10.3109/17518423.2015.1044132.

Grandin, T. (2012). *Different... not less: Inspiring stories of achievement and successful employment from adults*. Arlington, TX: Future Horizons.

Grandin, T. (2013). *The autistic brain*. New York: Houghton Mifflin Harcourt.

Grinker, R. R. (2008). *Unstrange minds: Remapping the world of autism*. New York: Basic Books.

Grinker, R. R. (2010). Commentary: On being autistic, and social. *Journal of the Society for Psychological Anthropology, 38*(1), 172–178. https://doi.org/10.1111/j.1548-1352.2009.01087.x.

Grinker, R. R. (2015). Reframing the science and anthropology of autism. *Culture, Medicine and Psychiatry, 39*(2), 345–350. https://doi.org/10.1007/s11013-015-9444-9.

Gross, L. (2009). A broken trust: Lessons from the vaccine–autism wars. *PLoS Biology, 7*(5), e1000114. https://doi.org/10.1371/journal.pbio.1000114.
Hallmayer, J., Cleveland, S., Torres, A., Phillips, J., Cohen, B., Torigoe, T., ... Risch, N. (2011). Genetic heritability and shared environmental factors among twin pairs with autism. *Archives of General Psychiatry, 68*(11), 1095–1102. https://doi.org/10.1001/archgenpsychiatry.2011.76.
Happé, F., & Frith, U. (2006). The weak coherence account: Detail-focused cognitive style in autism spectrum disorders. *Journal of Autism and Developmental Disorders, 36*(1), 5–25. https://doi.org/10.1007/s10803-005-0039-0.
Happé, F., & Ronald, A. (2008). The "Fractionable autism triad": A review of evidence from behavioural, genetic, cognitive and neural research. *Neuropsychology Review, 18*(4), 287–304. https://doi.org/10.1007/211065-008-9076-8.
Healy, C. M., & Pickering, L. K. (2011). How to communicate with vaccine-hesitant parents. *Pediatrics, 127*(Supplement 1), S127–S133. https://doi.org/10.1542/peds.2010-1722S.
Hilton, S., Petticrew, M., & Hunt, K. (2006). "Combined vaccines are like a sudden onslaught to the body's immune system": Parental concerns about vaccine "overload" and "immune-vulnerability". *Vaccine, 24*(20), 4321–4327. https://doi.org/10.1016/j.vaccine.2006.03.003.
Hinman, A. R., O'renstein, W. A., Schuchat, A., & CDC. (2011). Vaccine-preventable diseases, immunizations, and MMWR: 1961–2011. *MMWR Surveillance Summaries, 60*(Suppl 4), 49–57.
Holton, A., Weberling, B., Clarke, C. E., & Smith, M. J. (2012). The blame frame: Media attribution of culpability about the MMR-autism vaccination scare. *Health Communication, 27*(7), 690–701. https://doi.org/10.1080/10410236.2011.633158.
Honda, H., Shimizu, Y., & Rutter, M. (2005). No effect of MMR withdrawal on the incidence of autism: A total population study. *Journal of Child Psychology and Psychiatry, 46*(6), 572–579. https://doi.org/10.1111/j.1469-7610.2005.01425.x.
Hussain, H., Omer, S. B., Manganello, J. A., Kromm, E. E., Carter, T. C., Kan, L., ... Salmon, D. A. (2011). Immunization safety in US print media, 1995–2005. *Pediatrics, 127*(Suppl 1), S100–S106. https://doi.org/10.1542/peds.2010-1722o.
Hutton, J. (2016). Does rubella cause autism: A 2015 reappraisal? *Frontiers in Human Neuroscience, 10*(2016), 25. https://doi.org/10.3389/fnhum.2016.00025.
Hviid, A., Stellfeld, M., Wohlfahrt, J., & Melbye, M. (2003). Association between thimerosal-containing vaccine and autism. *Journal of American Medical Association, 290*(13), 1763–1766. https://doi.org/10.1001/jama.290.13.1763.
Institute of Medicine (IOM). (2012). *Adverse effects of vaccines: Evidence and causality*. Retrieved from Washington, DC.
Kata, A. (2010). A postmodern Pandora's box: Anti-vaccination misinformation on the Internet. *Vaccine, 28*(7), 1709–1716. https://doi.org/10.1016/j.vaccine.2009.12.022.
Kaye, J. A., del Mar Melero-Montes, M., & Jick, H. (2001). Mumps, measles and rubella vaccine and the incidence of autism recorded by general practitioners: A time trend analysis. *British Medical Journal, 322*(7254), 460–463. https://doi.org/10.1136/bmj.322.7284.460.
Klein, K. C., & Diehl, E. B. (2004). Relationship between MMR vaccine and autism. *Annals of Pharmacotherapy, 38*(7–8), 1297–1300. https://doi.org/10.1345/aph.1D293.
Landrigan, P. J. (2010). What causes autism? Exploring the environmental contribution. *Current Opinion in Pediatrics, 22*(2), 219–225. https://doi.org/10.1097/MOP.0b013e328336eb9a.
Langan, M. (2011). Parental voices and controversies in autism. *Disability & Society, 26*(2), 193–205. https://doi.org/10.1080/09687599.2011.544059.
Larson, H. J., Cooper, L. Z., Eskola, J., Katz, S. L., & Ratzan, S. (2011). Addressing the vaccine confidence gap. *The Lancet, 378*(9790), 526–535. https://doi.org/10.1016/s0140-6736(11)60678-8.
Leask, J., Booy, R., & McIntyre, P. B. (2010). MMR, Wakefield and the Lancet: What can we learn? *Medical Journal of Australia, 193*(1), 5–7.
Leask, J., Chapman, S., Hawe, P., & Burgess, M. (2006). What maintains parental support for vaccination when challenged by anti-vaccination messages? A qualitative study. *Vaccine, 24*(49–50), 7238–7245. https://doi.org/10.1016/j.vaccine.2006.05.010.

Lester, J. N., Karim, K., & O'Reilly, M. (2015). "Autism itself actually isn't a disability": Negotiating a "normal" versus "abnormal" autistic identity. *Communication & Medicine, 11*(2), 139–152. https://doi.org/10.1558/cam.v11i2.20371.

Madsen, K. M., Hviid, A., Vestergaard, M., Schendel, D., Wohlfahrt, J., Thorsen, P., … Melbye, M. (2002). A population-based study of measles, mumps, and rubella vaccination and autism. *The New England Journal of Medicine, 347*(19), 1477–1482. https://doi.org/10.1056/nejmoa021134.

Madsen, K. M., Lauritsen, M. B., Pedersen, C. B., Thorsen, P., Plesner, A. M., Andersen, P. H., et al. (2003). Thimerosal and the occurrence of autism: Negative ecological evidence from Danish population-based data. *Pediatrics, 112*(3), 604–606. https://doi.org/10.1542/peds.112.3.604.

Mäkelä, A., Nuorti, J. P., & Peltola, H. (2002). Neurologic disorders after measles-mumps-rubella vaccination. *Pediatrics, 110*(5), 957–963. https://doi.org/10.1542/peds.110.5.957.

Matson, J. L., & Kozlowski, A. M. (2011). The increasing prevalence of autism spectrum disorders. *Research in Autism Spectrum Disorders, 5*(1), 418–425. https://doi.org/10.1016/j.rasd.2010.06.004.

McCarthy, J. (2007). *Louder than words: A mother's journey into healing autism*. New York: Cutton.

McCarthy, J. (2008). *Mother warriors: A nation of parents healing autism against all odds*. New York: Dutton.

Miller, E., Andrews, N., Waight, P., & Taylor, B. (2003). Bacterial infections, immune overload, and MMR vaccine. *Archives of Disease in Childhood, 88*(3), 222–223. https://doi.org/10.1136/adc.88.3.222.

Milton, D. (2014). So what exactly are autism interventions intervening with? *Good Autism Practice, 15*(2), 6–14.

Mocarski, R. (2014). *Health mythologies: Developing an understanding of health myths and how they stick and spread through the vaccines cause autism myth* (Doctoral thesis, The University of Alabama). Retrieved from https://search-proquest-com.libraryproxy.griffith.edu.au/docview/1620540756?pq-origsite=summon.

Murch, S. H., Anthony, A., Casson, D. H., Malik, M., Berelowitz, M., Dhillon, A. P., … Walker-Smith, J. A. (2004). Retraction of an interpretation. *The Lancet, 363*(9411), 750. https://doi.org/10.1016/s0140-6736(04)15715-2.

Myers, B. J., Mackintosh, V. H., & Goin-Kochel, R. P. (2009). "My greatest joy and my greatest heart ache:" Parents' own words on how having a child in the autism spectrum has affected their lives and their families' lives. *Research in Autism Spectrum Disorders, 3,* 670–684. https://doi.org/10.1016/j.rasd.2009.01.004.

National Centre for Immunisation Research and Surveillance of Vaccine Preventable Diseases (NCIRS). (2009). *Thiomersal fact sheet*. Retrieved from http://www.ncirs.edu.au/assets/provider_resources/fact-sheets/thiomersal-fact-sheet.pdf.

O'Connor, K., & Kirk, I. (2008). Brief report: Atypical social cognition and social behaviours in autism spectrum disorder: a different way of processing rather than an impairment. *Journal of Autism and Developmental Disorders, 38*(10), 1989–1997. https://doi.org/10.1007/s10803-008-0559-5.

O'Roak, B. J., & State, M. W. (2008). Autism genetics: Strategies, challenges, and opportunities. *Autism Research, 1*(1), 4–17. https://doi.org/10.1136/adc.88.3.222.

Office of Special Masters. (2009). Michelle Cedillo v. Secretary of Health and Human Services. No. 98-916V. Retrieved from https://www.uscfc.uscourts.gov/cedillo-v-secretary-health-and-human-services-case-no-98916v-concluded-june-26-2007.

Offit, P. A. (2007). Thimerosal and vaccines—A cautionary tale. *New England Journal of Medicine, 357*(13), 1278–1279. https://doi.org/10.1056/NEJMp078187.

Offit, P. A. (2008). *Autism's false prophets: Bad science, risky medicine, and the search for a cure*. New York: Columbia University Press.

Offit, P. A. (2011). *Deadly choices: How the anti-vaccine movement threatens us all*. New York: Basic Books.

Offit, P. A., & Coffin, S. E. (2003). Communicating science to the public: MMR vaccine and autism. *Vaccine, 22*(1), 1–6. https://doi.org/10.1016/s0264-410x(03)00532-2.

Parker, S. K., Schwartz, B., Todd, J., & Pickering, L. K. (2004). Thimerosal-containing vaccines and autistic spectrum disorder: A critical review of published original data. *Pediatrics, 114*(3), 793–804. https://doi.org/10.1542/peds.2004-0434.

Pellicano, E., & Stears, M. (2011). Bridging autism, science and society: Moving toward an ethically informed approach to autism research. *Autism Research, 4*(4), 271–282. https://doi.org/10.1002/aur.201.

Phadke, V. K., Bednarczyk, R. A., Salmon, D. A., & Omer, S. B. (2016). Association between vaccine refusal and vaccine-preventable diseases in the United States: A review of measles and pertussis. *JAMA, 315*(11), 1149–1158. https://doi.org/10.1001/jama.2016.1353.

Poland, G. A. (2011, September). MMR vaccine and autism: Vaccine nihilism and postmodern science. In *Mayo Clinic Proceedings* (Vol. 86, No. 9, p. 869). Mayo Foundation.

Price, C. S., Thompson, W. W., Goodson, B., Weintraub, E. S., Croen, L. A., Hinrichsen, V. L., ... DeStefano, F. (2010). Prenatal and infant exposure to thimerosal from vaccines and immunoglobulins and risk of autism. *Pediatrics, 126*(4), 656–664. https://doi.org/10.1542/peds.2010-0309.

Rajendran, G., & Mitchell, P. (2007). Cognitive theories of autism. *Developmental Review, 27,* 224–260. https://doi.org/10.1016/j.dr.2007.02.001.

Rao, T. S., & Andrade, C. (2011). The MMR vaccine and autism: Sensation, refutation, retraction, and fraud. *Indian Journal of Psychiatry, 53*(2), 95–96. https://doi.org/10.4103/0019-5545.82529.

Richler, J., Luyster, R., Risi, S., Hsu, W. L., Dawson, G., Bernier, R., ... Lord, C. (2006). Is there a 'regressive phenotype' of autism spectrum disorder associated with the measles-mumps-rubella vaccine? A CPEA study. *Journal of Autism and Developmental Disorders, 36*(3), 299–316. https://doi.org/10.1007/s10803-005-0070-1.

Robinson, E. B., Koenen, K. C., McCormick, M. C., Munir, K., Hallett, V., Happé, F., ... Ronald, A. (2012). A multivariate twin study of autistic traits in 12-year-olds: Testing the fractionable autism triad hypothesis. *Behavior Genetics, 42*(2), 245–255. https://doi.org/10.1007/s10519-011-9500-3.

Rosen, B. N., Lee, B. K., Lee, N. L., Yang, Y., & Burstyn, I. (2015). Maternal smoking and autism spectrum disorder: A meta-analysis. *Journal of Autism and Developmental Disorders, 45*(6), 1689–1698. https://doi.org/10.1007/s10803-014-2327-z.

Sakamoto, A., Moriuchi, H., Matsuzaki, J., Motoyama, K., & Moriuchi, M. (2014). Retrospective diagnosis of congenital cytomegalovirus infection in children with autism spectrum disorder but no other major neurologic deficit. *Brain and Development, 37*(2), 200–205. https://doi.org/10.1016/j.braindev.2014.03.016.

Sarrett, J. C. (2011). Trapped children: Popular images of children with autism in the 1960s and 2000s. *Journal of Medical Humanities, 32*(2), 141–153. https://doi.org/10.1007/s10912-010-9135-z.

Scullard, P., Peacock, C., & Davies, P. (2010). Googling children's health: Reliability of medical advice on the internet. *Archives of Disease in Childhood, 95*(8), 580–582. https://doi.org/10.1136/adc.2009.168856.

Senier, L. (2008). "It's your most precious thing": Worst-case thinking, trust, and parental decision making about vaccinations. *Sociological Inquiry, 78*(2), 207–229. https://doi.org/10.1111/j.1475-682X.2008.00235.x.

Sharfstein, J. M. (2017). Vaccines and the Trump administration. *JAMA, 317*(13), 1305–1306. https://doi.org/10.1001/jama.2017.2311.

Singer, A. B., Aylsworth, A. S., Cordero, C., Croen, L. A., DiGuiseppi, C., Fallin, M. D., ... Daniels, J. L. (2017). Prenatal alcohol exposure in relation to autism spectrum disorder: Findings from the study to explore early development (SEED). *Paediatric and Perinatal Epidemiology, 31*(6), 573–582. https://doi.org/10.1111/ppe.12404.

Smith, M. J., Ellenberg, S. S., Bell, L. M., & Rubin, D. M. (2008). Media coverage of the measles-mumps-rubella vaccine and autism controversy and its relationship to MMR immunization rates in the United States. *Pediatrics, 121*(4), e836–e843. https://doi.org/10.1542/peds.2007-1760.

Stehr-Green, P., Tull, P., Stellfeld, M., Mortenson, P.-B., & Simpson, D. (2003). Autism and thimerosal-containing vaccines. *American Journal of Preventive Medicine, 25*(2), 101–106. https://doi.org/10.1016/s0749-3797(03)00113-2.

Suskind, R. (2016). *Life animated: A story of sidekicks, heroes and autism*. Glendale, CA: Kingswell.

Taylor, B., Miller, E., Farrington, C., Petropoulos, M.-C., Favot-Mayaud, I., Li, J., et al. (1999). Autism and measles, mumps, and rubella vaccine: No epidemiological evidence for a causal association. *The Lancet, 353*(9169), 2026–2029. https://doi.org/10.1016/s0140-6736(99)01239-8.

Taylor, L. E., Swerdfeger, A. L., & Eslick, G. D. (2014). Vaccines are not associated with autism: An evidence-based meta-analysis of case-control and cohort studies. *Vaccine, 32*(29), 3623–3629. https://doi.org/10.1016/j.vaccine.2014.04.085.

Tick, B., Bolton, P., Happé, F., Rutter, M., & Rijsdijk, F. (2016). Heritability of autism spectrum disorders: A meta-analysis of twin studies. *Journal of Child Psychology and Psychiatry, 57*(5), 585–595. https://doi.org/10.1111/jcpp.12499.

Uchiyama, T., Kurosawa, M., & Inaba, Y. (2007). MMR-vaccine and regression in autism spectrum disorders: Negative results presented from Japan. *Journal of Autism and Developmental Disorders, 37*(2), 210–217. https://doi.org/10.1007/s10803-006-0157-3.

Uno, Y., Uchiyama, T., Kurosawa, M., Aleksic, B., & Ozaki, N. (2015). Early exposure to the combined measles-mumps-rubella vaccine and thimerosal-containing vaccines and risk of autism spectrum disorder. *Vaccine, 33*(21), 2511–2516. https://doi.org/10.1016/j.vaccine.2014.12.036.

Varcin, K. J., Alvares, G. A., Uljarević, M., & Whitehouse, A. J. O. (2017). Prenatal maternal stress events and phenotypic outcomes in autisms spectrum disorder. *Autism Research, 10*(11), 1866–1877. https://doi.org/10.1002/aur.1830.

Venkatraman, A., Garg, N., & Kumar, N. (2015). Greater freedom of speech on Web 2.0 correlates with dominance of views linking vaccines to autism. *Vaccine, 33*(12), 1422–1425. https://doi.org/10.1016/j.vaccine.2015.01.078.

Verhoeff, B. (2012). What is this thing called autism? A critical analysis of the tenacious search for autism's essence. *BioSocieties, 7*(4), 410–432. https://doi.org/10.1057/biosoc.2012.23.

Vermeulen, P. (2015). Context blindness in autism spectrum disorder: Not using the forest to see the trees as trees. *Focus on Autism and Other Developmental Disabilities, 30*(3), 182–192. https://doi.org/10.1177/1088357614528799.

Verstraeten, T., Davis, R. L., DeStefano, F., Lieu, T. A., Rhodes, P. H., Black, S. B., … Chen, R. T. (2003). Safety of thimerosal-containing vaccines: A two-phased study of computerized health maintenance organization databases. *Pediatrics, 112*(5), 1039–1048.

Vyse, S. (2005). Where do fads come from? In J. Jacobson, R. Foxx, & J. A. Mulick (Eds.), *Controversial therapies for developmental disabilities: Fad, fashion, and science in professional practice* (pp. 3–18). Mahwah, NJ: Erlbaum.

Wakefield, A. J. (1999). MMR vaccination and autism. *The Lancet, 354*(9182), 949–950. https://doi.org/10.1016/S0140-6736(05)75696-8.

Wakefield, A. J. (2017). *Callous disregard: Autism and vaccines—The Truth Behind a Tragedy*. New York: Skyhorse Publishing Inc.

Wakefield, A. J., Harvey, P., & Linnell, J. (2004). MMR—Responding to retraction. *The Lancet, 363*(9417), 1327–1328. https://doi.org/10.1016/S0140-6736(04)16017-0.

Wakefield, A. J., Murch, S. H., Anthony, A., Linnell, J., Casson, D. M., Malik, M., … Walker-Smith, J. A. (1998). Ileal-lymphoid-nodular hyperplasia, non-specific colitis, and pervasive developmental disorder in children. *LANCET, 351*(9103), 637–641. https://doi.org/10.1016/s0140-6736(97)11096-0.

Wakefield, A. J., Stott, C., & Limb, K. (2006). Gastrointestinal comorbidity, autistic regression and measles-containing vaccines: Positive re-challenge and biological gradient. *Medical Veritas, 3*, 796–802.

Walsh, S., Thomas, D. R., Mason, B. W., & Evans, M. R. (2015). The impact of the media on the decision of parents in South Wales to accept measles-mumps-rubella (MMR) immunization. *Epidemiology and Infection, 143*(3), 550–560. https://doi.org/10.1017/S0950268814000752.

Wolff, J. J., Gu, H., Gerig, G., Elison, J. T., Styner, M., Gouttard, S., ... Network, I. (2012). Differences in white matter fiber tract development present from 6 to 24 months in infants with autism. *American Journal of Psychiatry, 169*(6), 589–600. https://doi.org/10.1176/appi.ajp.2011.11091447.

Xu, G., Jing, J., Bowers, K., Liu, B., & Bao, W. (2014). Maternal diabetes and the risk of autism spectrum disorders in the offspring: A systematic review and meta-analysis. *Journal of Autism and Developmental Disorders, 44*(4), 766–775. https://doi.org/10.1007/s10803-013-1928-2.

Yaqub, O., Castle-Clarke, S., Sevdalis, N., & Chataway, J. (2014). Attitudes to vaccination: A critical review. *Social Science and Medicine, 112,* 1–11. https://doi.org/10.1016/j.socscimed.2014.04.018.

Young, A. M., Elliston, A., & Ruble, L. A. (2015). Parents of children with autism: Issues surrounding childhood vaccination. *International Public Health Journal, 7*(3), 331–341.

Zerbo, O., Qian, Y., Yoshida, C., Grether, J. K., Van de Water, J., & Croen, L. A. (2015). Maternal infection during pregnancy and autism spectrum disorders. *Journal of Autism and Developmental Disorders, 45*(12), 4015–4025. https://doi.org/10.1007/s10803-013-2016-3.

Chapter 4
Establishing Contexts for Support: Undoing the Legacy of the "Refrigerator Mother" Myth

Abstract One of the earliest theories about the causes of autism is that it occurs from poor parenting or more specifically from the parents' failure to form an attachment or bond with their child in the early months of his/her life. Known as the "refrigerator mother" myth, this theory gained widespread popularity in the 1960s and led many parents and professionals to believe that parents of autistic children were negligent and responsible for their child's autistic symptomology. This chapter will explore the origins of the "refrigerator mother" myth, unpack the current research on interactions and attachment between parents and autistic children, and assess its current impact on autistic individuals, their parents and families. In particular, the resulting stress and isolation experienced by parents will be discussed. The chapter will conclude with recommendations for making the transition from placing the blame and burden on parents for their child's difficulties, towards creating supportive structures so that parents can build their child's competence.

Keywords Historical theories · Parents · Perceptions · Stigmatization
Stress and support

When autism was first identified, there was a limited understanding of its underlying nature or aetiology. For many years, it was thought to be a mental disorder, either related to or similar to schizophrenia. At the same time, Freud's psychoanalytical theory dominated the mental health field, with the result that mental health and behaviour disorders were often attributed to early experiences between parents and children. Eventually, this resulted in the hypothesis that autism was caused by cold and distant parents who failed to bond with their child in early infancy (Baker, 2010). Although this theory, later known as the "refrigerator mother" myth, has been scientifically disproven, its legacy continues to have an impact for autistic individuals and their families.

M. Bennett et al., *Life on the Autism Spectrum*,
https://doi.org/10.1007/978-981-13-3359-0_4

4.1 The Origin

Like many of the myths about autism, the "refrigerator mother" myth has its origins in the early history of research and public awareness of autism. In particular, this myth can be traced to two particular sources: Leo Kanner's early theories regarding the causes of autism and the publication of Bruno Bettelheim book, *The Empty Fortress: Infantile Autism and the Birth of Self* in 1967. Although Kanner first proposed the belief that autism was attributable to distant mothers, it was Bettelheim who was responsible for disseminating the "refrigerator mother" myth more widely to the public (Kroncke, Willard, & Huckabee, 2016).

In a follow-up to his 1943 study, in which he first identified a group of "autistic" children, Kanner suggested that their parents, particularly their mothers, were to blame for their children's developmental problems and difficult behaviours. Kanner observed that many of the mothers displayed a "genuine lack of maternal warmth" (1949, p. 422) and seemed unable to show affection towards their children. An example of this is his description of one mother, in which he states, "She is not by any means the mother type. Her attitude [towards her child] is more like toward a doll or pet than anything else" (Kanner, 1943, p. 230). Although Kanner did not directly state that disconnection between parents and their children was the cause of autism, his continued focus on the behaviour of parents, and questions about how these related to their child's issues, implied a connection. Interestingly, it was

Kanner, rather than Bettelheim, who first used the term "refrigerator" in connection with mothers, saying:

> I have dwelt at some length on the personalities, attitudes, and behaviour of the parents because they seem to throw considerable light on the dynamics of the children's psychopathologic condition. Most of the patients were exposed from the beginning to parental coldness, obsessiveness, and a mechanical type of attention to material needs only. They were the objects of observation and experiment conducted with an eye on fractional performance rather than with genuine warmth and enjoyment. They were kept neatly in refrigerators which did not defrost. Their withdrawal seems to be an act of turning away from such a situation to seek comfort in solitude. (Kanner, 1949, p. 425)

Kanner's hypothesis gained more momentum in 1967 when Bruno Bettelheim published his book, *The Empty Fortress and the Birth of Self,* which presented his theory that autism was caused by cold and distant mothers. In this book, Bettelheim claimed that children became autistic because their mothers were unable or refused to show them affection in early infancy, and thus failed to establish an emotional bond with their child (Baker, 2010; Greydanus & Toledo-Pereyra, 2012; Kroncke et al., 2016). Bettelheim, a Nazi concentration camp survivor, emigrated to the USA after WWII and became the director of the Orthogenic School in Chicago, Illinois. This school was a residential treatment centre for young people diagnosed with severe emotional disturbances. During his time at the school, Bettelheim became intrigued with children who were identified as displaying autistic behaviours (Baker, 2010; Greydanus & Toledo-Pereyra, 2012). Baker (2010) suggests that this interest might have been due to the connection he saw between the social isolation and aloofness demonstrated by these children and the social and emotional detachment he had observed in concentration camp prisoners.

In 1965, the Ford Foundation gave Bettelheim a grant to study a group of autistic children who were patients of the Orthogenic School. One of the patients whom Bettelheim studied was Joey (Baker, 2010; Greydanus & Toledo-Pereyra, 2012). Joey was identified by Bettelheim as a 9-year-old boy who acted more like a machine than a human (Bettelheim, 1959). At 18 months of age, he did not speak and was described by his family as being remote from them and hard to reach (Bettelheim, 1967). Bettelheim proposed that Joey's dysfunctional behaviour was caused by his parents' rejection of him. He justified this position by claiming that Joey's mother had been in denial during her pregnancy and did not want to see or nurse him after he was born. Consequently, this maternal rejection impacted Joey's ability to develop and socially connect with other people. Bettelheim also explained that Joey's father had punished his son when he cried during the night. Bettelheim argued that, under these circumstances, Joey had no choice but to reject his parents' social contact and amuse himself (Baker, 2010), eventually becoming detached and isolated from his social environment. This hypothesis led him to scrutinise other parents' behaviours towards their autistic children, saying that they needed to, "examine their part in problematic interactions with their children in order to determine their contribution to their children's difficult behaviours" (Silverman, 2012, p. 75).

In addition to offering an answer about the cause of autism, the "refrigerator mother" theory aligned with psychological theories about human behaviour that were prevalent during this time. During the years following WWII, Freudian theory dominated psychological practice, and children's disordered behaviours were felt to be a product of their early experiences with their parents (Courcy & des Rivières, 2017). Mothers were especially held accountable for their children's problems, including illness, mental disorders and disabilities. At the same time, the number of children identified as displaying "autistic behaviours" was increasing steadily. As public awareness of autism grew, people became concerned about this seemingly mysterious condition and sought answers and reassurances that their child would not be similarly affected. Bettelheim likened autistic children to concentration camp prisoners, saying their mothers were like camp commandants (Feinstein, 2011). This offered a powerful image to a public that was only just recovering from the atrocities of WWII. For a public who were already concerned about the rising numbers of children identified as autistic, this image along with Bettelheim's theories offered ready answers. More importantly, the "refrigerator mother" theory provided parents with reassurances that if they bonded and connected with their child, their child would not become autistic. It could be argued that Bettelheim's theory became so widespread as it fit with the public's need for reassurance that they could prevent their child from becoming autistic, a need which was addressed by finding a cause and someone to blame.

Bettelheim's theory was heavily criticised, especially by parents of children diagnosed with autism (Langan, 2011). Foremost among these critics were Bernard Rimland in the USA and John and Lorna Wing in the UK. In addition to being parents of autistic children, these individuals were some of the first researchers and professionals in the field of autism. Rimland, a psychologist, argued that Bettelheim's theory had been widely accepted without much evaluation or evidence (Langan, 2011), stating that parents often demonstrated some of the same behaviours as their autistic children, suggesting a biological rather than an environmental cause for autism. He added that many parents who were detached from their children also had children who did not display the behaviours associated with autism, while parents of autistic children often had other children who developed in a more typical fashion. Rimland cautioned that blaming parents was not productive and could only result in additional stress on families who were already under pressure (Rimland, 1965).

In the UK, psychiatrists John and Lorna Wing also expressed criticism of Bettelheim's theory, arguing that children who were abused and/or raised in deprived situations typically did not develop any autistic symptoms (Langan, 2011). Lorna Wing, along with Judith Gould, conducted a landmark study in which they identified the common characteristics unique to autistic individuals (Wing & Gould, 1979). These characteristics, identified as the triad of impairments, became the basis for the first diagnostic criteria for autism. Wing and Gould's study, more than any other, helped to establish autism as a neurodevelopmental, rather than a psychological disorder. Through their research, Wing and Gould determined that children diagnosed with autism demonstrated a spectrum of behaviours, with some described as very aloof, while others were described as either "passive" or "active, but odd" (Kroncke et al., 2016). The parents of these children were also diverse, which helped to negate the idea that they were all cold and distant from their children.

Similar to Rimland, Lorna Wing expressed her concern that blaming parents might prevent them from seeking help for their children and themselves (Langan, 2011). In response, both Rimland and the Wings established national autism advocacy organisations that aimed to foster collaboration and communication between parents and professionals. These organisations and others like them began to push for research into interventions that would help autistic children and their families. Subsequently, these organisations greatly influenced the shift in treatment to a more behavioural-based approach that occurred in autism research and practice in the 1970s and 80s (Feinstein, 2011). These organisations also helped to lay the foundation for current research on parent perspectives, which has explored the needs of parents of autistic children, and identified strategies and practices that parents can use to help their child grow and develop as they move from infancy into childhood.

4.2 The Research

Over the past 40 years, researchers have worked to determine the cause or causes of autism. Researchers have not yet been able to definitely identify a specific cause or causes for autism, but have ruled out a number of factors including both vaccinations and parental detachment (Landrigan, 2010). Current research suggests that most likely, there is not one cause for autism, but a variety of factors and causes that result in the combination of behaviours that meet the diagnostic criteria for autism spectrum disorder (Happe & Ronald, 2008; Verhoeff, 2012). Both genetic (Tick, Bolton, Happe, Rutter, & Rijsdijk, 2016) and environmental factors (Landrigan, 2010) have been associated with incidences of autism, while many researchers believe that it is the interconnection between genetic and environmental factors that is important (Hallmayer et al., 2011).

Although research has indicated that parents' actions are not to blame for their child's diagnosis, research does indicate that one of the primary risk factors for autism is the mother's exposure to disease or harmful substances during pregnancy. For example, several researchers have suggested that mothers who take valproate, a treatment for epilepsy, during pregnancy, may be at a higher risk of having a child diagnosed with autism (Christensen et al., 2013). It should be noted that the findings of these studies are very preliminary and do not necessarily demonstrate a causal link between valproate and autism, only that the two are correlated. Another explanation is that having a child diagnosed with autism, which has been linked to neurological differences in the brain, is more likely in mothers with epilepsy who also have neurological differences.

Other studies have suggested that prenatal exposure to certain diseases (Brown, 2012) or stressful situations (Kinney, Miller, Crowley, Huang, & Gerber, 2008), may be a risk factor for autism. Little is known, however, about the influence of these factors in a child's prenatal development, or whether they are just one of many factors that contribute to differences in development and thinking common in a neurodiverse society (Jaarsma & Welin, 2012). Although parents and autistic advocates sometimes disagree about the aetiology of autism, they do agree that focusing on causation and blame only has relevance in future (Pellicano, Dinsmore, & Charman, 2014). Instead, parents stress that they need strategies that will help their child and family now and directly impact their daily lives. This is particularly important for parents of children with more significant social communication and behavioural difficulties, who may find it challenging to connect with their children in their early years (Hall & Graff, 2010).

In recent years, researchers have begun to explore the complexities of parents' relationships with their autistic children. Myers, Mackintosh and Goin-Kochel (2009) surveyed 493 parents about the impact that their child's diagnosis and symptomology has had on their lives and the lives of their family. A number of parents expressed that their children enriched their lives, teaching them compassion and tolerance. For example, one parent stated, "I feel privileged that my son is autistic because it has opened up a whole new world and made me look at everything so differently" (Myers et al., 2009, p. 678). Others felt that dealing with their child's behaviour and sleep problems left them exhausted. This was compounded by the constant demands on them to take their child to therapies and to advocate for needed services, supports and the rights of their child. Consequently, they had less energy to give to their child, impacting on their interactions with their child and the rest of their family. In his essay recounting his experience with "autism quackery", Laidler (2004) reports that trying to get support and accessing services for his autistic son was extremely draining for his family. He contends that after making the decision to stop all therapies except one (i.e. speech therapy), he and his wife were able to spend more quality time with their child and family, which ultimately benefitted everyone including his autistic son who continued the same rate of progress as he had when attending all therapies.

Researchers have also examined the nature of attachments between autistic children and their parents. Rutgers, Bakermans-Kranenburg, van IJzendoorm and van Bercklelaer-Onnes (2004) conducted a literature review of 16 studies that examined the attachment of autistic children with their parents. Results indicated that at least half of the autistic children had secure attachments with their parents and most children sought their mothers, demonstrating secure attachment behaviours when distressed. As a group, autistic children were less attached to their parents than control groups of non-autistic children, although differences were less apparent for autistic children with higher IQ scores. In another study, Seskin et al. (2010) examined the association between parents' internal models of their attachment relationships and their children's functional and relational behaviours. They found that autistic children who had parents with more secure attachment representations demonstrated greater ability to initiate and respond in two-way communication, engage with others in joint problem-solving communication, and engage in symbolic play and imaginative thinking. They concluded that parents internal mental and emotional state may influence their child's social communication skills and recommended that professionals differentiate their interventions to support parents with differing internal resources.

Oppenheim et al. (2009) examined the association between a mother's ability to see her autistic child's point of view, the mother's sense of resolution with her child's diagnosis and her child's attachment to her. The researchers hypothesised that mothers with more insightfulness and resolution would have better attachment with their children. They found that 83% of children whose mothers demonstrated high insight and resolution also exhibited secure attachment with their mothers. In contrast, mothers who had either poor insightfulness or poor resolution had children who were less secure. Oppenheim et al. recommended that further research was needed to determine if these patterns continued over time or whether more mothers developed insightfulness and resolution, which allowed their children to become more securely attached. The researchers did caution that their findings only demonstrated a correlation, not a direct causation, between maternal insightfulness/resolution and autistic children's attachment. They added the possibility that both factors were related to a third factor such as genetic autistic traits that affected both mothers and children. The researchers also suggested that the children's lack of attachment may have led their mothers to develop less insightfulness or resolution. They felt this was unlikely, however, as the correlation between factors was not affected by the child's skill or functioning level.

In a similar study, van IJzendoorn et al. (2007) sought to determine whether parental sensitivity was associated with their child's attachment by comparing parental sensitivity and child attachment in children diagnosed with autism spectrum disorder, intellectual disability, language delay or with no diagnosis. Although parental sensitivity did not differ for parents of autistic children, children with a diagnosis of ASD were less secure and more disorganised than the other children. In addition, their involvement with parents during play was lower. This is not surprising given that play involves joint attention, which is an identified issue in autistic children as young as 2-years old (Bruinsma, Koegel, & Koegel, 2004). Van IJzendoorn et al. reasoned that their findings challenge the validity of attachment theory and that autistic children can attach, but may demonstrate this in different ways, and that parent–child attachment may be more related to social-communicative functioning. They also suggested that social communication issues commonly demonstrated by autistic children may mean that they and their parents may take more time and effort to develop sensitivity and attachment as they work out regular patterns and styles of interacting and communicating. This conclusion is consistent with those of Oppenheim et al. (2009) in that they confirm the importance of parents finding ways to connect with their autistic children.

In an effort to better understand the factors that shape early interactions between parents and autistic children, Wan et al. (2013) compared the interactions between parents and their infant children, who had been classified as at-risk of autism due to having an autistic older sibling, with those of parents and infant children with non-autistic older siblings. The researchers noted that differences appeared in parents' interactions with the at-risk group when the children were as young as 6 months-old. These differences did not predict a later diagnosis of ASD for the at-risk group of children. However, when comparisons were made between the two groups when children were 12 months of age, the interactions between the at-risk group and their parents was associated with a later diagnosis of ASD. At the same time, the researchers found that parent behaviours differed for the at-risk group at both age points, but did not relate to whether their infant child was diagnosed with ASD at a later point in time. Wan et al. concluded that parents may have changed their behaviour to suit their older autistic child, which impacted the ways they interacted with their infant children at both 6 and 12 months of age. Similar to Oppenheim et al. (2009), Wan et al. hypothesised that differences in parent behaviours could also have been an indication that parents of at-risk children were also more likely to exhibit at least some characteristics associated with autism. They suggested that as the older group of children had more distinctive differences in interactions, these may have reinforced parent behaviours, thereby reducing opportunities for social learning and increasing their child's difficulties in social interaction and communication.

Although researchers have certainly not found that distant parents are the cause of their child's autistic behaviours, the findings in studies such as those discussed above have indicated that attachment between autistic children and their parents may be influenced by both parent and child-related factors. It is also possible that parents may demonstrate some of the same issues with social interaction as their autistic children. Regardless of the directionality of factors, researchers have begun to explore strategies that will help parents to establish stronger connections with their autistic children. Thompson and McFerran (2013) found that following their participation in family centred music therapy, mothers of autistic children saw positive changes in their relationship with their child. These included improvements in quality of the relationship, parents' perception of the child and parents' response to the child. As these factors have all been found to be related to the attachment of autistic children and their parents, these findings are extremely encouraging. Even more noteworthy, Thompson and McFerran reveal that these changes were highly valued by the mothers and enabled them to have a stronger and more empathetic relationship with their autistic child. This research indicates that although parents may have differences in their early interactions and connections with their autistic children, engaging together in supportive activities can help them to learn how to relate with each other, and enable them to develop a stronger bond and more secure attachment with each other.

4.3 The Impact

At the time of its inception, the "refrigerator mother" theory appeared to be a plausible explanation for the development of autism. Few people understood the nature of autism and were inclined to attribute a child's behaviour or developmental issues to bad parenting. In the subsequent decades, researchers have established that parent behaviours do not cause autism (Farrugia, 2009), although they may influence the connections between parents and their autistic children. Despite this, the myth of the "refrigerator mother" continues to impact families of autistic children in the form of mother blaming and stigmatisation of mothers and parents (Courcy & des Rivières, 2017; Gill & Liamputtong, 2011; Neely-Barnes et al., 2011).

In a study of the experiences of 33 parents of autistic children, Gray (2002) found that the majority of parents reported they had experienced two types of stigma, enacted and felt stigma. Enacted stigma involved parents' experiences of direct rejection or discrimination by others. Parents discussed times they had not been invited over for social occasions or had dealt with negative reactions from others in public when their child demonstrated challenging behaviours. Parents reported they experienced felt stigma, which centred on parents' feelings of shame or fear of rejection, even more frequently. Parents felt that others judged them and made them feel embarrassed. Mothers reported more enacted stigma than fathers, revealing they often faced rude and hostile comments from others.

Similarly, other studies (Neely-Barnes et al., 2011) indicate that parents feel they are frequently blamed by community members and extended family for their child's issues. A systematic review of the literature (Corcoran, Berry, & Hill, 2015) revealed that not only do parents regularly encounter negative perceptions, but they also report that people try to interfere when they are dealing with their child's difficult behaviours. In another study, parents indicated that dealing with judgement from others was much more stressful than dealing with their child's challenging behaviours (Ludlow, Skelly, & Rohleder, 2011). This is evident in the statement of one mother who said she finds herself, "battling with the public all the time" (p. 705). These encounters impacted their family as well, as parents reported being hesitant about taking their child out in public. Interestingly, a few parents reported they tried to use these situations to educate others about autism (Ryan & Cole, 2009).

Courcy and des Rivières (2017) theorise that as more emphasis has been placed on obtaining early intervention and therapies for their children, mothers are confronting new forms of blame. These researchers interviewed 13 mothers and identified two forms of contemporary blaming experienced by the mothers. The first form involved blaming related to their child's diagnosis and behaviours and included being perceived as an over-reactive mother, an incapable mother and a complaining mother. This is similar to findings of other studies, but also illustrates the complexities and conflicting perceptions of mothers of autistic children. The second form of blaming involved perceptions that their child's development depended on the mother's involvement in intervention programs. Mothers reported being blamed for not detecting their child's needs earlier, not doing enough for their child, and conversely, doing too much for their child. Courcy and des Revieres concluded that although parents no longer were blamed for their child's autistic symptomology, they now perceived they were evaluated based on their ability to help their child. The researchers recommended that professionals try to understand parents' perspectives and find ways to support them without judgement.

Researchers suggest that one reason underlying the public's perception of parents of autistic children is the hidden or invisible nature of autism (Corcoran et al., 2015). In comparison with children with other types of disabilities, children diagnosed with autism look "normal". As a result, other people may attribute difficult behaviours, which might be caused by sensory overload or some other aspect of autism, to "bad parenting". Parents in another study (Neely-Barnes et al., 2011) related that the public found it difficult to see an autistic child, as all they could see was a "naughty" child. Gill and Liamputtong (2011) identified strategies that parents use to deal with stigma. A number of parents reported their child's diagnosis helped them and others to understand their child's behaviours, while other parents stated they just avoided certain social situations. A few parents felt they would always encounter ignorant people who would continue to judge them and their child. These parents had learned to adapt to the stigma, refusing to let it bother or upset them. More importantly, they had worked to develop better strategies to help their child, which enabled them to feel more confident and to deflect the comments of others. Farrugia (2009) found that parents resist stigma by employing medical discourse to educate community and family members. This strategy has had positive results as other people began to emulate the parents and use similar discourse when referring to the autistic child.

Carpenter and Austin (2007) stress that stigmatisation results in the social isolation and silencing of parents of autistic children. Mothers are particularly vulnerable as they are often the individual who is most responsible for advocating for their child with professionals on a daily basis. In addition, these researchers contend that mothers must also deal with the additional burden of what society perceives "good mothers" should be and should do. As a result, many mothers withdraw, which not only leaves them feeling less confident in supporting their child, but it also prevents them from accessing emotional support or information that might help them. This creates tensions for parents as they struggle to support their child, while simultaneously negotiating the expectations that society places on them, which ultimately creates a situation in which the parents themselves become "disabled".

A number of studies have examined the stress experienced by parents. Researchers indicate that parents of autistic children report much higher levels of stress than either parents of non-autistic children (Rao & Beidel, 2009) or parents of children with intellectual impairments (Dabrowska & Pisula, 2010). Moreover, stress levels are not significantly less for parents of autistic children with higher skill levels. Other studies (Freedman, Kalb, Zablotsky, & Stuart, 2012; Gau et al., 2012; Lutz, Patterson, & Klein, 2012) indicate that divorce rates and marital strain are high in families of autistic children, with mothers experiencing poorer health and well-being compared to mothers of children with other types of disabilities (Phetrasuwan & Shandor Miles, 2009; Safe, Joosten, & Molineux, 2012). Financial strain is also prevalent (Hassan & Inam, 2013). Mothers often report they are unable to work as they must be available to care for their child and take them to therapies and programs (Sharpe & Baker, 2007). This isolates them from other sources of support, which might help them to alleviate stress. The pressure to find money to pay for needed interventions and services is an additional source of financial stress. Financial issues appear to be a greater source of stress for fathers, whereas mothers report higher levels of overall stress (Hassan & Inam, 2013; Tehee, Honan, & Hevey, 2009). This is possible because mothers assume the bulk of responsibility for caring and advocating for their child and have less opportunity to do other things.

In addition to financial issues, parents have identified other factors that cause them the most stress. These include both environmental factors and child-related factors. Dealing with their child's behaviours is the primary source of child-related stress identified by parents (Argumedes, Lanovaz, & Larivee, 2018; Myers et al., 2009; Phetrasuwan & Shandor Miles, 2009), although several studies have found that parents are able to adapt and cope by accepting their children for who they are (Mohd & Magiati, 2012) and for their unique strengths (Myers et al., 2009). More complex are the environmental sources of stress experienced by parents of autistic children. These include difficulties with obtaining information and support following their child's diagnosis, and the interference and influence of others, including family members and friends (Moh & Magiati, 2012). For example, demands on their time as they seek support for their child and worry about how others perceive them, were two sources of significant stress mentioned by the mothers. Mothers relate that they struggle to balance multiple roles, acting as the family manager, the primary caregiver and advocate at the same time (Moh & Magiati, 2012; Safe et al., 2012), and that finding a balance is essential if they are to manage these roles (Woodgate, Ateah, & Secco, 2008). Mothers indicate that they need professionals to be aware of the pressures facing families and adapt their support so as not to cause them additional stress (Hall & Graff, 2010; Moh & Magiati, 2012).

After gathering narratives from 16 parents of autistic children and adults, Lutz et al. (2012) classified the mother's experiences as a "journey towards adaptation", in which they learned to adapt to their child's and families' changing needs. Through this journey, mothers developed different coping strategies in response to various stressors they experienced. At the beginning of their journey, they experienced feelings of grief and anger following their child's diagnosis of autism. In response, they sought answers and information about what they could do to help their child. Mothers also reported experiencing relationship strain as well as fear and anxiety, physical symptoms of stress and social isolation. To cope, they sought support, socialisation with others and comfort through spirituality. Faced with feelings of guilt and doubt, mothers focused on appreciating life and fulfilling multiple roles including becoming advocates for their child. Through their narratives, they explained how they revised their dreams and planned for the future to help them cope with disappointments they experienced along their journey. As they adapted, the mothers experienced personal growth and redefined their priorities, giving up on trying to fix their child and learning to focus on being with their child. This research illustrates the ongoing challenges and changing needs of parents of autistic children for different supports and strategies throughout their child and family's lifespan.

As previous researchers have demonstrated (Courcy & des Rivières, 2017), parents often feel a pressure to obtain the right services and strategies that will help their autistic children. Unfortunately, this can make them vulnerable to unproven therapies and practices (McDonald, Pace, Blue, & Schwartz, 2012). One of these, holding therapy, can be directly linked to the "refrigerator mother" myth. Holding therapy became popular during the 1970s and was offered as a cure for the lack of emotional bond that was believed to occur between autistic children and their parents (Mercer, 2013b). During holding therapy, the individual is physically restrained while their therapist or parent attempts to form an emotional bond by establishing eye and/or physical contact. In addition, their use of the toilet or diet may be restricted.

Since its inception, holding therapy has been controversial, with many questioning its safety. In 2000, international attention was focused on a 10-year-old American girl who died during a holding therapy session (Mercer, 2013c). More deaths followed, although these were less publicised. Others have raised concerns about the psychological damage that is inflected on individuals during holding therapy as they are forcibly restrained (Mercer, 2013a). In response, organisations such as the American

Psychological Association, the American Psychiatric Association and the National Association of Social Workers issued statements rejecting the use of holding therapy. Moreover, researchers (Fleming, Hurley, & Goth, 2015; Simpson, 2005) have classified holding therapy as a harmful practice and strongly advise against its use with autistic children.

It could be argued that the harm caused by holding therapy is a direct impact of the "refrigerator mother" myth. More significantly, the history of holding therapy as a treatment for autistic children provides an example of how stress and stigmatisation of parents can make them vulnerable to pressure from others to try dubious strategies in an attempt to help their children. Fortunately, the use of holding therapy has decreased dramatically over the past decade. However, the continued stigmatisation of parents and autistic individuals and the accompanying stress means that parents are still susceptible to trying other unsubstantiated, and potentially harmful, treatments.

Researchers (Lutz et al., 2012) have provided some insights into strategies that help parents to cope with stress and resist stigmatisation, but have also indicated that external pressure can impact the effectiveness of these strategies (Joosten & Safe, 2014). Researchers (Jones & Prinz, 2005) have indicated that parental self-efficacy may impact their child's social–emotional functioning and skill development. This can occur both directly as parents may lack knowledge and competence to utilise relevant strategies, but also indirectly as parents' capacity and parenting is diminished by fatigue or emotional exhaustion. As parents are the primary advocates and support system for their children, particularly in their children's formative years, their ability to deal with stress, stigmatisation and to adapt, is likely to have a significant impact on their children, not just in their early years, but as they move into adolescence and adulthood. Thus, building self-efficacy of parents of autistic children is important not just for their well-being, but for their child's future success in life.

4.4 The Future

Although the myth that "refrigerator mothers" or cold and distant parents are to blame for their child's autism is no longer widely believed, parents often face other types of blame and stigmatisation, which negatively impacts both them and their children (Courcy & des Rivières, 2017). Additionally, researchers have highlighted that support offered often focuses solely on the child's needs and ignores the needs of families and parents (Karst & Van Hecke, 2012). If the "refrigerator mother" myth is to be reconstructed, parents will need to be supported, rather than blamed, and empowered, rather than discounted. Not only will this decrease the external stress placed on parents and families, but it will enable them to connect better with their child. From the time of their child's diagnosis, families and autistic children need encouragement and guidance so they can obtain relevant information, access emotional support, revise their dreams and plan for the future (Lutz et al., 2012) and appreciate and redefine their lives and role as parents. To ensure that parents are supported in meaningful ways that enable them to guide their autistic children to be their best selves, traditional forms of professional support may need to be replaced with connections with the autistic community, transitioning the locus of support from remediation of deficits to envisioning possibilities.

Many parents cite their child's diagnosis as a time of significant stress and change, impacting both their child and family (Keenan et al., 2010; Martins et al., 2015; Valentine et al., 2010), and resulting in feelings of shock, guilt, anger, and for some, relief (Banach, Iudice, Conway, & Couse 2010; Fleischmann, 2004; Hutton & Caron, 2005). Parents' stress during this time has been found to be directly related to the type of information and support they receive (Moh & Magiati, 2012). Information presented by professionals can be helpful, but more often does not meet parents' needs at this time. Parents have reported that both during and after the diagnostic process, they either receive limited information (Ho et al., 2014; Keenan et al., 2010; Osborne & Reed, 2008), or the information provided is overly detailed and overwhelming (Abbott, Bernard, & Forge, 2012). Parents in one study (Keenan et al., 2010) reported a specific need for information on financial issues related to their child's diagnosis and felt that the information they received was not sufficient to enable them to identify strategies or develop a plan to support their child.

Professionals have also stressed the need for better supports for parents at the time of their child's diagnosis (Keenan et al., 2010), while parents report that supportive relationships with professionals is extremely important and influences their ability to cope with the overwhelming information and emotions they experience during this time (Abbott et al., 2012). In other research, parents felt that professionals' knowledge and interpersonal skills had an impact on them at this time (Osborne & Reed, 2008), and particularly valued optimism from professionals (Abbott et al., 2012). In contrast, a recent study (Finke et al., 2010) found that a majority of paediatricians surveyed indicated that they have had limited training on autism. This is significant as paediatricians are often the primary point of contact for parents throughout the diagnostic process. In addition, most of these individuals had not been able to access additional education or knowledge, either because they had little opportunity, or because they did not see it as a priority. Almost all of the paediatricians surveyed stated they did not recommend specific interventions, but suggested that parents look for information on the Internet, although they did caution parents about the importance of being informed consumers of the information they found on the web. This finding confirms the reports of parents that they are often left to navigate the complex information on autism with little support from professionals who are involved in the diagnostic process.

Several studies have explored the perceptions of parents about the types of support and information they feel would be the most helpful following their child's diagnosis of autism. Parents have identified that information provided needs to be matched with their needs and their child's needs at the time (Keenan et al., 2010). An essential component of making this happen is for professionals to listen to parents about their concerns at that time (De Alba & Bodfish, 2011). Parents also value information and support that will help them to make sense of their child's diagnosis and to choose appropriate interventions and strategies for their child (Moh & Magiati, 2012). They also feel that exploring these options over multiple sessions is more helpful as it allows them to fully digest the information they have heard in order to ask more relevant questions.

Barnett, Clements, Kaplan-Estrin and Fialka (2003) stress that adaptation is much more important for families than acceptance, as adaptation implies an ongoing process that enables them to keep adjusting and realigning their goals and priorities as their child faces new stages and milestones in their lives. Parents have related that the messages about autism they encounter when seeking information from the Internet or other sources such as autism charities are often very negative (Osborne & Reed, 2008), and have highlighted the need for messages of hope at the time of diagnosis (Nissenbaum et al., 2002). This includes the opportunity to hear stories of success. A sense of optimism and positivity has been highlighted as a key factor in parents' ability to adapt and support their autistic child (Abbott et al., 2012; Nissenbaum et al., 2002). Hearing positive messages is also essential if parents are to be able to develop new dreams for their child and realign their priorities to achieve this dream. Unfortunately, the physicians and professionals who first communicate with parents following their child's diagnosis may not be the best informed about future possibilities for autistic individuals. Furthermore, these individuals may not be the best placed to put parents in touch with relevant individuals who can support them to consider different options and make decisions that have the most relevance for their child and family. As social isolation has been found to inhibit parents' ability to adapt and support their child, finding a network of individuals that can offer parents hope and support is critical to both the parents' well-being and to that of their autistic child.

The myth of the "refrigerator mother" has had a significant impact on parents and the sense of blame and guilt they feel regarding their child's autism (Courcy & des Rivières, 2017). Current models of information and support often do little to alleviate these emotions and may even exacerbate them as they continually stress their child's limitations and needs. Thus, parents need access to information and support that enables them to envision a positive future for their child. One way to achieve this would be to link parents and children with the autistic community at the time of diagnosis. Autistic adults have increasingly highlighted the positive impact that diagnosis can have on their lives (Webster & Garvis, 2017), stating that it can help them to become more self-aware and to establish a sense of their own "autistic identity" (Lester et al., 2015). Others have stressed that it is autistic individuals who are the best sources of information and expertise regarding the autistic experience (Hurlbutt & Chalmers, 2002). More importantly, autistic adults have highlighted the importance of support to enable autistic children and their families to recognise their child's autistic abilities, rather than focus on achieving normalcy (Lester et al., 2015). Linking with autistic adults would enable parents to see more positive aspects of their child's diagnosis and to reconceptualise their images of their child's future. Not only would this help to alleviate some of the parents' concerns, but linking parents with autistic adults would have three additional benefits. First, it would give parents and families the opportunity to ask these adults about some of the challenges that their children might encounter as they age, for example, challenges in school. Second, conversations with autistic adults could help parents interpret their child's behaviours by providing them with an "insider's perspective" of autistic perceptions and thought processes. This would also give parents information about strategies and interventions that are most relevant to autistic individuals. Third, linking with the autistic community would provide parents with connections to autistic adults who could act as mentors for their children.

In addition to talking with autistic adults, connecting parents with more experienced parents of autistic children would provide them with support to negotiate services and advocate for their child within complex systems such as education and health programs. Support groups have been found to increase parents' self-efficacy as decision-makers for their child (Keen et al., 2010; Moh Roffeei et al., 2015). For some parents, attending face-to-face support groups may be impossible given their already demanding schedules and roles. Researchers (Clifford & Minnes, 2013) have found that online support groups can be as effective in supporting the needs of parents. Support groups can help to alleviate social isolation, but can also give parents strategies to advocate and challenge stigmatisation and societal barriers. It is these barriers that often cause parents the most ongoing stress and increase the perception they and their children have about the limitation or "disability" of autism. In addition, linking with others provides parents with connections that can help them to advocate and change the societal view of autism. It is only by creating this shift in societal thinking that parents will be freed from the culture of blame that has endured since the early days of Bettelheim and Kanner.

4.5 Conclusion

Early conceptualisations of autism were vague and often formulated around the notion of a child who had been damaged in some way. Due to the prevalence of Freudian theory during this time, early autism researchers were quick to blame parents for their child's autism symptomology. Subsequent research has thoroughly disproven this myth, demonstrating that autism is an intrinsic aspect of the child, most likely caused by a combination of biological and environmental factors. Despite this, parents continue to experience frequent blame, which has a detrimental impact both directly and indirectly on their child and family. Current models of information and support have been ineffective in giving parents the information they need to support their child's needs and to connect with their child in their own way. Rather than solely depending on professionals, it is recommended that parents be connected with members of the autistic community and other parents of autistic children. This will enable them to see the positive aspects of autism and to reformulate their dreams and goals for their child. More importantly, it will link parents with other advocates, so they can work together to create the societal change that is needed to mitigate their child's disability and strengthen their child's abilities.

References

Abbott, M., Bernard, P., & Forge, J. (2012). Communicating a diagnosis of Autism Spectrum Disorder-a qualitative study of parents' experiences. *Clinical Child Psychology and Psychiatry, 18*(3), 370–382. https://doi.org/10.1177/1359104512455813.

Argumedes, M., Lanovaz, M. J., & Larivee, S. (2018). Brief report: Impact of challenging behavior on parenting stress in mothers and fathers of children with autism spectrum disorders. *Journal of Autism and Developmental Disorders*. https://doi.org/10.1007/s10803-018-3513-1.

Baker, J. P. (2010). Autism in 1959: Joey the mechanical boy. *Pediatrics, 125*(6), 1101–1103. https://doi.org/10.1542/peds.2010-0846.

Banach, M., Iudice, J., Conway, L., & Couse, L. J. (2010). Family support and empowerment: Post autism diagnosis support group for parents. *Social Work With Groups, 33,* 69–83. https://doi.org/10.1080/01609510903437383.

Barnett, D., Clements, M., Kaplan-Estrin, M., & Fialka, J. (2003). Building new dreams: Supporting parents' adaptation to their child with special needs. *Infants and Young Children, 16*(3), 184–200.

Bettelheim, B. (1959). Joey: A "mechanical boy". *Scientific American, 200*(3), 116–120.

Bettelheim, B. (1967). *The empty fortress: Infantile autism and the birth of the self*. New York: Simon and Schuster.

Brown, A. S. (2012). Epidemiologic studies of exposure to prenatal infection and risk of schizophrenia and autism. *Developmental Neurobiology, 72*(10), 1272–1276. https://doi.org/10.1002/dneu.22024.

Bruinsma, Y., Koegel, R. L., & Koegel, L. K. (2004). Joint attention and children with autism: A review of the literature. *Developmental Disabilities Research Reviews, 10*(3), 169–175. https://doi.org/10.1002/mrdd.20036.

Carpenter, L., & Austin, H. (2007). Silenced, silence, silent: Motherhood in the margins. *Qualitative Inquiry, 13*(5), 660–674. https://doi.org/10.1177/1077800407301179.

Christensen, J., Grønborg, T. K., Sørensen, M. J., Schendel, D., Parner, E. T., Pedersen, L. H., et al. (2013). Prenatal valproate exposure and risk of autism spectrum disorders and childhood autism. *JAMA, 309*(16), 1696–1703. https://doi.org/10.1001/jama.2013.2270.

Clifford, T., & Minnes, P. (2013). Who participates in supportgroups for parents of children with autism spectrum disorders? The role of beliefs and coping style. *Journal of Autism and Developmental Disorders, 43*(1), 179–187. https://doi.org/10.1007/s10803-012-1561-5.

Corcoran, J., Berry, A., & Hill, S. (2015). The lived experience of US parents of children with autism spectrum disorders: A systematic review and meta-synthesis. *Journal of Intellectual Disabilities, 19*(4), 356–366. https://doi.org/10.1177/1744629515577876.

Courcy, I., & des Rivières, C. (2017). "From cause to cure": A qualitative study on contemporary forms of mother blaming experienced by mothers of young children with autism spectrum disorder. *Journal of Family Social Work, 20*(3), 233–250. https://doi.org/10.1080/10522158.2017.1292184.

Dabrowska, A., & Pisula, E. (2010). Parenting stress and coping styles in mothers and fathers of pre-school children with autism and Down syndrome. *Journal of Intellectual Disability Research, 54*(3), 266–280. https://doi.org/10.1111/j.1365-2788.2010.01258.x.

de Alba, M. J. G., & Bodfish, J. W. (2011). Addressing parental concerns at the initial diagnosis of autism spectrum disorders. *Research in Autism Spectrum Disorders, 5*(1), 633–639. https://doi.org/10.1016/j.rasd.2010.07.009.

Farrugia, D. (2009). Exploring stigma: Medical knowledge and the stigmatisation of parents of children diagnosed with autism spectrum disorder. *Sociology of Health & Illness, 31*(7), 1011–1027. https://doi.org/10.1111/j.1467-9566.2009.01174.x.

Feinstein, A. (2011). *A history of autism: Conversations with the pioneers*. West Sussex, U.K.: Wiley & Sons.

Finke, E. H., Drager, K. D. R., & Ash, S. (2010). Pediatricians' perspectives on identification and diagnosis of autism spectrum disorders. *Journal of Early Childhood Research, 8*(3), 254–268. https://doi.org/10.1177/1476718x10366773.

Fleischmann, A. (2004). Narratives published on the internet by parents of children with autism: What do they reveal and why is it important? *Focus on Autism and Other Developmental Disabilities, 19*(1), 35–43. https://doi.org/10.1177/10883576040190010501.

Fleming, B., Hurley, E., & Goth, T. (2015). *Choosing autism interventions: A research-based guide*. Brighton, UK: Pavilion Publishing and Media.

Freedman, B. H., Kalb, L. G., Zablotsky, B., & Stuart, E. A. (2012). Relationship status among parents of children with autism spectrum disorders: A population-based study. *Journal of Autism and Developmental Disorders, 42*(4), 539–548. https://doi.org/10.1007/s10803-011-1269-y.

Gau, S. S.-F., Chou, M.-C., Chiang, H.-L., Lee, J.-C., Wong, C.-C., Chou, W.-J., et al. (2012). Parental adjustment, marital relationship, and family function in families of children with autism. *Research in Autism Spectrum Disorders, 6*(1), 263–270. https://doi.org/10.1016/j.rasd.2011.05.007.

Gill, J., & Liamputtong, P. (2011). Being the mother of a child with Asperger's syndrome: Women's experiences of stigma. *Health Care for Women International, 32*(8), 708–722. https://doi.org/10.1080/07399332.2011.555830.

Gray, D. E. (2002). "Everybody just freezes. Everybody is just embarrassed": Felt and enacted stigma among parents of children with high functioning autism. *Sociology of Health and Illness, 24*(6), 734–749. https://doi.org/10.1111/1467-9566.00316.

Greydanus, D. E., & Toledo-Pereyra, L. H. (2012). Historical perspectives on autism: Its past record of discovery and its present state of solipsism, skepticism, and sorrowful suspicion. *Pediatric Clinics of North America, 59*(1), 1–11. https://doi.org/10.1016/j.pcl.2011.10.004.

Hall, H. R., & Graff, J. C. (2010). Parenting challenges in families of children with autism: A pilot study. *Issues in Comprehensive Pediatric Nursing, 33*(4), 187–204. https://doi.org/10.3109/01460862.2010.528644.

Hallmayer, J., Cleveland, S., Torres, A., Phillips, J., Cohen, B., Torigoe, T., et al. (2011). Genetic heritability and shared environmental factors among twin pairs with autism. *Archives of General Psychiatry, 68*(11), 1095–1102. https://doi.org/10.1001/archgenpsychiatry.2011.76.

Happe, F., & Ronald, A. (2008). The "fractionable autism triad": A review of evidence from behavioural, genetic, cognitive and neural research. *Neuropsychology Review, 18*(4), 287–304. https://doi.org/10.1007/s11065-008-9076-8.

Hassan, K., & Inam, A. (2013). Factors contributing to stress among parents of children with autism. *Nurture, 7*(1), 1–8.

Ho, H. S., Yi, H., Griffiths, S., Chan, D. F., & Murray, S. (2014). "Do It Yourself" in the parent-professional partnership for the assessment and diagnosis of children with autism spectrum conditions in Hong Kong: A qualitative study. *Autism, 18*(7), 832–844. https://doi.org/10.1177/1362361313508230.

Hurlbutt, K., & Chalmers, L. (2002). Adults with autism speak out: Perceptions of their life experiences. *Focus on Autism and Other Developmental Disabilities, 17*(2), 103–111. https://doi.org/10.1177/10883576020170020501.

Hutton, A. M., & Caron, S. L. (2005). Experiences of families with children with autism in rural New England. *Focus on Autism and Other Developmental Disabilities, 20*(3), 180–189. https://doi.org/10.1177/10883576050200030601.

Jaarsma, P., & Welin, S. (2012). Autism as a natural human variation: Reflections on the claims of the neurodiversity movement. *Health Care Analysis, 20*(1), 20–30. https://doi.org/10.1007/s10728-011-0169-9.

Jones, T. L., & Prinz, R. J. (2005). Potential roles of parental self-efficacy in parent and child adjustment: A review. *Clinical Psychology Review, 25*(3), 341–363. https://doi.org/10.1016/j.cpr.2004.12.004.

Joosten, A. V., & Safe, A. P. (2014). Management strategies of mothers of school-age children with autism: implications for practice. *Australian Occupational Therapy Journal, 61*(4), 249–258. https://doi.org/10.1111/1440-1630.12116.

Kanner, L. (1943). Autistic disturbances of affective contact. *Nervous Child, 2*(3), 217–250.

Kanner, L. (1949). Problems of nosology and psychodynamics of early infantile autism. *American Journal of Orthopsychiatry, 19*(3), 416–426. https://doi.org/10.1111/j.1939-0025.1949.tb05441.x.
Karst, J. S., & Van Hecke, A. V. (2012). Parent and family impact of autism spectrum disorders: A review and proposed model for intervention evaluation. *Clinical Child and Family Psychology Review, 15*(3), 247–277. https://doi.org/10.1007/s10567-012-0119-6.
Keen, D., Couzens, D., Muspratt, S., & Rodger, S. (2010). The effects of a parent-focused intervention for children with a recent diagnosis of autism spectrum disorder on parenting stress and competence. *Research in Autism Spectrum Disorders, 4*(2), 229–241. https://doi.org/10.1016/j.rasd.2009.09.009.
Keenan, M., Dillenburger, K., Doherty, A., Byrne, A., & Gallagher, S. (2010). The Experiences of parents during diagnosis and forward planning for children with autism spectrum disorder. *Journal of Applied Research in Intellectual Disabilities, 23*(4), 390–397. https://doi.org/10.1111/j.1468-3148.2010.00555.x.
Kinney, D. K., Miller, A. M., Crowley, D. J., Huang, E., & Gerber, E. (2008). Autism prevalence following prenatal exposure to hurricanes and tropical storms in Louisiana. *Journal of Autism and Developmental Disorders, 38*(3), 481–488. https://doi.org/10.1007/s10803-007-0414-0.
Kroncke, A. P., Willard, M., & Huckabee, H. (2016). What is autism? History and foundations. In *Assessment of autism spectrum disorder* (pp. 3–9). New York: Springer Cham.
Laidler, J. R. (2004). Through the looking glass: My involvement with autism quackery. *Autism Watch*. https://www.autism-watch.org/about/bio2.shtml.
Landrigan, P. J. (2010). What causes autism? Exploring the environmental contribution. *Current Opinion in Pediatrics, 22*(2), 219–225. https://doi.org/10.1097/MOP.0b013e328336eb9a.
Langan, M. (2011). Parental voices and controversies in autism. *Disability & Society, 26*(2), 193–205. https://doi.org/10.1080/09687599.2011.544059.
Lester, J. N., Karim, K., & O'Reilly, M. (2015). "Autism itself actually isn't a disability": Negotiating a "normal" versus "abnormal" autistic identity. *Communication & Medicine, 11*(2), 139–152. https://doi.org/10.1558/cam.v11i2.20371.
Ludlow, A., Skelly, C., & Rohleder, P. (2011). Challenges faced by parents of children diagnosed with autism spectrum disorder. *Journal of Health Psychology, 17*(5), 702–711. https://doi.org/10.1177/1359105311422955.
Lutz, H. R., Patterson, B. J., & Klein, J. (2012). Coping with autism: A journey toward adaptation. *Journal of Pediatric Nursing, 27*(3), 206–213. https://doi.org/10.1016/j.pedn.2011.03.013.
Martins, R., Bonito, I., Andrade, A., Albuquerque, C., & Chaves, C. (2015). The impact of the diagnosis of autism in parents of children. *Procedia—Social and Behavioral Sciences, 171,* 121–125. https://doi.org/10.1016/j.sbspro.2015.01.097.
McDonald, M. E., Pace, D., Blue, E., & Schwartz, D. (2012). Critical issues in causation and treatment of autism: Why fads continue to flourish. *Child and Family Behavior Therapy, 34*(4), 290–304. https://doi.org/10.1080/07317107.2012.732849.
Mercer, J. (2013a). Holding therapy in Britain: Historical background, recent events, and ethical concerns. *Adoption & Fostering, 37*(2), 144–156. https://doi.org/10.1177/0308575913490498.
Mercer, J. (2013b). Holding therapy: A harmful mental health intervention. *Focus on Alternative and Complementary Therapies, 18*(2), 70–76. https://doi.org/10.1111/fct.12024.
Mercer, J. (2013c). International concerns about holding therapy. *Research on Social Work Practice, 24*(2), 188–191. https://doi.org/10.1177/1049731513497518.
Moh, T. A., & Magiati, I. (2012). Factors associated with parental stress and satisfaction during the process of diagnosis of children with autism spectrum disorders. *Research in Autism Spectrum Disorders, 6*(1), 293–303. https://doi.org/10.1016/j.rasd.2011.05.011.
Mohd Roffeei, S. H., Abdullah, N., & Basar, S. K. (2015). Seeking social support on Facebook for children with autism spectrum disorders (ASDs). *International Journal of Medical Informatics, 84*(5), 375–385. https://doi.org/10.1016/j.ijmedinf.2015.01.015.
Myers, B. J., Mackintosh, V. H., & Goin-Kochel, R. P. (2009). "My greatest joy and my greatest heart ache:" Parents' own words on how having a child in the autism spectrum has affected their

lives and their families' lives. *Research in Autism Spectrum Disorders, 3*(3), 670–684. https://doi.org/10.1016/j.rasd.2009.01.004.

Neely-Barnes, S. L., Hall, H. R., Roberts, R. J., & Graff, J. C. (2011). Parenting a Child With an autism spectrum disorder: Public perceptions and parental conceptualizations. *Journal of Family Social Work, 14*(3), 208–225. https://doi.org/10.1080/10522158.2011.571539.

Nissenbaum, M. S., Tollefson, N., & Reese, R. M. (2002). The interpretative conference: Sharing a diagnosis of autism with families. *Focus on Autism and Other Developmental Disabilities, 17*(1), 30–43. https://doi.org/10.1177/108835760201700103.

Oppenheim, D., Koren-Karie, N., D'olev, S., & Yimiya, N. (2009). Maternal insightfulness and resolution of the diagnosis are associated with secure attachment in preschoolers with autism spectrum disorders. *Child Development, 80*(2), 519–527. https://doi.org/10.1111/j.1467-8624.2009.01276.x.

Osborne, L. A., & Reed, P. (2008). Parents' perceptions of communication with professionals during the diagnosis of autism. *Autism, 12*(3), 309–324. https://doi.org/10.1177/1362361307089517.

Pellicano, E., Dinsmore, A., & Charman, T. (2014). What should autism research focus upon? Community views and priorities from the United Kingdom. *Autism, 18*(7), 756–770. https://doi.org/10.1177/1362361314529627.

Phetrasuwan, S., & Shandor Miles, M. (2009). Parenting stress in mothers of children with autism spectrum disorders. *Journal for Specialists in Pediatric Nursing, 14*(3), 157–165. https://doi.org/10.1111/j.1744-6155.2009.00188.x.

Rao, P. A., & Beidel, D. C. (2009). The impact of children with high-functioning autism on parental stress, sibling adjustment, and family functioning. *Behavior Modification, 33*(4), 437–451. https://doi.org/10.1177/0145445509336427.

Rimland, B. (1965). *Infantile autism: The syndrome and its implications for a neural theory of behavior*. London: Methuen.

Rutgers, A. H., Bakermans-Kranenburg, M. J., van IJzendoorm, M. H., & Bercklelaer-Onnes, I. A. (2004). Autism and attachment: A meta-analytic review. *Journal of Child Psychology and Psychiatry, 45*(6), 1123–1134. https://doi.org/10.1111/j.1469-7610.2004.t01-1-00305.x.

Ryan, S., & Cole, K. R. (2009). From advocate to activist? Mapping the experiences of mothers of children on the autism spectrum. *Journal of Applied Research in Intellectual Disabilities, 22*(1), 43–53. https://doi.org/10.1111/j.1468-3148.2008.00438.x.

Safe, A., Joosten, A., & Molineux, M. (2012). The experiences of mothers of children with autism: Managing multiple roles. *Journal of Intellectual and Developmental Disability, 37*(4), 294–302. https://doi.org/10.3109/13668250.2012.736614.

Seskin, L., Feliciano, E., Tippy, G., Yedloutschnig, R., Sossin, K. M., & Yasik, A. (2010). Attachment and autism: Parental attachment representations and relational behaviors in the parent-child dyad. *Journal of Abnormal Child Psychology, 38*(7), 949–960. https://doi.org/10.1007/s10802-010-9417-y.

Sharpe, D. L., & Baker, D. L. (2007). Financial issues associated with having a child with autism. *Journal of Family and Economic Issues, 28*(2), 247–264. https://doi.org/10.1007/s10834-007-9059-6.

Silverman, C. (2012). *Understanding autism: Parents, doctors, and the history of a disorder*. Princeton, NJ: Princeton University Press.

Simpson, R. L. (2005). Evidence-based practices and students with autism spectrum disorders. *Focus on Autism and Other Developmental Disabilities, 20*(3), 140–149. https://doi.org/10.1177/10883576050200030201.

Tehee, E., Honan, R., & Hevey, D. (2009). Factors contributing to stress in parents of individuals with autistic spectrum disorders. *Journal of Applied Research in Intellectual Disabilities, 22*(1), 34–42. https://doi.org/10.1111/j.1468-3148.2008.00437.x.

Thompson, G., & McFerran, K. S. (2013). "We've got a special connection": Qualitative analysis of descriptions of change in the parent–child relationship by mothers of young children with autism spectrum disorder. *Nordic Journal of Music Therapy, 24*(1), 3–26. https://doi.org/10.1080/08098131.2013.858762.

Tick, B., Bolton, P., Happe, F., Rutter, M., & Rijsdijk, F. (2016). Heritability of autism spectrum disorders: A meta-analysis of twin studies. *Journal of Child Psychology and Psychiatry, 57*(5), 585–595. https://doi.org/10.1111/jcpp.12499.

Valentine, K., Rajkovic, M., Dinning, B., & Thompson, D. (2010). *Occasional paper no. 35: Post-diagnosis support for children with autism spectrum disorder, their families and carers*. Canberra: Research Publications Unit.

van IJzendoorn, M. H., Rutgers, A. H., Bakermans-Kranenburg, M. J., Swinkels, S. H., van Daalen, E., Dietz, C., et al. (2007). Parental sensitivity and attachment in children with autism spectrum disorder: Comparison with children with mental retardation, with language delays, and with typical development. *Child Development, 78*(2), 597–608. https://doi.org/10.1111/j.1467-8624.2007.01016.x.

Verhoeff, B. (2012). What is this thing called autism? A critical analysis of the tenacious search for autism's essence. *BioSocieties, 7*(4), 410–432. https://doi.org/10.1057/biosoc.2012.23.

Wan, M. W., Green, J., Elsabbagh, M., Johnson, M., Charman, T., Plummer, F., et al. (2013). Quality of interaction between at-risk infants and caregiver at 12-15 months is associated with 3-year autism outcome. *Journal of Child Psychology and Psychiatry, 54*(7), 763–771. https://doi.org/10.1111/jcpp.12032.

Webster, A. A., & Garvis, S. (2017). The importance of critical life moments: An explorative study of successful women with autism spectrum disorder. *Autism, 21*(6), 670–677. https://doi.org/10.1177/1362361316677719.

Wing, L., & Gould, J. (1979). Severe impairments of social interaction and associated abnormalities in children: Epidemiology and classification. *Journal of Autism and Developmental Disorders, 9*(1), 11–29. https://doi.org/10.1007/BF01531288.

Woodgate, R. L., Ateah, C., & Secco, L. (2008). Living in a world of our own: The experience of parents who have a child with autism. *Qualitative Health Research, 18*(8), 1075–1083. https://doi.org/10.1177/1049732308320112.

Chapter 5
Creating Inclusive Societies for Autistic Individuals: Negating the Impact of the "Autism Can Be Cured" Myth

Abstract Since Kanner completed the first study describing a group of individuals who demonstrated *"extreme autistic aloneness"*, the debate about the innate characteristics and aetiology of autism has raged. In the years following the publication of Kanner's study, researchers have made vast strides in identifying the core features of autism, but have not been able to definitively identify any physiological marker for autism. As a result, diagnosis is still dependent on behavioural measures and subjective evaluation. This has resulted in an inconsistency in diagnostic processes and support service provision for autistic children and adults. More importantly, researchers continue to expend a great deal of time and effort on identifying biological markers and causes of autism, rather than finding ways to maximise outcomes. This research focus is often driven by professionals and families who feel that finding a cause will generate a cure for autistic children. A different approach is needed in order to support and empower autistic individuals to capitalise on their individual strengths and learn the skills necessary to be successful in education, employment and community environments. This chapter will explore the myth that autism can be cured and will examine the origins and impact of this myth, which relates to a medical model of disability. As an alternative to focusing on a cure for autism, this chapter will present a more proactive and productive perspective by illustrating ways in which the community can support autistic children and adults to be their most successful selves.

Keywords Models of disability · Acceptance · Support and empowerment Physiological and behavioural characteristics

One of the myths about autism, which has caused a great deal of debate in recent years, is the myth that autism can be cured. In recent years, various individuals and groups have argued their opinion, not just about whether autism can be cured, but whether it should be cured. This debate has been at the centre of the neurodiversity movement and has prompted a great deal of discussion and deliberation between autism researchers, professionals, parents and autistic adults. Neurodiversity advocates argue against funds being spent on finding a cure (Bagatell, 2010), while organisations such as *Cure Autism Now* have focused on raising funds

M. Bennett et al., *Life on the Autism Spectrum*,
https://doi.org/10.1007/978-981-13-3359-0_5

specifically for this reason. Many other organisations such as the Autism Research Network promote "treatments" for autism, suggesting that it can be treated and possibly even eliminated (Singh, Illes, Lazzeroni, & Hallmayer, 2009). The search for a cure has led to a great deal of fad treatments and false claims and has perpetuated the "autism can be cured" myth by offering hope to parents whose primary desire is to help their autistic children to cope and achieve happiness and fulfilment in a non-autistic world.

5.1 The Origin

The origin of the myth that autism can be cured can be traced back to the 1960s when researchers and parents began to develop an understanding of autistic symptomology (Shandley & Austin, 2010). As parents became more vocal about the difficulties their children were experiencing, they also began to question theories about the causes of autism, which at the time was thought to be attributed to poor parenting (Greydanus & Toledo-Pereyra, 2012). As researchers and parents challenged prevailing theories of autism, they also began to explore the possibility of finding a cure for autism. Bernard Rimland, an early researcher and parent of an autistic son, was one of the first to not only question the poor parenting theory of autism, but to suggest that behavioural therapies could treat or recover children from autism (Broderick, 2009). The idea of recovering autistic individuals was promoted more widely to parents and professionals by Lovaas (1987) who suggested that treatments derived from the psychological theory, applied behaviour analysis (ABA), had resulted in the "recovery" of some autistic children.

The term "recovery" is defined in the *Merriam-Webster* dictionary as "regaining or returning to a normal or healthy state". The use of the word, recovery, implies that autistic children can be brought back or refound in some way. Claims of recovery from autism have been embraced by many individuals, but have also met with scepticism by others (Ozonoff, 2013), who point out that "recovered" children demonstrate characteristics similar to other autistic children who have attained higher levels of functioning through time, maturation and learning. Moreover, they argued that both recovered and non-recovered autistic individuals typically still met the criteria for autism. Questions have also been raised as to whether claims of "recovery" denote becoming like non-autistic individuals, or merely reducing the severity of autistic symptomology.

Since the publication of Lovaas's (1987) study, there have been a number of other reports from professionals and parents claiming they have cured or recovered children from autism. With the proliferation of the Internet, increased public awareness of autism, and the opportunity to profit from autism treatments, these claims have only increased. In 2005, Metz, Mulick, and Butter conducted an online search using the terms "autism" and "treatment". Their search revealed 65 treatments claiming to help or cure people of autism. These claims were often supported primarily by testimonials or stories from parents raising autistic children. For example, Jordan (2010) found that websites advertising vitamin supplements for autistic children contained many reports by parents who claimed their child's symptoms had vanished following vitamin treatment. However, these websites failed to offer any studies or scientific evidence to support these claims. Over the past decade, claims of autism cures have continued to mount and have become more readily accessible to parents and professionals. These claims target and prey upon the emotions of vulnerable parents who are searching the Internet to find answers or treatments for their children (McDonald, Pace, Blue, & Schwartz, 2012). For these parents, who may be regularly witnessing their child experiencing daily challenges, the offer of a cure provides hope for a more positive future for their child (Broderick, 2009). This provides even further incentive to believe the myth that autism can be cured (Ozonoff, 2013).

The myth of recovery has also been supported by claims from people in positions of authority or power. Vyse (2005) argues that celebrities or physicians have the power to shape public perception as these individuals are perceived as having a higher social status or specialised knowledge. When famous people, such as Jenny McCarthy, claim that a particular treatment has enabled them to cure their child's autism, their accounts attract a great deal of media attention, which adds further credibility to their claims. Parents, wanting to do all they can to help their child, may be enticed to try these treatments despite the lack of scientific evidence supporting their use. Researchers contend that persuasive accounts from celebrities, like Jenny McCarthy, can sway parents into believing that if they undertake the same treatments and follow their advice, they can also help their autistic child to recover (McDonald et al., 2012).

Support for fad treatments often comes from professionals, such as physicians or other health providers, who offer parents the option of approaches, which often have no evidence base for their effectiveness. Widder and Anderson (2015) suggest that the advice of physicians is given extra weight as many people have been taught to view a doctor as an expert who possesses exceptional knowledge and skills. Widder and Anderson call this perception the "doctor as God" perception (p. 291). Moreover, Newsome and Hovanitz (2005) argue that when doctors and other professionals fail to criticise treatments with no scientific base, they may be inadvertently supporting their use by parents hoping for a cure.

Researchers (Call, Delfs, Reavis, & Mevers, 2015; Matson & Williams, 2015; Miller, Schreck, Mulick, & Butter, 2012) have examined the reasons why parents are particularly susceptible to the claims of cures and recovery offered by "fad" treatments. Chief among these is the use of pseudoscience, in which individuals trying to sell products or treatments use statistics and terminology to provide the illusion that these treatments are supported by scientific evidence, when in reality they are not. Pseudoscience is very difficult to distinguish from legitimate scientific evidence, particularly for parents or professionals who may not be knowledgeable about scientific or research inquiry processes required to validate interventions. As Herbert, Sharp, and Gaudiano (2002) point out, pseudoscience tends to make exaggerated claims about the effectiveness of treatments, which are based on incredible theories that cannot be disproven. Often these claims are accompanied by facts and figures, which are used to mislead the consumer into thinking that scientific studies have been conducted to verify the effectiveness of the treatments. Parents, who are often very emotionally invested in finding help for their children, are particularly susceptible to pseudoscience, and in investing their time and energy into "fad" treatments. The combination of emotional vulnerability and investment of time, money and energy into a treatment can create a placebo effect in which parents or professionals believe that treatments have resulted in positive outcomes (Lilienfeld, Marshall, Todd, & Shane, 2014). This perceived effect, known as the "Hawthorne effect", often appears as short-term gains that result from the initial investment of parents and professionals, rather than from the treatment itself (Corbett et al., 2001). As a result, this may lead parents and professionals, who are already motivated to believe in the effectiveness of an intervention or treatment, to make claims that their child has dramatically improved or even been cured as a result of the treatment, despite limited evidence to support this belief. This is particularly likely if parents or professionals have invested a significant amount of time, energy or resources in the treatment with belief in the effectiveness of a treatment appearing to correspond to the level of investment in that treatment.

A final origin of the myth that autism can be cured can be found in the changing understanding and diagnostic criteria of autism. While initial studies on individuals identified as demonstrating "autism" were conducted in the 1940s, the first diagnostic criteria for autism was not finalised and included in the *DSM-III* until 1980 (Smith, Schaefer-Whitby, & Mrla, 2016). By this time, many misunderstandings about the nature and causes of autism had taken root in the public's perception. Since its initial inclusion in the *DSM-III*, the diagnostic criteria for autism has evolved to reflect the developing understanding of autism as comprising a spectrum of abilities and needs, changing repeatedly with each new version of the *DSM*. With each revision of the *DSM*, the public's understanding of autism has changed, resulting in confusion about its nature (Holt & Christensen, 2013). In addition, inconsistent diagnostic processes have resulted in a degree of false or misdiagnoses of autism over the years. As Helt et al. (2008) contend, you cannot recover from autism if you did not have it in the first place. These researchers point out that many claims of "recovering" or "curing autism" have been seen in cases where no standardised measures were used to confirm the validity of the diagnosis (Helt et al., 2008). Despite this, these stories of people who have recovered from autism have contributed to the perception that at least some individuals with autism can be cured.

5.2 The Research

Autism is defined as a neurodevelopmental disorder, but is viewed by proponents of a neurodiversity view as an intrinsic aspect of the identity of autistic individuals. This has led to a great deal of discussion among researchers, professionals, parents and autistic individuals about whether a cure is possible (Helt et al., 2008). While most researchers (Bölte, 2014) argue that autism is a lifelong condition, and autism advocates (Milton, 2014) contend that it is a description or label for their unique understanding and perception, a few researchers (Granpeesheh, Tarbox, & Dixon, 2009) have offered evidence that following treatment some autistic individuals have experienced decreased symptomology, or in a few cases, no longer met the diagnostic criteria for autism (Fein et al., 2013). Thus, they argue it is possible to "recover" from autism despite the contention of many that autism has been linked to biological and genetic factors (Lord, Bishop & Anderson, 2015). Helt et al. (2008) suggest that this contradiction is partly due to the lack of definition around what recovery constitutes. Traditionally, "recovery" has been defined as demonstrating skills or functioning in the normal range (Helt et al., 2008) and has been described with terms such as average, normal or typical (Ozonoff, 2013). Bölte (2014) offers a more detailed, clinical description of recovery, which he designates as an absence of psychopathology; absence of functional impairment in everyday life; a significant change in functioning level or psychopathology; no need for ongoing intervention; and no longer meeting diagnostic criteria. Both of these definitions, however, rely on behavioural observations and comparison to a perceived "norm" at a particular point in time. In the absence of a physiological test, it is almost impossible to definitively determine that a person is no longer "autistic", only that they no longer experience a degree of impact or impairment that is atypical or substantial.

Recently, researchers have suggested that recovery does not necessarily mean that a person is no longer autistic, but that they have merely achieved an optimal outcome (Fein et al., 2013; Helt et al., 2008). Fein et al. (2013) define optimal outcome as no longer demonstrating symptoms commonly associated with autism spectrum disorder (ASD) and no longer meeting the criteria for a diagnosis of ASD. In contrast to other descriptions of normalcy, Fein et al.'s (2013) definition emphasises a developmental progression of skills rather than typical performance. These researchers recently released a controversial study in which they compared characteristics of autistic children and adults in three groups: one group identified as achieving optimal outcome ($n = 34$); another group of autistic individuals identified as “high-functioning” ($n = 44$); and a third group of non-autistic individuals ($n = 34$). They found that the optimal outcome group demonstrated many skills commensurate with the non-autistic control group. Fein et al. concluded that optimal outcome was possible, although it did not mean this group did not still demonstrate some difference in social interaction and cognitive processing. Other researchers highlight the wide variation in outcomes for autistic individuals following the intervention (Szatmari et al., 2015) and point to the continued lack of evidence for many of these treatments and interventions (Bölte, 2014). Preliminary research also indicates that behaviourally based interventions, early involvement of parents and higher levels of intelligence are factors often associated with more positive outcomes (Bölte, 2014; Helt et al., 2008).

ABA-based and early intervention programs are two types of intervention that have often been linked to claims of recovery from autism (Bölte, 2014; Broderick, 2009; Dawson et al., 2012; Orinstein et al., 2014). Granpeesheh et al. (2009) reported that 38 autistic children achieved an optimal outcome after receiving intensive ABA. However, Bölte (2014) suggests that methodological limitations in these studies may compromise these findings, particularly claims that gains were solely the result of treatment. Unintended consequences of these types of interventions are also concerning for many autistic advocates, who cite that a focus on eliminating non-threatening behaviours because they are viewed as “autistic” in nature may result in long-term psychological harm as individuals are inhibited from expressing themselves in their own way (Kirkham, 2017).

In another study, Dawson et al. (2012) found that children who had been involved in the Early Start Denver Model (EDSM), an early intervention program, exhibited significant improvements in autism symptoms such as their Intelligent Quotient (IQ), language, adaptive skills and social behaviours, and demonstrated similar levels of brain activity on electroencephalograph (EEG) as a non-autistic control group. These researchers concluded that participation in the EDSM had altered the brain and behavioural development of the autistic children. Other researchers have made similar claims (Orinstein et al., 2014). Critics contend, however, that many of these interventions primarily involve individuals who demonstrated a higher level of skills even before the intervention was implemented (Helt et al., 2008).

Although researchers and professionals debate the possibility of a cure for autism, some factors have been associated with decreases in autistic symptomology. These can be divided into child-related factors and environmental factors. In a study examining the influence of both environmental and child-related factors, Turner and Stone (2007) found that children who achieved optimal outcomes had higher IQs, particularly on measures of verbal intelligence, and had milder social difficulties prior to any intervention. Interestingly, these researchers did not find any difference in children who achieved higher outcomes based on the amount of intervention they received. Other researchers (Harris & Handleman, 2000) have found that intervention is more effective if it starts at an earlier age. Helt et al. (2008) suggest that a combination of treatment and innate potential for cognition within the average range may result in the highest level of improvement for autistic children. These researchers also point out that although researchers have claimed that specific interventions have resulted in the recovery of autistic individuals, they have not explicitly assessed whether the individual still meets the criteria for ASD.

Although behaviourally based interventions have more of an evidence base, perhaps due to the higher number of studies in this area, a limited number of studies have compared the effectiveness of behaviourally based interventions with other types of interventions. In one study to do so, Boyd et al. (2014) compared the performance of children in the ABA-based LEAP early intervention program with a performance of children in a TEACCH early intervention program, which is based on cognitive social learning theory. They also compared these two groups with a third group of children who were enrolled in a non-model-specific early intervention program. The results of this study indicated no significant difference in outcomes for the three groups with children in all three groups demonstrating fairly similar outcomes. The researchers concluded that it was the common components of the three programs such as classroom organisation and structure, stimulating learning experiences and teacher interaction that contributed to these outcomes, more than the unique characteristics of each program. They also suggested that it was possibly more important to have a quality learning or special education program incorporating key components, than a specific intervention model. Although the findings of this study suggest that provided the right environmental and learning supports, autistic children can improve their skills in a number of areas, it does not indicate that these children recovered or were cured. Moreover, the researchers did not examine participants' outcomes over time.

The current research does indicate that a few young children diagnosed with autism in their early years may improve their skills to the point where they no longer meet the criteria for ASD (Lord et al., 2015). Although some professionals and researchers indicate that this supports the possibility of a reduction in symptomology or even recovery, current evidence more likely suggests that when provided with stimulating learning experiences and structure, autistic children can learn and develop new skills to negotiate their environments and interact more successfully with their neurotypical peers (Fecteau, Mottron, Berthiaume, & Burack, 2003; McGovern & Sigman, 2005), although outcomes still vary widely (Lord et al., 2015). Other researchers contend that early intervention is critical to improving outcomes (Koegel, Koegel, Ashbaugh, & Bradshaw, 2014) and may provide a small percentage of individuals diagnosed with ASD with enough skills that they no longer require additional support or individual intervention. Research indicates that even with support, the majority of autistic children and adults continue to experience challenges on a regular basis. However, autism advocates maintain that these challenges derive not solely from a lack of skills, but also from inflexible environments and societies that expect them to behave like their non-autistic peers (Milton, 2014). They argue that rather than focusing on the debate about the possibility of recovery, more discussion is needed as to whether recovery is even desirable.

5.3 The Impact

One of the reasons that the "autism can be cured" myth has endured is that it offers hope to parents who, following their child's diagnosis, are confronted with a host of negative information and images about autism and grim predictions for their child's future (Broderick, 2009). With professionals conveying the message that autism is a harmful disorder or condition, parents may feel that curing their autism is the only way their child will have a positive future. Broderick (2009) argues that treatment with the possibility of recovery is often the only type of hope offered to families, a message which is reinforced by the underlying assumption that "normalcy" is analogous to the quality of life. Thus, a primary impact of the "autism can be cured" myth is the promulgation of the belief that autism is a disease or disorder that needs to be cured and that autistic children are individuals who need to be returned to "normalcy". In addition, the continued promotion of this myth has resulted both in the stigmatisation of autistic children and adults, but also in the continued implementation of a medical model of treatment and normalisation (Aylott, 2000) in which the potential of autistic individuals is measured by the degree to which they can be recovered.

The belief that autism can be cured has resulted in a service delivery and support system, which focuses primarily on providing interventions and treatments that will enable autistic individuals to reduce their autism symptomology and to engage in behaviours and skills exhibited by the neurotypical population (Kapp, Gillespie-Lynch, Sherman, & Hutman, 2013). Despite an increased public discourse around social models of disability, a limited number of interventions or research has focused on the environmental factors that may prevent autistic children and adults from participating and achieving or which may cause them to engage in environmentally inappropriate behaviours (de Schipper et al., 2015). This has led to tensions between the autistic community and professionals, researchers and parents over the desired outcomes for autistic persons and the use of treatments to reduce their autistic symptomology. Nowhere is this more evident than in the debate regarding the use of applied behaviour analysis (ABA). Many in the autistic community feel that ABA has been marketed as a miracle cure designed to make them non-autistic (Milton, 2014) and "normal". In contrast, autistic advocates indicate the need for services and supports, which will allow them to embrace their "autistic" identity and achieve because of, rather than in spite of, their differences (Bagatell, 2010). As Mills (2016) states:

> We need to try to see the world from the autistic perspective and apply approaches based on a deeper and mutual understanding that are rational and ethical – which respect the right of the individual to be different – yet recognises and deals with distress and offers practical help. We should encourage and motivate the person to develop their interests and strengths

> rather than focus on 'deficits'. This will mean offering opportunity for development while supporting emotional stability. (p. 5)

This notion of autistic uniqueness and identity is supported by some researchers (Pellicano, Dinsmore, & Charman, 2014; Singh et al., 2009) who have revealed a second impact of the "autism can be cured" myth, namely the imbalance of research and funding that is being devoted to finding a cure for autism. In a review of autism research funding in the USA, Singh et al. (2009) found that although funding had increased substantially between 1997 and 2006, a significant proportion of funds went to projects undertaken by organisations such as the *National Alliance for Autism Research* and *Cure Autism Now* who are committed to funding biologically based research on the causes, treatments and cures for autism. These organisations have now merged into one organisation, *Autism Speaks*, which has repeatedly worked with parents to lobby the US government to find a cure for autism. Members of the autistic community have repeatedly criticised this organisation for its use of disease imagery to promote negative messages of autism stating that having autism is even worse than cancer (Broderick & Ne'eman, 2008). Autism advocates argue that through the use of shocking metaphor and other devices such as ominous music, these organisations are promoting a message of fear and stigma of autistic people (Krcek, 2013). More importantly, organisations such as *Autism Speaks* have been criticised for never including autistic individuals in their leadership structure or decision-making processes. More troubling is evidence that these sensationalist messages are capturing the public's attention as evidenced by Singh et al.'s (2009) estimate that these groups have successfully obtained $153 million in funding for research to find a cause and cure for autism.

In a more recent study, Pellicano et al. (2014) examined the current funding allocations for research in the UK. They found that little funds were allocated to the supports or services that would most directly impact autistic individuals and families. Only 5% of funding was spent on diagnostic support; 5% on creation of effective services; while only 1% was spent on addressing societal issues that posed a barrier for autistic people. In contrast, 56% of funds were spent on research to understand the biological and cognitive profiles of autistic people; 18% was spent on researching treatments; and 15% was spent on finding the causes of autism. Pellicano et al. (2014) surveyed various stakeholders including professionals, researchers, parents and autistic adults about their priorities for autism funding. Although there were differences of opinion between the groups, all agreed that too much funding was being spent on research aimed at preventing or curing autism. Moreover, all participants felt that more money should be spent on developing services and supports for individuals and their families. They stressed that they needed funds to go to services that would improve their lives now, rather than be concentrated on research that may or may not help autistic individuals in the future.

Parents have particularly expressed frustration at the lack of funding for services, while researchers have found that financial strain is a common source of stress for parents and families of autistic children (Hassan & Inam, 2013; Karst & Van Hecke, 2012). The difficulties and complexity of obtaining help for their child were emphasised by parents in a study conducted by Myers, Mackintosh, and Goin-Kochel (2009). These researchers identified 15 negative and 9 positive themes that characterised the experiences of parents of autistic children. While parents felt that having an autistic child enriched their lives and that their child possessed unique strengths and qualities they did not want to change, they also discussed the barriers they encountered in helping their child to access services and education programs and reported that their family experienced continual stress, isolation and stigmatisation from others in the community. This study highlights the tensions experienced by many parents, who do not wish to cure their child, but are unable to access appropriate services that will support their child to participate and achieve on their own terms within the constraints of current community environments. This study also indicates that for many parents the lack of helpful supports and services may make them feel that the only way to help their child is to "treat" them.

Unlike the parents in Myers et al. (2009) study, who stated they did not want to cure their child's autism, Bagatell (2010) found that a number of parents raising autistic children maintained a desire for a cure. These parents felt that autism was preventing their child from leading a happy and productive life and causing them to suffer harm. It is for parents such as these that the "autism cure" myth has had the most impact. In their search for a cure or solution to their child's difficulties, many parents are expending a great deal of time and money on unsubstantiated interventions and treatments. Autism advocates argue that these parents can unwittingly cause extreme psychological distress to their autistic children by making them feel that they are defective and not good enough (Milton & Moon, 2012). Goin-Kochel, Myers, and Mackintosh (2007) found that on average, parents had tried between seven and nine different therapies and were currently using between four and six different types of interventions. Bowker, D'Angelo, Hicks, and Wells (2011) also found that many parents report using multiple therapies, although a number had discontinued treatments they felt were ineffective. Several researchers (Carlon, Stephenson, & Carter, 2014; Levy & Hyman, 2015) have found that parents are just as likely to use alternative treatments as they are to use those that have a strong evidence base. Although some interventions may merely be ineffective, others can pose significant harm to those involved.

Two examples of harmful treatments, which have been offered as a miracle cure for autism, are chelation therapy and Lupron. Chelation therapy was originally designed as a medical treatment for people who were exposed to lead or other toxic metals and subsequently experienced lead or heavy metal poisoning. Chelation is administered through either injection or through a topical cream. It converts metals into harmless elements that are excreted in urine. The use of chelation has been justified by unfounded claims that metals such as mercury can cause autism. Others have speculated that autistic children do not process metals, which they are exposed to in the environment or through vaccines, and thus experience a build-up of toxic metals in their system (Shute, 2010). These individuals hypothesise that chelation will eliminate the excess metals and reduce or cure autism symptomology. Studies have found no evidence to support either these claims or any indication that chelation has therapeutic benefits for autistic children or adults (Davis et al., 2013;

James, Stevenson, Silove, & Williams, 2015). In contrast, chelation therapy has been attributed to the death of at least one autistic child (Beauchamp, Willis, Betz, & Villanacci, 2006) and has been linked to kidney failure in several other children (Shute, 2010). The National Autism Center (2015) and Simpson (2005) have now classified the use of chelation as a harmful practice and do not recommend its use at any time. Unfortunately, despite reports of harm or death, and the cancellation of a trial of chelation in 2006 due to safety concerns (National Capital Poison Center, 2010), chelation therapy continues to be used as a controversial treatment option for children with autism (Lofthouse, Hendren, Hurt, Arnold, & Butter, 2012).

Like chelation therapy, Lupron has been advertised as a cure for autism. Lupron inhibits testosterone production and has been used to treat prostate cancer and early onset puberty. It has also been used as a form of chemical castration for convicted rapists. The use of Lupron with autistic children was based on a theory that autism is related to elevated levels of testosterone and that testosterone magnifies the impact of mercury, which proponents of Lupron link to autism. Although a few studies have found a small correlation between autism and exposure to prenatal testosterone (Auyeung et al., 2009; Auyeung, Taylor, Hackett, & Baron-Cohen, 2010; Manning, Baron-Cohen, Wheelwright, & Sanders, 2001), this is not the same as causation. Neither testosterone nor mercury has been found to cause autism. Furthermore, Lupron has been shown to have many harmful side effects including breathing and swallowing problems, bone pain, testicular pain and osteoporosis (Singer, 2015), as well as bone damage and stunted growth (Shute, 2010). Although the original doctors, who promoted the use of Lupron as a cure for autism, have now lost their medical licenses (Gorski, 2011), Lupron continues to be prescribed by physicians who promote biomedical treatments for autism.

Parental desperation to help their child has also led them to try, and even endorse, other controversial approaches, such as holding therapy and electric shock therapy, with the hope of either recovery or a dramatic reduction in their child's autistic behaviours. These approaches are particularly targeted at getting rid of extreme behaviours such as aggression or self-harm, which often occur due to atypical interoception abilities. However, like chelation therapy and the use of Lupron, there is little evidence to support their use. Holding therapy was popular in the 1960s and early 1970s and was based on the refuted belief that autism is caused by a lack of parent–child bonding (Singer, 2015). Through the use of physical restraint and forced eye contact, the therapist works with the parent to repair this bond. As with chelation therapy and Lupron, holding therapy has been associated with several deaths as well as other adverse side effects such as Post-Traumatic Stress Disorder (Boris, 2003; Mercer, 2013). Consequently, holding therapy has been classified as a harmful practice (Simpson, 2005), although it continues to be carried out by some people as a treatment for autistic children with perceived attachment issues.

More recently, electric shock therapy has been used as a treatment for aggression and dangerous behaviours (Adams & Erevelles, 2017). In a highly controversial case, the Judge Rotenberg Education Center was recently shut down in the USA for using shock therapy to treat autistic children. This school, which had been in operation for several decades, utilised aversive punishment, including electroshocks, to decrease aggression and modify problematic behaviours of autistic children. Not only was this school supported by the state of New York, which had placed students there, but many parents and professionals defended its use of electroshock treatments as a justified solution for eliminating severe and harmful behaviours. Some proponents of the school even protested when the courts stepped in to restrict the use of this therapy (Morton-Bentley, 2010). In less severe cases, where the shock therapy has been used in clinics for self-injurious behaviours, parents have stated that although they were not happy about this treatment, they felt they had no alternative. This is evidenced in the statement of one parent, *"What is the alternative in my son's case?... He'd be dead right now; he'd be in a coma right now; he'd have a detached retina right now"* (Mandavilli, 2016). These cases indicate the desperate measures that some parents may take, particularly if their child is exhibiting extreme or excessively injurious behaviours.

Although these examples illustrate extreme cases, other researchers reveal that many parents have invested a significant amount of time and money on obtaining some type of treatment or cure for their child. Zane, Davis, and Rosswurm (2008) surveyed parents and found that the majority (70%) had tried at least one form of alternative treatment. In another study, Bowker et al. (2011) found that most parents were simultaneously using multiple therapies or treatments, but that at least 30% had abandoned the treatments they felt were ineffective or did not meet their expectations. Not only does this approach make it difficult to determine the efficacy of specific treatments or interventions, but it takes a significant toll on parents, families and autistic individuals. Dr. James Laidler describes the stress that accessing interventions placed on his family as he recounts his experiences with what he terms, "autism quackery" (Laidler, 2004). Laidler, who is himself a physician, found that he and his wife were convinced to try a number of treatments by claims of seemingly challenging and "hopeless" cases in which autistic children were miraculously cured after undergoing one treatment or another. After trying many approaches, Laidler found that his son had improved his skills, but was not cured. More importantly, their family was exhausted, financially depleted and had centred their life on implementing specific treatments, rather than enjoying their time together. After discontinuing all therapies and treatments, except speech and occupational therapies, Laidler noticed that not only did his son fail to deteriorate, but he continued to improve at the same rate. In contrast, the quality of their family life had improved dramatically. Without the stress of implementing a regimen of special diets and treatments, Laidler was able to spend more time with his son. He concludes his story by cautioning other parents about practitioners that market false cures and treatments and warns of the power these individuals have on vulnerable parents who are seeking support and messages of hope for their autistic children (Laidler, 2004).

Laidler's story is not unique. Matson, Adams, Williams, and Rieske (2013) found that parents from educated backgrounds are just as susceptible as uneducated parents to claims of miracle cures for their autistic children. Bagatell (2010) indicates that although many parents are joining with autistic adults in embracing the neurodiversity movement and advocating for their child's rights, parents face a number of barriers in accessing supports to help their child (Corcoran, Berry, & Hill, 2015; Myers et al.,

2009; Rao & Beidel, 2009). Unless these needs are acknowledged and supported, parents will continue to be susceptible to the claims of quick cures, while autistic organisations will continue to focus on allocating funds to preventing, treating and curing autism. To mitigate the impact of the "autism cure" myth, researchers and practitioners must shift their emphasis and concentrate on supporting rather than treating autistic individuals by building on their strengths and giving them skills to manage their own needs.

5.4 The Future

In a recent article examining the use of electroshock treatment at the Judge Rotenberg Center, Adams and Erevelles (2017) argue that the logic of a "state of exception" has enabled society to support the use of aversive and arguably abusive strategies for individuals with disabilities, including autistic persons. It is the contention of these researchers that the perception that autistic individuals are living a "bare life" has been used to justify the implementation of aversive treatments if these treatments offer these individuals the possibility of a "normal" existence. In other words, individuals diagnosed with autism or other identified disabilities have been exempted from the same protections or rights to humane treatment as other people. They are viewed as somehow "less than" other people, while harmful treatments are presented as posing less potential harm than suffering autism or other disabilities. If the "autism can be cured" myth is to be discredited, the view of the "autism sufferer" must be challenged. Establishing a positive future will necessitate the creation of environments in which autistic people as seen as having the potential to achieve meaningful outcomes while still maintaining their own identity as autistic persons, and their autistic differences are viewed as a strength rather than as a hindrance.

In her book, *Different Not Less*, Grandin (2012) recounts the stories of autistic adults who have used their unique characteristics to achieve success. Grandin suggests that the distinctive traits exhibited by autistic individuals offer an untapped potential for society in ways different from that of non-autistic people. Grandin proposes that it is not their ability to act like everyone else that enables these individuals to succeed, but their sense of their own unique characteristics and identity as autistic adults. Without denying the difficulties experienced by autistic individuals, Grandin argues that characteristics commonly associated with autism, such as focused interests and detail-orientated thinking, need to be nurtured, rather than eliminated. Grandin's own story is a testimony to this argument. When she was a young child, doctors recommended that her mother place her in an institution saying she would always need care, would not be able to do anything and would be a burden on her family (Grandin, 2013). Refusing to follow this advice, Temple's mother arranged for therapists to work with her daughter. Additionally, she organised for Temple to go to mainstream schools where she eventually met a teacher who nurtured her interest in animals. This interest and her unique way of seeing the world from the animal's perspective eventually led Temple Grandin to become one of the foremost animal scientists in the world. Rather than being cured, she contends that it was her "autistic brain" which helped her to achieve things other people could not (Grandin, 2013).

Grandin's story is an example of the possibilities when families and professionals take a positive view of autism and nurture the strengths and uniqueness of autistic individuals. Increasingly autistic adults are sharing their perceptions of the ways they have developed strategies and skills to alleviate or manage their challenges, while remaining innately "autistic". Many maintain that a key strategy has been to channel their special interests, passions and areas of expertise into careers or avenues for social interaction. In a recent study, Webster and Garvis (2017) found that autistic women were able to create alternative career pathways by building on their interests even after they had experienced failure in traditional job settings. Many of these women were self-employed, but all had found self-validation and fulfilment by following their passions. The findings of this study revealed that making sense of their autism diagnosis was critical in helping the women to develop a better self-awareness and sense of their own identity. This finding is supported by Aylott (2000) who suggests that autistic adults can find a positive identity if they are supported to see their difference as a strength, rather than as a deficit.

In another study (Ashby & Causton-Theoharis, 2009), autistic adults revealed that one of the primary challenges they faced is the low expectations of others. This constant pressure to prove themselves left them feeling exhausted. The researchers concluded that the traditional societal definition of autism as "abnormal" results in the disqualification of autistic individuals from society. Although the adults in this study felt that their challenges in sensory processing, communication and motor planning did sometimes prevent them from demonstrating their knowledge, they argued that a systemic view of them as incompetent was their greatest barrier. Participants suggested that supports for autistic people should focus on several factors including: presumption of competence, building on interests, forming trusting relationships and creating structured and supportive environments. The researchers conclude that the public's view of what is normal or competent needs to be expanded, and service delivery and supports should focus on the creation of contexts for supporting the competence of *"different forms of mind"* (p. 514).

Lawson (2011), an autistic researcher, has developed a theory of Single Attention and Associated Cognition in Autism (SAACA), which he proposes explains the ways in which attention, motivation and interest are intrinsically connected in cognitive processing of autistic individuals. Lawson suggests that in contrast to non-autistic individuals who can utilise polytropic attention to make sense of their world, autistic individuals exercise monotropic attention in which they focus all their attention on one particular point of interest. This makes them less able to shift their attention between stimuli or activities. Lawson contends that utilising interest and motivation is the key to enabling autistic individuals to more readily shift their focus as these interests can serve as a bridge from one focal point to another. He argues that building on interest and attention is not just important to motivate autistic individuals, but is essential to enabling them to learn (Prata, Coelho, & Lawson, 2018). This is consistent with the findings of Koegel, Singh, and Koegel (2010) who found that incorporating motivational variables of interest and choice increased autistic children's academic performance including both their initiation of tasks and rate of performance of tasks. It was also successful in decreasing their disruptive behaviours during tasks. The findings of this study confirm Lawson's suggestions that connecting interest, motivation and attention may be extremely important for supporting the achievement of autistic persons. When these are engaged, autistic individuals are better able to demonstrate their competence. Much more than more traditional interventions focusing on the deficits of autistic individuals, this approach has the potential to enable these individuals to achieve both outcomes valued by society as well as their own personal goals.

Another essential component of transforming the "autism can be cured" myth is the more relevant and timely provision of support that enables parents to obtain critical information regarding effective strategies to guide and help their autistic children. Not only will parents need access to information on effective strategies that build on their child's strengths as well as support their needs, they will also need to be provided with positive messages about what it means to be autistic and still have a positive future. Parents have reported that the diagnostic process for their children can be extremely stressful (Keenan, Dillenburger, Doherty, Byrne, & Gallagher, 2010), although this varies somewhat depending on parental knowledge and beliefs about autism (Martins, Bonito, Andrade, Albuquerque, & Chaves, 2015; Mercer, Creighton, Holden, & Lewis, 2006). Initially, some parents may experience a period of shock, but almost all express a deep concern for their child's future (Martins et al., 2015) and ask questions about what they need to do to help their child. Research has shown that the choices parents make about services and interventions for their child are usually influenced by their beliefs about the causes of autism and the possible future outcomes their child can achieve (Mercer et al., 2006). Unfortunately, parents often face an array of conflicting information (Mackintosh, Myers, & Goin-Kochel, 2005; Stephenson, Carter, & Kemp, 2012) and stigma about what it means to be on the autism spectrum (Russell & Norwich, 2012). To move forward, parents must be able to access more positive and accurate information about the autism spectrum as well as receive support from others to resist stigmatised notions of disability, and revise their vision for their child that enables them to see and support the positive aspects of their autistic difference (Farrugia, 2009).

Autistic women have reported that reading and hearing the diagnostic experiences of other autistic women helped them to develop a better image of themselves and a more positive identity for themselves (Webster & Garvis, 2017). Similarly, offering parents positive examples and stories may help them to work through their child's diagnosis and see the possibilities for their future (Cascio, 2012). More importantly, this could help parents to focus on their child's strengths and provide them with insights to help their child develop their skills and navigate the demands of the neurotypical world. Instead of focusing solely on treating the autistic child, services should concentrate on the creation of more flexible and supportive environments (Day, Michelson, Thomson, Penney, & Draper, 2012). This will include providing support to parents to teach their child new skills including self-management and communication skills needed to decrease challenging behaviours. Providing parents with more meaningful support will enable them to see the positive aspects of their child's differentness and will be less desperate for a cure. Research indicates that when parents undergo training and are involved in support programs, their stress is reduced while their feelings of confidence and self-efficacy are increased (Keen, Couzens, Muspratt, & Rodger, 2010). Furthermore, parents who are given access to information about autistic adults would be able to envision a positive future for their child and would counteract the view of their child's diagnosis as a tragedy and their future as hopeless.

Creating an alternative future for autistic children and adults that alters the "autism can be cured" myth will also involve altering community programs and environments in order to reduce current barriers and inequities that require autistic children and adults to become normal in order to participate and achieve (Milton & Moon, 2012). For example, creating school programs, which are flexible to allow students to move if needed and communicate in different ways, will increase participation and performance in schools. Similarly, adjusting workplace expectations so that autistic individuals can work in their own space when needed and provide information about unspoken social expectations would support the productivity of autistic adults. Developing more autism-friendly environments and communities may also have the added benefit of reducing the pressure on parents who must advocate for their child to be included and accommodated in their communities. In addition, positive advertising and images are needed to develop a more positive public view of autism and of autistic individuals as competent and capable of fully participating and contributing to society. It is only by enabling autistic individuals to engage as equal members of society and supporting them to participate and contribute in their own way (Ruble & Dalrymple, 1996) that they will be seen by the public as achievers rather than as sufferers who need to be cured.

5.5 Conclusion

The myth that autism can be cured has been one of the most debated autism myths over the years. Fuelled by hope, financial gain and media interest, the contention that autistic individuals can be cured or recovered continues to drive much of the current research and intervention programs. These are aimed primarily at treating the autistic person and are sustained by the desperation of parents who may feel that normalisation is the only hope for their child's future. To mitigate the impact of the myth and create a more positive future for autistic individuals, these underlying beliefs and perceptions need to be changed. Rather than focusing on research to find a cure or treatments to achieve optimal outcomes, researchers and governments need to focus on developing meaningful supports and services that will enable parents to see a more positive future for their children, which celebrates their unique strengths and empowers them to develop their own unique identity.

References

Adams, D. L., & Erevelles, N. (2017). Unexpected spaces of confinement: Aversive technologies, intellectual disability, and "bare life". *Punishment & Society, 19*(3), 348–365. https://doi.org/10.1177/1462474517705147.

Ashby, C. E., & Causton-Theoharis, J. N. (2009). Disqualified in the human race: A close reading of the autobiographies of individuals identified as autistic. *International Journal of Inclusive Education, 13*(5), 501–516. https://doi.org/10.1080/13603110801886673.

Auyeung, B., Baron-Cohen, S., Ashwin, E., Knickmeyer, R., Taylor, K., & Hackett, G. (2009). Fetal testosterone and autistic traits. *British Journal of Psychology, 100*(Pt 1), 1–22. https://doi.org/10.1348/000712608X311731.

Auyeung, B., Taylor, K., Hackett, G., & Baron-Cohen, S. (2010). Foetal testosterone and autistic traits in 18 to 24-month-old children. *Molecular Autism, 1*(1), 11. https://doi.org/10.1186/2040-2392-1-11.

Aylott, J. (2000). Autism in adulthood: the concepts of identity and difference. *British Journal of Nursing, 9*(13), 851–858. https://doi.org/10.12968/bjon.2000.9.13.5513.

Bagatell, N. (2010). From cure to community: Transforming notions of autism. *Ethos, 38*(1), 33–55. https://doi.org/10.1111/j.1548-1352.2009.01080.x.

Beauchamp, R. A., Willis, T. M., Betz, T. G., & Villanacci, J. (2006). Deaths associated with hypocalcemia from chelation therapy—Texas, Pennsylvania, and Oregon, 2003–2005. *Morbidity and Mortality Weekly Report, 55*(8), 204–207.

Bölte, S. (2014). Is autism curable? *Developmental Medicine and Child Neurology, 56*(10), 927–931. https://doi.org/10.1111/dmcn.12495.

Boris, N. W. (2003). Attachment, aggression and holding: A cautionary tale. *Attachment & Human Development, 5*(3), 245–247. https://doi.org/10.1080/14616730310001593947.

Bowker, A., D'Angelo, N. M., Hicks, R., & Wells, K. (2011). Treatments for autism: Parental choices and perceptions of change. *Journal of Autism and Developmental Disorders, 41*(10), 1373–1382. https://doi.org/10.1007/s10803-010-1164-y.

Boyd, B. A., Hume, K., McBee, M. T., Alessandri, M., Gutierrez, A., Johnson, L., … Odom, S. L. (2014). Comparative efficacy of LEAP, TEACCH and non-model-specific special education programs for preschoolers with autism spectrum disorders. *Journal of Autism and Developmental Disorders, 44*(2), 366–380. https://doi.org/10.1007/s10803-013-1877-9.

Broderick, A. A. (2009). Autism, "recovery (to normalcy)", and the politics of hope. *Journal of Intellectual and Developmental Disability, 47*(4), 263–281. https://doi.org/10.1352/1934-9556-47.4.263.

Broderick, A. A., & Ne'eman, A. (2008). Autism as metaphor: Narrative and counter-narrative. *International Journal of Inclusive Education, 12*(5–6), 459–476. https://doi.org/10.1080/13603110802377490.

Call, N. A., Delfs, C. H., Reavis, A. R., & Mevers, J. L. (2015). Factors influencing treatment decisions by parents for their children with autism spectrum disorder. *Research in Autism Spectrum Disorders, 15–16,* 10–20. https://doi.org/10.1016/j.rasd.2015.04.001.

Carlon, S., Stephenson, J., & Carter, M. (2014). Parent reports of treatments and interventions used with children with autism spectrum disorders (ASD): A review of the literature. *Australasian Journal of Special Education, 38,* 63–90. https://doi.org/10.1017/jse.2014.4.

Cascio, M. A. (2012). Neurodiversity: Autism pride among mothers of children with autism spectrum disorders. *Journal of Intellectual and Developmental Disability, 50*(3), 273–283. https://doi.org/10.1352/1934-9556-50.3.273.

Corbett, B., Khan, K., Czapansky-Beilman, D., Brady, N., Dropik, P., Goldman, D. Z., … Ziegler, R. (2001). A double-blind, placebo-controlled crossover study investigating the effect of porcine secretin in children with autism. *Clinical Pediatrics, 40*(6), 327–331. https://doi.org/10.1177/000992280104000604.

Corcoran, J., Berry, A., & Hill, S. (2015). The lived experience of US parents of children with autism spectrum disorders: A systematic review and meta-synthesis. *Journal of Intellectual Disabilities, 19*(4), 356–366. https://doi.org/10.1177/1744629515577876.

Davis, T. N., O'Reilly, M., Kang, S., Lang, R., Rispoli, M., Sigafoos, J., … Mulloy, A. (2013). Chelation treatment for autism spectrum disorders: A systematic review. *Research in Autism Spectrum Disorders, 7*(1), 49–55. https://doi.org/10.1016/j.rasd.2012.06.005.

Dawson, G., Jones, E. J. H., Merkle, K., Venema, K., Lowy, R., Faja, S., … Webb, S. J. (2012). Early behavioral intervention is associated with normalized brain activity in young children with autism. *Journal of the American Academy of Child and Adolescent Psychiatry, 51*(11), 1150–1159. https://doi.org/10.1016/j.jaac.2012.08.018.

Day, C., Michelson, D., Thomson, S., Penney, C., & Draper, L. (2012). Innovations in practice: Empowering parents, empowering communities: A pilot evaluation of a peer-led parenting programme. *Child and Adolescent Mental Health, 17*(1), 52–57. https://doi.org/10.1111/j.1475-3588.2011.00619.x.

de Schipper, E., Lundequist, A., Coghill, D., de Vries, P. J., Granlund, M., Holtmann, M., … Bölte, S. (2015). Ability and disability in autism spectrum disorder: A systematic literature review employing the international classification of functioning, disability and health-children and youth version. *Autism Research, 8*(6), 782–794. https://doi.org/10.1002/aur.1485.

Farrugia, D. (2009). Exploring stigma: Medical knowledge and the stigmatisation of parents of children diagnosed with autism spectrum disorder. *Sociology of Health & Illness, 31*(7), 1011–1027. https://doi.org/10.1111/j.1467-9566.2009.01174.x.

Fecteau, S., Mottron, L., Berthiaume, C., & Burack, J. A. (2003). Developmental changes of autistic symptoms. *Autism, 7*(3), 255–268. https://doi.org/10.1177/1362361303007003003.

Fein, D., Barton, M., Eigsti, I. M., Kelley, E., Naigles, L., Schultz, R. T., … Tyson, K. (2013). Optimal outcome in individuals with a history of autism. *Journal of Child Psychology and Psychiatry, 54*(2), 195–205. https://doi.org/10.1111/jcpp.12037.

Goin-Kochel, R. P., Myers, B. J., & Mackintosh, V. H. (2007). Parental reports on the use of treatments and therapies for children with autism spectrum disorders. *Research in Autism Spectrum Disorders, 1*(3), 195–209. https://doi.org/10.1016/j.rasd.2006.08.006.

Gorski, D. (2011). Chemical castration of autistic children leads to the downfall of Dr. Mark Geier. Retrieved from https://sciencebasedmedicine.org/chemical-castration-of-autistic-children-leads-to-the-downfall-of-dr-mark-geier/.

Grandin, T. (2012). *Different… not less: Inspiring stories of achievement and successful employment from adults*. Arlington, TX: Future Horizons.

Grandin, T. (2013). *The autistic brain*. New York: Houghton Mifflin Harcourt.

Granpeesheh, D., Tarbox, J., & Dixon, D. (2009). Retrospective analysis of clinical records in 38 cases of recovery from autism. *Annals of Clinical Psychiatry, 21*(4), 195–204.

Greydanus, D. E., & Toledo-Pereyra, L. H. (2012). Historical perspectives on autism: Its past record of discovery and its present state of solipsism, skepticism, and sorrowful suspicion. *Pediatric Clinics of North America, 59*(1), 1–11. https://doi.org/10.1016/j.pcl.2011.10.004.

Harris, S. L., & Handleman, J. S. (2000). Age and IQ at intake as predictors of placement for young children with autism: A four-to six-year follow-up. *Journal of Autism and Developmental Disorders, 30*(2), 137–142. https://doi.org/10.1023/A:1005459606120.

Hassan, K., & Inam, A. (2013). Factors contributing to stress among parents of children with autism. *Nurture, 7*(1), 1–8.

Helt, M., Kelley, E., Kinsbourne, M., Pandey, J., Boorstein, H., Herbert, M., et al. (2008). Can children with autism recover? If so, how? *Neuropsychology Review, 18*(4), 339–366. https://doi.org/10.1007/s11065-008-9075-9.

Herbert, J. D., Sharp, I. R., & Gaudiano, B. A. (2002). Separating fact from fiction in the etiology and treatment of autism: A scientific review of the evidence. *The Scientific Review of Mental Health Practice, 1*(1), 23–43.

Holt, J. M., & Christensen, K. M. (2013). Utahns' understanding of autism spectrum disorder. *Disability and Health Journal, 6*(1), 52–62. https://doi.org/10.1016/j.dhjo.2012.08.002.

James, S., Stevenson, S. W., Silove, N., & Williams, K. (2015). *Chelation for autism spectrum disorder (ASD)*. Retrieved from http://www.ncbi.nlm.nih.gov/pubmed/26106752.

Jordan, C. J. (2010). Evolution of autism support and understanding via the World Wide Web. *Journal of Intellectual and Developmental Disability, 48*(3), 220–227. https://doi.org/10.1352/1934-9556-48.3.220.

Kanner, L. (1943). Autistic disturbances of affective contact. *Nervous Child, 2*(3), 217–250.

Kapp, S. K., Gillespie-Lynch, K., Sherman, L. E., & Hutman, T. (2013). Deficit, difference, or both? Autism and neurodiversity. *Developmental Psychology, 49*(1), 59–71. https://doi.org/10.1037/a0028353.

Karst, J. S., & Van Hecke, A. V. (2012). Parent and family impact of autism spectrum disorders: A review and proposed model for intervention evaluation. *Clinical Child and Family Psychology Review, 15*(3), 247–277. https://doi.org/10.1007/s10567-012-0119-6.

Keen, D., Couzens, D., Muspratt, S., & Rodger, S. (2010). The effects of a parent-focused intervention for children with a recent diagnosis of autism spectrum disorder on parenting stress and competence. *Research in Autism Spectrum Disorders, 4*(2), 229–241. https://doi.org/10.1016/j.rasd.2009.09.009.

Keenan, M., Dillenburger, K., Doherty, A., Byrne, A., & Gallagher, S. (2010). The experiences of parents during diagnosis and forward planning for children with autism spectrum disorder. *Journal of Applied Research in Intellectual Disabilities, 23*(4), 390–397. https://doi.org/10.1111/j.1468-3148.2010.00555.x.

Kirkham, P. (2017). The line between intervention and abuse'–autism and applied behaviour analysis. *History of the Human Sciences, 30*(2), 107–126. https://doi.org/10.1177/0952695117702571.

Koegel, L. K., Koegel, R. L., Ashbaugh, K., & Bradshaw, J. (2014). The importance of early identification and intervention for children with or at risk for autism spectrum disorders. *International Journal of Speech-Language Pathology, 16*(1), 50–56. https://doi.org/10.3109/17549507.2013.861511.

Koegel, L. K., Singh, A. K., & Koegel, R. L. (2010). Improving motivation for academics in children with autism. *Journal of Autism and Developmental Disorders, 40*(9), 1057–1066. https://doi.org/10.1007/s10803-010-0962-6.

Krcek, T. E. (2013). Deconstructing disability and neurodiversity: Controversial issues for autism and implications for social work. *Journal of Progressive Human Services, 24*(1), 4–22. https://doi.org/10.1080/10428232.2013.740406.

Laidler, J. R. (2004). Through the looking glass: My involvement with autism quackery. *Autism Watch*. Retrieved from https://www.autism-watch.org/about/bio2.shtml.

Lawson, W. (2011). *The passionate mind: How people with autism learn*. London: Jessica Kingsley.

Levy, S. E., & Hyman, S. L. (2015). Complementary and alternative medicine treatments for children with autism spectrum disorders. *Child and Adolescent Psychiatric Clinics, 24,* 117–143. https://doi.org/10.1016/j.chc.2014.09.004.

Lilienfeld, S. O., Marshall, J., Todd, J. T., & Shane, H. C. (2014). The persistence of fad interventions in the face of negative scientific evidence: Facilitated communication for autism as a case example. *Evidence-Based Communication Assessment and Intervention, 8*(2), 62–101. https://doi.org/10.1080/17489539.2014.976332.

Lofthouse, N., Hendren, R., Hurt, E., Arnold, L. E., & Butter, E. (2012). A review of complementary and alternative treatments for autism spectrum disorders. *Autism Research and Treatment, 2012,* 870391. https://doi.org/10.1155/2012/870391.

Lord, C., Bishop, S., & Anderson, D. (2015). Developmental trajectories as autism phenotypes. *American Journal of Medical Genetics Part C: Seminars in Medical Genetics, 169*(2), 198–208. https://doi.org/10.1002/ajmg.c.31440.

Lovaas, O. I. (1987). Behavioral treatment and normal educational and intellectual functioning in young autistic children. *Journal of Consulting and Clinical Psychology, 55*(1), 3–9. https://doi.org/10.1037/0022-006X.55.1.3.

Mackintosh, V. H., Myers, B. J., & Goin-Kochel, R. P. (2005). Sources of information and support used by parents of children with autism spectrum disorders. *Journal of Developmental Disabilities, 12*(1), 41–51.

Mandavilli, A. (2016). How "Shock Therapy" is saving some children with autism: Electroconvulsive therapy is far more beneficial—and banal—than its torturous reputation suggests. Retrieved from https://www.theatlantic.com/health/archive/2016/10/how-shock-therapy-is-saving-some-children-with-autism/505448/.

Manning, J. T., Baron-Cohen, S., Wheelwright, S., & Sanders, G. (2001). The 2nd to 4th digit ratio and autism. *Developmental Medicine and Child Neurology, 43*(3), 160–164.

Martins, R., Bonito, I., Andrade, A., Albuquerque, C., & Chaves, C. (2015). The impact of the diagnosis of autism in parents of children. *Procedia - Social and Behavioral Sciences, 171,* 121–125. https://doi.org/10.1016/j.sbspro.2015.01.097.

Matson, J. L., Adams, H. L., Williams, L. W., & Rieske, R. D. (2013). Why are there so many unsubstantiated treatments in autism? *Research in Autism Spectrum Disorders, 7*(3), 466–474. https://doi.org/10.1016/j.rasd.2012.11.006.

Matson, J. L., & Williams, L. W. (2015). The curious selection process of treatments for autism spectrum disorders. *Research in Autism Spectrum Disorders, 9,* 21–25. https://doi.org/10.1016/j.rasd.2014.10.004.

McDonald, M. E., Pace, D., Blue, E., & Schwartz, D. (2012). Critical issues in causation and treatment of autism: Why fads continue to flourish. *Child & Family Behavior Therapy, 34,* 290–304. https://doi.org/10.1080/07317107.2012.732849.

McGovern, C. W., & Sigman, M. (2005). Continuity and change from early childhood to adolescence in autism. *Journal of Child Psychology and Psychiatry, 46*(4), 401–408. https://doi.org/10.1111/j.1469-7610.2004.00361.x.

Mercer, J. (2013). Holding therapy: A harmful mental health intervention. *Focus on Alternative and Complementary Therapies, 18*(2), 70–76. https://doi.org/10.1111/fct.12024.

Mercer, L., Creighton, S., Holden, J. J., & Lewis, M. E. (2006). Parental perspectives on the causes of an autism spectrum disorder in their children. *Journal of Genetic Counseling, 15*(1), 41–50. https://doi.org/10.1007/s10897-005-9002-7.

Metz, B., Mulick, J. A., & Butter, E. (2005). Autism: A late 20th century fad magnet. In J. Jacobson, R. Foxx, & J. A. Mulick (Eds.), *Controversial therapies for developmental disabilities: Fad, fashion and science in professional practice* (pp. 237–264). Larence: Erlbaum.

Miller, V. A., Schreck, K. A., Mulick, J. A., & Butter, E. (2012). Factors related to parents' choices of treatments for their children with autism spectrum disorders. *Research in Autism Spectrum Disorders, 6*(1), 87–95. https://doi.org/10.1016/j.rasd.2011.03.008.

Mills, R. (2016). Guidance for considering a treatment approach in autism. Retrieved from https://researchautism.net/publicfiles/word/guidance-treatment-approach-autism.doc.

Milton, D. (2014). So what exactly are autism interventions intervening with? *Good Autism Practice, 15*(2), 6–14.

Milton, D., & Moon, L. (2012). The normalisation agenda and the psycho-emotional disablement of autistic people. *Autonomy, the Critical Journal of Interdisciplinary Autism Studies, 1*(1), 1–12.

Morton-Bentley, D. W. (2010). On punishments: The continuing debate over aversive therapy on punishment: New York State, the Judge Rotenberg Center and the continuing debate over aversive therapy. *Holy Cross Journal of Law and Public Policy, 14,* 113.

Myers, B. J., Mackintosh, V. H., & Goin-Kochel, R. P. (2009). "My greatest joy and my greatest heart ache:" Parents' own words on how having a child in the autism spectrum has affected their lives and their families' lives. *Research in Autism Spectrum Disorders, 3*(3), 670–684. https://doi.org/10.1016/j.rasd.2009.01.004.

National Autism Center (NAC). (2015). *Findings and conclusions: National standards project Phase 2.* In N. A. Center (Series Ed.) & N. A. Center (Ed.). Retrieved from http://www.nationalautismcenter.org/national-standards-project/phase-2/.

National Capital Poison Center. (2010). *Chelation: Therapy or "therapy"?* Retrieved from http://www.poison.org/current/chelationtherapy.htm.

Newsome, C., & Hovanitz, C. A. (2005). The nature and values of empirically validated interventions. In J. Jacobson, R. Foxx, & J. A. Mulick (Eds.), *Controversial therapies for developmental disabilities: Fad, fashion, and science in professional practice* (pp. 31–44). Mahwah, NJ: Erlbaum.

Orinstein, A. J., Helt, M., Troyb, E., Tyson, K. E., Barton, M. L., Eigsti, I. M., … Fein, D. A. (2014). Intervention for optimal outcome in children and adolescents with a history of autism. *Journal of Developmental & Behavioral Pediatrics, 35*(4), 247–256. https://doi.org/10.1097/dbp.0000000000000037.

Ozonoff, S. (2013). Editorial: Recovery from autism spectrum disorder (ASD) and the science of hope. *Journal of Child Psychology and Psychiatry, 54*(2), 113–114. https://doi.org/10.1111/jcpp.12045.

Pellicano, E., Dinsmore, A., & Charman, T. (2014). What should autism research focus upon? Community views and priorities from the United Kingdom. *Autism, 18*(7), 756–770. https://doi.org/10.1177/1362361314529627.

Prata, J., Coelho, R., & Lawson, W. (2018). How the attitude of acceptance, enthusiasm and learning through motivation affects brain development in children with autism: A literature review. *Journal of Intellectual Disability - Diagnosis and Treatment, 6*(1), 14–24. https://doi.org/10.6000/2292-2598.2018.06.01.3.

Rao, P. A., & Beidel, D. C. (2009). The impact of children with high-functioning autism on parental stress, sibling adjustment, and family functioning. *Behavior Modification, 33*(4), 437–451. https://doi.org/10.1177/0145445509336427.

Ruble, L. A., & Dalrymple, N. J. (1996). An alternative view of outcome in autism. *Focus on Autism and Other Developmental Disabilities, 11*(1), 3–14. https://doi.org/10.1177/108835769601100102.

Russell, G., & Norwich, B. (2012). Dilemmas, diagnosis and de-stigmatization: Parental perspectives on the diagnosis of autism spectrum disorders. *Clinical Child Psychology and Psychiatry, 17*(2), 229–245. https://doi.org/10.1177/1359104510365203.

Shandley, K., & Austin, D. W. (2010). Reconceptualizing autism: Moving beyond the behavioral to address cause, cure and prevention. *Autism Insights, 2,* 25–30.

Shute, N. (2010). Desperate for an autism cure. *Scientific American, 303*(4), 80–85.

Simpson, R. L. (2005). Evidence-based practices and students with autism spectrum disorders. *Focus on Autism and Other Developmental Disabilities, 20*(3), 140–149. https://doi.org/10.1177/10883576050200030201.

Singer, A. (2015). Complementary and alternative treatments for autism part 2: Identifying and avoiding non-evidence-based treatments. *AMA Journal of Ethics, 17*(4), 375–380.

Singh, J., Illes, J., Lazzeroni, L., & Hallmayer, J. (2009). Trends in US autism research funding. *Journal of Autism and Developmental Disorders, 39*(5), 788–795. https://doi.org/10.1007/s10803-008-0685-0.

Smith, T. E., Schaefer-Whitby, P., & Mrla, T. (2016). Historical overview of the education and treatment of persons with autism. In *Autism spectrum disorders: Identification, education, and treatment* (pp. 23–40).

Stephenson, J., Carter, M., & Kemp, C. (2012). Quality of the information on educational and therapy interventions provided on the web sites of national autism associations. *Research in Autism Spectrum Disorders, 6*(1), 11–18. https://doi.org/10.1016/j.rasd.2011.08.002.

Szatmari, P., Georgiades, S., Duku, E., Bennett, T. A., Bryson, S., Fombonne, E., … & Volden, J. (2015). Developmental trajectories of symptom severity and adaptive functioning in an inception cohort of preschool children with autism spectrum disorder. *JAMA Psychiatry, 72*(3), 276–283. https://doi.org/10.1001/jamapsychiatry.2014.2463.

Turner, L. M., & Stone, W. L. (2007). Variability in outcome for children with an ASD diagnosis at age 2. *Journal of Child Psychology and Psychiatry, 48*(8), 793–802. https://doi.org/10.1111/j.1469-7610.2007.01744.x.

Vyse, S. (2005). Where do fads come from? In J. Jacobson, R. Foxx, & J. A. Mulick (Eds.), *Controversial therapies for developmental disabilities: Fad, fashion, and science in professional practice* (pp. 3–18). Mahwah, NJ: Erlbaum.

Webster, A. A., & Garvis, S. (2017). The importance of critical life moments: An explorative study of successful women with autism spectrum disorder. *Autism, 21*(6), 670–677. https://doi.org/10.1177/1362361316677719.

Widder, R. M., & Anderson, D. C. (2015). The appeal of medical quackery: A rhetorical analysis. *Research in Social and Administrative Pharmacy, 11*(2), 288–296. https://doi.org/10.1016/j.sapharm.2014.08.001.

Zane, T., Davis, C., & Rosswurm, M. (2008). The cost of fad treatments in autism. *Journal of Early and Intensive Behavior Intervention, 5*(2), 44.

Chapter 6
Understanding the "True" Potential of Autistic People: Debunking the Savant Syndrome Myth

Abstract In 1988, the movie *Rain Man* made its debut in cinemas across the world. This movie raised the public's awareness of autistic people including some of their strengths and common challenges. *Rain Man* also led many people to associate autism with savant abilities. This chapter begins with an introduction and history of savant syndrome, before discussing some of the ways that public attention on fictional and real-life autistic savants has contributed to the myth that all autistic people are savants. This is followed by an examination of the research on prevalence of savant abilities in the autistic population and of the cognitive differences, including strengths and difficulties, exhibited by autistic children and adults. The continued impact that the savant myth has on stereotyping and categorising autistic individuals will be examined and recommendations made for moving from a classification-based to an individual-based approach to supporting all autistic individuals to achieve their potential. The chapter will conclude with a discussion of the ways the savant myth can be transformed by changing the public representation, perception and engagement with autistic individuals of all abilities and needs.

Keywords Savant syndrome · Special skills · Splinter skills · Autistic thinking
High-/low-functioning · Individualised approach

Research indicates that a small proportion of the autistic population possesses exceptional skills, which could be classified as savant syndrome (Treffert, 2014). Nevertheless, savant syndrome has received a disproportionately large amount of attention, especially from the media and film industry. This attention has helped contribute to the creation of the myth that everyone on the autism spectrum has remarkable abilities and is a savant.

M. Bennett et al., *Life on the Autism Spectrum*,
https://doi.org/10.1007/978-981-13-3359-0_6

6.1 The Origins

To understand the origins of the "autistic savant" myth, it is helpful to examine the history of savant syndrome. One of the earliest accounts of savant syndrome was published in 1783 in Germany. In this article, Moritz described Jedediah Buxton, a man who could quickly calculate mathematical problems, but who was unable to live on his own. Since autism was not identified until 1943, it is difficult to conclude if Buxton was autistic (Treffert, 2009). A few years later in 1789, Benjamin Rush described Thomas Fuller, a man who like Jedediah Buxton could quickly perform complex mathematical calculations, but was described as unable to comprehend much of anything practical. Like Buxton, it is not possible to determine if Fuller was autistic, although the fact that he was a slave may mean that he was viewed at the time as having much lower intellectual abilities than he actually had.

In 1887, John Langdon Down was the first to use the term "idiot savant". Down, who is better known for the identification of Down syndrome, used the term to describe ten people he had observed at Earlswood Hospital who showed exceptional skills in a particular area, but who otherwise exhibited all of the characteristics associated with intellectual impairment (Howlin, Goode, Hutton, & Rutter, 2009; Miller, 1999; Treffert, 2014). For example, one man could read and recite *The Rise and Fall of The Roman Empire*, but required a substantial amount of assistance in his daily life (Treffert, 2014). Other individuals demonstrated exceptional musical, artistic or arithmetic abilities. Interestingly, Down also identified two groups of people who he felt demonstrated many of the signs of intellectual impairment, but who did not have any associated physiological traits. He described one group as being always delayed in their development, while the other seemed to develop in a typical fashion before suddenly demonstrating a regression of skills and loss of speech. Today, researchers (Treffert, 2009) are certain that this is a very early description of two different types of autism with the later group demonstrating regressive autism. Kanner (1944) would later recognise many of these same traits in the children profiled in his 1943 study, describing some as demonstrating special musical abilities.

The word "savant" is derived from the French word "savoir", which means "to know", and was combined with the word "idiot" to denote people with intelligence quotient (IQ) scores below 25 who also appeared to know or demonstrate exceptional abilities at a level considerably higher than their other abilities (Treffert, 2009, 2014). Since the majority of people with savant skills exhibit IQ scores higher than 40, the term idiot savant was actually a misnomer. To correct this inaccuracy, and to reflect changing attitudes about terminology for people with intellectual disability, the term "idiot savant" was replaced with "savant syndrome". This was felt to be preferable to the term autistic savant as many people with savant abilities have a diagnosis other than autism.

In 1973, the American Association on Mental Deficiency (AAMD) provided a formal description of savant syndrome:

> a person of low general intelligence who possesses an unusually high skill in some special tasks like mental arithmetic, remembering dates or numbers, or in performing other routine tasks at a remarkably high level. (Grossman, 1973, p. 143)

This definition was revised in 1983 to:

> persons with obvious mental retardation who are capable of performing remarkable feats in sharply circumscribed areas (e.g. arithmetic, calendar calculating) at a remarkably high level. (Grossman, 1983, p. 179)

While the wording of these definitions differs, they share two similarities. First, they specify that the individual must demonstrate abilities, which are unusually high compared to a normative sample, as well as compared to the individual's other abilities. Second, they stipulate that people with savant syndrome exhibit intellectual disability and/or significant challenges with adaptive behaviour (Miller, 1999). More recently, Miller (1998) proposed that the term savant be used to describe individuals who demonstrate exceptional skills in at least one area, with a clear difference between this skill and their overall level of functioning. This reflects the increasing recognition that some people who exhibit savant abilities do have IQ scores above 70 (i.e. the cut-off score for intellectual disability) and include individuals with other neurodevelopmental disabilities such as autism, Prader–Willi syndrome and Williams Syndrome (Howlin et al., 2009). Although some researchers have suggested that savants with a diagnosis of autism may have higher IQ scores than other savants (O'Connor & Hermelin, 1991), the majority do have at least a mild intellectual disability, and almost all have significant deficits in adaptive behaviour (Howlin et al., 2009).

Kanner was the first person to identify savant abilities in autistic individuals. In 1971, he published a paper following up on the original 11 children described in his

1943 study. He found that six of these individuals demonstrated exceptional skills in areas of music or rote memory, although they still exhibited deficits in adaptive behaviour and significant difficulties in a range of areas. Once his study was translated into English, researchers (Frith, 1991) realised that Asperger had also described two children who demonstrated savant skills. One exhibited remarkable calculation and spelling skills and the other demonstrated extraordinary spelling skills, which were incongruent with his other abilities (Asperger, 1944). Since then, researchers (Bölte & Poustka, 2004; Clark, 2016; Howlin et al., 2009; Miller, 1998) who have examined the characteristics of autistic children and adults have often noted that a proportion of these individuals seem to exhibit a similar profile in which one or two skills are quite extraordinary compared to either their other skills or to the norm.

As researchers have begun to explore and understand more about savant syndrome, public awareness has also increased. This can be at least partly attributed to the publication of high profile narratives or case studies of savants. These stories have helped to cultivate the public perception and myth that all autistics are savants. One of the most famous of these individuals was Kim Peek, who was the inspiration for the autistic character Raymond Babbitt, in the movie *Rain Man* (Treffert, 2009). Like Raymond, Peek had an exceptional memory, which enabled him to read and retain vast amounts of information. Researchers now know that Peek was not autistic, but had macrocephaly and brain abnormalities, although he was initially misdiagnosed with autism (Moran, 2010). In contrast, the movie clearly identifies Raymond Babbitt as being an autistic savant. The impact of *Rain Man* has been emphasised by several researchers (Conn & Bhugra, 2012; Nordahl-Hansen, Øien & Fletcher-Watson, 2017) who stress that more than any other image, the character of Raymond Babbitt both increased the public awareness of autism and forever solidified the perception that all autistic people are savants.

Daniel Tammet had seizures as a child, but was not diagnosed with Asperger's syndrome until he was in his early 20s (VanBergeijk, 2009). Widely recognised as a mathematical and linguistic genius, Tammet published his autobiography, *Born on a Blue Day* (Tammet, 2007) in which he offers insight into the way his mind works and how he experiences the world. This book became an international bestseller leaving its reader with a lasting impression of Tammet's amazing skills and contributing further to the way in which many people viewed autistic individuals (Draaisma, 2009). Although Tammet recounts many examples of difficulties he has experienced and continues to encounter, he does exhibit a higher level of adaptive behaviour than most savants (Gururangan, 2012) making him unusual in comparison with other savants. Other autistic individuals with savant abilities who have captured the public's attention include Stephen Wiltshire, who is able to reproduce cities by drawing them with a high degree of detail after seeing them only once (Waterhouse, 2013), and musical prodigy Derek Paravicini (Gururangan, 2012) who is both blind and autistic.

The public attention on individuals such as Stephen Wiltshire, Derek Paravicini and Daniel Tammet has also led to the creation of fictional characters who demonstrate savant abilities. Films have portrayed characters with learning disabilities (e.g. *Forrest Gump*), bipolar disorder (e.g. *Shine*) and schizophrenia (e.g. *A Beautiful Mind*) (Conn & Bhugra, 2012). The entertainment and literary communities have long been fascinated by characters who are different or eccentric in some way, particularly if they exhibit seemingly disparate skills and abilities (Belcher & Maich, 2014). Quasimodo in Hugo's *The Hunchback of Notre-Dame* and Lenny in Steinbeck's *Of Mice and Men* are examples of characters that exhibit a range of abilities and needs that prompt readers to both admire and pity them. The possibility of portraying characters who have exceptional skills in some areas, but who have severe difficulties in other areas, has presented an intriguing opportunity for characterisation in books, films and television. As a result, an increasing number of books, films and television shows have focused on a number of autistic characters who also have savant abilities (Nordahl-Hansen et al., 2017; Nordahl-Hansen, Oien, & Fletcher-Watson, 2018).

As mentioned previously, the most recognisable autistic character with savant syndrome is Raymond Babbitt, from the movie *Rain Man.* Like many autistic characters in films, Raymond displays a disparate set of skills, being able to quickly and accurately perform complex mathematical calculations and memorise and retain large amounts of information. At the same time, he is unable to perform simple daily tasks such as making a piece of toast on his own and becomes extremely agitated when his routine is interrupted. *Rain Man*, viewed by many people both in its original showing and in the years following, has won a number of awards including one for Dustin Hoffman, who was lauded by many who viewed his portrayal of the autistic Raymond as exceptional. Although it was pointed out in the movie that Raymond's skills were extremely unique, Hollywood has continued to regularly depict autistic people as having savant skills (Murray, 2006). Movies such as *Mercury Rising, Silent Fall* and *Mozart and the Whale* as well as television shows including *Parenthood, Criminal Minds* and *The Good Doctor* have all featured characters identified as both autistic and as exhibiting exceptional or savant abilities in some area.

Some researchers have suggested that virtually all fictional autistic characters display some savant abilities (Belcher & Maich, 2014; Draaisma, 2009), while others (Nordahl-Hansen et al., 2017) have stated that the percentage is closer to 50%. Even this more conservative figure, however, grossly overestimates the prevalence of savant abilities in the autistic population, which is estimated to be between 10 and 30% (Howlin et al., 2009; Rimland, 1978). The proliferation of autistic savants in movies and television has led many to believe that this is an accurate representation of the proportion of savants in the autistic community (Draaisma, 2009) and has helped to create unrealistic perceptions and expectations of autistic children and adults (Garner, 2014). For example, in 2007, the National Autistic Society conducted a large-scale study, which explored the public's awareness and knowledge of autism in the UK. They found that the "Rain Man myth" still exists, with 39% of respondents believing that most autistics had some type of special abilities (National Autistic Society, 2008).

Parents of autistic children have also attested to the effect these images have on the public's perception of autistic people. One father, Anthony Baker, relates that when he tells people his son is autistic, they ask about his special abilities. When he explains his son does not have savant skills, people typically view his son as doubly impaired (Baker, 2008). Stuart Murray contends that representing autistic characters as savants is an attempt to define the worth of these characters, adding that their savant skills often become pivotal to the plot as well as the character's ability to connect with others socially (Murray, 2008). Murray also suggests that movies and film often stress the computer-like thinking of autistic characters, rather than portraying them as complex individuals with both strengths and needs in a range of areas. Not only does this reinforce the stereotype of autistic people as unemotional, but it also diminishes the difficulties that autistic individuals often do experience in cognitive processing, and the variations in cognitive abilities demonstrated throughout the autistic population.

6.2 The Research

In recent years, researchers have begun to explore the cognitive profile of autistic children and adults and have examined the incidence of savant abilities. Estimates vary that between 10 and 30% of the autistic population may demonstrate some savant abilities. In an early study, Rimland (1978) surveyed 5,400 parents and found that 531, or 9.8%, reported their autistic child demonstrated exceptional skills in some area. These included musical abilities (53%), atypical memory skills (40%), mathematical abilities (25%) and artistic talent (19%). Bölte and Poustka (2004) reported a similar percentage identifying 33 of 254 (13%) of autistic individuals who demonstrated savant abilities. These individuals demonstrated exceptional abilities in memory, music, arithmetic, reading and drawing. The group varied widely in intelligence with IQ scores ranging from 36 to 128.

More recent research suggests that the percentage of savant skills in the autistic population may be higher than previous estimates. Howlin et al. (2009) investigated both the rates and types of savant skills demonstrated in a sample of 139 autistic adolescents and adults. They found that 28.5% of these individuals met the criteria for savant abilities, while at least 25% more demonstrated skills that, although not in the range of savant abilities, were above population norms and were high in comparison with the individual's other skills. These researchers concluded that estimates of savant abilities have probably been somewhat underestimated. Others (Hermelin & ProQuest, 2001; Waterhouse, 2013) disagree claiming that if these estimates were accurate, they would be observing these skills regularly in their work with autistic individuals, whereas they had only rarely encountered individuals with savant skills.

Treffert (2009, 2014), a well-known expert on savant syndrome, relates that although savant abilities are not unique to autistic individuals, researchers estimate that at least half of the identified people with savant abilities do have a diagnosis of autism, Asperger's syndrome, or autism spectrum disorder. Males are much more likely than females to exhibit savant abilities (Howlin et al., 2009; Miller, 1998). This may be partly related to the higher rates of autism diagnoses in males than females (Hall, 2013). Savant abilities have also been found to encompass a fairly limited range of skills (Treffert, 2009). The most common of these fall into five categories: music, mathematics, calendar calculating, art and mechanical or spatial skills. Other skills that have been reported less often include exceptional abilities with languages, atypical sensory discrimination, heightened awareness of time and knowledge in specific areas such as statistics or navigation. An enhanced memory appears to accompany the majority of these skills.

Researchers have proposed that there are three categories of savant abilities (Clark, 2016; Treffert, 2009). Savants who have *splinter skills* can often memorise rudimentary information such as birthdays, licence plate numbers or historical facts. These are by far the most common of the three categories of savant skills and may be exhibited by a number of autistic individuals. *Talented savants* possess highly refined abilities, such as artistic or musical abilities, which are more visible in contrast to their overall level of functioning as well as to their peers. These individuals often exhibit significant cognitive or adaptive impairments in association with their disability (Treffert, 2014). The character of Dr. Sean Murphy in *The Good Doctor* could be viewed as a talented savant. Although his skills are exceptional, they might be found in some very intelligent individuals in the non-autistic population. What makes his skills more exceptional is the contrast between his abilities in visualisation, memory and deduction and his abilities in social communication. The third type of savants is *prodigious savants*. These individuals have extraordinarily rare talents, which if exhibited by a person with no identified disability, would still result in them being considered a prodigy or genius. Stephen Wiltshire, Kim Peek and Daniel Tammet would be classified as prodigious savants. Interestingly, these individuals are also some of the most famous autistic savants. However, if Tammet's assertion is true, they are three of only about 100 individuals ever to demonstrate skills at this level.

Young (1995) examined the characteristics of 51 savants across the world. She found that 41 of these individuals also had a diagnosis of autism, while the rest had a diagnosis of intellectual disability. Twelve of these individuals were identified as prodigious savants; 20 were identified as talented savants; and 10 had splinter skills. Young cautions that the distinction between these categories remains unclear with the result that some individuals could be viewed as either talented or prodigious savants. Participants shared certain characteristics including particular needs such as neurological impairment with idiosyncratic abilities, impairments in language, intense interests, rigid ways of thinking and cognitive inflexibility. They also shared similar strengths in processing information, memory and encouragement and support from families and teachers. This study illustrates the complexity of skills demonstrated by savants, including the significant strengths and needs demonstrated by these individuals.

Researchers have also attempted to ascertain why special talents seem to co-occur more frequently with autism than with other neurocognitive conditions. Researchers have found differences in brain growth, structure and functioning of autistic individuals (Courchesne, Campbell, & Solso, 2011) although these traits have not consistently been found across all autistic individuals. Others acknowledge that autistic children demonstrate a different profile of cognitive skill development and cognitive processing than their non-autistic peers (Dawson, Mottron, & Gernsbacher, 2008). In addition, many autistic individuals demonstrate cognitive peaks related to visuospatial skills or rote memory, but have difficulty with abstract verbal concepts and comprehension tasks.

Two particular theories have been offered to explain why savant abilities are more common in individuals diagnosed with autism than in individuals with other disabilities. The first is that savant skills are supported by weak central coherence or to the hyper-attention to detail exhibited by many autistic individuals (Pring, Hermelin, & Heavey, 1995). The second hypothesis is that special skills are connected to restricted and repetitive behaviours (O'Connor & Hermelin, 1991). Happé and Vital (2009) examined the talents of autistic twins as reported by their parents. They found that restricted and repetitive behaviours and interests related to a hyper-attention to detail was more evident in children with special talents. They suggest that the detail-oriented cognitive style characteristic of many autistic individuals predisposes them to special talents. Happé and Vital argued that it is not autism itself, but this hyper-focus on detail that is related to special talents. Bennett and Heaton (2012) confirmed this hypothesis through case studies, which revealed that autistic children's special skills were associated with superior working memory and a highly focused attention to detail that was not accompanied by obsessionality.

Some researchers have suggested that savant abilities are driven by an autistic individual's special interests (Thioux, Stark, & Schultz, 2006), while others argue that implicit learning is a key element of savant abilities (Miller, 1999; Mottron, Dawson, Soulieres, Hubert, & Burack, 2006). Howlin et al. (2009) investigated the nature and prevalence of strengths and talents demonstrated by 137 autistic individuals at two different points in time. They found that 25.8% of these individuals' demonstrated talents, while 26.4% had cognitive strengths, and 28.5% had both types of skills. The majority of these individuals demonstrated unusual skills on a block design test, followed by digit span, object assembly and arithmetic. Howlin et al. found little evidence that specific talents correlated with the individual's special interests. The researchers concluded that the majority of participants demonstrated skills that met Treffert's (2009, 2014) definition of talented savants or splinter skills.

In another study, Meilleur, Jelenic and Mottron (2015) investigated special isolated skills in 254 autistic individuals and found that the prevalence for these skills was 62.5%. These researchers found that 58% of these individuals did very well on auditory or visual perceptual tasks (i.e. pitch and visual discrimination) that have been identified as areas of strength for many autistic individuals. They concluded that experience was a significant factor in the development of these strengths and talents, but that genetics was more related to perceptual discrimination skills. Both Meilleur et al. (2015) and Howlin et al. (2009) found that a fairly high percentage of autistic participants in their studies exhibited special skills or talents. Although these individuals did not exhibit the prodigious abilities typically associated with savant syndrome, it is possible that the unique cognitive profiles of autistic individuals do make them more likely to exhibit splinter skills, particularly in relation to difficulties they demonstrate in other areas of functioning.

In contrast to other researchers (Bennett & Heaton, 2012; Happé & Vital, 2009), Baron-Cohen, Ashwin, Ashwin, Tavassoli and Chakrabarti (2009) argued that attention to detail alone does not result in special skills, but that hyper-systemizing enables individuals to direct this attention to detail towards detecting "if *p*, then *q*' rules". Baron-Cohen et al. (2009) suggested that hyper-systemizing is a cognitive style common to autistic individuals that predisposes them to special talents. Systemizing is defined as the ability to recognise repeating patterns, which prompts the individual to construct systems or rules. It is this rule-based recognition of patterns that enable autistic individuals to develop talents in systemisable domains such as mathematics, reading and music, which are common areas of talent for autistic individuals. They also suggest that sensory sensitives affect cognitive processing in the early stages of development, eventually contributing to a heightened attention to detail, as children grow and mature. Baron-Cohen and colleagues conclude that the association between autism and talent begins with hyper-sensory sensitivities, which prompts the individual to focus on details and to engage in hyper-systemizing, which subsequently enables them to develop special skills and talents.

To better understand the ways in which autistic individuals with savant skills differ from those with no special abilities, Bölte and Poustka (2004) compared the cognitive profiles of two groups using the WISC-R. They found that autistic individuals with special skills performed significantly better on the WISC-R subscale of digit span. They concluded that autistic individuals' with special skills exhibit better working memory and executive functioning and that rote memory and low-level processing are a core characteristic of savant skills. Itzchak, Aviva and Zachor (2013) compared a group of autistic children with special skills with a matched group of autistic children with no special skills. They found that children with special skills demonstrated slightly less autism symptomology than the no-skill group. Another interesting finding was that children with special skills had a larger head circumference than the other group. The researcher's hypothesised that head circumference may relate to special abilities, but that restrictive and repetitive behaviours are probably not associated with special skills. Itzchak and colleagues concluded that individuals with savant abilities may represent a subgroup of autistic individuals.

Joseph, Tager-Flusberg and Lord (2002) have also attempted to ascertain whether the disparity in cognitive abilities demonstrated by many autistic individuals may be indicative of subgroups. These researchers found a high rate of uneven cognitive development in autistic children. Out of 73 participants, 35 had significant discrepancies in favour of non-verbal abilities, 32 had no discrepancy and 6 had a discrepancy in favour of verbal abilities. The researchers suggest that non-verbal and verbal profiles may indicate significant subtypes of autism. Other researchers (Happé & Ronald, 2008; Heaton, Williams, Cummins, & Happé, 2008) have also offered evidence for subgroups associated with different skills or abilities within the overall autistic population. Charman et al. (2011) argued that establishing a cognitive phenotype for autistic individuals is difficult because of the heterogeneity of the condition, as well as the focus on small sample sizes and subgroups of individuals with lower or higher IQ scores.

Mottron et al. (2006) suggested that savant skills may be the equivalent of expertise for non-autistic individuals. They offer the enhanced perceptual functioning theory of autism citing eight principles of learning that explain the unique perceptual processing demonstrated by autistic individuals. Mottron et al. contend these differences may be linked to special abilities for some autistic individuals and to the overall variability in the autistic population. It has also been conjectured that savant abilities demonstrated by autistic individuals could be viewed as extreme versions of strengths exhibited by a number of autistic individuals (Dawson et al., 2008). It is also possible that although true savantism is rare, the uneven profile of abilities common to autistic children and adults (Charman et al., 2011) could be viewed as special skills by others. For example, some have suggested that Dr. Temple Grandin has savant abilities. Grandin, however, states that it is her unique cognitive profile, which is characterised by enhanced visual perceptual abilities and a differing perspective that has allowed her to achieve substantial success in her field of expertise (Grandin, 2013a). She offers her theory that autistic individuals demonstrate three distinct thinking styles, which are different from non-autistic processing styles, but are all similar in a heightened awareness of patterns and detail for stimuli in specific areas. Grandin's three autistic thinking styles include: (1) a visual style for people like her who can visualise concepts in detail; (2) a music and mathematical style, which includes people who are highly attuned to music and mathematical patterns; and (3) a verbal logical style, which includes people who have a particular affinity for languages.

Although researchers have debated whether subgroups of autism can be identified, they do acknowledge that there has not yet been established if autistic individuals with different profiles can be definitively distinguished at the biological or genetic level (Mottron et al., 2006). Moreover, a lack of clear delineation between individuals diagnosed with Asperger's syndrome, and those diagnosed with either autistic disorder or "high-functioning" autism led to a major change in the diagnostic criteria in the fifth education of the *Diagnostic and Statistical Manual of Mental Disorders* (*DSM-V*) in 2013. Replacing the previous system of separating individuals by diagnostic category, the *DSM-V* specifies that individuals who meet the criteria for autism all receive one diagnosis of autism spectrum disorder. However, in recognition of the variations within the autism spectrum, a severity rating was added in which individuals are rated according to their level of need in each of the major criteria: social communication and restricted and repetitive interests and behaviours. Although it was originally designed to reflect the commonalities across the autistic population, this new classification may have actually created opportunity for greater divisions of autistic individuals by perceived ability levels.

6.3 The Impact

There are indications that a significant proportion of the population continues to believe the savant myth (National Autistic Society, 2008), which is evidenced by the continued perpetuation of the autistic savant stereotypes in movies, television and the news. Advocates have argued that the prevalence of this myth has placed unrealistic expectations on autistic individuals, many of who do not possess savant skills or abilities (Draaisma, 2009). Additionally, an argument can be made that the savant myth has encouraged a false categorisation of autistic individuals into fixed groups depending on the public's perception of their skills and ability to contribute to society (Murray, 2008).

As awareness has grown of the heterogeneity of the autistic population, researchers, professionals and even members of the autistic community have attempted to sort autistic people into specific groups or categories. This was reflected with the publication of the *Diagnostic and Statistical Manual of Mental Disorders—Fourth Edition (DSM-IV)* (American Psychiatric Association, 1994), which included five diagnostic categories under the umbrella term of pervasive developmental disorders. The publication of the *DSM-IV* revealed a significant change in thinking about autism (Silverman, 2012) following the publication of Asperger's research in English (Frith, 1991). Although each diagnostic category had its own specific diagnostic criteria, a fair degree of inconsistency was noted across individuals within the diagnostic process. In particular, researchers discerned a high degree of overlap between those individuals diagnosed with Asperger's syndrome and those diagnosed with high-functioning autism (Vivanti et al., 2013). The provision of diagnostic category was often more related to the individual conducting the diagnosis than to the specific symptoms demonstrated by the individual. Moreover, researchers identified that language, which was thought to be a core characteristic that distinguished between Asperger's syndrome and autistic disorder, was not a core symptomology inherent in autism spectrum disorders. Rather it was the way in which these individuals engaged in social communication with others that were identified as the primary symptom (Paul, 2008), with skills varying a great deal between individuals regardless of their other skills (Happé & Ronald, 2008; Joseph et al., 2002).

In 2013, the diagnostic criteria for autism were substantially revised in the *DSM-V* to reflect the growing belief that autism was actually one condition, which was manifested by a spectrum of symptoms (Young & Rodi, 2014), which was reflected by the inclusion of a severity rating. These changes met with a fair amount of concern and scepticism both from researchers (Ohan, Ellefson, & Corrigan, 2015; Vivanti et al., 2013) and members of the autistic community (Linton, Krcek, Sensui, & Spillers, 2013) who were concerned about the way in which these ratings would be applied and the impact on the ability of autistic individuals to receive needed supports and services. Additionally, some individuals, particularly those diagnosed with Asperger's syndrome, were concerned about losing a sense of identity following the change in diagnosis. These conversations often reflected a perceived division between individuals with a diagnosis of Asperger's syndrome and those with a diagnosis of autism. Some individuals in the former group expressed concern with having a label of autism and the perceived stigmatisation associated with this label (Giles, 2014). More were concerned, however, that the new diagnosis would diminish the needs of those individuals who were perceived as being "high-functioning" (Linton et al., 2013).

The terms "high-functioning" and "low-functioning" have been used by professionals and researchers for a number of years to distinguish between individuals with a range of characteristics who share the same diagnosis. Viewed as a much more positive alternative to previous labels, the use of these terms has nevertheless resulted in perpetuating misconceptions about autistic individuals. Building on the savant myth, these terms imply that autistic people display distinctive categories of symptomology and can be divided into distinct groups. However, research has indicated that autistic symptomology is varying, with some individuals exhibiting distinctive highs and lows across symptoms and skill areas (Joseph et al., 2002), while others demonstrate a more consistent level of ability across skills. Some individuals and researchers have argued that cognitive processing and language abilities clearly distinguish between high- and low-functioning groups (Jaarsma & Welin, 2012). This is problematic, however, as uneven profiles of cognitive and language functioning are the norm rather than the exception for autistic individuals (Charman et al., 2011). Thus, many autistic advocates reject the use of the terms "high-functioning" and "low-functioning", claiming they are false representations of their abilities and are based on a benchmark of what is considered "normal" (Gillespie-Lynch, Kapp, Brooks, Pickens, & Schwartzman, 2017). In addition, they contend that these terms force them into preconceived groups, which are primarily intended to classify them for funding and support purposes. This opinion has been expressed in a position statement published by the Autistic Self Advocacy Network (ASAN), which states:

> ASAN does not consider any neurological type to be superior or inferior to any other. We do not discriminate against or exclude any Autistic person because of their diagnostic category, support needs, or disabilities. We oppose the practice of separating Autistics into high- and low-functioning groups, which incorrectly suggests that people function at the same level across all areas. Each of us has a unique set of skills and challenges; a person who requires assistance in one area does not necessarily lack ability in another. Functioning labels significantly downplay the uniqueness of each individual, leading to artificial and inaccurate classifications that can cause Autistic people to be denied either services or opportunities. (Autistic Self-advocacy Network (ASAN), N.D.)

This statement clearly identifies the concern of many autistic individuals and their families that dividing autistic individuals into groups can have a detrimental impact affecting their ability to access services, as well as the discounting the unique profile of strengths and needs exhibited by these individuals.

Others have expressed their concern that the savant myth perpetuates two stereotypes associated with the categorisation of autistic individuals by the degree to which they exhibit special skills (Draaisma, 2009; Murray, 2008). Autistic individuals with savant abilities are often portrayed as exceptional eccentrics with superhuman abilities, while those individuals without special skills are presented as tragic figures whose disability causes them and their family ongoing suffering and heartache. Ironically, this has resulted in disadvantaging both groups. Individuals who are perceived as having better language and cognitive skills may be overlooked in services, while those individuals with more limited oral communication skills are often dismissed as intellectually disabled and incapable of speaking for themselves. The importance of recognising the difference between external characteristics and behaviours and internal cognition is explained by Amanda, an autistic adult:

> So, I'm all about our internal realities, not our external appearances. Even though I know our appearances (or what others decide our appearances mean) play a huge role in how we are treated. I just don't think someone's resemblance to someone else's appearance means they

> resemble each other inside at all, so I've never put a lot of stock in categories that people use to define us entirely by a small number of externally visible traits. (Savarese, 2010)

The division of autistic individuals into high- and low-functioning groups has also been reflected within the autism community (Bagatell, 2010). One of the criticisms of the neurodiversity movement has been that it is dominated by verbal and "high-functioning" autistics who do not understand the needs of more "low-functioning" individuals (Jaarsma & Welin, 2012). This debate has particularly centred on the contention of neurodiversity proponents that autism is not a disability, but rather a natural variation that is inseparable from the individual's identity. These individuals have eschewed any notion of a cure (Bagatell, 2010). In contrast, other autistic individuals have more complex feelings about this topic as evidenced in the following statement:

> The rift in the autism community basically is between what we label high-functioning and low-functioning people. High-functioning people talk and low-functioning people don't … I believe the idea that they (high-functioning people) should be cured is wrong. They are different, but basically are just a variation on the norm and should be accepted as such … As a low-functioning person who is still really awash in autism, I actually am aligned with the cure group, although I will not personally benefit if a cure is found. Low-functioning people are just trying to get through the day without hurting, tapping, flailing, biting, screaming, etc. The thought of a gold pot of a potion with a cure really would be wonderful. (Rubin, 2005)

Amanda and Sue's statements both illustrate the complexities involved in quantifying the needs of autistic individuals and underscore the problems with categorising these individuals into predetermined groups, which ultimately misrepresent their abilities and needs. Not only does this prevent them from getting the appropriate services and supports they need, it also promotes stigmatization of both groups. While individuals with limited spoken language or lower cognitive skills may be viewed as limited in their ability to engage fully in different settings and subsequently denied opportunities, individuals with special abilities may not be recognised as having significant needs in other areas and may be expected to perform in situations that they are not able to manage without support. Thus, a more individual approach is needed.

6.4 The Future

The savant myth has promoted stereotypes of autistic individuals and has encouraged the categorisation of these individuals into groups that do not accurately represent their strengths and needs (Baker, 2008; Draaisma, 2009; Murray, 2006). Transforming this myth will involve a number of changes in both the public's perception and representation of autistic individuals with and without savant abilities as well as the ways that members of the community, including professionals and researchers, engage with these individuals. To construct a preferred future, researchers and professionals will need to work with autistic people of all abilities to examine their shared experiences and to find ways to bring the autistic community together to develop supports and services that build on the unique strengths and interests of each individual. Rather than focusing on differences in individuals who have lower or higher skills, addressing their commonalities will better enable others to create a community of support for each individual no matter their abilities.

It is important that professionals recognise the impact of separating individuals by ability groups. Ironically, there is some indication that severity ratings included in the *DSM-V*, which were intended as a way of recognising the uneven profile of needs and heterogeneity of symptoms across individuals, may be used to place people into categories. In its text, the *DSM-V* clearly states that the ratings for social communication and restricted and repetitive behaviours should be applied independently of each other (American Psychiatric Association, 2013). This reflects current research on the uneven profile of symptomology common to many autistic individuals (Charman et al., 2011; Happé & Ronald, 2008). Despite this, autistic individuals and families have reported that funding agencies and government programs have not adopted this approach. For example, recent news reports indicate that autistic individuals in Australia are being classified as level 1, 2 or 3 under the National Disability Insurance Scheme (Ryan, 2018). These classifications are being used to determine funding, which has caused consternation for a number of autistic individuals and their families who are concerned that their needs are being unrecognised and potentially dismissed (Wroe, 2018). An alternative approach would not rely on classification of groups, but would examine each individual's strengths and needs to determine how their strengths could be used as a foundation for support and to identify additional services and supports the individual would need to enable them to overcome barriers, manage challenges and achieve their goals.

Providing an individually based approach also requires a shift in both the perception and representation of autistic individuals. For instance, rather than referring to the individual as "a level 1 autistic man", he might be described as "an autistic man who has an excellent memory and attention to detail but experiences more difficulties in language comprehension". Similarly, instead of saying "a low-functioning woman with autism", an individualised approach would describe this individual as "an autistic woman who utilises augmentative communication, is knowledgeable about horses, and experiences difficulties with sensory overload and anxiety". This approach has the advantage of providing a much more accurate description of the individual's strengths and needs, as well as providing a humanistic alternative to reducing the individual to a label associated with a specific group or level. In addition, this approach has the advantage of ensuring that the difficulties experienced by individuals with savant abilities are not overlooked, and the strengths of individuals with complex needs are acknowledged.

Changes will also need to be made to the public representation or "face" of autism. Instead than portraying autistic individuals as either tragic sufferers who are limited by their disability or quirky eccentrics with exceptional abilities, autistic individuals need to be represented as the complex individuals they are. One way to do this would be to include autistic characters in books, films and media whose autism is not highlighted as a potential asset or liability, but just one aspect of their character. An analogy can be drawn to a character that is divorced. This is certainly an aspect of their character and may play a role in certain plotlines, but is not critical to the majority of these plotlines. Nor does it define the character who is portrayed as a complex individual with a range of assets and limitations.

Creating autistic characters that demonstrate self-advocacy would also help to change the public's perception of autism as an obstacle to be overcome. Currently, many autistic characters have a limited voice, with their perspective being provided by other characters such as family. The difficulties autistic individuals experience in social communication and restricted and repetitive behaviours are often the source of jokes and serve to provide humour in the storylines of television shows and movies. For example, Raymond's need for routine was the source of much of the humour in *Rain Man*. Giving autistic characters an opportunity to express their thoughts and feelings about what it means to be autistic, and to be portrayed as able to solve problems and advocate for necessary supports in their environment, would enable others to see them as capable and competent.

Even more importantly, the representation of autistic characters needs to encompass the full range of autistic individuals. This would entail the creation of more three-dimensional autistic characters that demonstrate a range of interests, abilities and strengths in a proportion more representative of the autistic community. Children and adults would be portrayed as well as autistic individuals who are highly verbal and those who use augmentative and alternative communication to interact with others. Some characters would be good at computers and maths, but others might be adept at languages, art or music. Others might be still working to identify their particular strengths and interests. Recently, some television shows have employed autism consultants in order to accurately portray autistic characters. However, criticism has been raised that autistic consultants are needed in order to capture an accurate representation of the autistic experience. As the experiences of autistic individuals are varying, an even better approach might be to establish an autistic advisory board for the film industry. This would help to encourage the representation of different experiences and perspectives across characters and productions.

Changing the way that the public engages with autistic individuals is another critical element in altering the savant myth. Both individuals with and without savant abilities need a stronger voice in their community and in determining the types of services, supports and strategies that are most relevant to them. Organisations such as the National Autistic Society and others have provided suggestions for facilitating the engagement of individuals who are not able to communicate through typical means or who might experience other barriers to participation because of sensory issues or social anxiety (Nicolaidis et al., 2015). These include provision of written materials in advance to allow the individual time for consideration and processing, enabling the individual to take notes and ask questions at a later time, reducing distracting sensory aspects of the environment, such as lighting or perfumes, incorporation of technology such as closed captioning services, and support for the use of alternative communication. Most important, though, is that the individual be given the means to express the way they wish to communicate and interact with others. This is extremely important as not only do autistic individuals vary widely in their own personalities, interests, abilities and needs, but so do their support systems and networks. For example, an autistic adolescent whose family all works in the family restaurant may not require the same types of support as another individual with the same skills, but less support.

To facilitate the full engagement of autistic individuals, consideration must also be given to the power imbalance that may place this individual at a disadvantage. The need for researchers and professionals to consider the expertise of autistic individuals has been highlighted by a number of individuals (Gillespie-Lynch et al., 2017; Milton & Moon, 2012). They stress the importance of this approach in ensuring that services and supports are not driven by a "normalisation" agenda, but support the rights of autistic individuals to make their own choices and to succeed because of, rather than in spite of, their differences. To ensure that autistic individuals feel others' value their knowledge and participation, the role of the different individuals needs to be outlined. However, providing equity of role and responsibility does not mean that all individuals are recognised as having similar expertise or responsibilities. Milton and Bracher (2013) suggest that facilitating co-learning and capacity building of all individuals, including those autistic participants, can help facilitate more equitable participation. Additionally, Milton offers two barriers that need to be considered (Milton, 2014). Firstly, the common misperception of autistic individuals as socially disengaged or lacking empathy may cause others to dismiss their participation in group decision-making as something autistic individuals would not want or be able to do. Milton stresses that this perception must be corrected before participatory equity can be achieved. Secondly, Milton reports that distrust of autistic individuals regarding research and service professionals, which has developed out of their experiences over time, poses a significant barrier to the way they perceive the intent of others in the group. Thus, finding ways to help autistic and non-autistic individuals to identify shared goals and develop mutual trust, is also critical if autistic individuals are to be engaged fully in productive processes.

Lastly, building a positive future to transform the savant myth will entail recognising and building on the inherent perceptions and cognitive profiles of autistic individuals. Studies have shown that autistic children and adults exhibit a range of skills regardless of whether they have savant abilities or not (Happé & Vital, 2009). Foremost among these is a high attention to detail (Bennett & Heaton, 2012) including enhanced perceptual abilities (Mottron et al., 2006). Heightened sensory sensitivities and a tendency to hyper-systemizing have also been cited as factors in the special abilities exhibited by many autistic individuals (Baron-Cohen et al., 2009). Although estimates vary regarding the number of autistic individuals who exhibit skills that could be classified as being in the savant or talented range, researchers agree that the majority of autistic individuals exhibit splinter skills or an uneven profile of abilities, with some skills being much higher than others (Charman et al., 2011; Heaton et al., 2008; Joseph et al., 2002). Temple Grandin (2013b) suggests that autistic thinking styles can be areas of strength that set them apart from non-autistic individuals. She cites creative thinking, associative thinking and bottom-up thinking as three areas in which autistic individuals are particularly adept.

Like Temple Grandin, John Elder Robison believes that his particular style of autistic thinking and attention to detail enabled him to perform skills that others may find challenging. Diagnosed with Asperger's syndrome in his 30s, Robison spent much of his early 20s creating highly technical sound and light shows for bands. He maintains that his ability to focus on small details was essential to his success in this area as evidenced by the following quote:

> As I recall my own development, I can see how I went through periods where my ability to focus inward and do complex calculations in my mind developed rapidly. When that happened, my ability to solve complex technical or mathematical problems increased, but I withdrew from other people. Later, there were periods where my ability to turn toward other people and the world increased by leaps and bounds. At those times, my intense powers of focused reasoning seemed to diminish. (Robison, 2007, p. 208)

Interestingly, this quote also illustrates Robison's belief that his ability to intensely concentrate diminished as he developed more social awareness. Nevertheless, both Grandin and Robison highlight the ways in which they were able to translate their particular "autistic thinking" into avenues for successful careers. As Grandin explains:

> In some ways, I credit my autism for enabling me to understand cattle ... I have been lucky, because my understanding of animals and visual thinking led me to a satisfying career in which my autistic traits don't impede my progress. (Grandin, 1992, p. 111)

Helping autistic people to reach their full potential should begin by recognising each person's unique profile of strengths and the way that these can be used to create future opportunities and success. Unfortunately, researchers have indicated that even autistic individuals with savant abilities are often challenged to do this (Howlin et al., 2009). One critical factor appears to be the degree to which these individuals are provided with encouragement and support to pursue their passions and build on their strengths, rather than focusing primarily on their difficulties. Grandin (1992) credits one of her teachers for fostering her interest in science, while others have stressed the critical role that parents and friends have had in enabling them to develop their abilities and advocate for themselves (Webster & Garvis, 2017). One program that aims to accomplish this is the Dandelion program, which places autistic individuals in jobs by matching their strengths to job requirements. The program's founder, Thorkil Sonne, explains their mission saying:

> A Dandelion is seen as a weed if in an unwanted place. But if you take that plant to a wanted place you'll see it as an herb and as one of the most valuable plants in nature. That's what we're doing. We're putting people in places where they are welcomed and where they can excel. (Hedley, Uljarević, & Hedley, 2017, p. 302)

Thus, changing perceptions of the community also play an essential role in providing autistic individuals with the opportunity and reinforcement to believe in themselves and to showcase their talents. This will then allow others to view them as autistic individuals rather than as members of specific categories or groups.

6.5 Conclusion

The image of the autistic savant has been a common representation of autistic individuals in public forums such as books, television and films. This has resulted in the stigmatisation of all autistic individuals who are categorised as either having skills of value or needing substantial support that creates a burden on others. Although researchers are divided on the actual prevalence of savant abilities in the autistic population, they do agree that the popular representation of these individuals markedly exceeds the actual number. Researchers have determined that only a very small proportion of autistic individuals have the truly exception abilities that are often highlighted in films. More common is the demonstration of special skills that are disproportionate and demonstrated at a higher level than their other skills. Autistic advocates argue that instead of recognising the complex nature of their abilities, categorising them by groups has resulted in unrealistic expectations for some and lack of expectations for others. To mitigate the impact of the savant myth, autistic individuals need to be viewed as individuals, rather than as members of preordained groups. This will involve changing the public representation to incorporate a variety of autistic characters, with strengths and needs, who are able to participate fully and advocate for themselves in a range of settings. This will enable others to see them as three-dimensional characters who can achieve if they are encouraged and provided with the opportunity to utilise their strengths and interests.

References

American Psychiatric Association. (1994). *Diagnostic and statistical manual of mental disorders—Fourth edition*. Washington, DC: American Psychiatric Publishing. Retrieved from http://www.terapiacognitiva.eu/dwl/dsm5/DSM-IV.pdf.

American Psychiatric Association. (2013). *Diagnostic and statistical manual of mental disorders—Fifth edition*. Washington, DC: American Psychiatric Publishing.

Asperger, H. (1944). "Die, Autistischen Psychopathen" im Kindesalter. *Archiv für psychiatrie und nervenkrankheiten, 117*(1), 76–136. https://doi.org/10.1007/BF01837709.

Autistic Self-advocacy Network (ASAN). (N.D.). Position statements: The autistic community and allies. Retrieved from http://autisticadvocacy.org/about-asan/position-statements/.

Bagatell, N. (2010). From cure to community: Transforming notions of autism. *Ethos, 38*(1), 33–55. https://doi.org/10.1111/j.1548-1352.2009.01080.x.

Baker, A. D. (2008). Recognizing Jake: Contending with formulaic and spectacularized representations of autism in film. In M. Osteen (Ed.), *Autism and representation* (pp. 229–243), New York: Taylor & Francis.

Baron-Cohen, S., Ashwin, E., Ashwin, C., Tavassoli, T., & Chakrabarti, B. (2009). Talent in autism: Hyper-systemizing, hyper-attention to detail and sensory hypersensitivity. *Philosophical Transactions of the Royal Society B: Biological Sciences, 364*(1522), 1377–1383. https://doi.org/10.1098/rstb.2008.0337.

Belcher, C., & Maich, K. (2014). Autism spectrum disorder in popular media: Storied reflections of societal views. *Brock Education, 23*(2), 97–115. https://doi.org/10.26522/BROCKED.V23I2.311.

Bennett, E., & Heaton, P. (2012). Is talent in autism spectrum disorders associated with a specific cognitive and behavioural phenotype? *Journal of Autism and Developmental Disorders, 42*(12), 2739–2753. https://doi.org/10.1007/s10803-012-1533-9.

Bölte, S., & Poustka, F. (2004). Comparing the intelligence profiles of savant and nonsavant individuals with autistic disorder. *Intelligence, 32*(2), 121–131. https://doi.org/10.1016/j.intell.2003.11.002.

Charman, T., Jones, C. R., Pickles, A., Simonoff, E., Baird, G., & Happé, F. (2011). Defining the cognitive phenotype of autism. *Brain Research, 1380,* 10–21. https://doi.org/10.1016/j.brainres.2010.10.075.

Clark, T. (2016). *Exploring giftedness and autism: A study of a differentiated educational program for autistic savants*. New York: Routledge.

Conn, R., & Bhugra, D. (2012). The portrayal of autism in Hollywood films. *International Journal of Culture and Mental Health, 5*(1), 54–62. https://doi.org/10.1080/17542863.2011.553369.

Courchesne, E., Campbell, K., & Solso, S. (2011). Brain growth across the life span in autism: Age-specific changes in anatomical pathology. *Brain Research, 1380,* 138–145. https://doi.org/10.1016/j.brainres.2010.09.101.

Dawson, M., Mottron, L., & Gernsbacher, M. A. (2008). Learning in autism. In H. L. Roediger III (Ed.), *Cognitive psychology of memory* (Vol. 2). Oxford: Elsevier.

Draaisma, D. (2009). Stereotypes of autism. *Philosophical Transactions of the Royal Society B: Biological Sciences, 364*(1522), 1475–1480. https://doi.org/10.1098/rstb.2008.0324.

Frith, U. (1991). Asperger and his syndrome. *Autism and Asperger Syndrome, 14,* 1–36.

Garner, A. (2014). *What's showing: Film industry portrayals of autism spectrum conditions and their influences on preservice teachers in Australia.* (Ph.D.), Retrieved from http://ro.uow.edu.au/theses/4282/.

Giles, D. C. (2014). DSM-V is taking away our identity: The reaction of the online community to the proposed changes in the diagnosis of Asperger's disorder. *Health (London), 18*(2), 179–195. https://doi.org/10.1177/1363459313488006.

Gillespie-Lynch, K., Kapp, S. K., Brooks, P. J., Pickens, J., & Schwartzman, B. (2017). Whose expertise is it? Evidence for autistic adults as critical autism experts. *Frontiers in Psychology, 8,* 438. https://doi.org/10.3389/fpsyg.2017.00438.

Grandin, T. (1992). *Thinking in pictures and other reports from my life with autism.* London: Bloomsbury.

Grandin, T. (2013a). *The autistic brain*. New York: Houghton Mifflin Harcourt.

Grandin, T. (2013b). Temple Grandin: What's right with the autistic mind. *Time*. Retrieved from http://content.time.com/time/subscriber/article/0,33009,2153096-1,00.html.

Grossman, H. (1973). *Manual on terminology and classification in mental retardation*. Washington, DC: American Association on Mental Deficiency.

Grossman, H. (1983). *Classification in mental retardation*. Washington, DC: American Association on Mental Deficiency.

Gururangan, K. (2012). Savant syndrome: Growth of empathy and creativity. *Berkeley Scientific Journal, 15*(1), 1–9.

Hall, L. J. (2013). *Autism spectrum disorders: From theory to practice*. Boston: Pearson.

Happé, F., & Ronald, A. (2008). The "fractionable autism triad": A review of evidence from behavioural, genetic, cognitive and neural research. *Neuropsychology Review, 18*(4), 287–304. https://doi.org/10.1007/s11065-008-9076-8.

Happé, F., & Vital, P. (2009). What aspects of autism predispose to talent? *Philosophical Transactions of the Royal Society B: Biological Sciences, 364*(1522), 1369–1375. https://doi.org/10.1098/rstb.2008.0332.

Heaton, P., Williams, K., Cummins, O., & Happé, F. (2008). Autism and pitch processing splinter skills: A group and subgroup analysis. *Autism, 12*(2), 203–219. https://doi.org/10.1177/1362361307085270.

Hedley, D., Uljarević, M., & Hedley, D. F. (2017). Employment and living with autism: Personal, social and economic impact. In S. Halder & L. C. Assaf (Eds.), *Inclusion, disability and culture* (pp. 295–311). Cham, Switzerland: Springer.
Hermelin, B., & ProQuest, E. (2001). *Bright splinters of the mind: A personal story of research with autistic savants*. London: Jessica Kingsley Publishers.
Howlin, P., Goode, S., Hutton, J., & Rutter, M. (2009). Savant skills in autism: Psychometric approaches and parental reports. *Philosophical Transactions of the Royal Society B: Biological Sciences, 364*(1522), 1359–1367. https://doi.org/10.1098/rstb.2008.0328.
Itzchak, E.-B., Aviva, B., & Zachor, D. A. (2013). Are special abilities in autism spectrum disorder associated with a distinct clinical presentation? *Research in Autism Spectrum Disorders, 7*(9), 1122–1128. https://doi.org/10.1016/j.rasd.2013.05.003.
Jaarsma, P., & Welin, S. (2012). Autism as a natural human variation: Reflections on the claims of the neurodiversity movement. *Health Care Analysis, 20*(1), 20–30. https://doi.org/10.1007/s10728-011-0169-9.
Joseph, R. M., Tager-Flusberg, H., & Lord, C. (2002). Cogntiive profiles and social-communicative functioning in children with autism spectrum disorder. *Journal of Child Psychology and Psychiatry, 43*(6), 807–821. https://doi.org/10.1111/1469-7610.00092.
Kanner, L. (1944). Early infantile autism. *The Journal of Pedatrics, 25*(3), 211–217. https://doi.org/10.1016/S0022-3476(44)80156-1.
Kanner, L. (1971). Follow-up study of eleven autistic children originally reported in 1943. *Journal of autism and Childhood Schizophrenia, 1*(2), 119–145. https://doi.org/10.1007/BF01537953.
Linton, K. F., Krcek, T. E., Sensui, L. M., & Spillers, J. L. H. (2013). Opinions of people who self-identify with autism and Asperger's on DSM-5 criteria. *Research on Social Work Practice, 24*(1), 67–77. https://doi.org/10.1177/1049731513495457.
Meilleur, A. A., Jelenic, P., & Mottron, L. (2015). Prevalence of clinically and empirically defined talents and strengths in autism. *Journal of Autism and Developmental Disorders, 45*(5), 1354–1367. https://doi.org/10.1007/s10803-014-2296-2.
Miller, L. K. (1998). Defining the savant syndrome. *Journal of Developmental and Physical Disabilities, 10*(1), 73–85. https://doi.org/10.1023/A:1022813601762.
Miller, L. K. (1999). The savant syndrome: Intellectual impairment and exceptional skill. *Psychological Bulletin, 125*(1), 31–46. https://doi.org/10.1037/0033-2909.125.1.31.
Milton, D., & Moon, L. (2012). The normalisation agenda and the psycho-emotional disablement of autistic people. *Autonomy, the Critical Journal of Interdisciplinary Autism Studies, 1*(1), 1–12.
Milton, D. E. (2014). Autistic expertise: A critical reflection on the production of knowledge in autism studies. *Autism, 18*(7), 794–802. https://doi.org/10.1177/1362361314525281.
Milton, D. E., & Bracher, M. (2013). Autistics speak but are they heard. *Medical Sociology online, 7*, 61–69.
Moran, M. (2010). Autistic savant made famous by "Rain man" dies—What is new in understanding of syndrome? *Neurology Today, 10*(3), 14–15. https://doi.org/10.1097/01.NT.0000368614.59951.d2.
Mottron, L., Dawson, M., Soulieres, I., Hubert, B., & Burack, J. (2006). Enhanced perceptual functioning in autism: An update, and eight principles of autistic perception. *Journal of Autism and Developmental Disorders, 36*(1), 27–43. https://doi.org/10.1007/s10803-005-0040-7.
Murray, S. (2006). Autism and the contemporary sentimental: Fiction and the narrative fascination of the present. *Literature and Medicine, 25*(1), 24–45. https://doi.org/10.1353/lm.2006.0025.
Murray, S. (2008). *Representing autism: Culture, narrative, fascination*. Liverpool, UK: Liverpool University Press.
National Autistic Society. (2008). *Think differently—Act positively*. Retrieved from London http://www.nas.org.uk.
Nicolaidis, C., Raymaker, D. M., Ashkenazy, E., McDonald, K. E., Dern, S., Baggs, A. E., ... Boisclair, W. C. (2015). Respect the way I need to communicate with you: Healthcare experiences of adults on the autism spectrum. *Autism, 19*(7), 824–831. http://doi.org/10.1177/1362361315576221.

Nordahl-Hansen, A., Oien, R. A., & Fletcher-Watson, S. (2018). Pros and cons of character portrayals of autism on TV and film. *Journal of Autism and Developmental Disorders, 48*(2), 635–636. https://doi.org/10.1007/s10803-017-3390-z.

Nordahl-Hansen, A., Tondevold, M., & Fletcher-Watson, S. (2017). Mental health on screen: A DSM-5 dissection of portrayals of autism spectrum disorders in film and TV. *Psychiatry Research, 262,* 351–353. https://doi.org/10.1016/j.psychres.2017.08.050.

O'Connor, N., & Hermelin, B. (1991). Talents and preoccupations in idiots-savants. *Psychological Medicine, 21*(4), 959–964. https://doi.org/10.1017/S0033291700029949.

Ohan, J. L., Ellefson, S. E., & Corrigan, P. W. (2015). Brief report: The impact of changing from DSM-IV 'Asperger's' to DSM-5 "autistic spectrum disorder" diagnostic labels on stigma and treatment attitudes. *Journal of Autism and Developmental Disorders, 45*(10), 3384–3389. https://doi.org/10.1007/s10803-015-2485-7.

Paul, R. (2008). Interventions to improve communication in autism. *Child and Adolescent Psychiatric Clinics of North America, 17*(4), 835–856. https://doi.org/10.1016/j.chc.2008.06.011.

Pring, L., Hermelin, B., & Heavey, L. (1995). Savants, segments, art and autism. *Journal of Child Psychology and Psychiatry, 36*(6), 1065–1076. https://doi.org/10.1111/j.1469-7610.1995.tb01351.x.

Rimland, B. (1978). Savant capabilities of autistic children and their cognitive implications. In G. Serban (Ed.), *Cognitive deficits in the development of mental illness* (pp. 43–65). Oxford, England: Brunner/Mazel.

Robison, J. E. (2007). *Look me in the eye: My life with Asperger's*. New York: Random House.

Rubin, S. (2005). Acceptance versus cure. Retrieved from http://edition.cnn.com/CNN/Programs/presents/shows/autism.world/notebooks/sue/notebook.html.

Rush, B. (1789). Account of a wonderful talent for arithmetical calculation in an African slave, living in Virginia. *American Museum, 5*, 62–63.

Ryan, M. (30 May, 2018). Profoundly irresponsible: How the NDIS is failing the autistic. *The Sydney Morning Herald*. Retrieved from https://www.smh.com.au/healthcare/profoundly-irresponsible-how-the-ndis-is-failing-the-autistic-20180520-p4zge7.html#comments.

Savarese, E. T. (2010). What we have to tell you: A roundtable with self-advocates from AutCom. *Disability Studies Quarterly, 30*. Retrieved from http://dsqsds.org/article/view/1073/1239.

Silverman, C. (2012). *Understanding autism: Parents, doctors, and the history of a disorder*. Princeton, NJ: Princeton University Press.

Tammet, D. (2007). *Born on a blue day: Inside the extraordinary mind of an autistic savant*. London: Hodder & Soughton.

Thioux, M., Stark, D. E., & Schultz, R. T. (2006). The day of the week when you were born in 700 is: Calendar computation in an autistic savant. *Journal of Experiential Psychology: Human Perception and Performance, 32*(5), 1155–1168. https://doi.org/10.1037/0096-1523.32.5.1155.

Treffert, D. A. (2009). The savant syndrome: An extraordinary condition. A synopsis: Past, present, future. *Philosophical Transactions of the Royal Society B: Biological Sciences, 364*(1522), 1351–1357. https://doi.org/10.1098/rstb.2008.0326.

Treffert, D. A. (2014). Savant syndrome: Realities, myths and misconceptions. *Journal of Autism and Developmental Disorders, 44*(3), 564–571. https://doi.org/10.1007/s10803-013-1906-8.

VanBergeijk, E. (2009). Daniel Tammet: Born on a blue day: Inside the extraordinary mind of an autistic savant. *Journal of Autism and Developmental Disorders, 40*(10), 1293. https://doi.org/10.1007/s10803-009-0868-3.

Vivanti, G., Hudry, K., Trembath, D., Barbaro, J., Richdale, A., & Dissanayake, C. (2013). Towards the DSM-5 criteria for autism: Clinical, cultural, and research implications. *Australian Psychologist, 48,* 258–261. https://doi.org/10.1111/ap.12008.

Waterhouse, L. (2013). *Rethinking autism: Variation and complexity*. London: Elsevier.

Webster, A. A., & Garvis, S. (2017). The importance of critical life moments: An explorative study of successful women with autism spectrum disorder. *Autism, 21*(6), 670–677. https://doi.org/10.1177/1362361316677719.

Wroe, D. (19 May, 2018). Autism advocates blast proposed "cutbacks" to NDIS access. *The Sydney Morning Herald*. Retrieved from https://www.smh.com.au/politics/federal/autism-advocates-blast-proposed-cutbacks-to-ndis-access-20180519-p4zgbf.html.

Young, R. L. (1995). *Savant syndrome: Processes underlying extraordinary abilities.* (Doctoral thesis, University of Adelaide, Adelaide, South Australia) Retrieved from https://digital.library.adelaide.edu.au/dspace/bitstream/2440/18543/1/01front.pdf.

Young, R. L., & Rodi, M. L. (2014). Redefining autism spectrum disorder using DSM-5: The implications of the proposed DSM-5 criteria for autism spectrum disorders. *Journal of Autism and Developmental Disorders, 44*(4), 758–765. https://doi.org/10.1007/s10803-013-1927-3.

Chapter 7
Creating Contexts for Interaction in a Neurotypical World: Confronting Myths of Social Communication and Empathy

Abstract Deficits in language and social communication comprise an essential part of the diagnostic criteria for autism and Asperger's disorder since autism was first described by Kanner and Asperger in the 1940s. Although it was originally believed that most autistic children had significant language delays, a wider understanding of the autism spectrum has revealed that it is social communication that is the primary difficulty, rather than language. Despite this, images of uncommunicative autistic children continue to promote myths such as you can't have autism if you can talk and autistic people lack empathy for others. This chapter starts with an overview of descriptions and portrayals of autistic individuals as uncommunicative and withdrawn, which is followed by an examination of development of social communication by autistic children and the variance in social–emotional expression demonstrated by these individuals as they grow to adulthood. The impact of these myths on perpetuating disengagement of both verbal and non-verbal autistic individuals from their communities will be explored, and questions will be raised about the appropriateness of focusing primarily on increasing these individual's social skills. Suggestions will be made for alternative approaches that bridge the communication gap through the use of technology and alternative approaches in which people are encouraged to expand their conceptualisation of what constitutes autistic communication styles. Additionally, recommendations will be offered about ways that better enable autistic individuals to develop awareness of their own emotions and the impact of their signals on others in order to connect better with others and demonstrate more complex layers of empathy.

Keywords Social communication · Empathy · Social–emotional awareness
Augmentative and alternative communication · Joint attention · Theory of mind

M. Bennett et al., *Life on the Autism Spectrum*,
https://doi.org/10.1007/978-981-13-3359-0_7

The ability to communicate with others is critical in most aspects of life. For some autistic individuals, deficits in social communication often present them with challenges when they interact with non-autistic members of society. These challenges are compounded by the assumptions that others make about the communication abilities and social–emotional traits of autistic individuals. A common misperception is that autistic individuals do not talk or have severely delayed language. This has led to the myth that you cannot have autism if you talk well. An associated myth is the common belief that autistic people cannot feel empathy. Both of these myths are derived from early stereotypes of autistic children and are based on a specific view of communication and social interaction.

7.1 The Origins

Like many of the common myths about autism, the roots of the myths that autistic people don't talk or feel empathy can be found in Kanner's early research. In his original study, Kanner presented case studies of children whom he described as all sharing a "disability to relate themselves in the ordinary way to people and situations from the beginning of life" (Kanner, 1944, p. 211). He discussed the ways in which these children ignored people around them and were limited in their ability to communicate with others. Kanner concluded that the shared traits exhibited by these children demonstrated a new syndrome, which he called "extreme autistic aloneness", of which the most defining feature was their "inability to relate themselves in the ordinary way to people". These terms would have a powerful impact on people's early perceptions of autism and autistic children. Not only did Kanner establish a lack of communication as a core characteristic of autistic individuals, but by identifying autism as an affective disorder, he associated autism with a lack of emotion or empathy with the emotions of others.

Kanner's (1943) case studies provide an in-depth look at 11 children who all demonstrated the core features later identified by Wing and Gould as the triad of impairment (1979). These would eventually constitute the original diagnostic criteria for autism in the *Diagnostic and Statistical Manual of Mental Disorders—Third Edition (DSM-III)*. These characteristics include a marked difference in social–emotional affect, difficulties with language and communication, and a tendency towards rigid and repetitive behaviours and interests (Kanner). Many of these repetitive behaviours involved ritualistic use of language or sounds. For example, one boy, Donald, was described as being indifferent to people and having a literal and inflexible approach to language. He also displayed a number of rituals repeating some of the same words throughout the day.

Despite the overall impression of autistic children as lacking language, a number of children in Kanner's (1943) study did exhibit a fair amount of expressive language and vocabulary. For example, Kanner describes Paul as having clear enunciation and a clear vocabulary. Another boy, Alfred, was reported to ask obsessive questions and provide detailed information about certain topics. Of the 11 children described in Kanner's case studies, only three had almost no language. A further two used limited language with others speaking in single words or short phrases. These individuals, as well as the other six children who demonstrated higher language skills, all displayed unusual response to or use of language including ritualistic use of words and phrases, non-reciprocal dialogue and marked repetition of the language from others in their environment. Although it was not known at the time, Asperger (1944) reported similar behaviours, describing the children in his study as exhibiting unusual language patterns and poor reciprocal communication.

What is evident in both Kanner's (1943) and Asperger's (1944) case studies is that most of the children demonstrated pronounced difficulties in communicating and interacting with other people. For instance, Kanner reported that John did not respond to commands, while Herbert's parents assumed he was deaf as he made no attempt to talk with them, and Alfred did not share his experiences although he did have language. Even more noticeable were Kanner's descriptions of these children as withdrawn or detached from the people around them. Charles was described as acting hypnotised, Elain as appearing vague and detached and Virginia as having no interest in people. Similarly, Asperger described Hellmuth as always being in another world and Haroo as being aloof from people. Although Asperger's study would not be widely read until it was translated in 1991, Kanner's descriptions were quite detailed and helped to create a future image of autistic children as withdrawn and unwilling or unable to communicate with those around them.

The publication of Kanner's (1943) study certainly had an impact on the scientific and medical community's awareness of autism. However, it is possible that the stereotype of the aloof uncommunicative child might not have developed if it had not been for Bruno Bettelheim. In 1967, Bettelheim published his book, *The empty fortress: Infantile autism and the birth of self*. In this book, he presented his theory that autism was caused by cold and detached parents. More significantly, he argued that the early disconnect with their parents, resulted in the emotional detachment of the children who were subsequently unable to connect and reciprocate the emotions and communications of others. Bettelheim's theories have been disproven, but the images of emotionally detached and unresponsive children helped to solidify the myths that autistic people do not talk and cannot feel empathy.

Following the release of Bettelheim's (1967) study, popular and contemporary representations of autistic individuals have portrayed them as aloof, uncommunicative and unconcerned about the emotional well-being of others. For example, in the 1988 movie *Rain Man*, the autistic character, Raymond Babbitt, responds adversely when his brother tries to hug him and appears to not notice that his brother is becoming increasingly frustrated and agitated as they travel together. In addition, although Raymond can talk, he demonstrates little reciprocal communication and uses many repetitive and idiosyncratic phrases. Other movies have portrayed characters who are even more withdrawn. The television series, *St. Elsewhere,* which aired from 1982 to 1988, featured a reoccurring character who was unable to speak, communicating only in noises and challenging behaviours. This character also perpetuated the stereotype of the trapped child as the ending scene implied that the entire series was a product of this child's imagination as he gazed at a snow globe. More recently, the movie *The Black Balloon* focused on the relationship between an adolescent autistic boy and his brother. During the movie, the brother was shown trying to connect with his autistic brother who was non-verbal and demonstrated a number of problematic and potentially harmful behaviours. Garner (2014) found that this movie had a significantly negative impact on viewers, which persists well after they have seen the movie. Teachers who viewed the movie responded that it sent a very negative image about the communication abilities of autistic individuals as it did not provide any example of the use of alternative communication such as visuals.

In the movie, *Snowcake*, the central character, Linda, is portrayed as an autistic woman who is able to live somewhat independently and communicate with other people. In two of the film's most powerful scenes, however, Linda is shown as being indifferent when she views her daughter's dead body and attends her daughter's funeral. Even more impactful is a scene where she becomes distressed at the post-funeral gathering, because people are disturbing the items in her home. The lasting impression is that Linda is uncaring or incapable of feeling typical emotions. The film contains many scenes which reinforce this image, including one in which Linda displays no emotional response after another character expresses his sorrow at being involved in her daughter's death. Although one could argue that Sigourney Weaver's portrayal of Linda, who was based on a real person, is much more complex and that she does give little signs of her distress during the film, these may not be evident to the viewer who knows little about autism or has never met an autistic person. Particularly missing from the film is Linda's perspective. The viewer is only able to see Linda through the other characters who often react poorly to Linda's unusual communication and affect.

In addition to televised characters, researchers (Broderick & Ne'eman, 2008; Sarrett, 2011) have noted the number of images and news stories that have portrayed autistic children as detached and unable to connect with others due to being trapped or isolated by their autism. Rarely are these individuals portrayed communicating with others, expressing emotions, or demonstrating empathy. The power of these stereotypical images of autistic individuals was revealed in a recent study, in which Huws and Jones (2010) examined community members' knowledge and perceptions about autism and autistic people. They found that a common view was that autistic people were trapped and unable to communicate with others. They described autistic people as "living in their own world" (p. 339) and felt they were not able to relate to others or the outside world. Parents have also expressed concerns that having an autistic child would mean they would not be able to communicate or be affectionate (Senier, 2008).

Examinations of public images and stereotypes of autism indicate two additional factors that have contributed to the myths that autistic people don't talk and are unable to show empathy for others. The first of these is related to stories of children who have seemingly developed "normally" only to experience sudden and unexplained regression of skills, most noticeable of which is a loss of language. Although these cases are in the minority and comprise roughly 20–30% of the autistic population (Barger, Campbell, & McDonough, 2013; Meilleur & Fombonne, 2009), stories of children who have suddenly lost their language have received a great deal of media attention, particularly following the release of Wakefield et al.'s (1998) study suggesting that the measles, mumps and rubella vaccine was responsible. Parents were shown describing how their child became withdrawn, emotionally distant and unable to speak (Offit & Coffin, 2003). This added to the public perception that autistic children were not able to talk or connect.

A final factor contributing to these myths is the emotional expressions of autistic individuals. The stereotypical image of autistic children is of an individual with a vacant or distant expression and a flat affect. Although this is certainly an exaggerated image, researchers have found that autistic children and adults can exhibit atypical facial expressions in response to emotions. For example, Loveland et al. (1994) found that children diagnosed with autism demonstrated many more unusual and mechanical facial expressions than children diagnosed with Down syndrome. More recently, Stagg, Slavny, Hand, Cardoso, and Smith (2014) asked adults to rate the facial expressions of videos of autistic and non-autistic children. Participants were not told which children had a diagnosis of autism spectrum disorder. Overall, the adults rated the autistic children as being much less expressive than the non-autistic controls. Similarly, children rated the autistic group as less friendly based solely on their facial expressions. This suggests that facial expressions can significantly impact the way others perceive and respond to autistic children or adults. It is also important to note that the children in the videos were all asked to talk about positive experiences in their lives with the intent that they would demonstrate positive expressions. In spite of this, the autistic group was less effective in conveying these positive feelings.

In his book, *Look Me in the Eye*, autistic author John Elder Robison explains that for him, thoughts, emotions and facial expressions were not necessarily connected. He relates that he was continuously in trouble for his weird facial expressions, which made people think he lacked compassion and feeling for others. In reality, he was experiencing a variety of thoughts and emotions, but did not reflect these with the typically expected facial expression. This example demonstrates the multifaceted nature of communication and empathy in which the outward behaviours may not match the individual's intent. For autistic children and adults, there is often an atypical relationship between language and communication and facial expressions and emotions. It is this disconnect that is at the foundation of misperceptions and myths about the ways in which autistic individuals communicate with others, including the ways in which they demonstrate emotions and empathy for others.

7.2 The Research

> The newly published criteria for autism spectrum disorder in the *Diagnostic and Statistical Manual of Mental Disorder – Fifth Edition (DSM-5)* specifies that individuals demonstrate persistent deficits in social communication and social interaction to include: 1) deficits in social-emotional reciprocity, 2) deficits in nonverbal communicative behaviours used for social interaction, and 3) deficits in developing, maintaining and understanding relationships (American Psychiatric Association, 1994). These provide insight into the factors that affect the ways that autistic individuals communicate and engage in social-emotional interactions with others.

According to these criteria, individuals may demonstrate difficulties with language, but this is not essential to receive a diagnosis of autism spectrum disorder. This represented a significant change from the previous edition. The *DSM-IV* included five different diagnoses, which were all categorised as pervasive developmental disorders (American Psychiatric Association, 1994). Of these, autistic disorder and Asperger's syndrome were the most common diagnoses given. The main difference between these two diagnoses was that individuals did not need to demonstrate a delay in language to receive a diagnosis of Asperger's syndrome. They did, however, still need to demonstrate a marked deficit in communication skills. A lack of consistency of diagnosis and clear delineation between the two diagnoses led to them being merged into one diagnosis of autism spectrum disorder in the *DSM-V*. More important was the realisation that the core difficulty experienced by autistic individuals was not language, but communication (Vivanti et al., 2013). In addition, researchers recognised that as communication always involves another person, social interaction and communication were interlinked. Thus, the two criteria became one criterion specifying deficits in social communication.

To help understand the origins of the myth that autistics don't talk, it is important to clarify the distinction between *language* and *communication.* Communication involves the way that people convey and receive information with each other. Prizant, Wetherby, Rubin, Laurent, and Rydell (2005) note that autistic children may communicate for the purposes of regulating another's behaviour, such as requesting or rejecting objects, but are less likely to communicate for the purpose of social relatedness or to connect with others. Social communication is distinguished by its purpose. People engage in social communication to develop social relationships. According to Wetherby, Watt, Morgan, and Shumway (2007, p. 960), "social communication skills include a broad array of verbal and nonverbal behaviours used in reciprocal social interaction". In addition, social communication involves the ability to use socially appropriate verbal and non-verbal behaviours and to change those behaviours as needed to suit the environment and listener. Non-verbal behaviours can include the use of facial expressions, body language and voice quality or tone to engage in or enhance communication with another person (Hall, 2018). In contrast, language is a symbolic abstract system with formalised rules for word representation, production and use (Heflin & Alaimo, 2007). Generally, this takes the form of oral language, but it can be a visual language such as American Sign Language or Auslan, or a written symbol system that uses drawings or words to represent specific meanings.

Researchers (Twachtman-Cullen, 2014) have stated that for many autistic children and adults, there is a disconnect between language and communication. This is evident in Kanner's (1943) and Asperger's (1944) descriptions of children who used language not to socially interact, but to calm themselves or to engage in verbal rituals and routines. For example, Kanner described Donald who appeared to derive pleasure from repeating specific words to himself. Likewise, Asperger described Charles who constantly asked himself, "what is this?" as he moved around his environment. Since these early studies, researchers have examined the communication and language development of autistic children to understand the ways in which these differ from non-autistic children.

Researchers are somewhat unclear about the exact number of autistic children and adults who have little to no speech, particularly as they move into adulthood (Tager-Flusberg & Kasari, 2013). Before autism and Asperger's syndrome were merged in the *DSM-V*, researchers thought as many as 50% of all individuals diagnosed with autism had limited or no speech (Seltzer, Shattuck, Abbeduto, & Greenberg, 2004). Currently, estimates are that approximately 25–30% of all autistic children, including those previously diagnosed with autism or Asperger's syndrome, have limited or no spoken language (Hall, 2018; Tager-Flusberg & Kasari, 2013). Researchers have also stated that up to 25% of autistic individuals may initially develop language, but then regress and lose some or all of their spoken language (Kim, Paul, Tager-Flusberg, & Lord, 2014; Meilleur & Fombonne, 2009). By adulthood, estimates are that approximately 10–15% may have little functional spoken language (Magiati, Tay, & Howlin, 2014) with the majority having comorbid intellectual or physical disabilities. Individuals with limited spoken language are described as being at the pre-linguistic and/or pre-intentional level of communication (Heflin & Alaimo, 2007). To be at the pre-intentional stage means that the individual does not yet recognise the importance of communicating with others. These individuals may respond to requests or directions, but do not initiate communication, either verbally or non-verbally. It is also important to note that even individuals who speak or use language can still be considered pre-intentional communicators if they do not use language to interact with others. A unique characteristic of autistic children compared to children with other developmental disabilities is that they will often use language with no communicative intent (Alpern, 2012). In contrast, individuals who are identified as pre-linguistic will use non-verbal means to communicate and interact, but do not yet have the ability to use formal language systems such as oral language or sign language (Heflin & Alaimo, 2007). Knowing which stage the individual is at is extremely important in determining the best type of intervention.

Language skills vary widely across the autistic population (Hall, 2018; Kim et al., 2014). Most autistic children and adults do have functional language skills, although the majority demonstrate at least some language delays. The language profiles of autistic children vary substantially, which has led some researchers to suggest the existence of different language subgroups (Joseph, Tager-Flusberg, & Lord, 2002; Kim et al., 2014). Furthermore, researchers have found that many autistic children continue to increase their language skills through their childhood years, particularly with intervention (Howlin, Savage, Moss, Tempier, & Rutter, 2014). One study (Howlin, 2003) compared the language performance of autistic adults who had demonstrated language delays as children with those of non-autistic adults. They found that both groups demonstrated similar expressive language in their adult years. As a result of studies like these, researchers (Gernsbacher, Morson, & Grace, 2015) have concluded that a number of autistic children may demonstrate a delayed profile of language development in childhood but a more typical profile in adulthood. This is a particularly interesting finding given that language skills were one of the primary characteristics that were previously used to distinguish between a diagnosis of autism and one of Asperger's syndrome. Depending on their age, the child may have received a different diagnosis. Inconsistency of diagnosis was one of the factors in the change to autism spectrum disorder in the *DSM-V* (Vivanti et al., 2013).

One of the most common language differences exhibited by autistic children and adults is the use of echolalia. Echolalia involves the idiosyncratic use of language in which the individual repeats words or phrases either immediately after they hear the phrase, or at a later time (Hall, 2018). Often the individual repeats these words or phrases a number of times in sequence. Originally, people believed that echolalia was an inappropriate behaviour that served no function and was either a form of vocal tic or a sign that the individual was perseverating on a topic. Researchers have now identified that echolalia serves a number of functions for the autistic child or adult. Immediate echolalia has been found to aid comprehension, while delayed echolalia appears to be an aid in social interaction (Heflin & Alaimo, 2007). Other functions include turn taking, affirmative answers, requests and self-regulation (Kim et al., 2014). Typically, individuals with high levels of echolalia have more limited vocabularies. With a limited repertoire to choose from, these individuals repeat words and phrases in an attempt to communicate with others. For individuals with more advanced language skills, echolalia can take on the form of repetitive scripts, which they use to navigate social contexts.

A minority of autistic children do not demonstrate any noticeable delays in language development (Kim et al., 2014). These individuals may also have strengths in using written language or in public speaking. Some also have special interests and talents in foreign languages or language systems (Hall, 2018). Despite their language abilities, by definition, all individuals diagnosed with autism spectrum disorder under the *DSM-V* will demonstrate difficulties and differences in the way they use language or non-verbal behaviours to communicate with others (Kim et al., 2014). Noticeable differences include the use of and response to non-verbal communication behaviours, restricted communicative intent, repetitive or idiosyncratic use of language, poor reciprocal communication, difficulties with literal comprehension and use of figurative language, and difficulties with syntax and semantics of language (Hall, 2018; Heflin & Alaimo, 2007; Kim et al., 2014; Mody & Belliveau, 2013). In general, parents become most concerned about their child's language development between the ages of 2 and 3 (Prelock, Paul, & Allen, 2011). However, the majority of these children would have actually demonstrated differences in their early communication at a much earlier age.

One of the earliest indicators that a child might be autistic is an inability to follow their parents' gaze or to share their parents' attention on an object or activity, known as joint attention (Hall, 2018). Joint attention involves the coordination of one individual's attention with another in order to share a point of reference and exchange information (Mundy, 2018). Imitation and coordination of attention typically develops by around 9 months of age, with children demonstrating some aspects of joint attention by 6 months of age (Toth, Munson, Meltzoff, & Dawson, 2006). It is through joint attention that children learn to imitate and later to communicate and engage in social interactions with others. Difficulties with joint attention are so common in young autistic children that lack of these is now being used as identifiers in early autism screeners (Hall, 2018). Researchers have found that early joint attention predicts later language development as well as conversation skills and social reciprocity (Twachtman-Cullen, 2014).

Being able to understand and respond to non-verbal cues such as interpreting facial expressions, body language and vocal inflexions are another core area of difficulty identified in the diagnostic criteria for autism spectrum disorder (American Psychiatric Association, 2013). The use of non-verbal communication is particularly cited as a source of frustration and challenge for autistic individuals with more advanced language skills (Heflin & Alaimo, 2007). Not only do limitations in non-verbal communication pose a barrier to social communication, but they are also integral in the demonstration of skills, such as empathy, needed for developing social relationships. For example, researchers (Brewer et al., 2016; Faso, Sasson, & Pinkham, 2015) have investigated how well autistic individuals are able to use facial expressions and emotions to communicate compared to their non-autistic peers. Faso et al. (2015) found that non-autistic adults felt the expressions of autistic adults were more intense and less natural than those of their non-autistic peers. Despite these differences, the non-autistic participants had few difficulties interpreting the expressions of either group, possibly as a result of the context that was provided. In contrast, Brewer et al. (2016) found that both autistic and non-autistic participants had greater difficulty interpreting the facial emotions of autistic individuals than they did non-autistic individuals. Researchers have also examined the ways that autistic children utilise voice tone and rhythm, known as prosody, in their communication with others. McCann, Peppe, Gibbon, O'Hare, and Rutherford (2007) compared the prosody of autistic and non-autistic children, finding that autistic children demonstrated much poorer use of prosody than the non-autistic group. Similarly, Chevallier, Noveck, Happé, and Wilson (2011) revealed that autistic children had more difficulty than their non-autistic peers in using voice tone to discern the speaker's mental or emotional state.

Research has shown that autistic individuals generally have a literal interpretation of language and experience far more difficulty in understanding figurative language (Kim et al., 2014). Figurative language refers to language where the literal and intended meanings of words, sentences, and expressions are inconsistent (Glucksberg, 2001). Common types of figurative language include metaphors, irony, and sarcasm. Kalandadze, Norbury, Naerland, Naess, and Naess (2016) conducted a meta-analysis of 41 studies, which compared the figurative language abilities of autistic and non-autistic participants. They found that autistic participants had more limited comprehension of figurative language, demonstrating more difficulty with comprehension of metaphors than of ironic or sarcastic statements. This is an interesting finding as it suggests that in isolation, individuals may have difficulty with figurative language or voice tone, but that they may be able to use a combination of cues more effectively to discern the speaker's intent.

Theory of mind is a social cognitive skill that has been linked both to difficulties in non-verbal communication and empathy (Baron-Cohen, 2000). For a speaker to successfully engage in social communication and to form social–emotional connections with others, they must be aware of the listener's mental states, including their previous experiences, knowledge and interests (Eigsti, de Marchena, Schuh, & Kelley, 2011) as well as their emotional states (Koegel, Ashbaugh, Navab, & Koegel, 2016). Empathy, which has been identified as a critical communication skill required for developing positive relationships, is the ability to recognise and appropriately respond to another person's emotional state. Theory of mind, sometimes identified as cognitive empathy, involves the ability to recognise another person's intentions, beliefs, desires and emotions, which are often expressed through their vocal tones, body posture and facial expressions (Blair, 2005; Reniers, Corcoran, Drake, Shryane, & Völlm, 2011). In contrast, affective empathy encompasses the skills needed to respond to another person's emotional state in a contextually relevant manner (Blair, 2005). In addition, for an emotional response to be considered socially appropriate, it needs to show that the observer *cares* about how the other person feels (Baron-Cohen, Richler, Bisarya, Gurunathan, & Wheelwright, 2003).

To demonstrate empathy, an individual must be able to both recognise the other person's emotional state and be able to provide a response that is meaningful to the other person. Rogers, Dziobek, Hassenstab, Wolf, and Convit (2007) explored both the cognitive and affective empathic abilities of individuals diagnosed with Asperger's syndrome and compared their responses on measures of cognitive and affective empathy with that of a non-autistic group. They concluded that the autistic participants demonstrated much lower cognitive empathy than the non-autistic group but had similar outcomes on measures of affective empathy. In another study, Jones, Happé, Gilbert, Burnett, and Viding (2010) compared the cognitive and affective empathic abilities of autistic boys with boys with either psychopathic tendencies, conduct problems or no issues. They found that autistic boys were more empathetic than the boys with psychopathic tendencies, exhibiting more fear and concern for victims of aggression. Jones et al. (2010, p. 1188) concluded that, "Psychopathic tendencies are associated with difficulties in resonating with other people's distress, whereas ASD is characterised by difficulties in knowing what other people think".

These studies both suggest that although autistic individuals do experience difficulty with discerning the mental or emotional state of others, they are often able to respond appropriately once they realise what the other person is thinking or feeling.

The challenges involved in cognitive empathy are illustrated by autistic individuals who have shared their perceptions. Chris, an autistic student attending Cambridge University, explains some of the difficulties he experiences in perceiving other people's emotions saying:

> Some emotions are more difficult than others: fear and anger, surprise, because it can be quite similar in the way people express them—especially when they are mild. There are small cues (clues or differences) between them, which I guess I'm not picking up. (Barrett, 2006, p. 103)

Likewise, Edgar Schneider writes:

> I am an emotional idiot … I have an important component of the human psyche missing: the ability to connect emotionally with other human beings […] It is not that I am totally unfeeling, but that I just cannot read other people's signals. (Schneider, 1999, pp. 25–26)

Another common theme illustrated in the narratives of autistic individuals is that they feel a variety of emotions during social interactions with others, but have difficulty discerning what they are expected to do or say (Adams et al., 2009; Barrett, 2006; Chamak, Bonniau, Jaunay, & Cohen, 2008; Davidson & Smith, 2009). As Davidson and Smith (2009) explain:

> What they 'lack' is not, on their own accounts, an emotional capacity as such, although it may appear to others to be so, but certain capabilities concerning interpretative intuitions that are more usually assumed as 'second nature' and hence to constitute a shared ground for the interpretative community. (p. 906)

This statement also highlights another aspect of empathy, that is, whether the other person is willing and able to discern and respond to the autistic individual's mental and emotional state.

In a recent study, Sheppard, Pillai, Wong, Ropar, and Mitchell, (2016) found that the failure of non-autistic individuals to interpret and respond to the communication of autistic individuals is a barrier to effective social communication and interaction. Researchers (Heasman & Gillespie, 2018) also found that family members had difficulty identifying with the perspective of their autistic children, which caused difficulty in their ability to communicate and connect socially and emotionally with their child. The findings of these studies suggest that an inability of autistic individuals to communicate and demonstrate empathy can be attributed not just to their lack of skills, but also to the failure of both individuals to communicate and interact in a manner that is meaningful to both. Autistic researcher, Damien Milton, identifies this as the "double empathy" problem (Milton, 2012).

7.3 The Impact

As evident in the previous discussion, current research shows that, like many stereotypes, the myths that you can't talk if you have autism and autistic people don't feel empathy, do have some basis in fact. There are some autistic individuals who are never able to talk, although the vast majority can speak quite well. Moreover, research does indicate that in general autistic people do poorer on measures of cognitive empathy than their non-autistic counterparts. This research also demonstrates that these myths are a gross oversimplification of the ways in which autistic individuals utilise communication and language skills and demonstrate empathy. Unfortunately, these myths continue to impact autistic individuals by shaping the expectations placed on them by others.

The primary impact of the autistics can't talk and don't have empathy myths is that it misrepresents the social communication and social–emotional skills of autistic children and adults as these myths fail to distinguish between communication and language. As a result, specific expectations are placed on autistic individuals depending on whether they have a high level of language or minimal or no language. Individuals who are minimally verbal often face very low expectations from others who view their limited language as an indicator that they are unable to engage with people or activities. This problem is compounded by people who assume that minimally verbal autistic people need someone to speak for them. These individuals, while well meaning, can prevent the autistic individual from expressing themselves ensuring that their voice, opinions and values are recognised. Even more importantly, another person may not accurately represent the autistic person's perspectives and may result in them accepting or undergoing treatment or activities, which are against their wishes or interests.

This issue has been the focus of controversy surrounding one intervention aimed at minimally verbal autistic individuals. Facilitated communication is a type of augmentative communication in which the individual is assisted by a trained facilitator to use a keyboard or other device to type (Lilienfeld, Marshall, Todd, & Shane, 2015). This approach is based on a theory that the physical connection between the two individuals unlocks the ability of the autistic person to communicate. Facilitated communication has been extensively evaluated and reviewed and has now been discredited. The primary reason for this was that researchers determined that it was the facilitator and not the autistic individual who was actually guiding the communication (Boynton, 2012; Trembath, Paynter, Keen, & Ecker, 2015). This resulted in multiple allegations, which caused harm to a number of individuals. However, facilitated communication should not be confused with other forms of alternative or augmentative communication, which trains the autistic individual to utilise technology to communicate. Individuals such as Naoki Higashida, who wrote the book *The Reason I Jump*, communicate by using technology such as keyboards and symbol boards. The primary difference is that these individuals do not rely on a facilitator, which ensures that it is their voice that is being heard (Chan & Nankervis, 2014; Welch, Polatajko, Rigby, & Fitch, 2018).

Another issue faced by minimally verbal autistic persons is that language is often seen as an indicator of intelligence or capacity to socially interact with other people. As a result, the perceptions and opinions of autistic individuals who have minimal language are often not considered in research or service delivery (Tager-Flusberg & Kasari, 2013). While verbal language is often correlated with higher IQ scores and the majority of minimally verbal autistic individuals do have some degree of intellectual disability (Howlin, Savage, Moss, Tempier, & Rutter, 2014), this does not mean that these individuals do not have the capacity to think and speak for themselves in a variety of settings. Courchesne, Meilleur, Poulin-Lord, Dawson, and Soulieres (2015) found that when they utilised a strength-based assessment rather than a traditional measurement of intelligence and performance, 26 of 30 autistic children with minimal verbal skills were able to complete the task and, in some cases, performed better than non-autistic peers. The researchers concluded that individuals with minimal language are at a risk of being significantly underestimated if they are not provided with relevant opportunities to demonstrate their skills in a manner that best suits them. This finding was echoed by Welch et al. (2018) who gathered memoirs written by autistic youths who utilised a variety of technological supports to communicate. These individuals expressed that what they are like on the inside is very different from what people often perceive on the outside and stressed the difference that technology and augmentative communication had made in their lives. Naoki Higashida likens this to allowing him to "exist in this world as a human being" (Welch et al., 2018, p. 6).

In contrast, autistic individuals with a high level of language skills face a different type of expectation. The belief that language is the primary indicator of competence leads people to believe that highly verbal autistic children and adults experience no difficulties in communicating. Consequently, their social communication needs are often overlooked. As one autistic person stated:

> Usually when I demonstrate a large vocabulary or some fundamentals, my needs especially around communication are then ignored. My choice is then to pretend to be less intelligent and accept their infantilism, or to be confused, frustrated, and stressed out. (Nicolaidis et al., 2015, p. 828)

As this quote illustrates, autistic individuals who have high-level language skills can still experience a number of needs in communication, which impact their ability to engage in different settings. Autistic adults often report that problems with social communication are one of the primary areas of difficulty they encounter in university and employment settings (Griffith, Totsika, Nash, & Hastings, 2012; Ward & Webster, 2018). These difficulties may lead to misunderstandings with others in the environment (Portway & Johnson, 2005) or cause them to become anxious or behave in a manner not appropriate to the setting (Bogdashina, 2005). Because their communication needs are not recognised, autistic individuals with higher language skills may be labelled as difficult, defiant or problematic if they fail to follow directions or behave in ways that meet other people's expectations (Portway & Johnson, 2005). Moreover, these individuals are at an even greater risk of not receiving services as they may often not meet the criteria for funding, which is based on traditional measures of language and intelligence (Griffith et al., 2012). Researchers (Alpern, 2012) stress the importance of measures of pragmatic language and social communication in determining needs and supports for autistic individuals as these individuals may do well with expressive and receptive language, but still experience a great deal of difficulty in communicating with others. This, in turn, can result in autistic individuals becoming marginalised as they fail to develop the social communication skills and abilities necessary to interact with others and be successful in different settings. This is expressed by Anna who relates:

> I have been trying to get [support] because I've been to the JobCentre (…) but because it's not a physical problem really, she can't help me. So, if you're in a wheelchair, it's visible, isn't it? But because I'm intelligent, and I think most people who have Asperger's are intelligent, they don't expect you to have problems with things. It's so stupid. (Griffith et al., 2012, p. 540)

Empathy is another aspect of social communication that is reported to cause confusion and difficulties for a number of autistic individuals, particularly those with higher language skills (Bogdashina, 2005). Reports from autistic adults highlight that they often find it difficult to discern what their communicative partners expect from them. However, the myth that autistic people are unable to feel empathy has resulted in a deficit model in which they are viewed as impaired and in need of intervention (Milton, 2012). Traditional approaches have concentrated on building the autistic individual's social skills, particularly focusing on skills such as interpreting facial expressions, knowing how to respond when someone is distressed and identifying their own emotions. Milton argues that these strategies are based on a foundation of normalisation and are developed by people with a non-autistic perspective, which may not meet the needs of autistic individuals who have a differing perspective. This approach also fails to recognise the bidirectionality of the social communication process and to develop the ability of both parties to interpret and respond to the other. Milton suggests that rather than focusing primarily on the limitations of the autistic individual, strategies need to address the current barriers involved in autistic to non-autistic communication.

7.4 The Future

> It takes more work to communicate with someone whose native language isn't the same as yours. And autism goes deeper than language and culture; autistic people are 'foreigners' in any society. You're going to have to give up your assumptions about shared meanings. You're going to have to learn to back up to levels more basic than you've probably thought about before, to translate, and to check to make sure your translations are understood. You're going to have to give up the certainty that comes of being on your own familiar territory, of knowing you're in charge, and let your child teach you a little of her language, guide you a little way into his world. (Sinclair, 1993, p. 2)

In this quote, autistic advocate, Jim Sinclair, likens the communication of autistic people to speaking a foreign language, which requires others to take on a different perspective in order to communicate with that individual. Bogdashina (2005) continues with this analogy saying:

> It is like learning to speak a foreign language. When we find ourselves among foreigners, we do not assume that they have nothing to say or that they cannot communicate. If we want to understand them and to establish communication with them, we have to learn their language or find an interpreter. (p. 15)

The myths that autistic people cannot speak or show empathy are based on an assumption that they lack these skills. These statements highlight a differing view suggesting that autistic individuals are communicating, but in a manner that is different to those around them. This point is stressed by O'Neill (1999) who states:

> [Non-autistics] can be ignorant of the autistic's struggles to communicate. In this case, more care must be taken to learn how to interpret autistic languages … Communication in autism is not a "failure". It is not non-existent. It's simply different, in some way eccentric in an interesting way, and in some cases dormant. (p. 47)

Transforming these myths will require a change in viewpoint in which the belief in the competence of autistic individuals provides a foundation from which autistic and non-autistic people work together to translate each other's language, so they may share their perspectives and knowledge.

Bogdashina (2005) suggests that communication requires people to engage in shared experiences using a shared language or tool of communication. What makes this possible is a shared knowledge of ways to interact. If the parties do not acknowledge their differing knowledge, they are unable to communicate. Therefore, if autistic and non-autistic individuals are to engage in successful communication experiences, they must acknowledge that they think differently and use different forms of language and beliefs about communication. To communicate they must develop an awareness of their own forms of communication in order to establish a shared communication system.

Researchers (Prizant et al., 2005; Samson, Huber, & Gross, 2012) have indicated that autistic individuals may lack awareness of the ways in which their body language or facial expressions communicate information to others. Two possible reasons are offered for this. The first is that when they unwittingly communicate through expressions and body language, theory of mind deficits prevent them from discerning the ways in which the other individual's actions indicate how this was received. More recently, some researchers (Fiene & Brownlow, 2015) have suggested that autistic individuals lack an interoceptive sense, which diminishes their awareness of what their body is doing, including interpreting their own emotions or body indications of these emotions. Current research indicates that interoception, emotion and empathy may be linked in autistic individuals (Mul, Stagg, Herbelin, & Aspell, 2018). Interoception is the physiological sense of the body. Current research suggests that interoceptive awareness is slower to develop for autistic individuals, which can lead to difficulties in understanding emotions and demonstration of empathy. Difficulties with interoception and/or alexithymia impact the ability to be empathetic as well as the ability to respond in socially appropriate ways. Researchers (Mul et al., 2018) suggest that by developing interoceptive awareness, autistic individuals will be more aware of their own emotions and will be better able to respond to the emotions of others. Singer, Critchley and Preuschoff (2009) suggest that there is a common role in empathy, interoception and alexithymia centred on the insula. It has been suggested that the brain structures required to process interoceptive signals are also used to process and respond to vicarious emotions (Singer, 2009). It would seem logical that if someone does not experience the feeling of happiness or sadness, then it would be difficult for them to both envisage and empathise with those emotions in others.

A number of evidence-based approaches have focused on facilitating the ability of autistic individuals to monitor their emotions and behaviours and to determine the way they may need to modify the expression of these to fit specific situations (Buron & Myles, 2014). The SCERTS model developed by Prizant et al. (2005) focuses on utilising partner support and environmental support to facilitate the shared attention and communication of young autistic children and a communication partner. The SCERTS model incorporates the use of differing means such as symbols and words to ensure that a communication system is used that allows both partners to understand

and convey their thoughts and emotions. Another system that has been supported by a number of studies is the *5-point scale* developed by Buron and Curtis (2012). The 5-point scale is a self-monitoring and communication tool, which is used to monitor and communicate different emotions. Using visual or written cues, the individual is prompted to check their body for signs of different emotions, and then to take action to change these if necessary. For example, an autistic adolescent might identify that an increased heart rate, sweaty palms and clenched teeth are his body's indicators that he is becoming quite agitated. He could also check to see what expression his face was currently conveying and use the scale to communicate how he was feeling to others around him. Lastly, he could check the scale to determine what action he could take to decrease his agitation. However, this scale is less useful if the individual lacks interoceptive awareness of the physical indicators of their stress and/or distress as they would not be aware of their increased heart rate, sweaty palms or clenched teeth or may not even present those signs. Atypical interoception often results in atypical presentation of emotions, as is often noted in autistics.

In addition to developing the self-awareness of autistic individuals, non-autistic individuals also need to develop an awareness of the ways in which their communication is perceived if they are to address Milton's "double empathy" problem (Milton, 2012). Jim Sinclair describes the importance of this:

> When people make assumptions about my perspective without taking the trouble to find out such things as how I receive and process information or what my motives and priorities are, those assumptions are almost certain to be wrong … If I know that I do not understand people and I devote all this energy and effort to figuring them out, do I have more or less empathy than people who not only do not understand me, but who do not even notice that they do not understand me? (Bogdashina, 2005, p. 191)

This statement underscores that empathy must be a two-way process for successful and reciprocal social communication.

Researchers and autistic individuals (Bagatell, 2010; Bogdashina, 2005; Welch et al., 2018) have highlighted that both highly verbal and minimally verbal autistic individuals communicate in different ways than non-autistic people. People like Temple Grandin have provided some insights into the different way that they process words and language explaining, "When I talk to other people I translate my pictures into stock phrases or sentences I have 'on tape' in my head" (Grandin & Johnson, 2009, p. 18). In order to promote social communication and empathy, autistic and non-autistic individuals need to develop a shared communication system. For more verbal autistic individuals, this may mean an understanding of the ways that each needs to communicate. For example, working out how specific the language needs to be for each autistic individual may be important, while non-autistic individuals may need some ideas expanded to connect with other ideas. These issues are compounded further by the fact that autistic individuals do not have the same communication needs. Some, like Temple Grandin, state they see concepts in pictures, whereas the late Donna Williams says she attends more to sound patterns and the feeling of words (Bogdashina, 2005).

For individuals who have minimal language, the need for a shared communication system is more obvious, but also more challenging. As Temple Grandin explains:

> To understand the mind of a child or adult who is completely nonverbal, you must leave the world of thinking in words. This can be quite challenging for many people … For the majority of people, words are their "native language." It is difficult for them to step outside this very basic way of relating and imagine something else. (Grandin, 2011, p. 107)

In recent years, the use of assistive technology and augmentative and alternative communication have provided a promising way forward. This includes low-tech systems such as the Picture Exchange Communication System, which has been established as an evidence-based practice for teaching intentionality to pre-intentional communicators (Tager-Flusberg & Kasari, 2013). Other systems include voice-output communication aids (Kasari et al., 2014) and manual signs (Hall, 2018). It should also be noted that research has consistently demonstrated that the use of communication systems can facilitate the oral language abilities of many autistic individuals (Paul, Orlovski, Marcinko, & Volkmar, 2009; Schaefer-Whitby, Lorah, Love, & Lawless, 2017; Tager-Flusberg & Kasari, 2013). Functional communication training has also been highly effective in providing these individuals with better alternatives, replacing inappropriate communicative behaviours (Heflin & Alaimo, 2007). Critical to the success of these systems, however, is that both individuals in the communication exchange are able to use and understand them and that they can be reliably and feasibly used in multiple settings.

Both research and reports of autistic advocates clearly indicate that autistic individuals vary widely in their language abilities, communicating styles and ways in which they learn new language. Thus, no one approach will work for all individuals, nor even for subgroups of people who are either highly verbal or minimally verbal. Researchers have stressed the importance of communication assessments in determining the current abilities and needs of autistic individuals (Paul, 2008; Schaefer-Whitby et al., 2017). The "voice" of autistic individuals is critical to transforming myths about autistic communication and empathy. Additionally, the role of the environment and skills of communication partners needs to be considered to facilitate reciprocity of communication between autistic individuals and others in their environment (Prizant et al., 2005). Most important, though, is that the perceptions and thoughts of autistic individuals are sought, in order to understand the communication system that is more relevant for them. The use of photographs and videos has been found to help autistic individuals to communicate their perspectives in ways they are unable to express in words (Harte, 2009). In essence, these can be viewed as a means of translating the disconnect between the typical or non-autistic way of communicating and the foreign or differing communication style utilised by the autistic person. Although this may be challenging and involve extra effort, this will reap benefits by facilitating better communication and social–emotional connections for everyone.

7.5 Conclusion

Common misconceptions about the social communication of autistic individuals include the myths that they lack the ability to talk and that they do not feel empathy. These beliefs originate from Kanner's early descriptions of autistic children, which described them as being distant and unresponsive to others. This image was further perpetuated by researcher Bruno Bettelheim, who suggested that cold and distant parents produced autistic children who were detached and unable to communicate with others. Although this theory has been discredited, the image of the distant and unemotional autistic child has continued to be promoted through photographs, characters and reports of parents. In contrast, research indicates that autistic people do communicate and convey emotions, but that they do so in a manner that is not readily understood by others. This has resulted in misperceptions about the abilities and needs of both autistic individuals who are highly verbal as well as those who are minimally verbal. To better understand the specific needs of these individuals, they need to have a "voice" in their own lives. To facilitate a positive future and transform the myths about language and empathy, autistic and non-autistic people need to recognise the ways in which they differ. This will provide a foundation from which they can develop a shared system of communication and use this to create shared understandings and knowledge.

References

Adams, J. B., Baral, M., Geis, E., Mitchell, J., Ingram, J., Hensley, A., … El-Dahr, J. (2009). Safety and efficacy of oral DMSA therapy for children with autism spectrum disorders: Part B—Behavioral results. *BMC Clinical Pharmacology, 9*(1), 17. https://doi.org/10.1186/1472-6904-9-16.

Alpern, C. (2012). Enhancing language and communication development. In D. Zager, M. L. Wehmeyer, & R. L. Simpson (Eds.), *Educating students with autism spectrum disorders* (pp. 282–294). New York: Routledge.

American Psychiatric Association. (1994). *Diagnostic and statistical manual of mental disorders—Fourth edition*. Washington, DC: American Psychiatric Publishing. Retrieved from http://www.terapiacognitiva.eu/dwl/dsm5/DSM-IV.pdf.

American Psychiatric Association. (2013). *Diagnostic and statistical manual of mental disorders—Fifth edition*. Washington, DC: American Psychiatric Publishing.

Asperger, H. (1944). Die "Autistischen Psychopathen" im Kindesalter. *Archiv für psychiatrie und nervenkrankheiten, 117*(1), 76–136.

Bagatell, N. (2010). From cure to community: Transforming notions of autism. *Ethos, 38*(1), 33–55. https://doi.org/10.1111/j.1548-1352.2009.01080.x.

Barger, B. D., Campbell, J. M., & McDonough, J. D. (2013). Prevalence and onset of regression within autism spectrum disorders: A meta-analytic review. *Journal of Autism and Developmental Disorders, 43*(4), 817–828. https://doi.org/10.1007/s10803-012-1621-x.

Baron-Cohen, S. (2000). Theory of mind and autism: A review. *International Review of Mental Retardation, 23,* 169–184. https://doi.org/10.1016/s0074-7750(00)80010-5.

Baron-Cohen, S., Richler, J., Bisarya, D., Gurunathan, N., & Wheelwright, S. (2003). The systemizing quotient: An investigation of adults with Asperger syndrome or high-functioning autism, and normal sex differences. *Philosophical Transactions of the Royal Society of London. Series B, Biological Sciences, 358*(1430), 361–374. https://doi.org/10.1098/rstb.2002.1206.

Barrett, M. (2006). "Like dynamite going off in my ears": Using autobiographical accounts of autism with teaching professionals. *Educational Psychology in Practice, 22*(2), 95–110. https://doi.org/10.1080/02667360600668170.

Bettelheim, B. (1967). *The empty fortress: Infantile autism and the birth of the self*. New York: Simon and Schuster.

Blair, R. (2005). Responding to the emotions of others: Dissociating forms of empathy through the study of typical and psychiatric populations. *Consciousness and Cognition, 14*(4), 698–718. https://doi.org/10.1016/j.concog.2005.06.004.

Bogdashina, O. G. (2005). *Communication issues in autism and Asperger syndrome: Do we speak the same language?* London; Philadelphia: Jessica Kingsley Publishers.

Boynton, J. (2012). Facilitated communication—What harm it can do: Confessions of a former facilitator. *Evidence-Based Communication Assessment and Intervention, 6*(1), 3–13.

Brewer, R., Biotti, F., Catmur, C., Press, C., Happé, F., Cook, R., et al. (2016). Can neurotypical individuals read autistic facial expressions? Atypical production of emotional facial expressions in autism spectrum disorders. *Autism Research, 9*(2), 262–271. https://doi.org/10.1002/aur.1508.

Broderick, A. A., & Ne'eman, A. (2008). Autism as metaphor: Narrative and counter-narrative. *International Journal of Inclusive Education, 12*(5–6), 459–476. https://doi.org/10.1080/13603110802377490.

Buron, K. D., & Curtis, M. B. (2012). *The incredible 5-point scale: The significantly improved and expanded second edition: Assisting students in understanding social interactions and controlling their emotional responses*. Shawnee Mission, KS: AAPC Publishing.

Buron, K. D., & Myles, B. S. (2014). Emotional regulation. In K. D. Buron & P. Wolfberg (Eds.), *Learners on the autism spectrum: Preparing highly qualified educators* (2nd ed., pp. 239–263). Shawnee Mission, Kansas: AAPC.

Chamak, B., Bonniau, B., Jaunay, E., & Cohen, D. (2008). What can we learn about autism from autistic persons? *Psychotherapy and Psychosomatics, 77*(5), 271–279. https://doi.org/10.1159/000140086.

Chan, J., & Nankervis, K. (2014). Stolen voices: Facilitated communication is an abuse of human rights. *Evidence-Based Communication Assessment and Intervention, 8*(3), 151–156. https://doi.org/10.1080/17489539.2014.1001549.

Chevallier, C., Noveck, I., Happé, F., & Wilson, D. (2011). What's in a voice? Prosody as a test case for the Theory of Mind account of autism. *Neuropsychologia, 49*(3), 507–517. https://doi.org/10.1016/j.neuropsychologia.2010.11.042.

Courchesne, V., Meilleur, A. A., Poulin-Lord, M. P., Dawson, M., & Soulieres, I. (2015). Autistic children at risk of being underestimated: School-based pilot study of a strength-informed assessment. *Molecular Autism, 6*(12). https://doi.org/10.1186/s13229-015-0006-3.

Davidson, J., & Smith, M. (2009). Autistic autobiographies and more-than-human emotional geographies. *Environment and Planning D: Society and Space, 27*(5), 898–916. https://doi.org/10.1068/d4308.

Eigsti, I. M., de Marchena, A. B., Schuh, J. M., & Kelley, E. (2011). Language acquisition in autism spectrum disorders: A developmental review. *Research in Autism Spectrum Disorders, 5*(2), 681–691. https://doi.org/10.1016/j.rasd.2010.09.001.

Faso, D. J., Sasson, N. J., & Pinkham, A. E. (2015). Evaluating posed and evoked facial expressions of emotion from adults with autism spectrum disorder. *Journal of Autism and Developmental Disorders, 45*(1), 75–89. https://doi.org/10.1007/s10803-014-2194-7.

Fiene, L., & Brownlow, C. (2015). Investigating interoception and body awareness in adults with and without autism spectrum disorder. *Autism Research, 8*(6), 709–716. https://doi.org/10.1002/aur.1486.

Garner, A. (2014). *What's showing: Film industry portrayals of autism spectrum conditions and their influences on preservice teachers in Australia* (Ph.D.). Retrieved from http://ro.uow.edu.au/theses/4282/.

Gernsbacher, M. A., Morson, E. M., & Grace, E. J. (2015). Language development in autism. In G. Hickok & S. Small (Eds.), *Neurobiology of language* (Vol. 879–886). London: Academic Press.

Glucksberg, S. (2001). *Understanding figurative language: From metaphor to idioms*. Oxford: Oxford University Press.

Grandin, T. (2011). *The way I see it: A personal look at autism & Asperger's*. Arlington, TX: Future Horizons.

Grandin, T., & Johnson, C. (2009). *Animals in translation: Using the mysteries of autism to decode animal behavior*. New York: Scribner.

Griffith, G. M., Totsika, V., Nash, S., & Hastings, R. P. (2012). 'I just don't fit anywhere': Support experiences and future support needs of individuals with Asperger syndrome in middle adulthood. *Autism, 16*(5), 532–546. https://doi.org/10.1177/1362361311405223.

Hall, L. J. (2018). *Autism spectrum disorders: From theory to practice* (3rd ed.). Boston: Pearson.

Harte, H. A. (2009). What teachers can learn from mothers of children with autism. *Teaching Exceptional Children, 42,* 24–30.

Heasman, B., & Gillespie, A. (2018). Perspective-taking is two-sided: Misunderstandings between people with Asperger's syndrome and their family members. *Autism., 22*(6), 740–750. https://doi.org/10.1177/1362361317708287.

Heflin, J., & Alaimo, D. F. (2007). *Students with autism spectrum disorders: Effective instructional practices*. Upper Saddle River, NJ: Pearson/Merrill Prentice Hall.

Howlin, P. (2003). Outcome in high-functioning adults with autism with and without early language delays: Implications for the differentiation between autism and Asperger syndrome. *Journal of Autism and Developmental Disorders, 33*(1), 3–13. https://doi.org/10.1023/a:1022270118899.

Howlin, P., Savage, S., Moss, P., Tempier, A., & Rutter, M. (2014). Cognitive and language skills in adults with autism: A 40-year follow-up. *Journal of Child Psychology and Psychiatry, 55*(1), 49–58. https://doi.org/10.1111/jcpp.12115.

Huws, J. C., & Jones, R. S. P. (2010). 'They just seem to live their lives in their own little world': Lay perceptions of autism. *Disability & Society, 25*(3), 331–344. https://doi.org/10.1080/09687591003701231.

Jones, A. P., Happé, F. G., Gilbert, F., Burnett, S., & Viding, E. (2010). Feeling, caring, knowing: Different types of empathy deficit in boys with psychopathic tendencies and autism spectrum disorder. *Journal of Child Psychology and Psychiatry, 51*(11), 1188–1197. https://doi.org/10.1111/j.1469-7610.2010.02280.x.

Joseph, R. M., Tager-Flusberg, H., & Lord, C. (2002). Cognitive profiles and social-communicative functioning in children with autism spectrum disorder. *Journal of Child Psychology and Psychiatry, 43*(6), 807–821. https://doi.org/10.1111/1469-7610.00092.

Kalandadze, T., Norbury, C., Naerland, T., & Naess, K. A. B. (2016). Figurative language comprehension in individuals with autism spectrum disorder: A meta-analytic review. *Autism, 22*(2), 99–117. https://doi.org/10.1177/1362361316668652.

Kanner, L. (1943). Autistic disturbances of affective contact. *Nervous Child, 2*(3), 217–250.

Kanner, L. (1944). Early infantile autism. *The Journal of Pedatrics, 25*(3), 211–217.

Kasari, C., Kaiser, A., Goods, K., Nietfeld, J., Mathy, P., Landa, R., ... Almirall, D. (2014). Communication interventions for minimally verbal children with autism: A sequential multiple assignment randomized trial. *Journal of the American Academy of Child and Adolescent Psychiatry, 53*(6), 635–646. https://doi.org/10.1016/j.jaac.2014.01.019.

Kim, S. H., Paul, R., Tager-Flusberg, H., & Lord, C. (2014). Language and communication in autism. In F. Volkmar, S. Rogers, R. Paul, & K. A. Pelphrey (Eds.), *Handbook of autism and pervasive developmental disorders*. Hoboken, NJ: Wiley.

Koegel, L. K., Ashbaugh, K., Navab, A., & Koegel, R. L. (2016). Improving empathic communication skills in adults with autism spectrum disorder. *Journal of Autism and Developmental Disorders, 46*(3), 921–933. https://doi.org/10.1007/s10803-015-2633-0.

Lilienfeld, S. O., Marshall, J., Todd, J. T., & Shane, H. C. (2015). The persistence of fad interventions in the face of negative scientific evidence: Facilitated communication for autism as a case example.

Evidence-Based Communication Assessment and Intervention, 8(2), 62–101. https://doi.org/10.1080/17489539.2014.976332.
Loveland, K. A., Tunali-Kotoski, B., Pearson, D. A., Brelsford, K. A., Ortegon, J., & Chen, R. (1994). Imitation and expression of facial affect in autism. *Development and Psychopathology, 6*(3), 433–444. https://doi.org/10.1017/s0954579400006039.
Magiati, I., Tay, X. W., & Howlin, P. (2014). Cognitive, language, social and behavioural outcomes in adults with autism spectrum disorders: A systematic review of longitudinal follow-up studies in adulthood. *Clinical Psychology Review, 34*(1), 73–86. https://doi.org/10.1016/j.cpr.2013.11.002.
McCann, J., Peppe, S., Gibbon, F. E., O'Hare, A., & Rutherford, M. (2007). Prosody and its relationship to language in school-aged children with high-functioning autism. *International Journal of Language & Communication Disorders, 42*(6), 682–702. https://doi.org/10.1080/13682820601170102.
Meilleur, A. A., & Fombonne, E. (2009). Regression of language and non-language skills in pervasive developmental disorders. *Journal of Intellectual Disability Research, 53*(2), 115–124. https://doi.org/10.1111/j.1365-2788.2008.01134.x.
Milton, D. E. M. (2012). On the ontological status of autism: The 'double empathy problem'. *Disability & Society, 27*(6), 883–887. https://doi.org/10.1080/09687599.2012.710008.
Mody, M., & Belliveau, J. W. (2013). Speech and language impairments in autism: Insights from behavior and neuroimagining. *North American Journal of Medicine and Science, 5*(3), 157–161.
Mul, C. L., Stagg, S. D., Herbelin, B., & Aspell, J. E. (2018). The feeling of me feeling for you: Interoception, alexithymia and empathy in autism. *Journal of Autism and Developmental Disorders, 48*(9), 2953–2967. https://doi.org/10.1007/s10803-018-3564-3.
Mundy, P. (2018). A review of joint attention and social-cognitive brain systems in typical development and autism spectrum disorder. *European Journal of Neuroscience, 47*(6), 497–514. https://doi.org/10.1111/ejn.13720.
Nicolaidis, C., Raymaker, D. M., Ashkenazy, E., McDonald, K. E., Dern, S., Baggs, A. E., ... Boisclair, W. C. (2015). "Respect the way I need to communicate with you": Healthcare experiences of adults on the autism spectrum. *Autism, 19*(7), 824–831. https://doi.org/10.1177/1362361315576221.
O'Neill, J. L. (1999). *Through the eyes of aliens, A book about autistic people*. London: Jessica Kingsley.
Offit, P. A., & Coffin, S. E. (2003). Communicating science to the public: MMR vaccine and autism. *Vaccine, 22*(1), 1–6. https://doi.org/10.1016/s0264-410x(03)00532-2.
Paul, R. (2008). Interventions to improve communication in autism. *Child and Adolescent Psychiatric Clinics of North America, 17*(4), 835–856. https://doi.org/10.1016/j.chc.2008.06.011.
Paul, R., Orlovski, S. M., Marcinko, H. C., & Volkmar, F. (2009). Conversational behaviors in youth with high-functioning ASD and Asperger syndrome. *Journal of Autism and Developmental Disorders, 39*(1), 115–125. https://doi.org/10.1007/s10803-008-0607-1.
Portway, S. M., & Johnson, B. (2005). Do you know I have Asperger's syndrome? Risks of a non-obvious disability. *Health, Risk & Society, 7*(1), 73–83. https://doi.org/10.1080/09500830500042086.
Prelock, P. A., Paul, R., & Allen, E. M. (2011). Evidence-based treatments in communication for children with autism spectrum disorders. In F. Volkmar & B. Reichow (Eds.), *Evidence-based treatments for children with ASD* (pp. 93–169). New York: Springer.
Prizant, B., Wetherby, A., Rubin, E., Laurent, A., & Rydell, P. (2005). *The SCERTS model: A comprehensive educational approach for children with autism spectrum disorders* (Vol. 1 Assessment). Baltimore, MD: Brookes Publishing Company.
Reniers, R. L., Corcoran, R., Drake, R., Shryane, N. M., & Völlm, B. A. (2011). The QCAE: A questionnaire of cognitive and affective empathy. *Journal of Personality Assessment, 93*(1), 84–95. https://doi.org/10.1080/00223891.2010.528484.

Rogers, K., Dziobek, I., Hassenstab, J., Wolf, O. T., & Convit, A. (2007). Who cares? Revisiting empathy in Asperger syndrome. *Journal of Autism and Developmental Disorders, 37*(4), 709–715. https://doi.org/10.1007/s10803-006-0197-8.

Samson, A. C., Huber, O., & Gross, J. J. (2012). Emotion regulation in Asperger's syndrome and high-functioning autism. *Emotion, 12*(4), 659–665. https://doi.org/10.1037/a0027975.

Sarrett, J. C. (2011). Trapped children: Popular images of children with autism in the 1960s and 2000s. *Journal of Medical Humanities, 32*(2), 141–153. https://doi.org/10.1007/s10912-010-9135-z.

Schaefer-Whitby, P., Lorah, E., Love, J., & Lawless, H. (2017). Enhancing communication and language development. In D. Zager, D. F. Cihak, & A. Stone-Macdonald (Eds.), *Autism spectrum disorders: Identification, education and treatment* (p. 1). New York: Routledge.

Schneider, E. (1999). *Discovering my autism*. London: Kingsley Publishers.

Seltzer, M. M., Shattuck, P., Abbeduto, L., & Greenberg, J. S. (2004). Trajectory of development in adolescents and adults with autism. *Mental Retardation and Developmental Disabilities, 10*(4), 234–247. https://doi.org/10.1002/mrdd.20038.

Senier, L. (2008). It's your most precious thing: Worst-case thinking, trust and parental decision making about vaccinations. *Sociological Inquiry, 78*(2), 207–229. https://doi.org/10.1111/j.1475-682x.2008.00235.x.

Sheppard, E., Pillai, D., Wong, G. T., Ropar, D., & Mitchell, P. (2016). How easy is it to read the minds of people with autism spectrum disorder? *Journal of Autism and Developmental Disorders, 46*(4), 1247–1254. https://doi.org/10.1007/s10803-015-2662-8.

Sinclair, J. (1993). Don't mourn for us. *Our Voice, 1*(3), 1–4.

Singer, W. (2009). The brain, a complex self-organizing system. *European Review, 17*(2), 321–329. https://doi.org/10.10107/S1062798709000751

Singer, T., Critchley, H. D., & Preuschoff, K. (2009). A common role of insula in feelings, empathy and uncertainty. *Trends in Cognitive Sciences, 13*(8), 334–340.

Stagg, S. D., Slavny, R., Hand, C., Cardoso, A., & Smith, P. (2014). Does facial expressivity count? How typically developing children respond initially to children with autism. *Autism, 18*(6), 704–711. https://doi.org/10.1177/1362361313492392.

Tager-Flusberg, H., & Kasari, C. (2013). Minimally verbal school-aged children with autism spectrum disorder: The neglected end of the spectrum. *Autism Research, 6*(6), 468–478. https://doi.org/10.1002/aur.1329.

Toth, K., Munson, J., Meltzoff, A. N., & Dawson, G. (2006). Early predictors of communication development in young children with autism spectrum disorder: Joint attention, imitation, and toy play. *Journal of Autism and Developmental Disorders, 36*(8), 993–1005. https://doi.org/10.1007/s10803-006-0137-7.

Trembath, D., Paynter, J., Keen, D., & Ecker, U. K. (2015). "Attention: Myth Follows!" Facilitated communication, parent and professional attitudes towards evidence-based practice, and the power of misinformation. *Evidence-Based Communication Assessment and Intervention, 9*(3), 113–126.

Twachtman-Cullen, D. (2014). Symbolic communication: Common pathways and points of departure. In K. D. Buron & P. Wolfberg (Eds.), *Learners on the autism spectrum: Preparing highly qualified educators* (2nd ed., pp. 58–81). Shawnee Mission, Kansas: AAPC.

Vivanti, G., Hudry, K., Trembath, D., Barbaro, J., Richdale, A., & Dissanayake, C. (2013). Towards the DSM-5 criteria for autism: Clinical, cultural, and research implications. *Australian Psychologist, 48,* 258–261. https://doi.org/10.1111/ap.12008.

Wakefield, A. J., Murch, S. H., Anthony, A., Linnell, J., Casson, D. M., Malik, M., … Walker-Smith, J. A. (1998). Ileal-lymphoid-nodular hyperplasia, non-specific colitis, and pervasive developmental disorder in children. *LANCET, 351*(9103), 637–641. https://doi.org/10.1016/s0140-6736(97)11096-0.

Ward, D., & Webster, A. (2018). Understanding the lived experiences of university students with autism spectrum disorder (ASD): A phenomenological study. *International Journal of Disability, Development and Education, 65*(4), 373–392. https://doi.org/10.1080/1034912x.2017.1403573.

Welch, C., Polatajko, H., Rigby, P., & Fitch, M. (2018). Autism inside out: Lessons from the memoirs of three minimally verbal youths. *Disability and Rehabilitation*, 1–9. https://doi.org/10.1080/09638288.2018.1465133.

Wetherby, A., Watt, N., Morgan, L., & Shumway, S. (2007). Social communication profiles of children with autism spectrum disorders late in the second year of life. *Journal of Autism and Developmental Disorders, 37*(5), 960–975. https://doi.org/10.1007/s10803-006-0237-4.

Wing, L., & Gould, J. (1979). Severe impairments of social interaction and associated abnormalities in children: Epidemiology and classification. *Journal of Autism and Developmental Disorders, 9*(1), 11–29. https://doi.org/10.1007/bf01531288.

Chapter 8
Constructing Contexts for Success in a Social Society: Undoing the Impact of the Behaviour/Mental Disorder Myth

Abstract Autistic individuals often experience heightened levels of anxiety as they encounter new settings, expectations and hidden curriculum. This anxiety can be manifested in the form of challenging behaviours, particularly for children who are still learning social communication, self-management and coping skills. This has led many people to believe that behavioural difficulties are a core characteristic of autism spectrum disorder and that autistic individuals demonstrate mental or behaviour disorders. Such conceptualisations portray autistic individuals as having behaviour disorders that need to be remediated or treated, and who need to learn social skills to fit into society. The myth of autism as a behaviour/mental disorder will be examined by tracing its early history and associations with schizophrenia. This will be followed by a review of the research and current theory about the link between behaviour challenges demonstrated by autistic children and adults, autistic symptomology and the environment. The current impact of the myth for autistic individuals will be discussed and an alternative view will be offered in which social skills and problem behaviours are viewed as a product of the interaction and mismatch between the needs of individuals and the demands of the community. The chapter will conclude by offering examples of autism-friendly environments and strategies that can support the processing styles of autistic children and adults and enable them to manage the anxiety that often leads them to engage in problematic and potentially isolating behaviours.

Keywords Anxiety and behaviour · Constructing autism-friendly environments Historical perspectives · Schizophrenia

Since it was first identified, autism has been linked with unusual and seemingly unexplainable behaviours and characteristics. With no clear biological or physiological explanation, the outward manifestation of atypical behaviours has led to the myth that autism is fundamentally a mental illness or behaviour disorder. This myth has resulted in a great deal of stigmatisation of autistic individuals as unpredictable, mad or dangerous. In order to mitigate the impact of this myth, it is important to explore its early origins, particularly its early association with schizophrenia.

M. Bennett et al., *Life on the Autism Spectrum*,
https://doi.org/10.1007/978-981-13-3359-0_8

8.1 The Origin

The origins of the myth that autism is a mental illness or behaviour disorder can be largely linked to its diagnostic history and observation of atypical behaviours in the first groups of autistic children described by researchers as well as to early beliefs about behaviour and mental illness. As early as 1867, British psychiatrist, Henry Maudsley, suggested that children who exhibited strange or unexplained behaviour were suffering from a type of child psychosis (Wing, 1997). By the turn of the century, medical professionals and scientists had begun to divide these individuals into different groups. These included one group who seemed to develop in a typical fashion before suddenly losing their language and social interaction skills and another group, which demonstrated a marked difference from early infancy in the ways they expressed emotion and affection towards their parents. Medical professionals understood little about the reasons for these behaviours and classified these children, who exhibited many behaviours and characteristics now commonly associated with autism, as having a type of schizophrenia or other mental illness.

The term "autism" was introduced in 1911 by Swiss psychiatrist Eugene Bleuler (Smith, Schaefer-Whitby, & Mrla, 2016) to describe an aspect of schizophrenia associated with a person's withdrawal from reality. It was Kanner (1943) who first used the term autism to describe a group of individuals who exhibited behaviours that are now classified under the diagnostic criteria for autism spectrum disorder. These behaviours included difficulties with social interaction and communication with others, and rigid and fixated behaviours. Shortly after Kanner identified these behaviours, Hans Asperger described another group of children whom he called "little professors". These children exhibited many of the same characteristics described by Kanner, although they had higher levels of language and cognitive skills (Smith et al., 2016). Like Kanner, Asperger also used the term autism to describe the children he observed and described as having lost contact with their environment (Asperger, 1938). Although both Kanner and Asperger appeared to initially question the link between autism and schizophrenia, they later made a clear distinction between the two conditions. Both believed that these children's isolation was not related to a desire to retreat from the world, as would be expected in schizophrenia, but was the manifestation of a lack of contact with the world from infancy (Feinstein, 2011). In spite of this, autism continued to be associated with schizophrenia in the medical and psychiatric literature, and in the public perception until the 1980s (Smith et al., 2016).

Researchers now recognize that autism is neither linked to or a subset of schizophrenia (Billstedt, 2000), although there is no doubt that both autism and schizophrenia share several common symptoms. Both individuals diagnosed with schizophrenia and those diagnosed with autism spectrum disorder can exhibit aggressive or self-injurious behaviours. However, severe behaviours are exhibited by only a small minority of autistic individuals (Billstedt, 2000) and are more commonly exhibited by children than by adolescents or adults, while aggressive and self-injurious behaviours are much more common for individuals with limited communication skills. These behaviours can be quite frightening to other people, particularly if they are not familiar with the individual or with autism.

Autism and schizophrenia also differ in terms of their developmental trajectories. Parents usually notice the first indicators of autism when their child is less than three years of age (Crane, Chester, Goddard, Henry, & Hill, 2015; Sansosti, Lavik, & Sansosti, 2012; Siklos & Kerns, 2007). In contrast, people typically experience the first symptoms of schizophrenia during adolescence (Gogtay, Vyas, Testa, Wood, & Pantelis, 2011; Häfner & an der Heiden, 1997). Despite these differences, there is still diagnostic confusion between the two conditions. A study of the medical records of Indigenous Australian adults (Roy & Balaratnasingam, 2010) found that 13 of 14 patients, who had been diagnosed with schizophrenia, also met the criteria for autism. The researchers concluded that many of these individuals may have been misdiagnosed with schizophrenia and cautioned the need for more understanding of autism in minority groups, particularly when accompanied by intellectual disability.

An examination of the history of the diagnostic criteria for autism provides some insight into the confusion between autism and schizophrenia. In 1980, the *Diagnostic and Statistical Manual of Mental Disorders—Third Edition* (*DSM-III*) was published. This marked the first time that autism was identified as a condition separate from schizophrenia. Prior to this time, both the *DSM-I* and *DSM-II* classified autism as a form of childhood schizophrenia. Even though autism was officially categorised as a developmental disorder in the *DSM-III*, some people have argued that its inclusion in a manual of mental disorders continues to imply that autism is a mental illness. Fear of stigmatisation has been a particular concern of some autistic individuals, particularly since the announcement of one single diagnostic label of autism spectrum disorder, which was introduced in the *DSM-V* in 2013 (Ohan, Ellefson, & Corrigan, 2015). Consequently, some autistic advocates have argued for the term "autism spectrum condition" rather than "autism spectrum disorder", feeling that this term more accurately reflects their view that autism is a part of their identity rather than a label that is used to identify them as defective or disordered (Kenny et al., 2016).

Another mental disorder that is sometimes confused with autism is reactive attachment disorder (RAD). This condition is often linked to poor bonding with others in their formative years, a cause that was originally attributed to autism (Hanson & Spratt, 2000). Sadiq et al. (2012) compared autistic individuals and those diagnosed with RAD on measures of social interaction, use of language, and repetitive and stereotyped behaviours. They found that individuals diagnosed with RAD demonstrated behaviours consistent with the diagnostic criteria for ASD. Children diagnosed with ASD, however, had sub-clinical scores in all areas on standardized measures of ASD, whereas children with RAD only exhibited low scores in repetitive and stereotyped behaviours. In addition, the two groups demonstrated similar difficulties in some areas of social interaction. The researchers concluded that parent report is essential to distinguishing between these two difficulties.

In another study, Akdemir, Pehlivantürk, Unal, and Ozusta (2009) found that attachment behaviours of autistic children were similar to those of children with other developmental disabilities. Attachment behaviours of autistic children were correlated with the severity of autism symptomology, and particularly with language skills. These findings indicate that differences in social communication skills demonstrated by autistic children may lead parents or others to believe that they are not forming attachments and may confuse these behaviours with those of children who fail to form attachments with others such as those with RAD. In a related study, Cath, Ran, Smit, van Balkom, and Comijs (2008) found that individuals diagnosed with ASD differed from patients with obsessive–compulsive disorder (OCD) or social anxiety disorder on autism-related problem behaviours, but did suggest that an overlap in behaviours between the groups may reflect overlapping aetiologies between the conditions. These studies indicate that although ASD cannot be categorised as a mental disorder, some of the behavioural manifestations or symptoms associated with autism may be similar to those of other mental or developmental disorders. The underlying mechanisms of autism, however, are unique, which means that the needs of autistic children and adults are distinct from individuals with other conditions such as social anxiety disorder, RAD, or obsessive–compulsive disorder.

The pervasiveness of the perception that autism is a mental health disorder was confirmed in a recent study (John, Knott, & Harvey, 2018) in which university students and members of the public were asked about their beliefs about individuals diagnosed with autism. Two of the most common beliefs reported by participants were that: (1) autistic individuals are mad and (2) autistic individuals are dangerous. The term "mad" was used to denote instability linked to mental illness. Participants stated their opinions were influenced by hearing autistic individuals described in terms associated with mental illness, but changed their opinion once they got to know someone diagnosed with ASD. Other participants shared experiences of meeting people diagnosed with autism who were aggressive. This made them hesitant to interact with other autistic individuals in the future. In another study, Jensen et al. (2016) asked members of the public if they were able to distinguish between autism and schizophrenia. They found that people associated schizophrenia with danger and autism with intelligence and creativity. Despite this, participants were still hesitant about interacting with either group, perceiving both as exhibiting negative or problematic behaviours.

Historically, individuals who exhibited aggressive or unexplainable behaviours were labelled as being mentally ill. The primary method for dealing with these individuals was to place them into mental institutions, where they were often subjected to aversive treatments or drugs, in an attempt to cure them or make them more "normal" (Dekker, 1990; Morrissey & Goldman, 1986). Not only were institutionalisation and segregation used both for people suffering from psychosis, but these measures were also a primary course of treatment for individuals who demonstrated intellectual disabilities, or behavioural differences now associated with ASD (Gray, 2002). Today the majority of these institutions have been closed, but this has not lessened the discomfort that people feel when someone engages in unusual or "dangerous" behaviours. This has resulted in a different kind of segregation for autistic individuals, in the form of exclusion from social activities (Causton-Theoharis, Ashby, & Cosier, 2009), workplace settings (Costley, Baldwin, & Bruck, 2016) and schools (Krezmien, Travers, & Camacho, 2017; Lilley, 2012).

Since Kanner's initial study (Kanner, 1943), the diagnosis of autism (or autism spectrum disorder) has been based on the observation of atypical and, sometimes extreme, behaviours. These include a lack of typical emotional response to stimuli, perceived lack of connection with others, and sudden behaviour outbursts (Zwaigenbaum et al., 2005). Influenced by the teachings of Freud, researchers such as Bruno Bettelheim and even Kanner himself, initially attributed these behaviours to a mental disorder caused by a failure of parents to bond with their children (White, Smith, Smith, & Stodden, 2012). This theory, subsequently identified as the "refrigerator mother" theory, helped to solidify the perception that autism was a mental illness. Although the theory that autism is caused by "refrigerator mothers" has been disproven, the diagnosis of autism spectrum disorder is still based on observations of behaviours, rather than on any physiological or genetic test. As a result, autism has come to be associated with problematic behaviours, rather than with specific physical or intrinsic differences or disabilities.

The uneven pattern of skills demonstrated by autistic individuals also creates difficulties in interpreting or addressing challenging behaviours (Hart & Whalon, 2012), with professionals often mistakenly believing that if a child is able to cope one day, they should be able to demonstrate the appropriate behaviours every day. A lack of obvious emotional affect is interpreted to mean that the individual is unfeeling or unable to connect with others (Brewer et al., 2016), and the need for repetition and routine is perceived to indicate that the person suffers compulsions they cannot control (Paula-Perez, 2013). These behaviours have also contributed to the diagnostic overlap with a number of other psychological conditions, such as RAD (Davidson et al., 2015), OCD, social anxiety disorder (Cath et al., 2008), oppositional defiant disorder, attention deficit disorder (Gadow, Devincent, & Drabick, 2008) and, of course, schizophrenia (Fitzgerald, 2013).

The early links between autism spectrum disorder and schizophrenia and the similarity of symptoms and behaviours demonstrated by autistic individuals and those diagnosed with other disorders have all contributed to the myth that autism is primarily a mental or behaviour disorder. Although autistic individuals may exhibit some of the same behaviours as individuals diagnosed with other conditions, the past 30 years have seen researchers (Wing, 1997) move from an initial identification of the phenomena of autism to a greater understanding of the characteristics and underlying physiological and cognitive processes unique to autistic children and adults. Understanding these is an essential step in discrediting the myth that autism is a mental or behaviour disorder.

8.2 The Research

In 1979, Wing and Gould published a landmark study describing behaviours common to individuals identified as autistic. This study was the first to systematically define the distinct symptomology of autism and established the "triad of impairments" that formed the basis of the first diagnostic criteria for autism in the *DSM-III.* Since then, researchers have continued to investigate the experiences of autistic individuals and to determine the characteristics that differentiate autism spectrum disorder from other conditions. Although autism has been classified as a neurodevelopmental disorder with a unique cognitive profile, researchers (Billstedt, 2000; Leyfer et al., 2006; Mattila et al., 2010; Simonoff et al., 2008) have determined that a number of autistic children and adults do experience comorbid psychiatric conditions as well as behaviour difficulties leading credence to the "autism mental/behaviour disorder" myth.

Billstedt (2000) contends that comorbidity rates may be high in the autistic population and may be the cause of more severe behaviours such as self-injurious behaviours and aggression. Simonoff et al. (2008) assessed 112 children, aged 10–14, diagnosed with autism, for comorbid disorders. They found that at least 70% of the children had at least one comorbid disorder and 41% had two or more. The most common comorbid conditions were social anxiety disorder, attention deficit hyperactivity disorder (ADHD) and oppositional defiant disorder. Some children had more than one comorbid diagnosis, leading Simonoff et al. to recommend that routine clinical assessments be conducted with autistic children to rule out comorbid conditions. Similarly, Leyfer et al. (2006) recommend the use of differential diagnosis for autistic children and adults in order to identify potential comorbid conditions and determine appropriate interventions. In a more recent study, Gargaro, Rinehart, Bradshaw, Tonge, and Sheppard (2011) questioned whether the overlapping behaviours of these conditions meant that they were not actually conditions comorbid with autism, but were indicative of the need for a more detailed differential diagnosis to determine the correct diagnosis.

Other studies have indicated that sleep disorders are common among autistic children and can have a significant impact on both the children and their families (Richdale & Schreck, 2009). Children deprived of sleep can exhibit a variety of behaviour difficulties. Richdale and Schreck (2009) conducted a review of relevant research and found that sleep disorders are common and persistent in the majority of autistic children, with parents reporting that 50–80% of children regularly demonstrate disturbed sleep patterns. The aetiology of sleep problems appears to be partly attributed to atypical physiological development associated with the autism spectrum, including differences in melatonin production, circadian patterns and epilepsy. Richdale and Schreck also suggest a relationship between daytime behaviour difficulties including hyperactivity, anxiety and mood disorders, and chronic sleep disorders. Autistic children deprived of sleep are less able to self-manage and are more prone to tantrums and other challenging behaviours, while their sleep-deprived parents have less resources for coping with these challenging behaviours (Billstedt, 2000).

Anxiety, depression and ADHD are three other conditions with high rates of comorbidity with autism. Kim, Szatmari, Bryson, Streiner, and Wilson, (2016) found that in comparison to a non-autistic cohort, autistic children had a higher rate of all three of these conditions. Interestingly, the presence of comorbid conditions was not correlated with early autistic symptoms, but was linked to the difference between children's early verbal and non-verbal IQ scores. Children with a greater discrepancy between the two scores also exhibited higher levels of anxiety and mood difficulties. Similar to sleep disorders, the presence of comorbid anxiety or mood disorders can have a significant impact on adaptive or disruptive behaviours. Thus, although autism itself may not be a mental or behaviour disorder, a number of autistic individuals do exhibit comorbid disorders, such as sleep problems, anxiety and depression, which may be outwardly manifested in difficult behaviours.

No matter the cause, research indicates that some autistic children and adolescents do exhibit challenging behaviours. This can impact them in a number of ways and may prevent them from accessing education programs, employment or social opportunities (Levy & Perry, 2011; Sansosti et al., 2012). Horner, Carr, Strain, Todd and Reed (2002) conducted a review of interventions used to address the behaviour difficulties exhibited by young autistic children. They found that the majority of interventions were directed at tantrums (76%), aggression (59%), stereotypical behaviours (14%) and self-injury (11%). Other targeted behaviours included destructive behaviours and inappropriate verbal and social behaviours. Matson et al. (2011) suggested that behaviour difficulties are often described as the most frequent and challenging issues for autistic children. In a review of 173 studies, Matson et al. discovered that 94.3% of autistic children were reported to display some form of challenging behaviour. Similar to those identified by Horner et al. these behaviours included aggression, tantrums, handmouthing, property destruction, stereotypical behaviour, and self-injurious behaviour. Studies that analysed the purpose of these behaviours found that children engaged in them to: obtain attention, acquire an object, avoid or escape negative tasks or environments, and obtain sensory stimulation. A few studies also found that behaviours had a biological or cognitive origin. It is important to note that although a number of studies have been conducted to examine behaviour problems exhibited by autistic individuals, the majority of this research has been conducted with younger children. Less is known about behaviours exhibited by adolescents, while even more limited research has been conducted on the behaviour difficulties demonstrated by autistic adults. Researchers have suggested that behaviour difficulties may decrease as autistic individuals move into adulthood (Howlin & Magiati, 2017), although there is substantial evidence to indicate that a fairly significant percentage of autistic adults experience comorbid psychiatric or mood disorders (Croen et al., 2015).

Researchers have also sought to determine the risk factors for behaviour problems in populations of autistic children (Griffith, Hastings, Nash, & Hill, 2010; Totsika, Hastings, Emerson, Lancaster, & Berridge, 2011). Totsika et al. found that children diagnosed with ASD, both with and without ID, were more likely to demonstrate challenging behaviours in comparison to either typically developing children or children diagnosed only with ID, although both ASD and ID were identified to be separate risk factors for hyperactivity or emotional and/or behaviour problems. Researchers have also determined that parents of children diagnosed with autism and intellectual disability (ID) are more likely to report their child exhibits problem behaviours. These parents were more likely to experience higher levels of stress, and lower positive perceptions of their children than mothers of autistic children with higher intellectual abilities. Additionally, mothers of autistic children were found to be much more likely to experience emotional disorders, although positive well-being was not influenced by diagnosis. Totsika et al. recommended that interventions targeting challenging behaviours should also address maternal well-being in order to have the most impact for autistic individuals and their families.

In addition to their impact on parents, challenging behaviours effect the participation and achievement of autistic children at school (Ashburner, Ziviani, & Rodger, 2010), including the relationships they have with their teachers and peers (Machalicek, O'Reilly, Beretvas, Sigafoos, & Lancioni, 2007; Martinez, Werch, & Conroy, 2016). Some researchers have argued that challenging behaviours pose the most significant threat to autistic children's participation in, or exclusion from, education settings, community activities and social relationships (Dunlap, Iovannone, Wilson, Kincaid, & Strain, 2010). Certainly, behaviour problems are the primary reason cited for suspensions or the exclusion of autistic children from schools (Beauchamp, 2012; Dickson, 2008). Teachers report that understanding and managing the behaviours of autistic children negatively impact their ability to include these children in education programs (Lindsay, Proulx, Thomson, & Scott, 2013). Teachers add they lack knowledge about ASD and require more training and strategies to engage autistic children in academic work, help them manage unstructured time, and expand on these students' restricted interests. A number of interventions have been trialled in school settings to reduce problem behaviours such as physical and verbal aggression, property destruction, non-compliance and self-injury (Machalicek et al., 2007; Martinez et al., 2016). Many of these interventions have resulted in a reduction of problem behaviours, although it should be noted that many of these interventions have been implemented by researchers or outside staff. More research is needed to validate interventions that can be conducted by teachers within the context of classroom programs (Kasari & Smith, 2013).

Researchers have attempted to unpack some of the factors that make autistic children susceptible to exhibiting behaviour problems. As has already been mentioned, comorbid conditions such as sleep disorders, anxiety or ID can make an individual more likely to exhibit challenging behaviours. Severity of difficulties in skills areas such as intellectual processing, language and communication has also been linked to more severe behaviours including self-injurious behaviours (Matson, Wilkins, & Macken, 2008). Two areas that have been repeatedly linked to challenging behaviours are communication and sensory needs. Autistic children often experience significant difficulties in developing the social communication skills required for successfully navigating both school and community environments. Conroy, Dunlap, Clarke and Alter (2016) contend that children diagnosed with ASD are at risk for developing challenging behaviours as they often lack the communication skills to indicate their basic needs and thoughts. Out of frustration, they communicate through behaviour. For example, lacking the words or means to indicate he is in pain, a young autistic boy may bang his head on the floor. Researchers have established that an effective method for addressing problem behaviours is to implement functional communication training (Koegel, Matos-Freden, Lang, & Koegel, 2012; Tiger, Hanley, & Bruzek, 2008), which will help provide autistic children with more appropriate ways to communicate their needs.

Sensory processing differences are another factor in challenging behaviours. Ashburner, Ziviani and Rodger (2008) explored the relationship between sensory processing issues and emotional and behavioural difficulties exhibited by autistic students in school settings. Their findings indicate that children's inability to regulate auditory input was related to inattention to academic tasks, as was sensory sensitivity to tactile input. On the other hand, movement or vestibular and proprioceptive sensitivity was related to oppositional behaviours, while auditory processing was linked to non-participation and underachievement. Sensory processing difficulties have also been linked to self-injurious behaviour. Duerden et al. (2012) ascertained that abnormal sensory processing was the greatest single predictor for self-injurious behaviour in children diagnosed with ASD and had a greater relationship to self-injury than either cognitive or social ability factors. Duerden et al. concluded that for some children, self-injurious behaviours may be a form of sensory seeking behaviour and recommend that interventions for these behaviours include provision for alternative means of sensory input.

Current research indicates that some autistic individuals, particularly children, do exhibit a number of challenging behaviours, which can impact the way that others perceive their abilities (Ashburner et al., 2010), and result in stigmatisation and segregation. As opposed to the myth that autism is a mental/behaviour disorder, these behaviours are not intrinsic to ASD, but are most likely a result of the individual's needs in areas such as communication, sensory processing and emotional regulation. Alternatively, they may be related to other disorders such as sleep or anxiety disorders. Functional assessment of behaviour is critical to determine the function of a particular behaviour for an individual in different contexts (von der Embse, Brown,

& Fortain, 2011). In a review of the literature, Matson, Mahan, Hess, Fodstad and Neal (2010) found that functional assessment revealed that most behaviours served several primary functions: to get or get away from an object or activity, attention from others, or sensory stimulus. More importantly, all behaviours can be viewed as a form of communication, which, when interpreted, can provide insight into the best means of creating environments that support autistic individuals to achieve their goals.

8.3 The Impact

One of the main impacts of the "autism is a mental/behaviour disorder" myth is the public perception that autistic individuals are deviant and dangerous. This has created a stigmatisation of autism and led some to justify the exclusion of autistic individuals from community settings and programs. Historically, individuals who were deemed to be mentally ill or dangerous were incarcerated in mental institutions. In today's society, residential mental health facilities are far less common, but individuals seen as exhibiting problematic, unpredictable or dangerous behaviours are still excluded and segregated on a regular basis. Mythologising autism as a mental or behaviour disorder has created fear and prompted the segregation and exclusion of autistic individuals under the justification that this action is necessary to maintain their safety and the safety of those around them (McCarthy, Wiener, & Soodak, 2010). A primary example of this type of thinking can be seen in the continued exclusion and segregation of autistic students from school programs. In a recent study, Lilley (2012) found that parents experienced stigma and both direct and indirect discrimination when they attempted to enrol their autistic children in school for the first time. While some were specifically told the school could not provide support for their child's needs, others were encouraged to go to other schools or special schools, where it was suggested they would be more able to provide the right type of support for their child. Similarly, in another study (Carpenter & Austin, 2007), mothers of children diagnosed with autism or ADHD revealed they were silenced and judged for their child's behaviours, which resulted in both their child and them being excluded from social gatherings as well as school functions.

Although many countries have anti-discrimination laws and have signed international agreements supporting the right of individuals with disability to be included (Peters, 2007), the reality is that many autistic children regularly experience segregation or exclusion. Researchers (Humphrey, 2008; Krezmien et al., 2017; Parsons, Lewis, & Ellins, 2009) indicate that many autistic students have been excluded from school at some point. Additionally, autistic students experience higher rates of suspension and exclusion than students with other types of disabilities, and significantly higher rates than students without disabilities. Researchers (McCarthy et al., 2010) have found that many school administrators still have a bias about autistic students, and feel that these students should be placed in segregated settings due to the danger they pose to peers. Some studies suggest that the rate of segregation and suspension of autistic students has increased (Beauchamp, 2012), with more specialised classes being created even after education systems have launched inclusive school policies and initiatives (Graham & Jahnukainen, 2011).

Unfortunately, exclusion is not just limited to school settings. A review of the literature suggests that many employers do not view autistic individuals as employable, which has resulted in many autistic individuals being indirectly excluded in the workplace as they are unable to obtain employment (Richards, 2012). Employers are often hesitant to provide support to employees that they feel might be difficult. In contrast, the evidence from this research suggests that rather than experiencing difficulties because of mental health problems, individuals may develop mental health problems as a result of being excluded.

Another belief underpinning the "autism as a mental disorder" myth is the pervasive belief among professionals and researchers that autistic individuals are disordered and need to be treated so that they can become more "normal". This belief has had a significant impact on the way that services and supports are offered to autistic individuals and their families, and has led to a proliferation of treatments designed to "fix" the individual. The primary example of this has been the use of applied behaviour analysis (ABA) to eliminate dangerous or socially unacceptable behaviours demonstrated by autistic individuals. The use of "ABA programs" has become quite controversial in the autistic community (Milton, 2014) as they are perceived to focus primarily on eradicating autistic characteristics, and subsequently on eliminating autistic identity.

Applied behaviour analysis (ABA) developed as a psychological theory during the 1950s, developing from the work of B.F. Skinner. ABA has been defined as the "utilization of the basic principles of learning and motivation to address socially important problems" (Olive, Boutot, & Tarbox, 2011, p. 142). Three principles of behaviour underlie ABA. These include: all behaviour is learned; all behaviour serves a purpose; and all behaviour is contextual. In addition, a fourth principle, all behaviour is a form of communication, is often added as integral to understanding an individual's behaviours and actions (Tiger et al., 2008). According to the principles and theory of ABA, behaviours are created and subsequently maintained by the interaction between the individual and their environment (Olive et al., 2011). Supporting the learning of new behaviours involves the manipulation of aspects of the environment in order to provide a stimulus for desired behaviour and motivation for engaging in the behaviour again in the future. It is important to note that the use of the term "behaviours" in this example does not refer only to challenging or problematic behaviours, but as any outward action that can be observed by others. Thus, it could be argued that behaviours are the external manifestations of motivation, knowledge or learning.

Applied behaviour analysis was first suggested as a treatment for autistic children by early autism researchers, Bernard Rimland and Ivor Lovaas (Feinstein, 2011). These researchers were among the first to challenge the idea that autism was an untreatable mental illness and to suggest that autistic individuals could learn new knowledge and skills with the right training. Their ideas had a significant impact on the field of autism knowledge. Unfortunately, their interpretation of ABA and subsequent practices led them to also utilise negative and harmful practices, in the belief that autism was associated with aberrant behaviours that needed to be eradicated, so the individual could achieve typical milestones and outcomes. For Rimland, a father of an autistic son who had significant needs in a number of areas, the motivation to help his son be "normal" propelled him to try a number of treatments in an effort to cure his son of autism (Silverman, 2012). In contrast, Lovaas had a much more significant impact on the physical and mental well-being of a number of individuals and their families. With the aim of eliminating what he saw as dangerous or aberrant behaviours, Lovaas employed the use of highly aversive techniques such as electroshock. Justifying these treatments with the contention that their use was less aversive than identified problematic behaviours, Lovaas offered parents the potential to save their child from what he stated was a terrible (autistic) life (Feinstein, 2011). Although Lovaas' practices were highly problematic, his research was one of the first studies to show that strategies based on ABA theory could be used to teach autistic individual's new skills, including those that as meaningful and relevant to them. One example of these skills is toileting skills. Toileting issues are a significant barrier to inclusion of autistic individuals in many settings. Helping them to gain these skills can greatly increase their opportunities in many aspects of life. One strategy that is effective in supporting toileting skills is discrete trial training, which is an ABA-based strategy.

More recently, as researchers have developed an understanding of the role, which the environment plays in the problem behaviours demonstrated by autistic children, ABA-based approaches have been utilised to understand the environmental factors that are triggering these behaviours. By understanding these factors, steps can then be taken to modify or adjust the environment to better support the needs of the individual (Matson et al., 2011). For example, excessive noise and glaring lights may cause an autistic student with sensory sensitives to withdraw or even leave the room. Changing these factors or giving the student a way to modulate or block them may help him/her to concentrate and complete their work to a much higher standard. Although the positive benefits of ABA-based approaches have been well documented and some shift has occurred in the way that behaviour difficulties are viewed and addressed, it has to be acknowledged that a number of these interventions and programs are still focused primarily on remediating the problems of autistic individuals rather than on understanding and altering the reasons for these behaviours (Milton, 2014).

The continued focus on "disordered behaviours" has also impacted families. Research reveals that one of the most commonly cited issues reported by parents of autistic children is the challenge of managing their child's difficult and often seemingly unpredictable behaviours (Myers, Mackintosh, & Goin-Kochel, 2009; Pozo & Sarriá, 2014). Not only do parents face these challenges in their own homes, but they are also often the first point of call for schools or other programs when the child demonstrates behaviours the organisation views as problematic (Myers et al., 2009). As a result, parents experience significant emotional and financial stress (Karst & Van Hecke, 2012). Emotionally, they may become isolated from family or friends whom they feel do not understand their child's needs. They also have to deal with judgement from others when their child engages in extreme behaviours, such as tantrums or meltdowns in public (Gill & Liamputtong, 2011). Financial stress is a major concern for many families as they seek to find funds to pay for recommended treatments and therapies. The proliferation of early intervention or so-called ABA programs marketed as miracle treatments make parents fearful that if they do not raise the funds for these treatments, their child will suffer. Parents and mothers in particular frequently report that they have had to leave their jobs to care for their autistic children who are excluded from school or community programs (Baker & Drapela, 2010). This creates additional difficulties as parents are told their child cannot access these programs until they develop the appropriate behaviours, while simultaneously excluding them from the environments in which they can develop and practice these behaviours. Research (Happé & Frith, 2006) indicates that autistic children often have difficulty with generalisation and need to be taught new skills in the environment in which they will use them. Thus, the culture of exclusion perpetuates the belief that it is the child who is disordered and needing treatment, rather than on identifying and adjusting the features of the environment that might be leading to the behaviours.

Another feature of ABA is the use of a scientific process to systematically determine that change in behaviours, or development of knowledge and skills, is the direct result of manipulation of the environment or other intervention, rather than from other factors (Heflin & Alaimo, 2007). Understanding the environmental factors that create and maintain behaviours is a key component of ABA. This has led to the development of the use of functional behaviour analysis, in which data is gathered and a hypothesis created, about the function of the behaviour for the individual in a particular context. Functional analysis of behaviour has been identified as an important element of learning programs for autistic individuals (Iovannone, Dunlap, Huber, & Kincaid, 2003). The impact of focussing on the deficits of the individual means that supports and services are not developed to help parents or professionals understand their child's behaviours in order to address them. Currently, the focus of many funded programs, such as the Helping Children with Autism initiative in Australia, is on treating the autistic child, rather than on creating appropriate environments where they can thrive. It could be argued that current funding is often based on a medical model, which focuses on treating a disorder, rather than on a social or human rights model, which focuses on creating supportive environments and enabling practices that protect the rights of everyone to fully participate in society.

The focus on the individual has meant less money that has been spent on examining the aspects of environments and programs that pose a barrier to the successful engagement or achievement of autistic individuals. De Schipper et al. (2015) conducted a review of studies, which had examined the ways in which barriers to participation of autistic individuals were assessed. They found that most assessments focused on the individual's characteristics and not on environmental factors. Few studies have examined adaptations of environments and programs to meet the needs of autistic individuals, but many have focused on the use of medications to treat problematic behaviours of autistic individuals (McPheeters et al., 2011). As behaviour is a result of the interaction between the individual and the environment, it is concerning that less attention has been paid to the contexts to determine what aspects may increase or decrease the likelihood of challenging behaviours. In particular, further attention needs to be paid to creating environments, which are flexible to meet the communication, sensory and cognitive processing needs of autistic individuals. This will not only have the primary benefit of increasing their motivation, participation and achievement, but also reduce the emotional distress and anxiety that are often the trigger for many problematic behaviours.

Researchers have identified key features of environments that enable autistic children and adults to fully participate, contribute and achieve. The most important feature of any environment is that it is flexible to adjust to the needs of the people in the environment (Australian Advisory Board on Autism Spectrum Disorders, 2012). For instance, although there may be a uniform required in a school, the school policy incorporates some flexibility to allow individuals to wear short or long sleeves or to wear a shirt underneath the uniform to decrease sensitivity to certain materials. Another frequently cited aspect of autism-friendly environments is the provision of information and structure to support the processing style of autistic individuals (Aspy & Grossman, 2011; Mesibov, Shea, & Schopler, 2005). This includes providing specific visual and structural supports to communicate the expectations for the individuals in that environment including the rules, both stated and implied, different actions required, places that are designated for different activities, and expectations for interacting with others in the environment. Mesibov, Shea and McGCaskill (2012) stressed that autistic individuals need to know what they are expected to do, how they are supposed to do it, when they will know they have completed expected tasks, and what they should do next. The ability to manage sensory stimuli and access communication in different ways is also important to facilitating participation of many autistic individuals. Participating in environments that do not support sensory and communication needs is often cited as a source of distress, anxiety and behaviour difficulties for autistic children (Ashburner et al., 2008). Finally, it is important that environments support the interests of autistic individuals (Koegel, Kim, Koegel, & Schwartzman, 2013) and help them to build connections and trust with others (Koegel et al., 2013). Not only will this facilitate a greater sense of belonging, but it will also connect them to a wider community of support and enhance their ability to adapt in different settings.

A final impact of the "autism as a mental/behaviour disorder" myth is the lack of services to address the comorbid mental health issues experienced by many autistic individuals. As researchers (Leyfer et al., 2006; Mattila et al., 2010) have demonstrated that rates of comorbid mental health conditions are high for this population, it is interesting that mental health issues have not been the focus of more research and services. Anxiety and sleep disorders are particularly prevalent and are often cited as directly related to mood or emotional difficulties and behaviour problems (Gillott & Standen, 2007; Green, Gilchrist, Burton, & Cox, 2000; Richdale & Schreck, 2009). Perceiving these issues and behaviours as part of autism, rather than ancillary to autism, may actually prevent them from being adequately addressed. Researchers and practitioners need to recognise these symptoms as distinct, in order to ascertain the best course of action that will enable the individual to get the help they need (Simonoff et al., 2008).

8.4 The Future

If future practitioners and researchers are to alter the impact of the "autism as a mental/behaviour disorder" myth, the current perspective and support system must shift from focusing on the deficits to building the competence of autistic individuals. This will mean creating environments and services underpinned by an alternative view of autism and of autistic individuals as unique individuals, possessing strengths and needs, who struggle to navigate the "neurotypical" world around them and to make sense of and regulate their own emotions and actions. Enacting this change will also require a change in the way that behaviour difficulties are managed and funds are allocated to support autistic individuals and their families. Until the public's perception of autism is changed and autism is viewed as a difference, rather than as a disorder or deficit, autistic individuals will continue to be treated as somehow "less than" their neurotypical peers and in need of treatment rather than support.

Shifting the current focus on the disordered individual also means that "autistic ways" of social interaction and communication need to be supported, rather than remediated. For example, individuals may need to be allowed to have the flexibility to communicate in writing in school or workplace settings, rather than having to answer or respond quickly in direct social interactions. In addition, helping autistic individuals to build connections with others through shared interests may be the best pathway for facilitating social relationships, instead of the more common approach of teaching social skills. Research also suggests that some autistic individuals have reported they do better with navigating social interactions with one or two friends, but find larger groups more challenging (Vine Foggo & Webster, 2017). Similarly, environments that support the sensory needs of autistic individuals will help to reduce anxiety and behavioural outbursts. These could include the provision of quiet spaces where the individuals can get away when they are overwhelmed. Rather than engaging in disruptive behaviours to escape sensory stimuli, these individuals can be supported to utilise more functional means of communication to access the calming space. Lastly, and by no means, least, researchers have demonstrated that engaging the interests of autistic individuals is a powerful motivator that can help them to tolerate activities and tasks they would otherwise find difficult (Lanou, Hough, & Powell, 2012).

Changing the future direction of the "autism as a mental/behaviour" myth will also require significant modifications in the way that resources and treatments are used to address the behavioural needs of autistic individuals. A capability perspective rather than a deficit approach needs to be taken, in which individuals are met with high expectations that they can achieve if they are given the instruction and support they require. This type of approach will include developing environments and practices to support the development of social and emotional skills, not based on a scale of normal development, but that are necessary for individuals to successfully navigate and be successful in different environments. These include skills such as navigating hidden curriculum, communicating with others and regulating their emotions, which will enable them to accomplish their own goals. Focusing on skills and support that will allow them to take charge of their own lives, make their own decisions, and solve their own problems, will also help to decrease problematic behaviours that may be serving as obstacles to their participation in these environments. Researchers have identified a number of promising practices for supporting autistic children in different environments (National Autism Center (NAC), 2015; Prior, Roberts, Rodger, Williams, & Sutherland, 2011; Wong et al., 2015). These include the use of cognitive behavioural therapy and exercise for anxiety, and the use of self-management training to increase self-regulation and self-monitoring. Scripting and peer training have been effective in helping autistic individuals to make sense of hidden curriculum and expectations in different environments, while modelling and behaviour packages have helped children and adults learn alternative behaviours and forms of communication. Increasingly, these approaches are relying on naturalistic teaching strategies which place an emphasis on contextual learning or the teaching of key skills through the use of pivotal response training which is based on using the principles of ABA in naturalistic settings.

Less is known about strategies that are effective for adults. However, behavioural interventions have enabled adults to acquire skills and reducing problematic barriers that impede their participation in community settings (NAC, 2015). Many strategies and programs that have been established for children or adolescents have not been researched for adults, and much more research is needed for this population. There is emerging evidence that practices, which incorporate behaviour principles and create supportive environments and the development of self-awareness and self-regulation, will be effective for adults, although these strategies may need to be adjusted for the particular needs of adults of different ages and abilities (Hendricks, 2010). Providing support and teaching within employment or community settings has also resulted in improved outcomes for adults (Hendricks, 2010). Recent research (Webster & Garvis, 2017) indicates that some of the best strategies are those that are developed by the adults themselves and are those which help them to utilise decision-making and problem-solving practices and provide them with encouragement and support to self-manage the environmental elements such as sensory stimuli that cause them anxiety and distress. Identified factors that help autistic adults to better utilise problem solving strategies include the provision of emotional support and a belief in their competence from a trusted person as well as access to role models and information. The narratives of autistic adults emphasise the importance of having access to contexts and professionals who provide opportunities for them to learn new strategies and believe that autistic individuals are capable of directing their own learning and problem-solving processes. Creating these types of environments and supports will fashion a future in which autistic individuals are seen as competent contributors to society rather than disordered individuals who need to be treated to be a part of that society.

8.5 Conclusion

Since its first link with schizophrenia, autism has been perceived as a mental illness and a behaviour disorder. Although research has clearly determined that autism spectrum disorder is a unique condition characterised by differences in the way that the individual processes and reacts to environmental stimuli, autistic individuals have continued to be seen as deviants who need to be segregated from others until they can learn the appropriate behaviours. As a result, treatments have focused on treating the individual, rather than on creating contexts and environments in which the individual can succeed in their own way. Although there is little doubt that autistic individuals can exhibit challenging behaviours, a more positive and forward-thinking approach is needed. Acceptance and promotion of an individual's strengths and potential will help enable them to participate more fully and achieve greater success in workplace, education and community settings. Seeing autistic individuals as capable of creating their own solutions offers more potential for success, with resultant benefits for both the individuals and greater society. Thus, to truly transform the myth of "autism as a mental/behaviour disorder" will require a focus not just on supporting individuals, but on creating supportive environments.

References

Akdemir, D., Pehlivantürk, B., Unal, F., & Ozusta, S. (2009). Comparison of attachment-related social behaviors in autistic disorder and developmental disability. *Turkish Journal of Psychiatry, 20*(2), 105–117.

Ashburner, J., Ziviani, J., & Rodger, S. (2008). Sensory processing and classroom emotional, behavioral and educational outcomes in children with autism spectrum disorder. *The American Journal of Occupational Therapy, 62,* 564–573. https://doi.org/10.5014/ajot.62.5.564.

Ashburner, J., Ziviani, J., & Rodger, S. (2010). Surviving in the mainstream: Capacity of children with autism spectrum disorders to perform academically and regulate their emotions and behavior at school. *Research in Autism Spectrum Disorders, 4*(1), 18–27. https://doi.org/10.1016/j.rasd.2009.07.002.

Asperger, H. (1938). Das psychisch abnormale kind. *Wiener Klinische Wochenschrift, 2,* 217–253.

Aspy, R., & Grossman, B. G. (2011). *The Ziggurat model: A framework for designing comprehensive interventions for individuals with high-functioning autism and Asperger Syndrome*. Shawnee Mission, KS: AAPC Publishing.

Australian Advisory Board on Autism Spectrum Disorders. (2012). *Education and autism spectrum disorders in Australia: The provision of appropriate educational services for school-age students with autism spectrum disorders in Australia.* Retrieved from http://www.autismadvisoryboard.org.au/uploads/file/pdfs/Education%20Position%20Paper%20Final%202010%20Final.pdf.

Baker, D. L., & Drapela, L. A. (2010). Mostly the mother: Concentration of adverse employment effects on mothers of children with autism. *The Social Science Journal, 47*(3), 578–592. https://doi.org/10.1016/j.soscij.2010.01.013.

Beauchamp, T. (2012). *Addressing high rates of school suspension*, UnitingCare Children, Young People and Families. Retrieved from https://core.ac.uk/download/pdf/30677748.pdf.

Billstedt, E. (2000). Autism and Asperger syndrome: Coexistence with other clinical disorders. *Acta Psychiatrica Scandinavica, 102*(5), 321–330. https://doi.org/10.1034/j.1600-0447.2000.102005321.x.

Brewer, R., Biotti, F., Catmur, C., Press, C., Happe, F., Cook, R., et al. (2016). Can neurotypical individuals read autistic facial expressions? Atypical production of emotional facial expressions in autism spectrum disorders. *Autism Research, 9*(2), 262–271. https://doi.org/10.1002/aur.1508.

Carpenter, L., & Austin, H. (2007). Silenced, silence, silent: Motherhood in the margins. *Qualitative Inquiry, 13*(5), 660–674. https://doi.org/10.1177/1077800407301179.

Cath, D. C., Ran, N., Smit, J. H., van Balkom, A. J., & Comijs, H. C. (2008). Symptom overlap between autism spectrum disorder, generalized social anxiety disorder and obsessive-compulsive disorder in adults: A preliminary case-controlled study. *Psychopathology, 41*(2), 101–110. https://doi.org/10.1159/000111555.

Causton-Theoharis, J., Ashby, C., & Cosier, M. (2009). Islands of loneliness: Exploring social interaction through the autobiographies of individuals with autism. *Journal of Intellectual and Developmental Disability, 47*(2), 84–96. https://doi.org/10.1352/1934-9556-47.2.84.

Conroy, M. A., Dunlap, G., Clarke, S., & Alter, P. J. (2016). A descriptive analysis of positive behavioral intervention research with young children with challenging behavior. *Topics in Early Childhood Special Education, 25*(3), 157–166. https://doi.org/10.1177/02711214050250030301.

Costley, D., Baldwin, S., & Bruck, S. (2016). *Shining a light on the autism spectrum: Experiences and aspirations of adults*. New York: Taylor & Francis.

Crane, L., Chester, J. W., Goddard, L., Henry, L. A., & Hill, E. (2015). Experiences of autism diagnosis: A survey of over 1000 parents in the United Kingdom. *Autism, 20*(2), 153–162. https://doi.org/10.1177/1362361315573636.

Croen, L. A., Zerbo, O., Qian, Y., Massolo, M. L., Rich, S., Sidney, S., et al. (2015). The health status of adults on the autism spectrum. *Autism, 19*(7), 814–823. https://doi.org/10.1177/1362361315577517.

Davidson, C., O'Hare, A., Mactaggart, F., Green, J., Young, D., Gillberg, C., et al. (2015). Social relationship difficulties in autism and reactive attachment disorder: Improving diagnostic validity through structured assessment. *Research in Developmental Disabilities, 40,* 63–72. https://doi.org/10.1016/j.ridd.2015.01.007.

de Schipper, E., Lundequist, A., Coghill, D., de Vries, P. J., Granlund, M., Holtmann, M., … Bölte, S. (2015). Ability and disability in autism spectrum disorder: A systematic literature review employing the International Classification of Functioning, Disability and Health-Children and Youth Version. *Autism Research, 8*(6), 782–794. https://doi.org/10.1002/aur.1485.

Dekker, J. J. H. (1990). The fragile relation between normality and marginality. Marginalization and institutionalization in the history of education. *Paedagogica Historica, 26*(2), 13.

Dickson, E. (2008). The inclusion and exclusion of students with disability related problem behaviour: The contrasting approaches of Australia and the United States of America. *Australia and New Zealand Journal of Law and Education, 13*(2), 49–63.

Duerden, E. G., Oatley, H. K., Mak-Fan, K. M., McGrath, P. A., Taylor, M. J., Szatmari, P., et al. (2012). Risk factors associated with self-injurious behaviors in children and adolescents with autism spectrum disorders. *Journal of Autism and Development Disorders, 42*(11), 2460–2470. https://doi.org/10.1007/s10803-012-1497-9.

Dunlap, G., Iovannone, R., Wilson, K. J., Kincaid, D. K., & Strain, P. S. (2010). Prevent-Teach-Reinforce: A standardized model of school-based behavioral intervention. *Journal of Positive Behavior Interventions, 12*(1), 9–22. https://doi.org/10.1177/1098300708330880.

Feinstein, A. (2011). *A history of autism: Conversations with the pioneers*. West Sussex, U.K.: Wiley.

Fitzgerald, M. (2013). Overlap between autism and schizophrenia: History and current status. *Advances in Mental Health and Intellectual Disabilities, 8*(1), 15–23. https://doi.org/10.1108/amhid-09-2013-0058.

Gadow, K. D., Devincent, C. J., & Drabick, D. A. (2008). Oppositional defiant disorder as a clinical phenotype in children with autism spectrum disorder. *Journal of Autism and Developmental Disorders, 38*(7), 1302–1310. https://doi.org/10.1007/s10803-007-0516-8.

Gargaro, B. A., Rinehart, N. J., Bradshaw, J. L., Tonge, B. J., & Sheppard, D. M. (2011). Autism and ADHD: How far have we come in the comorbidity debate? *Neuroscience and Biobehavioral Reviews, 35*(5), 1081–1088. https://doi.org/10.1016/j.neubiorev.2010.11.002.

Gill, J., & Liamputtong, P. (2011). Being the mother of a child with Asperger's syndrome: Women's experiences of stigma. *Health Care for Women International, 32*(8), 708–722. https://doi.org/10.1080/07399332.2011.555830.

Gillott, A., & Standen, P. J. (2007). Levels of anxiety and sources of stress in adults with autism. *Journal of Intellectual Disabilities, 11*(4), 359–370. https://doi.org/10.1177/1744629507083585.

Gogtay, N., Vyas, N. S., Testa, R., Wood, S. J., & Pantelis, C. (2011). Age of onset of schizophrenia: Perspectives from structural neuroimaging studies. *Schizophrenia Bulletin, 37*(3), 504–513. https://doi.org/10.1093/schbul/sbr030.

Graham, L. J., & Jahnukainen, M. (2011). Wherefore art thou, inclusion? Analysing the development of inclusive education in New South Wales, Finland and Alberta. *Journal of Education Policy, 26*(2), 263–388. https://doi.org/10.1080/02680939.2010.493230.

Gray, D. E. (2002). Ten years on: A longitudinal study of families of children with autism. *Journal of Intellectual and Developmental Disability, 27*(3), 215–222. https://doi.org/10.1080/136682502100000863.

Green, J., Gilchrist, A., Burton, D., & Cox, A. (2000). Social and psychiatric functioning in adolescents with Asperger syndrome compared with conduct disorder. *Journal of Autism and Developmental Disorders, 30*(4), 279–293. https://doi.org/10.1023/A:1005523232106.

Griffith, G. M., Hastings, R. P., Nash, S., & Hill, C. (2010). Using matched groups to explore child behavior problems and maternal well-being in children with Down Syndrome and autism. *Journal of Autism and Developmental Disorders, 40*(5), 610–619. https://doi.org/10.1007/s10803-009-0906-1.

Häfner, H., & an der Heiden, W. (1997). Epidemiology of schizophrenia. *The Canadian Journal of Psychiatry, 42*(2), 139–151. https://doi.org/10.1177/070674379704200204.

Hanson, R. F., & Spratt, E. G. (2000). Reactive attachment disorder: What we know about the disorder and implications for treatment. *Child Maltreatment, 5*(2), 137–145. https://doi.org/10.1177/1077559500005002005.

Happé, F., & Frith, U. (2006). The weak coherence account: Detail-focused cognitive style in autism spectrum disorders. *Journal of Autism and Developmental Disorders, 36*(1), 5–25. https://doi.org/10.1007/s10803-005-0039-0.

Hart, J. E., & Whalon, K. (2012). Misbehavior or missed opportunity? Challenges in interpreting the behavior of young children with autism spectrum disorder. *Early Childhood Education Journal, 41*(4), 257–263. https://doi.org/10.1007/s10643-012-0527-8.

Heflin, J., & Alaimo, D. F. (2007). *Students with autism spectrum disorders: Effective instructional practices*. Upper Saddle River, N.J: Pearson/Merrill Prentice Hall.

Hendricks, D. (2010). Employment and adults with autism spectrum disorder: Challenges and strategies for success. *Journal of Vocational Rehabilitation, 32,* 125–134. https://doi.org/10.3233/JVR-2010-0502.

Horner, R. H., Carr, E. G., Strain, P. S., Todd, A. W., & Reed, H. K. (2002). Problem behavior interventions for young children with autism: A research synthesis. *Journal of Autism and Developmental Disorders, 32*(5), 423–446. https://doi.org/10.1023/A:1020593922901.

Howlin, P., & Magiati, I. (2017). Autism spectrum disorder: Outcomes in adulthood. *Current Opinion in Psychiatry, 30*(2), 69–76. https://doi.org/10.1097/YCO.0000000000000308.

Humphrey, N. (2008). Including pupils with autistic spectrum disorders in mainstream schools. *Support for Learning, 23*(1), 41–47. https://doi.org/10.1111/j.1467-9604.2007.00367.x.

Iovannone, R., Dunlap, G., Huber, J., & Kincaid, D. (2003). Effective educational practices for students with autism spectrum disorders. *Focus on Autism and Other Developmental Disabilities, 18*(3), 150–165. https://doi.org/10.1177/10883576030180030301.

Jensen, C. M., Martens, C. S., Nikolajsen, N. D., Skytt Gregersen, T., Heckmann Marx, N., Goldberg Frederiksen, M., et al. (2016). What do the general population know, believe and feel about

individuals with autism and schizophrenia: Results from a comparative survey in Denmark. *Autism, 20*(4), 496–508. https://doi.org/10.1177/1362361315593068.
John, R., Knott, F. J., & Harvey, K. N. (2018). Myths about autism: An exploratory study using focus groups. *Autism, 22*(7), 845–854. https://doi.org/10.1177/1362361317714990.
Kanner, L. (1943). Autistic disturbances of affective contact. *Nervous Child, 2*(3), 217–250.
Karst, J. S., & Van Hecke, A. V. (2012). Parent and family impact of autism spectrum disorders: A review and proposed model for intervention evaluation. *Clinical Child and Family Psychology Review, 15*(3), 247–277. https://doi.org/10.1007/s10567-012-0119-6.
Kasari, C., & Smith, T. (2013). Interventions in schools for children with autism spectrum disorder: Methods and recommendations. *Autism, 17*(3), 254–267. https://doi.org/10.1177/1362361312470496.
Kenny, L., Hattersley, C., Molins, B., Buckley, C., Povey, C., & Pellicano, E. (2016). Which terms should be used to describe autism? Perspectives from the UK autism community. *Autism, 20*(4), 442–462. https://doi.org/10.1177/1362361315588200.
Kim, J. A., Szatmari, P., Bryson, S. E., Streiner, D. L., & Wilson, F. J. (2016). The prevalence of anxiety and mood problems among children with autism and Asperger syndrome. *Autism, 4*(2), 117–132. https://doi.org/10.1177/1362361300004002002.
Koegel, L., Matos-Freden, R., Lang, R., & Koegel, R. (2012). Interventions for children with autism spectrum disorders in inclusive school settings. *Cognitive and Behavioral Practice, 19*(3), 401–412. https://doi.org/10.1016/j.cbpra.2010.11.003.
Koegel, R., Kim, S., Koegel, L., & Schwartzman, B. (2013). Improving socialization for high school students with ASD by using their preferred interests. *Journal of Autism and Developmental Disorders, 43*(9), 2121–2134. https://doi.org/10.1007/s10803-013-1765-3.
Krezmien, M. P., Travers, J. C., & Camacho, K. (2017). Suspension rates of students with autism or intellectual disabilities in Maryland from 2004 to 2015. *Journal of Intellectual Disability Research, 61*(11), 1011–1020. https://doi.org/10.1111/jir.12406.
Lanou, A., Hough, L., & Powell, E. (2012). Case studies on using strengths and interests to address the needs of students with autism spectrum disorders. *Intervention in School and Clinic, 47*(3), 175–182.
Levy, A., & Perry, A. (2011). Outcomes in adolescents and adults with autism: A review of the literature. *Research in Autism Spectrum Disorders, 5*(4), 1271–1282. https://doi.org/10.1016/j.rasd.2011.01.023.
Leyfer, O. T., Folstein, S. E., Bacalman, S., Davis, N. O., Dinh, E., Morgan, J., … Lainhart, J. E. (2006). Comorbid psychiatric disorders in children with autism: Interview development and rates of disorders. *Journal of Autism and Developmental Disorders, 36*(7), 849–861. https://doi.org/10.1007/s10803-006-0123-0.
Lilley, R. (2012). It's an absolute nightmare: Maternal experiences of enrolling children diagnosed with autism in primary school in Sydney, Australia. *Disability and Society, 28,* 514–526. https://doi.org/10.1080/09687599.2012.717882.
Lindsay, S., Proulx, M., Thomson, N., & Scott, H. (2013). Educators' challenges of including children with autism spectrum disorder in mainstream classrooms. *International Journal of Disability, Development and Education, 60*(4), 347–362. https://doi.org/10.1080/1034912x.2013.846470.
Machalicek, W., O'Reilly, M. F., Beretvas, N., Sigafoos, J., & Lancioni, G. E. (2007). A review of interventions to reduce challenging behavior in school settings for students with autism spectrum disorders. *Research in Autism Spectrum Disorders, 1*(3), 229–246. https://doi.org/10.1016/j.rasd.2006.10.005.
Martinez, J. R., Werch, B. L., & Conroy, M. A. (2016). School-based interventions targeting challenging behaviors exhibited by young children with autism spectrum disorder: A systematic literature review. *Education and Training in Autism and Developmental Disabilities, 51*(3), 265–280.
Matson, J. L., Kozlowski, A. M., Worley, J. A., Shoemaker, M. E., Sipes, M., & Horovitz, M. (2011). What is the evidence for environmental causes of challenging behaviors in persons with intellectual disabilities and autism spectrum disorders? *Research in Developmental Disabilities, 32*(2), 693–698. https://doi.org/10.1016/j.ridd.2010.11.012.

Matson, J. L., Mahan, S., Hess, J. A., Fodstad, J. C., & Neal, D. (2010). Progression of challenging behaviors in children and adolescents with autism spectrum disorders as measured by the Autism Spectrum Disorders-Problem Behaviors for Children (ASD-PBC). *Research in Autism Spectrum Disorders, 4*(3), 400–404. https://doi.org/10.1016/j.rasd.2009.10.010.

Matson, J. L., Wilkins, J., & Macken, J. (2008). The relationship of challenging behaviors to severity and symptoms of autism spectrum disorders. *Journal of Mental Health Research in Intellectual Disabilities, 2*(1), 29–44. https://doi.org/10.1080/19315860802611415.

Mattila, M. L., Hurtig, T., Haapsamo, H., Jussila, K., Kuusikko-Gauffin, S., Kielinen, M., ... Moilanen, I. (2010). Comorbid psychiatric disorders associated with Asperger syndrome/high-functioning autism: A community- and clinic-based study. *Journal of Autism and Developmental Disorders, 40*(9), 1080–1093. https://doi.org/10.1007/s10803-010-0958-2.

McCarthy, M. R., Wiener, R., & Soodak, L. C. (2010). Vestiges of segregation in the implementation of inclusion policies in public high schools. *Educational Policy, 26*(2), 309–338. https://doi.org/10.1177/0895904810386596.

McPheeters, M. L., Warren, Z., Sathe, N., Bruzek, J. L., Krishnaswami, S., Jerome, R. N., et al. (2011). A systematic review of medical treatments for children with autism spectrum disorders. *Pediatrics, 127*(5), e1312–e1321. https://doi.org/10.1542/peds.2011-0427.

Mesibov, G. B., Shea, V., & McGCaskill, S. (2012). Structured teaching and the TEACCH program. In D. Zager, M. L. Wehmeyer, & R. L. Simpson (Eds.), *Educating students with autism spectrum disorders* (pp. 99–112). New York: Taylor & Francis.

Mesibov, G. B., Shea, V., & Schopler, E. (2005). *The TEACCH approach to autism spectrum disorders*: Springer Science & Business Media.

Milton, D. (2014). So what exactly are autism interventions intervening with? *Good Autism Practice, 15*, 6–14.

Morrissey, J. P., & Goldman, H. H. (1986). Care and treatment of the mentally ill in the United States: Historical developments and reforms. *The Annals of the American Academy of Political and Social Science, 484*(1), 12–27. https://doi.org/10.1177/0002716286484001002.

Myers, B. J., Mackintosh, V. H., & Goin-Kochel, R. P. (2009). "My greatest joy and my greatest heart ache:" Parents' own words on how having a child in the autism spectrum has affected their lives and their families' lives. *Research in Autism Spectrum Disorders, 3*(3), 670–684. https://doi.org/10.1016/j.rasd.2009.01.004.

National Autism Center (NAC). (2015). *Findings and conclusions: National standards project Phase 2*. In N. A. Center (Series Ed.) & N. A. Center (Ed.). Retrieved from http://www.nationalautismcenter.org/national-standards-project/phase-2/.

Ohan, J. L., Ellefson, S. E., & Corrigan, P. W. (2015). Brief report: The impact of changing from DSM-IV "Asperger's" to DSM-5 "autistic spectrum disorder" diagnostic labels on stigma and treatment attitudes. *Journal of Autism and Developmental Disorders, 45*(10), 3384–3389. https://doi.org/10.1007/s10803-015-2485-7.

Olive, M., Boutot, E. A., & Tarbox, J. (2011). Teaching students with autism using the principles of applied behavior analysis. In E. A. Boutot & B. S. Myles (Eds.), *Autism spectrum disorders: Foundations, characteristics and effective strategies* (pp. 141–162). Upple Saddle River, NJ: Pearson Education, Inc.

Parsons, S., Lewis, A., & Ellins, J. (2009). The views and experiences of parents of children with autistic spectrum disorder about educational provision: Comparisons with parents of children with other disabilities from an online survey. *European Journal of Special Needs Education, 24*(1), 37–58. https://doi.org/10.1080/08856250802596790.

Paula-Perez, I. (2013). Differential diagnosis between obsessive compulsive disorder and restrictive and repetitive behavioural patterns, activities and interests in autism spectrum disorders. *Revista de Psiquiatría y Salud Mental (English Edition), 6*(4), 178–186.

Peters, S. J. (2007). 'Education for All?' A historical analysis of international inclusive education policy and individuals with disabilities. *Journal of Disability Policy Studies, 18*(2), 98–108. https://doi.org/10.1177/10442073070180020601.

Pozo, P., & Sarriá, E. (2014). Prediction of stress in mothers of children with autism spectrum disorders. *The Spanish Journal of Psychology, 17,* 1–12. https://doi.org/10.1017/sjp.2014.6.

Prior, M., Roberts, J. M. A., Rodger, S., Williams, K., & Sutherland, R. (2011). *A review of the research to identify the most effective models of practice in early intervention of children with autism spectrum disorders*. Australia: Australian Government Department of Families, Housing, Community Services and Indigenous Affairs.

Richards, J. (2012). Examining the exclusion of employees with Asperger syndrome from the workplace. *Personnel Review, 41*(5), 630–646. https://doi.org/10.1108/00483481211249148.

Richdale, A. L., & Schreck, K. A. (2009). Sleep problems in autism spectrum disorders: Prevalence, nature, & possible biopsychosocial aetiologies. *Sleep Medicine Reviews, 13*(6), 403–411. https://doi.org/10.1016/j.smrv.2009.02.003.

Roy, M., & Balaratnasingam, S. (2010). Missed diagnosis of autism in an Australian indigenous psychiatric population. *Australas Psychiatry, 18*(6), 534–537. https://doi.org/10.3109/10398562.2010.498048.

Sadiq, F. A., Slator, L., Skuse, D., Law, J., Gillberg, C., & Minnis, H. (2012). Social use of language in children with reactive attachment disorder and autism spectrum disorders. *European Child and Adolescent Psychiatry, 21*(5), 267–276. https://doi.org/10.1007/s00787-012-0259-8.

Sansosti, F. J., Lavik, K. B., & Sansosti, J. M. (2012). Family experiences through the autism diagnostic process. *Focus on Autism and Other Developmental Disabilities, 27*(2), 81–92. https://doi.org/10.1177/1088357612446860.

Siklos, S., & Kerns, K. A. (2007). Assessing the diagnostic experiences of a small sample of parents of children with autism spectrum disorders. *Research in Developmental Disabilities, 28*(1), 9–22. https://doi.org/10.1016/j.ridd.2005.09.003.

Silverman, C. (2012). *Understanding autism: Parents, doctors, and the history of a disorder*. Princeton, NJ: Princeton University Press.

Simonoff, E., Pickles, A., Charman, T., Chandler, S., Loucas, T., & Baird, G. (2008). Psychiatric disorders in children with autism spectrum disorders: Prevalence, comorbidity, and associated factors in a population-derived sample. *Journal of the American Academy of Child and Adolescent Psychiatry, 47*(8), 921–929. https://doi.org/10.1097/CHI.0b013e318179964f.

Smith, T. E., Schaefer-Whitby, P., & Mrla, T. (2016). Historical overview of the education and treatment of persons with autism. In: *Autism spectrum disorders: Identification, education, and treatment* (pp. 23–40).

Tiger, J. H., Hanley, G. P., & Bruzek, J. (2008). Functional communication training: A review and practical guide. *Behavior Analysis in Practice, 1*(1), 16–23. https://doi.org/10.1007/BF03391716.

Totsika, V., Hastings, R. P., Emerson, E., Lancaster, G. A., & Berridge, D. M. (2011). A population-based investigation of behavioural and emotional problems and maternal mental health: Associations with autism spectrum disorder and intellectual disability. *Journal of Child Psychology and Psychiatry, 52*(1), 91–99. https://doi.org/10.1111/j.1469-7610.2010.02295.x.

Vine Foggo, R. S., & Webster, A. A. (2017). Understanding the social experiences of adolescent females on the autism spectrum. *Research in Autism Spectrum Disorders, 35,* 74–85. https://doi.org/10.1016/j.rasd.2016.11.006.

von der Embse, N., Brown, A., & Fortain, J. (2011). Facilitating inclusion by reducing problem behaviors for students with autism spectrum disorders. *Intervention in School and Clinic, 47*(1), 22–30. https://doi.org/10.1177/1053451211406545.

Webster, A. A., & Garvis, S. (2017). The importance of critical life moments: An explorative study of successful women with autism spectrum disorder. *Autism, 21*(6), 670–677. https://doi.org/10.1177/1362361316677719.

White, M. L., Smith, J. D., Smith, T. E. C., & Stodden, R. A. (2012). Autism spectrum disorders: Historical, legislative and current perspectives. In D. Zager, M. L. Wehmeyer, & R. L. Simpson (Eds.), *Educating students with autism spectrum disorders* (pp. 3–12). New York: Routledge.

Wing, L. (1997). The history of ideas on autism. *Autism, 1*(1), 13–23. https://doi.org/10.1177/1362361397011004.

Wing, L., & Gould, J. (1979). Severe impairments of social interaction and associated abnormalities in children: Epidemiology and classification. *Journal of Autism and Developmental Disorders, 9*(1), 11–29. https://doi.org/10.1007/BF01531288.

Wong, C., Odom, S. L., Hume, K. A., Cox, A. W., Fettig, A., Kucharczyk, S., … Schultz, T. R. (2015). Evidence-based practices for children, youth, and young adults with autism spectrum disorder: A comprehensive review. *Journal of Autism and Developmental Disorders, 45*(7), 1951–1966. https://doi.org/10.1007/s10803-014-2351-z.

Zwaigenbaum, L., Bryson, S., Rogers, T., Roberts, W., Brian, J., & Szatmari, P. (2005). Behavioral manifestations of autism in the first year of life. *International Journal of Developmental Neuroscience, 23*(2–3), 143–152. https://doi.org/10.1016/j.ijdevneu.2004.05.001.

Chapter 9
Establishing Social Inclusion the Autism Way: Denying the "They Don't Want Friends" Myth

Abstract Autistic individuals experience difficulties in social communication as well as differences in social-cognitive processing. These skills are required for successful interpretation of social cues and utilisation of non-verbal communication during social interactions. In addition, restricted interests often mean that autistic children and adults are not as flexible in their leisure interests and conversation topics as their neurotypical peers. These challenges may cause autistic children and adults to experience frustration and negative consequences when they attempt to engage in interactions and form social relationships with others, particularly with those who are not autistic. This has led some autistic individuals to feel that engaging in social relationships with others is "too hard" and has perpetuated the common misperception that autistic people do not want friends. This chapter will examine the foundations of this myth as well as the research that has described the social relationships and friendships experienced by autistic individuals across different age groups. The characteristics of successful friendships and relationships will be explored, and the features of conducive environments to facilitate friendships will be identified. Finally, recommendations will be made to help create the right environments to support individuals with autism to form good relationships with both autistic and neurotypical peers in school and community settings.

Keywords Peer-mediated supports · Social communication · Social relationships
Special interests

Friendships and other social relationships play a key part in a person's overall quality of life. Not only do friends contribute to a person's enjoyment of life, but they can help them connect to the community and provide a sense of belonging within that community. Friends also serve as a source of learning and support in times of stress. For many autistic individuals, relating to others is difficult, and forming friendships and social relationships is often more problematic than it is for their non-autistic peers (Petrina, Carter, & Stephenson, 2014; Webster & Garvis, 2017a). Consequently, a number of autistic children and adults have few friends, contributing to the common misperceptions that they are social isolates who prefer their own company or lack the emotional capacity to bond with others (Aylott, 2000). The myth that autistics

M. Bennett et al., *Life on the Autism Spectrum*,
https://doi.org/10.1007/978-981-13-3359-0_9

do not want friends has become fairly widespread (John, Knott, & Harvey, 2018), creating even more stigma and isolation for autistic children and adults. The origins of the "don't want friends" myth and the beliefs behind them have a long history. To counteract this myth, it is essential to recognise the way these beliefs have been shaped over time and to develop an understanding of what it means to be "autistic".

9.1 The Origins

The origins of the "don't want friends" myth can be traced to the early 1900s when psychiatrist Eugen Bleuler, first used the term "autism" to describe children who demonstrated social–emotional disorders (White, Smith, Smith, & Stodden, 2012). Although Bleuler first used the term, autism, in 1911, it was not until the 1940s that this term became more widely recognised when Kanner used it to categorise a group of children whom he described as exhibiting "profound aloneness that dominates all behaviour" (Kanner, 1943, p. 247). Interestingly, Asperger (1944), working in Vienna, also used the word autistic in his description of a group of children who demonstrated somewhat similar behaviours to those observed by Kanner. Although his work was relatively unknown until it was translated into English over 40 years later, it is now apparent that Asperger, like Kanner, believed that the children he observed were characterised by an inability to establish normal relationships with their peers (Frith, 2003). Their use of the word autism may be linked to Bleuler's use of "autism", to denote observed behaviours which demonstrated, a "narrowing of relationships to people and to the outside world, a narrowing so extreme that it seemed to exclude everything except the person's own self" (Frith, 2003, p. 5).

In contrast to Bleuler who observed individuals that appeared to withdraw as a means of escaping reality into fantasy (Greydanus & Toledo-Pereyra, 2012), the children described by both Kanner and Asperger appeared to exhibit core deficits in social interaction and communication from early infancy. Kanner described this as "autistic aloneness" writing that "the outstanding pathognomonic, fundamental disorder is the children's inability to relate themselves in the ordinary way to people and situations from the beginning of life" (Kanner, 1943, p. 242). In another paper, he described one boy's social interaction differences saying, "he has a good relation to objects … the child's relation to people is altogether different … profound aloneness dominates all behaviour". Although identified as exhibiting isolated and disordered behaviour, these children did not regress further and had increased some skills.

Since the publication of these early studies, the word autism, which means "self", has been associated with a state of aloneness or isolation. Davidson (2008) suggests that this perception has been strengthened further by the description of autistic children as being withdrawn in a world of their own. For many, autism evokes an image of an individual sitting and rocking in a corner, locked in their own world (Broderick & Ne'eman, 2008; Grinker, 2010). Over the years, this stereotype has been repeatedly reinforced through media, literature, photographs and by early autism researchers and professionals. Broderick and Ne'eman (2008) conducted an analysis of the ways that metaphors were used in popular books to describe autism. These included books such as Bettelheim's *Empty Fortress* (1967), Clara Claiborne Park's *The Siege* (1967) and Judy and Sean Barron's *There's a Boy in Here* (1992). They found that many of these texts used words such as "fortress", "wall" or "emergence" to portray the autistic child as someone who is trapped behind a barrier that prevents them from interacting with others. This suggests that autism involves being removed to another place, from which autistic children have to be rescued or retrieved. Media images also help to promote the stereotype of the autistic individual as isolated or trapped. Images of children confined behind windows or physically separated from a group are common (Broderick & Ne'eman, 2008; Sarrett, 2011). These images have helped create the perception of the autistic child or adult as a person who is trapped in a shell or prison of autism. Moreover, these images send the message that it is autism, which prevents these individuals from interacting with others.

Another image commonly presented in visual and print media is that of the autistic individual as alienated from the world around them. This depiction focuses on the isolation of the autistic individual and their social disconnection from others (Holton, 2013). An example is seen in the popular television show, *Parenthood*. After conducting an analysis of all the episodes in the first season of this series, Holton (2013) found that Max, a character diagnosed with Asperger's syndrome, is often portrayed as being socially isolated from his family and others around him. He is also frequently shown as exhibiting behavioural difficulties that impact others around him, although the impact that others have on him is not portrayed. Max is defined by his differentness, which is viewed by his family as a barrier to his ability to make friends. His family are regularly shown trying to mitigate these differences and also expressing their fear of them. This link between social deficits and fear is not uncommon. Holton, Farrell, and Fudge (2014) found that the fictional autistic characters are rarely presented as capable individuals with their own perspectives and voices, but rather are portrayed as unstable social outcasts who exhibit a number of social skills deficits and engage in violent behaviours. Holton et al. conclude that these images provide cues and promote stigmatisation of autism and autistic people, creating a "threatening space" in which autistic people are devalued and discounted until they overcome their autism and become capable of "normal" social interaction.

The prevalence of the myth that autistic individuals do not want friends has been established in a recent study that explored the public's perception of autism and autistic individuals. John, Knott and Harvey (2017) conducted focus groups with people from a range of backgrounds and ages, to identify the myths and misperceptions they held about autistic people. Results revealed seven commonly held beliefs about autistic individuals. Four of these related to perceptions about the ability of autistic individuals to socially interact with others. These included beliefs that autistic individuals: (1) are disinterested in social relationships; (2) do not like to be touched; (3) are introverts and (4) are unable to notice social rejection. The researchers concluded that information and contact with autistic people played the most pivotal role in participants' attitude formation. The researchers added that with frequent exposure to images of autistic individuals as social isolates and limited real-life contact with autistic people, the public is unlikely to see the heterogeneity of autism or the diverse skills exhibited by autistic individuals.

Another factor that has contributed to the "don't want friends" myth can be found in the diversity of characteristics demonstrated by autistic children and adults. Deficits in social communication and social interaction are essential criteria for a diagnosis of ASD (American Psychiatric Association, 2013). This includes difficulties in developing and maintaining social relationships and in social–emotional reciprocity and communication behaviours for social interaction. Researchers (Orsmond, Krauss, & Seltzer, 2013), parents (Knott, Dunlop, & Mackay, 2006) and autistic adults (Vincent et al., 2016) have discussed the difficulties that autistic individuals experience as they engage with others and seek friendship. Autistic adults have especially highlighted the challenges they experience in navigating social environments and expectations of others (Causton-Theoharis, Ashby, & Cosier, 2009), expressing that they find it difficult to interpret social cues and communicate with others, particularly in new situations (Vincent et al., 2016). This may lead them to be slow to respond to peers' social initiations or to respond in odd or unexpected ways, leading others to believe they do not wish to interact with others.

Difficulties with using and interpreting non-verbal communication also contribute to this misconception. For example, autistic children may use misleading facial expressions or body language, such as maintaining a flat expression or failing to look at the peer when they are talking. They may also not respond with social comments when expected or may initiate conversation or comments in such a way that they are missed by peers. Difficulties with knowing what other people are thinking (i.e. theory of mind) may also cause problems. Autistic children and adults report they often experience difficulty in discerning what their peers want them to say or the ways in which their communication is interpreted by others (Müller, Schuler, & Yates, 2008). Finally, autistic children and adults may not engage in reciprocal conversations in the same way as their peers and may dominate conversations with discussion of favourite topics or ignore information or questions they deem "irrelevant". Together, these issues may give the appearance that the autistic individual is disengaged from social interaction. Misleading social communication skills, however, should not be misinterpreted as a lack of interest in social engagement and relationships.

9.2 The Research

Friendship has been defined as a bond between two people that is characterised by shared interests, mutual liking and mutual enjoyment and which persists over time (Howes, 1983, 1996). Researchers (Bukowski, Hoza, & Boivin, 1994; Parker & Asher, 1993) have described essential qualities of friendship. These include companionship, validation and caring, intimacy, help and conflict. Each of these qualities serves a different purpose and change over time, with companionship playing a larger role in early childhood, and intimacy assuming greater importance as children grow older (Ladd, 1988; Newcomb & Bagwell, 1996). Additionally, friendships differ for males and females, with girls engaging in more activities involving conversation and intimate exchange of information, while boys are more likely to engage with friends in specific activities such as games or sports (Underwood, 2007). Research indicates that people have different types of relationships with others in their social networks including friends, best friends and acquaintances (Meyer et al., 1998). There is also evidence to suggest that children diagnosed with ASD, or with other developmental disabilities, may experience atypical relationships characterised by special treatments or high amounts of helping (Meyer et al., 1998; Webster & Carter, 2012b).

Several researchers have explored the social relationships of autistic children and adolescents (Chamberlain, Kasari, & Rotheram-Fuller, 2007; Kasari, Locke, Gulsrud, & Rotheram-Fuller, 2011; Webster & Carter, 2012a, c). These studies have shown that, in general, these individuals demonstrate a desire to connect with others and to develop a variety of social relationships and friendships. Howard, Cohn, and Orsmond (2006) conducted a case study in which a 12-year-old boy diagnosed with Asperger's syndrome utilised photographs and interviews to convey his perceptions of friendship. He expressed his desire to have friendships and expressed the enjoyment and benefits he experienced from spending time with his best friend. In another study, Cook, Ogden and Winstone (2018) interviewed 11 adolescent autistic girls and found that all were motivated to have friends. A similar finding was obtained by Vine Foggo and Webster (2017) in an analysis of the online discussions of adolescent and young adult autistic females. In an examination of the influence of gender on friendships, Sedgewick, Hill, Yates, Pickering, and Pellicano (2016) suggested that autistic girls seemed to be more motivated than autistic boys to have friends, while an analysis of the friendship experiences of adolescent autistic boys (O'Hagan & Hebron, 2017) revealed a gap between their desire for friendships and their ability to make friends.

Although most of the studies about friendship have been conducted with autistic children or adolescents, a few studies indicate that the majority of autistic adults also express a strong desire for relationships. Causton-Theoharis et al. (2009) analysed autobiographical accounts of seven autistic adults to explore their experiences with social interaction. All demonstrated a strong desire for social connections with others but reported they often experienced feelings of loneliness. Similarly, a large-scale study conducted by Costley, Baldwin, and Bruck (2016) revealed that many autistic adults sought friendships and social experiences, but were frustrated at their lack of opportunity to interact with others. Adults in another study (Vincent et al., 2016) reported feeling alienated from their peers, despite their desire to form relationships with them. In addition, they reported experiencing difficulties and anxiety when it came to initiating contact or engaging in social interactions with others.

In a study of successful autistic women, Webster and Garvis (2017a) explored the role that others played in enabling the self-efficacy of participants. Three women reported they desired social relationships but stated that a lack of social awareness had resulted in them experiencing abusive relationships. Other participants discussed the ways that friends had helped them to believe in themselves at critical points in their lives. All participants expressed the deep satisfaction they felt when they could mentor or help other autistic girls and women. In contrast, a related study (Webster & Garvis, 2017b) revealed that autistic men primarily interacted with others through structured activities and formed fewer intimate relationships, more akin to acquaintanceships than friendships. Similarly, Underwood (2007) found that autistic boys utilise games or sports to engage with peers, whereas girls are more likely to interact through less structured social activities involving conversation and sharing of experiences.

A larger body of research has been devoted to examining the qualities that characterise friendships and social relationships of autistic children. Petrina et al. (2014) conducted an extensive review of 24 studies that explored the friendship of autistic children. They concluded that although many autistic children reported having friends, these friendships were somewhat different in nature to those demonstrated by non-autistic children. Autistic children had fewer friends, met their friends less frequently outside of school and had lower stability in their friendships than their non-autistic peers. They also had more friends who had a diagnosis of ASD or another disability. Other studies have also indicated that autistic children have friendships that are poorer in quality than those of children with other identified disabilities (Rowley et al., 2012), encompassing less mutuality of engagement and behaviours. Some researchers (Chang, Shih, & Kasari, 2016) have suggested that these differences may be attributed in part to early difficulties in development of joint attention and language commonly demonstrated by many autistic children.

Another key finding is that autistic children can identify the features of a friend or friendships but tend to use simpler descriptions than their non-autistic peers. In an early study (Bauminger, Shulman, & Agam, 2004), autistic children and adolescents were able to select pictures that demonstrated friendships, identifying them simply as friends. In contrast, their non-autistic peers gave more detailed descriptions describing the reciprocal affective and intimate features of the friendships. Additionally, autistic children reported less intimacy as well as lower levels of companionships in their friendships than their non-autistic peers. Petrina et al. (2014) found that autistic children often use words associated with companionship to describe their friendships. In comparison, non-autistic children tend to provide fuller descriptions of the features of their friendships, describing aspects reflecting other common characteristics of friendships such as caring and validation, intimate exchange of information, helping behaviours, conflict and conflict resolution (Parker & Asher, 1993). In another study, Kuo, Orsmond, Cohn, and Coster (2011) found that autistic adolescents and their parents agreed on the characteristics of their friendships. Identified friends tended to be the same gender, and many were younger than the autistic child, although this gap was not usually greater than one year. The researchers in this study did not find that autistic children with lower skill levels had less friends than those with higher skills. Autistic adolescents and their parents did differ in their perception of the reciprocal nature of the friendship with autistic adolescents perceiving more reciprocity in their friendships than their parents.

In a recent study examining the friendships of autistic secondary students, O'Hagan and Hebron (2017) found that parents disagreed with their autistic teenagers about the importance of different friendship qualities. The researchers concluded that this was due to the different way parents viewed friendships. Whereas the adolescents felt engaging together in shared interests was a key quality of friendships, their parents felt that intimacy was a more important feature of friendships, which was not represented in their child's friendships. Interestingly, the adolescents in this study all nominated other students in the special education program as their friends, rather than peers in the regular education program. In another study, Petrina, Carter, Stephenson, and Sweller (2016) compared the friendships of autistic children both with other autistic children and with non-autistic peers. They found that the majority of friendships were reciprocated. However, autistic children differed significantly from their non-autistic peers in their description of the quality of their friendships, particularly in the areas of conflict resolution and intimate exchange. This was reflected in the lower numbers of best friendships reported by autistic children. Best friendships inherently involve disclosure of more intimate information such as an exchange of secrets. A failure to engage in these types of behaviours may inhibit the development of closer relationships.

Researchers have also explored the different types of interactions and relationships which autistic children develop with their peers. Chamberlain et al. (2007) examined the social networks of elementary school children. They found that autistic children experienced lower centrality in social networks, as well as lower rates of social acceptance, companionship and reciprocity with peers. Students' level of involvement with peers varied considerably. Some autistic students were described as being at the centre of social networks, while others were found to be very isolated. Interestingly, participants' perception of loneliness did not correspond to their involvement in social networks. The researchers concluded that autistic children may not always be aware of their status with peers. In a similar study, Kasari et al.

(2011) measured the involvement of autistic children in social networks in inclusive schools. They found that 20% of the children had a high network status and reciprocated friendships, but the remaining 80% were more often on the periphery of social networks and had fewer friendships.

A few researchers have examined the degree to which autistic children are satisfied with their friendships. Calder, Hill and Pellicano (2013) found that most autistic children they interviewed reported being satisfied with their friendships, although they did identify fewer friends than their non-autistic peers. Findings also indicated that social motivation varied among the children in this study, with parents and teachers reporting this as a significant factor in whether the child had friends or not. Similarly, Petrina et al. (2016) examined the friendship satisfaction of both autistic children and their nominated friends. Both groups reported high levels of agreement regarding their satisfaction with the relationship. Moreover, levels of satisfaction were no different for autistic or non-autistic peers. Comparatively, Chamberlain et al. (2007) reported that although autistic children reported less companionships and reciprocity in their relationships, they did not report higher levels of loneliness than their non-autistic peers.

Age has been linked to friendship, with friendship numbers decreasing as autistic individuals move into adulthood (Orsmond et al., 2004). In a recent review of studies examining outcomes for autistic adults (Howlin & Moss, 2012), only a quarter of participants reported having at least one friend, and even fewer (15%) were in a long-term romantic relationship. A comprehensive study conducted by Costley et al. (2016) is even more revealing. In this research, 300 autistic adults, 165 parents and 20 service providers contributed information and data about the lived experiences of autistic adults in Australia. Many of the autistic adults in this study related happy experiences in their childhood, which were often associated with friendships and social interactions with peers. Unfortunately, less than 50% reported they currently had any friends, and many parents felt their children had not received the support needed to make social connections with others. Over 30% of autistic adults stated they needed support to access social opportunities including social groups and interest groups. Even more troubling, 70% of adults and 75% of parents reported their child had experienced isolation and bullying earlier in life, which continued to impact them in their adult years. Others had less traumatic experiences, but most relayed a feeling that they never quite fit in.

In another study (Causton-Theoharis et al., 2009), autistic adults discussed the loneliness they often felt and related their difficulties with "navigating the world of people" (p. 87). Their narratives revealed these challenges were related to several factors including: a need for predictability, communication and social disorientation, atypical responses to sensory information, intense interests and having to work to engage socially and withdrawing and using imagination as a substitute for interaction. The last was a particularly surprising finding as adults discussed their attempts to create their own social partners when faced with the difficulty and frustration of dealing with others. Similarly, (Webster & Garvis, 2017a, b) autistic men and women who considered themselves successful in many aspects discussed the difficulties they had experienced in their social lives, finding this was the area in their lives where they felt the least confident or successful. As one man related:

> The technical side is easy for me. I've been grateful that I've got a good IQ and all my inventions and ideas and that just come to me. I don't really have to, all I have to do is engage in my mind and … I wake up in the morning and the ideas come to me. So, all the challenges have been dealing with people and learning the skills, the social skills to be able to engage with other people. (Perry)

Historically, autism is diagnosed in boys at four times the rate of girls (Werling & Geschwind, 2013). Recently there has been a large amount of interest in the differences between autistic males and females and the ways that specific characteristics and experiences are unique to each gender. As with the research on social interactions and friendships in the non-autistic population, researchers have found differences in the social relationships and friendships of autistic males and females. Kuo et al. (2011) found that autistic boys and their friends spent more time on activities such as video games, whereas autistic girls were more likely to have conversations with their friends. Moreover, some evidence suggests that autistic girls may demonstrate greater levels of social and communication skills and awareness than autistic boys (Head, McGillivray, & Stokes, 2014), although they still exhibit lower skills in these areas than their non-autistic female peers. Other researchers have found differences in sociability of autistic girls and boys, with boys exhibiting lower social motivation and friendship quality (Sedgewick et al., 2016). In addition, autistic boys rated their friendships as having less intimacy than autistic girls, while girls reported lower levels of conflict, but experienced higher levels of relational aggression, such as being excluded and having their friends stolen. The researchers concluded that the girls' friendships were more like those of their non-autistic peers than they were similar to the friendships of autistic boys.

In an effort to determine if autistic girls had social expectations similar to those of their non-autistic female peers, Vine Foggo and Webster (2017) interviewed seven adolescent autistic girls about their social experiences. Participants revealed that they enjoyed spending time with female peers and that they engaged in activities typical to teenage girls, such as going shopping or to a party. They also indicated that these experiences were stressful for them, particularly when they involved interacting with a group of peers. The girls found that spending time on activities they enjoyed, such as reading or drawing, helped them to be able to cope with the demands of complex social interactions. In contrast to research conducted primarily with males (Knott et al., 2006), the girls in this study appeared to have a good understanding of what other girls liked to do, although they were more hesitant in describing what their peers thought of them. Overall, they felt that the benefits of having friends far outweighed the difficulties they encountered.

In contrast, Daniel and Billingsley (2010) found that adolescent autistic boys reported that one of their primary issues was establishing friendships and felt that sharing interests was extremely important in friendships. Only half of the boys in this study had stable friendships. This is in contrast to the girls in the study conducted by Vine Foggo and Webster (2017) in which all of the girls reported having at least one friend. Similarly, research conducted by Webster and Garvis (2017a) found that autistic men and women demonstrated a number of differences in their social relationships. When asked what had helped them to achieve success in their lives, the women often talked about a friend or colleague who had helped them to believe in themselves. In comparison, the men were extremely hesitant to say that friends or others had helped them to achieve. Rather, they indicated that they felt they had to succeed through their own efforts. They mostly talked about friends as someone they shared activities with, like sports or other activities, whereas the women discussed the emotional connection they had with their friends. These findings indicate that autistic men and women may have different views regarding the roles that peers and social relationships play in their lives.

Research clearly indicates that autistic children and adults do desire social interactions and friendships but may experience challenges with social navigation and negotiation. This may result in them becoming frustrated and isolated. Unfortunately, the opportunities for interaction and development of friendships appear to decrease as autistic adolescents move into adulthood and lose the structure and access to peers they may get in school or other community activities. Thus, research is needed to determine the type of supports that will enable autistic adults to make and maintain social relationships and friendships in which they can explore their shared interests and enjoy mutual engagement and affection.

9.3 The Impact

Although the impact of the “don’t want friends” myth has been more understated than that of other myths, such as the “vaccination causes autism” myth, this myth has still had a significant impact on the lives of both autistic children and adults. For children, the primary impact of this myth has been the focus on interventions to develop their social skills, rather than finding ways to support them in social relationships. Researchers have repeatedly found that having good social skills does not necessarily result in having friends (Finke, 2016; Webster & Carter, 2010). For example, parents in a study conducted by Petrina, Carter, and Stephenson (2015) rated development of social and emotional skills as important as, or more important than, developing friendships. This is despite research that demonstrates that having good social skills does not necessarily result in having friends (Finke; Webster & Carter). Moreover, interventions have concentrated on friendship difficulties demonstrated by autistic children, rather than finding ways to develop mutual understanding between autistic children and their peers. Thus, it can be argued that the focus on developing skills for friendship is often based on a neurotypical conceptualisation of friendship. As research indicates that autistic individuals may have different perceptions of, and needs from, their social relationships and friends, the focus on “typical” friendships may prevent them from developing the types of relationships that are most meaningful to them.

Previous research has indicated that autistic individuals understand and can describe friendships, but often do not include some of the same qualities as their peers (Bauminger et al., 2004; Petrina et al., 2014). Most noticeably they do not often talk about behaviours associated with intimacy or reciprocity of friends (Kuo et al., 2011). Whether or not this is a barrier to friendship has yet to be explored. Some research indicates it is not a barrier, as autistic individuals in these studies (Chamberlain et al., 2007; Petrina et al., 2016) have reported that they have some stable friendships. Overall, studies do suggest that autistic children and adolescents have less friends than their neurotypical peers. This is particularly noticeable for boys who have reported difficulty with making friends (Daniel & Billingsley, 2010). In addition, boys generally exhibit lower social communication skills than girls (Head et al., 2014), which may prevent them from engaging in the required exchange of information in order to develop deeper friendships. Girls, on the other hand, report more difficulty with navigating conflict and understanding how peers perceive them (Vine Foggo & Webster, 2017). This has led them to take on the role of peacekeeper in an effort to diminish conflict, sometimes at the cost of their own preferences and satisfaction, which also provides a threat to the reciprocity of the relationship. Together, these findings suggest that supporting the dynamic between the individual and their peer is critical to the formation and maintenance of friendships.

Friendship is inherently a mutual construct involving the actions and emotions of both people, not just in isolation, but as they engage and respond to the other person. To date, social skills interventions have primarily been directed solely at the autistic child. This is possibly attributable to the association of social skills with the deficits in social communication that must be present for an individual to receive a diagnosis of ASD. Social skills interventions include social skills groups, social stories, video modelling, peer-mediated interventions and behavioural interventions, all of which are designed to increase the social skills that are believed to prevent autistics from successfully interacting with others (Finke, 2016). They fail, however, to address the core skills that are involved in developing relationships, which at their very essence involve mutuality of behaviours demonstrated by both parties. Not only must the autistic individual be able to interpret their peer's social cues, but the peer must be able to interpret and respond to the social communication of the autistic individual, which may appear quite different in form than "typical" social communication. For example, to engage in successful interactions, individuals and peers must be able to communicate using a shared system of verbal and non-verbal structures. Autistic individuals may have difficulty understanding a peer's use of colloquialisms, whereas the peer may have difficulty interpreting the body language of the autistic child. Milton (2012) refers to this as the double empathy problem. Unless this is addressed, the mutual exchange of information and deeper understanding needed for long-lasting relationships will not occur.

The second impact of the "don't want friends" myth is the limited amount of research and practice that has focused on providing opportunities for autistic individuals to find and engage with peers around a shared interest. Shared interest has been identified as the first step to forming friendships (Newcomb & Bagwell, 1996). Researchers have also demonstrated that for autistic individuals, shared interests provide an essential foundation for connecting with peers (Bauminger & Shulman, 2003; Howard et al., 2006). This is particularly true for boys, for whom shared interests often facilitate mutual engagement and enjoyment of activities (Daniel & Billingsley, 2010). Moreover, researchers have found that when individuals share an interest and are motivated to interact with that peer, they will often develop the social awareness and social skills they need to be successful (Bauminger et al., 2008). Interventions that bring individuals together over a shared hobby have been particularly effective in enabling autistic children to develop the social communication skills needed in social environments. More importantly, these activities provide peers with a context to develop the skills they need to successfully engage and communicate with their autistic peers. These skills are promoted when social situations are set up that allow autistic children and their peers to self-select whom and what they will do together. This is in contrast to traditional social skills groups in which the facilitator determines the group and the activity.

Not only do autistic individuals and their peers need the opportunity to connect over shared interests, they also need structure and support in order to negotiate the social dynamics of these activities and overcome the double empathy problem. Due to differences in their social communication skills and development of theory of mind, many autistic individuals may experience challenges in the initial stages of establishing friendships. Over time, these difficulties can multiply and become more complex, eroding the confidence of the autistic child or adult and preventing them from initiating contact with others (Daniel & Billingsley, 2010). With a little guidance, however, autistic children and their peers can work through these challenges. The integrated playgroup approach developed by Wolfberg (2009) has been effective in providing different levels of structure and support to autistic children and peers via mutually rewarding activities. This approach has led to increased social skills and friendships between autistic children and their peers in primary and high school settings (Wolfberg et al., 2012). School is a natural place to provide opportunities and support for interaction. Unfortunately, researchers indicate that teachers may not be aware of the friendships of children with disabilities, have limited time to promote interactions or lack skills to provide the type of support and learning required (Barned, Knapp, & Neuharth-Pritchett, 2011). Chang et al. (2016) found that early childhood teachers used few strategies to support interactions and friendships between autistic children and their peers, relying primarily on behavioural regulation. These teachers rarely engaged in behaviour or classroom management and did not provide cues for social interaction. Thus, autistic children are at risk of becoming socially isolated, even in situations such as school, where they regularly encounter several peers who may share their interests.

Although it could be argued that autistic children have lacked appropriate support to facilitate meaningful relationships, the impact of the "don't want friends" myth for adults has been that their friendship needs have been virtually ignored (Costley et al., 2016; Mazurek, 2014). Autistic adults are even more likely to be socially isolated, as they may not have a regular activity like school to bring them into contact with peers. Furthermore, high unemployment and underemployment rates mean that these individuals are more likely to spend large amounts of time by themselves or with family members (Eaves & Ho, 2008; Howlin & Magiati, 2017). Becoming isolated may contribute to anxiety and depression, which are estimated to have high comorbidity rates for autistic adults (Croen et al., 2015). In general, priorities for autistic adults have primarily focused on support related to employment or independent living. As Vermeulen (2014) points out, however, higher employment and independence may not equate to happiness and well-being if the person is isolated from others. The high rates of anxiety and depression reported by autistic adults suggest that a different approach is needed. Instead of focusing solely on skill development, helping autistic adults to find meaningful connections with others in their community may provide them with natural supports and pathways to employment and traditional measures of success.

Further attention is needed to ascertain the strategies and supports that will build the self-efficacy of autistic adults to connect with peers in adult environments. This is particularly important as many of these environments would entail new social dynamics and requirements that are not formally acknowledged, but are expected. As many autistic adults report their foremost challenges tend to involve navigating the complexities of social interaction, this might result in high levels of anxiety and cause them to withdraw or retreat into themselves. For example, an autistic male might want to try a social club to meet girls but might be intimidated by what he perceives are unspoken rules that others understand, but he does not. After going one time, he might give up and stay home. The "don't want friends" myth has perpetuated the image of the autistic adult as choosing to be alone and thus provides a justification for not providing support to those autistic adults who desire relationships but need support and guidance to develop meaningful connections and relationships.

Friendship has been linked to several positive outcomes and provides vital sources of support for children and adults as they manage transitions and encounter new challenges throughout their lives. A final impact of the "don't want friends" myth is that it has not only resulted in a lack of support for social interactions, it has prevented autistic children and adults from obtaining a vital source of support and experiences that would help them to deal with negative social experiences, solve problems and advocate for themselves. Friendships serve a number of functions, including providing individuals with affection, intimacy, trust and companionship (Bauminger et al., 2004). Although some autistic individuals have reported they are socially isolated and bullied by peers (Humphrey & Symes, 2010), others have reported that their friends accept them and provide them with a key source of support that helps them to navigate social situations and to believe in themselves (Humphrey & Lewis, 2008; Webster & Garvis, 2017a). Researchers have also found that friendships can increase the feelings of self-worth of autistic children and adolescents (Bauminger et al., 2004) and can be an effective source of protection and emotional stability as they move through life (Sreckovic, Hume, & Able, 2017). More importantly, developing social relationships can help them to feel a sense of belonging and affiliation with their community, which has been identified as a core component of well-being and happiness (Sebastian, Blakemore, & Charman 2009; Vermeulen, 2014)

9.4 The Future

Current research indicates that autistic children and adults have less friends (Chamberlain et al., 2007; Petrina et al., 2016) than their non-autistic peers and are more likely to be socially isolated (Orsmond, Shattuck, Cooper, Sterzing, & Anderson, 2013) and to have relationships that have a lasting negative impact (Humphrey & Symes, 2010; Sebastian et al., 2009). These challenges have often been attributed to the autistic individual's deficits in social and communication, which has resulted in a large amount of attention on support and interventions to develop these skills. This approach has had limited success in increasing the social relationships of autistic individuals, particularly as they move into adulthood. To mitigate the impact of the "don't want friends" myth, an alternative perspective on the social lives of autistic individuals is needed, which focuses on social inclusion rather than social deficits. Transforming this perspective will shift the focus of support from the current model which asks, "how can we support this individual to develop the skills they need to successfully interact with others?", to a new approach, which is based on the question, "what do autistic individuals need so that they, and their peers, can connect and form relationships?" This change of perspective places the focus of support not just on the autistic individual, but on developing the capacity of peers and the community to understand their perspective and style of social communication in order to connect with autistic individuals in meaningful and equitable ways.

Gottman (1983) identified the stages that individuals go through when they form friendships. First, they meet and connect over shared interests, and then they progress to exchanging information at increasingly intimate levels. They also engage in conflict and learn to negotiate and resolve these issues. As Finke (2016) contends, friendship is a mutual relationship, which involves the active engagement of two people. Strategies are needed that will support autistic individuals and their peers as they move through the different stages of friendship development. To support this process, Finke (2016) suggests that three factors should be considered: equal status, equally motivating and authentic opportunities for interaction and planning for frequent and repeated interaction within a mutually preferred activity.

Equal status refers to ensuring that both participants in a relationship are equal participants in the interaction. This involves removing any barriers, such as preconceived notions, that may prevent the peer from seeing the autistic individual as someone who can contribute equally to the relationship. Programs such as peer buddy programs, although well intentioned, may actually prevent friendships as they establish an inequity in relationships whereby one individual is always perceived as receiving help from the other. Although helping has been identified as a key quality in friendships (Parker & Asher, 1993), both parties have to have opportunities to help the other. For example, working together on projects which build on the autistic individual's special interest would enable peers to see them offer key information they might otherwise not have. Similarly, the peer might bring knowledge about how best to communicate this information to others. By building on each other's strengths, both the peer and the autistic child would contribute equally, although differently, and would help the other.

Another important factor in supporting the mutual equality of both parties is to support mutual communication and empathy. As Milton (2012) suggests, it is important to address the double empathy problem in order to support meaningful connections between autistic individuals and their peers. Successful programs incorporate skill development in multiple areas of social communication, such as perspective taking, responding to teasing, conversation skills and understanding and expressing emotions (Petrina et al., 2014). These still may not result in desired outcomes if individuals have different expectations about the nature of friendships. In order to help autistic children and adults to develop more intimate and sustained friendships, support needs to be in place to help both parties to understand the expectations of the other and to engage in a more intimate exchange of information.

Motivation for friends is another important variable in friendship intervention (Finke, 2016). To support friendships, research (Daniel & Billingsley, 2010) has indicated that providing opportunities for autistic individuals to connect with their peers over shared interests is critical. Even more important is recognition by the community that friendships do not have to follow a typical pattern and can take many different forms. Brownlow, Bertilsdotter Rosqvist, and O'Dell, (2015) argue that facilitating relationships for autistic children and adults necessitates a broader conceptualisation of friendship. These include non-traditional interactions such as social networking, which allow autistic individuals to express themselves in their own way and time. These researchers also contend that although these relationships look different, they may offer many of the same benefits for the individuals involved. Although research is limited, a few studies have begun to explore the unique social worlds of autistic adolescents and adults. In one study, Mazurek (2013) examined the social media use of 108 autistic adults, correlating their engagement in these forums with measures of friendship and loneliness. Findings revealed that most adults used social media to connect with others and that those who utilised social media had more close friends. In contrast, those individuals who had more friends outside of social media were more likely to report lower levels of loneliness. This suggests that connections through social media may serve a purpose but may not be sufficient in addressing all of the social and emotional needs of autistic adults. However, it is possible that alternative forms of connecting with others could serve as the initial basis of friendships, which if supported by frequent opportunities for deeper engagement could develop into more meaningful and long-lasting relationships. This may be a particularly helpful approach for autistic adults who often have limited access to social environments after they leave school.

Finke's (2016) final factor in supporting friendships is planning for repeated opportunities for interaction. Repeated interactions provide the necessary opportunity and support that individuals need to engage with peers for sustained periods during which they build trust to share more intimate information. As they spend more time with each other, they also begin to experience conflict and to find ways to resolve these differences. These experiences are critical to transmute casual friendships into deeper relationships. In addition, to the opportunity to engage in repeated social interactions with peers, autistic children and adults may require additional mentoring or guidance to navigate these steps. For instance, autistic children often engage in somewhat circumspective conversations and may need to be coached to provide more meaningful information to peers not just about the activity but about their thoughts and feelings. Autistic children may not realise this is expected in social situations. Similarly, the peer may need some coaching to identify and respond to the different non-verbal communication of the autistic child such as not expecting the child to look directly at them when they are talking.

Conflict resolution has been cited as a particular area of difficulty (Vine Foggo & Webster, 2017) with autistic girls indicating they would rather take the blame than experience conflict. Providing ideas to autistic adolescents and peers about mediating conflict in relationships might help them to understand that this is a normal part of developing lasting friendships and provide them with strategies they can use to deal with these differences when they occur. Support for autistic adults may involve engaging them in more reflective and problem-solving strategies, which will also support them to develop strategies for future social interactions. For example, Vine Foggo and Webster (2017) suggest that if given time on their own to de-stress, autistic females were better able to navigate more complex group situations. Additionally, autistic females and males may need different types of support with research, indicating that social expectations may be different for males and females and thus pose different challenges (Webster & Garvis, 2017a). Males tend to need more support to accept help from others (Webster & Garvis, 2017b), whereas females are more hesitant to express their own desires when with peers (Vine Foggo & Webster, 2017).

Any development of a new approach to support should involve the input and ideas of autistic people about the strategies and supports they feel will be most effective in helping them to develop sustainable relationships. This may mean developing and supporting autistic individuals to engage in alternative social avenues, such as social media, or may mean empowering them to create new forums for social interaction. Working with autistic adolescents and adults will facilitate the creation of supports that allow them to connect with others in their own way, rather than to conform to traditional notions of friendships. Even more importantly, gaining their perspectives will provide insights necessary to create environments where autistic individuals are included in social networks throughout the community and valued for the unique contributions they can offer for others in the community.

9.5 Conclusion

The perception of autistic individuals as social isolates, who avoid interacting with others, is a myth that has developed and strengthened over time. In reality, however, research indicates that autistic individuals desire and benefit from social interactions and friendships. Despite this, autistic individuals often report fewer opportunities to engage with peers and experience higher levels of loneliness than their non-autistic peers, particularly as they mature to adulthood. Although these individuals may have friendships that do not fit traditional definitions, they are still meaningful and offer many benefits to both parties. Typically, strategies to support friendship have focused on remediating and improving the perceived social skill deficits of autistic individuals. Not only has this approach not resulted in significantly increasing friendships, but it has failed to take into account the reciprocal nature of social relationships. Thus, alternative approaches are needed, which focus on creating opportunities for autistic children and adults to connect with peers through shared interests and which provides support for both parties to navigate the complexities of the social dynamic. This would include supporting them to engage in mutual social communication behaviours to share more intimate information and work through differences and conflicts. An alternative future will empower autistic individuals to create connections that are meaningful and relevant to them and which provide social–emotional benefit and enjoyment to them and their peers. It is this transformation of perspective that will truly mitigate the impact of the myth that autistic people do not want friends.

References

American Psychiatric Association. (2013). *Diagnostic and statistical manual of mental disorders—Fifth edition*. Washington, DC: American Psychiatric Publishing.

Asperger, H. (1944). Die "Autistischen Psychopathen" im Kindesalter. *Archiv für psychiatrie und nervenkrankheiten, 117*(1), 76–136.

Aylott, J. (2000). Understanding children with autism: Exploding the myths. *British Journal of Nursing, 9*(2), 779–784. https://doi.org/10.12968/bjon.2000.9.12.6248.

Barned, N. E., Knapp, N. F., & Neuharth-Pritchett, S. (2011). Knowledge and attitudes of early childhood preservice teachers regarding the inclusion of children with autism spectrum disorder. *Journal of Early Childhood Teacher Education, 32*(4), 302–321. https://doi.org/10.1080/10901027.2011.622235.

Bauminger, N., & Shulman, C. (2003). The development and maintenance of friendship in high-functioning children with autism. *Autism, 7*(1), 81–97. https://doi.org/10.1177/1362361303007001007.

Bauminger, N., Shulman, C., & Agam, G. (2004). The link between perceptions of self and of social relationships in high-functioning children with autism. *Journal of Developmental and Physical Disabilities, 16*(2), 193–214. https://doi.org/10.1023/b:jodd.0000026616.24896.c8.

Bauminger, N., Solomon, M., Aviezer, A., Heung, K., Gazit, L., Brown, J., et al. (2008). Children with autism and their friends: A multidimensional study of friendship in high-functioning autism spectrum disorder. *Journal of Abnormal Child Psychology, 36*(2), 135–150. https://doi.org/10.1007/s10802-007-9156-x.

Broderick, A. A., & Ne'eman, A. (2008). Autism as metaphor: Narrative and counter-narrative. *International Journal of Inclusive Education, 12*(5–6), 459–476. https://doi.org/10.1080/13603110802377490.

Brownlow, C., Bertilsdotter Rosqvist, H., & O'Dell, L. (2015). Exploring the potential for social networking among people with autism: Challenging dominant ideas of 'friendship'. *Scandinavian Journal of Disability Research, 17*(2), 188–193. https://doi.org/10.1080/15017419.2013.859174.

Bukowski, W. M., Hoza, B., & Boivin, M. (1994). Measuring friendship quality during pre and early adolescence: The development and psychometric properties of the friendship qualities scale. *Journal of Social and Personal Relationships, 11*(3), 471–484. https://doi.org/10.1177/0265407594113011.

Calder, L., Hill, V., & Pellicano, E. (2013). 'Sometimes I want to play by myself': Understanding what friendship means to children with autism in mainstream primary schools. *Autism, 17*(3), 296–316. https://doi.org/10.1177/1362361312467866.

Causton-Theoharis, J., Ashby, C., & Cosier, M. (2009). Islands of loneliness: Exploring social interaction through the autobiographies of individuals with autism. *Journal of Intellectual and Developmental Disability, 47*(2), 84–96. https://doi.org/10.1352/1934-9556-47.2.84.

Chamberlain, B., Kasari, C., & Rotheram-Fuller, E. (2007). Involvement or isolation? The social networks of children with autism in regular classrooms. *Journal of Autism and Developmental Disorders, 37*(2), 230–242. https://doi.org/10.1007/s10803-006-0164-4.

Chang, Y. C., Shih, W., & Kasari, C. (2016). Friendships in preschool children with autism spectrum disorder: What holds them back, child characteristics or teacher behavior? *Autism, 20*(1), 65–74. https://doi.org/10.1177/1362361314567761.

Cook, A., Ogden, J., & Winstone, N. (2018). Friendship motivations, challenges and the role of masking for girls with autism in contrasting school settings. *European Journal of Special Needs Education, 33*(3), 302–315. https://doi.org/10.1080/08856257.2017.1312797.

Costley, D., Baldwin, S., & Bruck, S. (2016). *Shining a light on the autism spectrum: Experiences and aspirations of adults*. New York: Taylor & Francis.

Croen, L. A., Zerbo, O., Qian, Y., Massolo, M. L., Rich, S., Sidney, S., et al. (2015). The health status of adults on the autism spectrum. *Autism, 19*(7), 814–823. https://doi.org/10.1177/1362361315577517.

Daniel, L. S., & Billingsley, B. S. (2010). What boys with an autism spectrum disorder say about establishing and maintaining friendships. *Focus on Autism and Other Developmental Disabilities, 25*(4), 220–229. https://doi.org/10.1177/1088357610378290.

Davidson, J. (2008). 'In a World of her Own…': Re-presenting alienation and emotion in the lives and writings of women with autism. *Gender, Place & Culture, 14*(6), 659–677. https://doi.org/10.1080/09663690701659135.

Eaves, L. C., & Ho, H. H. (2008). Young adult outcomes of autism spectrum disorders. *Journal of Autism and Developmental Disorders, 38*(4), 739–747. https://doi.org/10.1007/s10803-007-0441-x.

Finke, E. H. (2016). Friendship: Operationalizing the intangible to improve friendship-based outcomes for individuals with autism spectrum disorder. *American Journal of Speech-Language Pathology, 25*(4), 654–663. https://doi.org/10.1044/2016_ajslp-15-0042.

Frith, U. (2003). *Autism: Explaining the enigma* (2nd ed.). Malden, MA; Oxford: Blackwell.

Gottman, J. M. (1983). How children become friends. *Monographs for the Society for Research in Child Development, 48*(3), 1–82.

Greydanus, D. E., & Toledo-Pereyra, L. H. (2012). Historical perspectives on autism: Its past record of discovery and its present state of solipsism, skepticism, and sorrowful suspicion. *Pediatric Clinics of North America, 59*(1), 1–11. https://doi.org/10.1016/j.pcl.2011.10.004.

Grinker, R. R. (2010). Commentary: On being autistic, and social. *Journal of the Society for Psychological Anthropology, 38*(1), 172–178. https://doi.org/10.1111/j.1548-1352.2009.01087.x.

Head, A. M., McGillivray, J. A., & Stokes, M. A. (2014). Gender differences in emotionality and sociability in chidlren with autism spectrum disorders. *Molecular Autism, 5*(19). https://doi.org/10.1186/2040-2392-5-19.

Holton, A. E. (2013). What's wrong with Max? Parenthood and the portrayal of autism spectrum disorders. *Journal of Communication Inquiry, 37*(1), 45–63. https://doi.org/10.1177/0196859912472507.

Holton, A. E., Farrell, L. C., & Fudge, J. L. (2014). A threatening space?: Stigmatization and the framing of autism in the news. *Communication Studies, 65*(2), 189–207. https://doi.org/10.1080/10510974.2013.855642.

Howard, B., Cohn, E., & Orsmond, G. I. (2006). Understanding and negotiating friendships: Perspectives from an adolescent with Asperger syndrome. *Autism, 10*(6), 619–627. https://doi.org/10.1177/1362361306068508.

Howes, C. (1983). Patterns of friendship. *Child Development, 54,* 1041–1053.

Howes, C. (1996). The earliest friendships. In W. M. Bukowski, A. F. Newcomb, & W. W. Hartup (Eds.), *The company they keep: Friendship in childhood and adolescence* (pp. 66–86). New York: Cambridge University Press.

Howlin, P., & Magiati, I. (2017). Autism spectrum disorder: Outcomes in adulthood. *Current Opinion in Psychiatry, 30*(2), 69–76. https://doi.org/10.1097/yco.0000000000000308.

Howlin, P., & Moss, P. (2012). Adults with autism spectrum disorders. *Canadian Journal of Psychiatry, 57*(5), 275–283. https://doi.org/10.1177/070674371205700502.

Humphrey, N., & Lewis, S. (2008). 'Make me normal': The views and experiences of pupils on the autistic spectrum in mainstream secondary schools. *Autism, 12*(1), 23–46. https://doi.org/10.1177/1362361307085267.

Humphrey, N., & Symes, W. (2010). Perceptions of social support and experience of bullying among pupils with autistic spectrum disorders in mainstream secondary schools. *European Journal of Special Needs Education, 25*(1), 77–91. https://doi.org/10.1080/08856250903450855.

John, R., Knott, F. J., & Harvey, K. N. (2018). Myths about autism: An exploratory study using focus groups. *Autism, 22*(7), 845–854. https://doi.org/10.1177/1362361317714990.

Kanner, L. (1943). Autistic disturbances of affective contact. *Nervous Child, 2*(3), 217–250.

Kasari, C., Locke, J., Gulsrud, A., & Rotheram-Fuller, E. (2011). Social networks and friendships at school: Comparing children with and without ASD. *Journal of Autism and Developmental Disorders, 41*(5), 533–544. https://doi.org/10.1007/s10803-010-1076-x.

Knott, F., Dunlop, A. W., & Mackay, T. (2006). Living with ASD: How do children and their parents assess their difficulties with social interaction and understanding? *Autism, 10*(6), 609–617. https://doi.org/10.1177/1362361306068510.

Kuo, M. H., Orsmond, G. I., Cohn, E. S., & Coster, W. J. (2011). Friendship characteristics and activity patterns of adolescents with an autism spectrum disorder. *Autism, 17*(4), 481–500. https://doi.org/10.1177/1362361311416380.

Ladd, G. W. (1988). Friendship patterns and peer status during early and middle childhood. *Development and Behavioral Pediatrics, 9*(4), 229–238. https://doi.org/10.1097/00004703-198808000-00010.

Mazurek, M. O. (2013). Social media use among adults with autism spectrum disorders. *Computers in Human Behavior, 29*(4), 1709–1714. https://doi.org/10.1016/j.chb.2013.02.004.

Mazurek, M. O. (2014). Loneliness, friendship, and well-being in adults with autism spectrum disorders. *Autism, 18*(3), 223–232. https://doi.org/10.1177/1362361312474121.

Meyer, L. H., Minondo, S., Fisher, M., Larson, M. J., Dunmore, S., Black, J. W., et al. (1998). Frames of friendship: Social relationships among adolescents with diverse abilities. In L. H. Meyer, H.-S. Park, M. Grenot-Scheyer, I. S. Schwartz, & B. Harry (Eds.), *Making friends: The influences of culture and development* (pp. 189–221). Baltimore: Paul H. Brookes.

Milton, D. E. M. (2012). On the ontological status of autism: The 'double empathy problem'. *Disability & Society, 27*(6), 883–887. https://doi.org/10.1080/09687599.2012.710008.

Müller, E., Schuler, A., & Yates, G. B. (2008). Social challenges and supports from the perspective of individuals with Asperger syndrome and other autism spectrum disabilities. *Autism, 12*(2), 173–190. https://doi.org/10.1177/1362361307086664.

Newcomb, A. F., & Bagwell, C. L. (1996). The developmental significance of children's friendship relations. In W. M. Bukowski, A. F. Newcomb, & W. W. Hartup (Eds.), *The company they keep: Friendship in childhood and adolescence* (pp. 289–321). New York: Cambridge University Press.

O'Hagan, S., & Hebron, J. (2017). Perceptions of friendship among adolescents with autism spectrum conditions in a mainstream high school resource provision. *European Journal of Special Needs Education, 32*(3), 314–328. https://doi.org/10.1080/08856257.2016.1223441.

Orsmond, G. I., Krauss, M. W., & Seltzer, M. M. (2004). Peer relationships and social and recreational activities among adolescents and adults with autism. *Journal of Autism and Developmental Disorders, 34*(3), 245–256. https://doi.org/10.1023/b:jadd.0000029547.96610.df.

Orsmond, G. I., Shattuck, P. T., Cooper, B. P., Sterzing, P. R., & Anderson, K. A. (2013). Social participation among young adults with an autism spectrum disorder. *Journal of Autism and Developmental Disorders, 43*(11), 2710–2719. https://doi.org/10.1007/s10803-013-1833-8.

Parker, J. G., & Asher, S. R. (1993). Friendship and friendship quality in middle childhood: Links with peer group acceptance and feelings of loneliness and social dissatisfaction. *Developmental Psychology, 29,* 611–621. https://doi.org/10.1037/0012-1649.29.4.611.

Petrina, N., Carter, M., & Stephenson, J. (2014). The nature of friendship in children with autism spectrum disorders: A systematic review. *Research in Autism Spectrum Disorders, 8*(2), 111–126. https://doi.org/10.1016/j.rasd.2013.10.016.

Petrina, N., Carter, M., & Stephenson, J. (2015). Parental perception of the importance of friendship and other outcome priorities in children with autism spectrum disorder. *European Journal of Special Needs Education, 30*(1), 61–74. https://doi.org/10.1080/08856257.2014.943566.

Petrina, N., Carter, M., Stephenson, J., & Sweller, N. (2016). Perceived friendship quality of children with autism spectrum disorder as compared to their peers in mixed and non-mixed dyads. *Journal of Autism and Developmental Disorders, 46*(4), 1334–1343. https://doi.org/10.1007/s10803-015-2673-5.

Rowley, E., Chandler, S., Baird, G., Simonoff, E., Pickles, A., Loucas, T., et al. (2012). The experience of friendship, victimization and bullying in children with an autism spectrum disorder: Associations with child characteristics and school placement. *Research in Autism Spectrum Disorders, 6*(3), 1126–1134. https://doi.org/10.1016/j.rasd.2012.03.004.

Sarrett, J. C. (2011). Trapped children: Popular images of children with autism in the 1960s and 2000s. *Journal of Medical Humanities, 32*(2), 141–153. https://doi.org/10.1007/s10912-010-9135-z.

Sebastian, C., Blakemore, S. J., & Charman, T. (2009). Reactions to ostracism in adolescents with autism spectrum conditions. *Journal of Autism and Developmental Disorders, 39*(8), 1122–1130. https://doi.org/10.1007/s10803-009-0725-4.

Sedgewick, F., Hill, V., Yates, R., Pickering, L., & Pellicano, E. (2016). Gender differences in the social motivation and friendship experiences of autistic and non-autistic adolescents. *Journal of Autism and Developmental Disorders, 46*(4), 1297–1306. https://doi.org/10.1007/s10803-015-2669-1.

Sreckovic, M. A., Hume, K., & Able, H. (2017). Examining the efficacy of peer network interventions on the social interactions of high school students with autism spectrum disorder. *Journal of Autism and Developmental Disorders, 47*(8), 2556–2574. https://doi.org/10.1007/s10803-017-3171-8.

Underwood, M. K. (2007). Introduction to the special issue gender and children's friendships: Do girls' and boys' friendships constitute different peer cultures, and what are the trade-offs for development? *Merrill-Palmer Quarterly, 53*(3), 319–324.

Vermeulen, P. (2014). The practice of promoting happiness in autism. *Promoting happiness and wellbeing in autism.* Birmingham: British Institute of Learning Difficulties.

Vincent, J., Potts, M., Fletcher, D., Hodges, S., Howells, J., Mitchell, A., … Ledger, T. (2016). 'I think autism is like running on Windows while everyone else is a Mac': Using a participatory action research approach with students on the autistic spectrum to rearticulate autism and the lived experience of university. *Educational Action Research, 25*(2), 300–315. https://doi.org/10.1080/09650792.2016.1153978.

Vine Foggo, R. S., & Webster, A. A. (2017). Understanding the social experiences of adolescent females on the autism spectrum. *Research in Autism Spectrum Disorders, 35*, 74–85. https://doi.org/10.1016/j.rasd.2016.11.006.

Webster, A. A., & Carter, M. (2010). Observations of relationships between children with developmental disabilities and peers in inclusive settings. *Special Education Perspectives, 19*(2), 7–23.

Webster, A. A., & Carter, M. (2012a). Characteristics of the closest relationships between children with developmental disabilities and peers in inclusive settings. *Australasian Journal of Special Education, 34*(01), 61–78. https://doi.org/10.1375/ajse.34.1.61.

Webster, A. A., & Carter, M. (2012b). A descriptive examination of the types of relationships formed between children with developmental disability and their closest peers in inclusive school settings. *Journal of Intellectual and Developmental Disability, 38*(1), 1–11. https://doi.org/10.3109/13668250.2012.743650.

Webster, A. A., & Carter, M. (2012c). Mutual liking, enjoyment, and shared interactions in the closest relationships between children with developmental disabilities and peers in inclusive school settings. *Journal of Developmental and Physical Disabilities, 25*(4), 373–393. https://doi.org/10.1007/s10882-012-9319-8.

Webster, A. A., & Garvis, S. (2017a). The importance of critical life moments: An explorative study of successful women with autism spectrum disorder. *Autism, 21*(6), 670–677. https://doi.org/10.1177/1362361316677719.

Webster, A. A., & Garvis, S. (2017b). *Creating success fo men on the autism spectrum: The role of identity and logic*. Paper presented at the Asia Pacific Autism Conference: Growing with Autism (7–9 September), Autism Spectrum Australia, Sydney, Australia.

Werling, D. M., & Geschwind, D. H. (2013). Sex differences in autism spectrum disorders. *Current Opinion in Neurology, 26*(2), 146–153. https://doi.org/10.1097/wco.0b013e32835ee548.

White, M. L., Smith, J. D., Smith, T. E. C., & Stodden, R. A. (2012). Autism spectrum disorders: Historical, legislative and current perspectives. In D. Zager, M. L. Wehmeyer, & R. L. Simpson (Eds.), *Educating students with autism spectrum disorders* (pp. 3–12). New York: Routledge.

Wolfberg, P., Bottema-Beutel, K., & DeWitt, M. (2012). Including children with autism in social and imaginary play with typical peers: Integrated play groups model. *American Journal of Play, 5*(1), 55.

Wolfberg, P. J. (2009). *Play and imagination in children with autism*. Overland Park, KS: Autism Asperger.

Chapter 10
Intimacy and Romance Across the Autism Spectrum: Unpacking the "Not Interested in Sex" Myth

Abstract Prior to the 1970s, it was a common misconception that autistic individuals were neither interested in, nor capable of, engaging in romantic and sexual relationships. It was thought that the core social difficulties frequently experienced by autistic adults had a positive correlation with asexuality. It is likely that some of these attitudes and assumptions came about because of a view of autistic individuals as childlike or socially immature. This chapter will explore the myth that autistic individuals are asexual, including related stereotypes regarding sexual and relationship behaviours. The current literature on and relationship preferences, engagement, and behaviours of autistic adolescents and adults will be reviewed, and the impact of current stereotypes on the sexual rights and knowledge of autistic individuals will be examined. Finally, an argument will be made for recognition of autistic sexuality as a difference rather than a deficit in which autistic adolescents and adults are seen as individuals with a range of preferences and needs who, if provided with information and support they require, will be able to connect with others in mutually beneficial relationships.

Keywords Asexuality · Autistic sexuality · Intimacy · Relationships Sex education · Sexual differences · Sexual stereotypes

For many people, forming romantic attachments and engaging in intimate relationships is a key part of their journey as they move through adolescence and into adulthood. For autistic adolescents and adults, a common misconception, or myth, is that they are asexual and are not interested in sexual or intimate relationships (MacKenzie, 2018). Conversely, another belief is that autistic adolescents and adults frequently engage in problematic sexual behaviours. This has led many parents and professionals to deny or ignore the sexuality of autistic individuals. This has resulted in a limited knowledge base about the sexuality and relationships of autistic individuals which has likely contributed to, and perpetuated, these myths. It is only recently that researchers have challenged this stereotype and have begun to explore the intimate relationships and sexuality of autistic individuals.

M. Bennett et al., *Life on the Autism Spectrum*,
https://doi.org/10.1007/978-981-13-3359-0_10

10.1 The Origins

The myth that autistic people are asexual and not interested in sex, like many other autism myths, cannot be linked to a specific origin, but has developed over time through a combination of influences. To understand the ways in which this myth has evolved, an examination of societal views regarding sexuality and disability is needed. Historically, sexuality and relationships among people with disability were generally regarded as taboo in many cultures (Koegel, Detar, Fox, & Koegel, 2014). This is partially due to the fact that in many cultures, and particularly before the advent of effective contraception, sexuality was for many synonymous with child rearing. Individuals diagnosed with autism and other disabilities were viewed as incapable of caring for themselves and requiring society to care for them in public and private facilities. Consequently, public concern was raised over the prospect of individuals with disability reproducing and creating further societal burden. Individuals with disability were also frequently believed to be sexual deviants, with abnormal sexual impulses and drives. At a time when sexual difference was not widely accepted, the sexuality of individuals with disability was not only discouraged, but sometimes was actively restricted (Saxe & Flanagan, 2013; Taylor Gomez, 2012). Those autistic individuals who lived more independently experienced barriers such as societal and social isolation and stigmatisation as sexual deviants (Gougeon, 2010).

In addition to fears regarding procreation, the need to protect vulnerable individuals was used as a reason for limiting the sexual rights of individuals with disability, including those with autism (Gougeon, 2010). This justification was underpinned by a perception of individuals with autism as perpetually childlike, and incapable of developing the social–emotional maturity to engage in intimate sexual relationships (Stevenson et al., 2011) and incapable of normal sexuality and relationships (Konstantareas & Lunsky, 1997). This was compounded by the overwhelming number of images that associated autism with childhood (Stevenson et al., 2011), a conceptual imagery that still dominates public displays and discourse. In an examination of public images of autism, Stevenson et al. found that 90% of fictional books, 95% of organisational websites and 68% of television and film programs depicted autism with the face or character of a child. Researchers have also concentrated primarily on researching issues experienced by autistic children. This was highlighted by Jang et al. (2014) who found that 70% of studies about autism published between 1994 and 2014, focused on children or adolescents. Stevenson et al. (2011) contend that the continued association of autism with childhood has the effect of silencing autistic adults by denying their existence. This also results in a disregard and discounting of adult needs such as the need for romance, intimate relationships and sex.

Parents may also perpetuate stereotypes denying their autistic child's sexuality by having an inability to see their children as future adults who are interested in sex and relationships. Early studies indicated that parents believed their autistic children were not capable of participating in mature sexual relationships (Ruble & Dalrymple, 1993). These parents were concerned that when their autistic children became adults, they would not be aware of socially appropriate sexual behaviours and viewed the potential sexuality of their child as a problem to be solved. In more recent years, parents have begun to recognise that sexuality may be a part of their child's adult life, but express apprehension and concern about the complexities of working through the difficulties of helping their child to navigate intimate relationships and sexual behaviours (Ballan, 2012; Nichols & Blakeley-Smith, 2009). These parents have reported that they struggle to communicate with their child about these topics. Given that research indicates parents of autistic children often experience high levels of daily stress in dealing with their child's needs and behaviours (Corcoran, Berry, & Hill, 2015), ignoring or unconsciously denying their child's sexuality may present them with a more manageable alternative in the short term.

Differences in social communication may have also contributed to the asexuality myth. Social communication deficits are part of the diagnostic criteria for autism spectrum disorder and can include difficulties in social–emotional reciprocity, non-verbal communication and developing and maintaining relationships (Wilson et al., 2013). Many autistic individuals experience difficulties in communicating with others, finding it particularly challenging to understand and utilise non-verbal communication associated with emotional interactions (Brewer et al., 2016). This may make it appear that they are unemotional or unresponsive to the emotions of others. However, just because autistic individuals cannot effectively express themselves does not mean that they are not interested in having intimate relationships. As the excerpt from the autistic magazine *Empowerment* indicates:

> It often happens that the professional world of doctors and psychologists reads people with autism/AS improperly. For example, they may believe that a person is indifferent to a relationship just because her/his facial expressions say it. In fact, it just so happens that what you feel is rarely matched with what you signal with your body language. (Bertilsdotter-Rosqvist, 2014, p. 360)

Additionally, autistic adolescents and adults often struggle to develop and maintain social relationships. Research indicates that they experience higher rates of social isolation and loneliness than their non-autistic peers (Locke, Ishijima, Kasari, & London, 2010). They also have fewer friends and frequently have difficulty initiating social interactions (Müller, Schuler, & Yates, 2008; Orsmond, Shattuck, Cooper, Sterzing, & Anderson, 2013). This does not mean, however, that they do not want to interact with others. Many autistic adults stress that they wish to connect with others (Causton-Theoharis, Ashby, & Cosier, 2009) and long for greater intimacy, in spite of their challenges with navigating social environments (Müller et al., 2008). Daniel Tammet, a 27-year-old autistic man, provides evidence of this, stating:

> No relationship is without its difficulties and this is certainly true when one or both of the persons involved has an autistic spectrum disorder. Even so, I believe what is truly essential to the success of any relationship is not so much compatibility, but love. When you love someone, virtually anything is possible. (Tammet, 2007, p. 155)

Moreover, researchers (Mazurek, 2014) have found that autistic adults can be significantly affected by loneliness, which has been associated with increased depression, anxiety and dissatisfaction with life. In contrast, autistic adolescents and adults who have more friends and involvement in social networks, experience greater self-esteem and emotional well-being. It is also interesting to note that although many autistic individuals are using the Internet to connect with others, these relationships do not appear to reduce their level of loneliness (Mazurek, 2013). This suggests that autistic individuals need the contact of face-to-face interactions to gain the full emotional benefits from a relationship.

Although intimate connections appear to be important to many autistic adolescents and adults, there are some autistic individuals, including more well-known autistic authors, who have stated that they are not interested in romantic or sexual relationships (Baggs, 2009; Kim, 2011). A few studies have found that there does seem to be a greater percentage of people who identify as asexual in the autistic population than in the non-autistic population (Dewinter, De Graaf, & Begeer, 2017; Gilmour, Schalomon, & Smith, 2012; Strunz et al., 2016). Researchers have found that autistic women, in particular, report higher rates of asexuality than non-autistic women (Dewinter et al., 2017). Despite this finding, asexuality is only indicated by a small minority of autistic individuals, while the majority indicate that sexuality and romantic relationships are important to them (Gilmour et al., 2012).

The entertainment industry has recently incorporated a number of autistic characters in television series and films. A disproportionate number of these individuals are depicted as asexual eccentrics who find the idea of sex to be unnecessary, weird or distasteful (Loftis, 2015). Characters such as Sheldon on *The Big Bang Theory* and Spencer Reid on *Criminal Minds* have helped to solidify the public's association of autism with asexuality. Fortunately, there is some indication that this is changing. The character of Sheldon has been allowed to formulate a meaningful romantic and sexual relationship, while the movie, *Mozart and the Whale*, tells the story of two autistic adults who meet and fall in love. Interestingly this movie is loosely based on the true story of Jerry and Mary Newport, which may have enabled the writer to see beyond the stereotype of asexuality. This couple has subsequently published their own book, providing information about sexuality and relationships for other autistic adults (Newport & Newport, 2002).

10.2 The Research

As autistic adults have begun to share their stories, researchers have begun to more comprehensively explore the romantic and sexual relationships of autistic adolescents and adults. These studies (Barnett & Maticka-Tyndale, 2015; Byers, Nichols, Voyer, & Reilly, 2012; Pecora, Mesibov, & Stokes, 2016; Strunz et al., 2016) indicate that autistic adults and adolescents engage in a diverse range of sexual behaviours and a range of relationships. Renty and Roeyers (2006) examined the quality of life of 58 autistic adults living in Belgium all of whom had intelligence quotient (IQ) scores in the average range. Only 8.6% of these individuals were married, while another 19% were currently involved in an ongoing intimate relationship. The majority (67%) were single, which may have been related to the finding that more than 66% lived either with their parents or in supported living. No relationship was found between autism symptomology and relationship status. The researchers concluded that relationship status and support for relationships was a significant factor in the participant's overall quality of life. Subsequent studies (Cederlund, Hagberg, Billstedt, Gillberg, & Gillberg, 2008; Costley, Baldwin, & Bruck, 2016; Hofvander et al., 2009) have also found that a majority of autistic adults are not currently or have not previously been involved in intimate relationships. Moreover, these individuals often express a desire to be in a relationship and are frustrated with the difficulties they experience in establishing and maintaining relationships (Hellemans, Colson, Verbraeken, Vermeiren, & Deboutte, 2007).

In a recent study, Strunz et al. (2016) surveyed over 200 autistic adults about their romantic relationships and experiences. They found that 73% of these adults reported they had previously or were currently involved in a romantic relationship, while 7% stated that they had no desire to be in a relationship. Participants who were in a relationship with an autistic partner were significantly more satisfied with their relationship than participants whose partner was not autistic. A portion of participants who were not in a relationship (65%) reported that relationships left them too exhausted and were afraid they would not be able to meet their partner's expectations (61%). A number of individuals (57%) stated that they did not know how to find a romantic partner or did not know what would be expected of them (50%). These findings suggest that rather than not wanting to be in a relationship, many autistic individuals find the complexities involved to be fairly daunting. These findings are supported by Costley et al. (2016), who conducted an extensive study of the experiences and perceptions of autistic adults across Australia. Although only a minority were married or in a long-term relationship (21%), a number of individuals (23%) expressed a desire for more fulfilling relationships in the future. More significantly, 64% of participants who were not currently in a relationship felt they needed better support to help with dating and relationships. The researchers also noted that some of the individuals who were in a relationship expressed a need for support to help them maintain their current relationships. The findings of these studies indicate that although currently a minority of autistic adults are in a relationship, they do want to have relationships, but feel they need support to do so.

Studies have shown that autistic individuals are interested in sex and engage in a variety of sexual behaviours (Gilmour et al., 2012). This is true even for participants diagnosed both with autism and intellectual impairment (Konstantareas & Lunsky, 1997). In a study conducted by Hellemans et al. (2007), 96% of autistic adolescents and adults interviewed stated they were interested in sex and most had engaged in some type of sexual behaviour (e.g. touching others, kissing others, touching themselves, masturbation). In another study, Byers, Nichols and Voyer (2013) investigated the sexual functioning of single autistic adults. They found that most participants were positive about their sexual functioning, and those participants who had no previous experience with sexual relations tended to be younger, male and identify as heterosexual. Other researchers have indicated that individuals who are older and exhibit less autistic symptomology report greater sexual functioning including greater sexual satisfaction and desire and fewer sexual problems or anxiety (Nichols & Byers, 2008). Similarly, autistic adults who are in a relationship report greater sexual satisfaction and more frequent sexual engagement (Byers et al., 2012).

Several researchers have compared the relationships and sexual behaviours of autistic males and females (Byers et al., 2012; Dewinter et al., 2017; Gilmour et al., 2012). Other studies have indicated (Byers et al., 2012; Pecora et al., 2016) that in comparison with autistic women, autistic men have less sexual knowledge, but report more desire and engagement in both solitary sexual behaviours (e.g., more sexual thoughts and sexual desires, more solitary sexual experiences) and dyadic sexual relations. Byers et al. (2013) explored the sexuality of single autistic adults revealing that men reported greater anxiety about sexual relationships, but better sexual functioning than the women. Other researchers (Gilmour et al., 2012) suggest that autistic females report higher rates of asexuality and homosexuality than do autistic men and are more subject to adverse sexual experiences than either autistic men or non-autistic females (Pecora et al., 2016).

Another group of researchers have compared the sexual behaviours of autistic and non-autistic individuals. Mehzabin and Stokes (2011) hypothesised that autistic individuals would have less sexual experiences, behaviours and understanding of privacy than their non-autistic counterparts. Reports from both groups showed similar levels of knowledge about privacy and public displays of appropriate sexual behaviours (i.e. holding hands). However, autistic adults engaged in fewer sexual behaviours and had fewer sexual experiences, suggesting that these individuals faced additional barriers in engaging in sexual relations. Assessment data revealed that autistic adults had much lower social behaviours, less sex education, and were more concerned about their future than the non-autistic participants. The researchers concluded that these factors were likely a contributing factor in the lower sexual activity of the autistic adults.

Dewinter, Vermeiren, Vanwesenbeeck, Lobbestael and Van Nieuwenhuizen (2015) compared the sexual behaviours, interests, experiences and attitudes of autistic adolescent boys with those of non-autistic adolescent boys. Groups were matched on age and intelligence. Dewinter et al. found little difference in the sexual behaviours of autistic and non-autistic adolescents. Both groups engaged in the same types of sexual behaviours and were of a similar age when they started to engage in sexual behaviours. In contrast, Barnett and Maticka-Tyndale (2015) found that autistic adults were more likely to have had their first romantic or sexual experience at a later age (after 18) than their non-autistic peers. They were also less likely to identify as heterosexual or gender conforming.

Other researchers have also investigated whether autistics are more likely to identify as homosexual or bisexual than would be typically expected in the general population (Barnett & Maticka-Tyndale, 2015; Byers et al., 2013; Dewinter et al., 2017; Gilmour et al., 2012). Byers et al. (2013) found that 24% of 129 single autistic adults identified as being homosexual or bisexual. Similarly, in a meta-analysis of nine studies of autistic adolescents and adults, Pecora et al. (2016) found that 15–35% of all participants identified as either homosexual or bisexual. These are significantly higher percentages than those found in the general population. In contrast, in a comparative study (Gilmour et al., 2012), autistic individuals, and females in particular, reported greater rates of homosexuality, than did their same-sex non-autistic peers. Additionally, researchers have found that autistic adolescents and adults express wider variability and less rigidity in their sexual attraction than the non-autistic population. For example, 55% of the autistic adults in Byers et al.'s (2013) study stated they were somewhat attracted to both men and women. This corresponds with the findings in another study (Dewinter et al., 2017) in which autistic adults, and women in particular, were more likely than non-autistic adults to report being attracted to people of both sexes and to having gender non-conforming feelings. In addition, autistic men and women are more likely to be bisexual than their non-autistic peers (Byers et al., 2013; Dewinter et al., 2017; Gilmour et al., 2012; Strunz et al., 2016).

In order to better understand the sexuality of autistic adolescents and adults, researchers have examined how the sexual knowledge of autistic adolescents and adults compares to that of their non-autistic peers. Mehzabin and Stokes (2011) found that despite having fewer sexual encounters and experiences than their non-autistic peers, autistic adults had similar levels of knowledge about privacy and public displays of appropriate sexual behaviours (e.g., holding hands). Likewise, Gilmour et al. (2012) found no difference in the sexual knowledge of autistic and non-autistic adults regarding their amount of sexual knowledge. Additionally, researchers have investigated the sources accessed by autistic adolescents and adults to acquire this knowledge. Brown-Lavoie, Viecili and Weiss (2014) found that most autistic adults used non-social sources such as the Internet to learn about sexually transmitted diseases and contraception. In contrast, non-autistic adults accessed information from social sources, including peers and teachers. They also found that autistic adults had less actual knowledge of sex than non-autistic adults.

Stokes, Newton and Kaur (2007) suggest that compared to non-autistic peers, autistic adolescents and adults engage in a wider variety of courtship behaviours. In addition, they exhibit more inappropriate behaviours such as inappropriate touching, showing obsessional interest, making inappropriate comments and pursing potential partners in a manner that may sometimes be considered threatening (i.e. stalking). Other researchers (Gougeon, 2010) have indicated that autistic individuals may have difficulty distinguishing between public and private sexual behaviours and may lag behind their non-autistic peers in knowledge of privacy behaviours and sexual behaviour. Other researchers (Mehzabin & Stokes, 2011) indicate that autistic and non-autistic adults demonstrate similar levels of privacy, knowledge and public sexualised behaviours. However, Stokes and Kaur (2005) found that autistic adolescents do not show the same growth in knowledge about privacy behaviours as they age as their non-autistic peers. Given the findings of these studies, it would seem that although autistic adults eventually develop awareness of public and private sexual behaviours, they take longer to do so than their non-autistic peers. Parents have also expressed concern that their autistic children might misinterpret other people's intentions and engage in inappropriate behaviours as a result (Nichols & Blakeley-Smith, 2009), while others worry that other people might misinterpret their child's behaviours, which although benign in intent, might be viewed by some as signs of sexual deviancy (Ballan, 2012). For example, one mother felt that if her son touched someone's clothes because he liked the texture, this might be misinterpreted as inappropriate sexual touching. These parents stress the importance of comprehensive sexual education in adolescents, which can help them to not just learn about sex, but how to navigate social relationships with others as a prelude to more intimate relationships.

The research clearly indicates that the majority of autistic adolescents and adults are interested in romantic and sexual relationships and engage in a wide variety of relationships and sexual behaviours. However, even those individuals who are in a relationship often state they need support to navigate the complexities involved. More concerning is the finding that autistic adolescents and adults often lack the appropriate knowledge or skills to pursue these interests in an appropriate or feasible manner. This has left them frustrated and may have even added to the stigmatisation of autistic individuals as either sexually disinterested or sexually problematic. Conversely, this continued perception may pose the greatest barrier to providing the support necessary to enable autistic individuals to connect with others in meaningful and mutually beneficial ways.

10.3 The Impact

Advocates argue that myths about autism and sexuality have caused discrimination and marginalisation of autistic adults by continuing to deny their rights to be fully functioning and sexual adults (Gougeon, 2010; MacKenzie, 2018). They contend that not only has this impacted previous knowledge and understanding in this area, but it has positioned the sexuality of autistic adolescents and adults as a problem to be treated or managed, rather than as a basic need to be supported. As a result, autistic individuals have not been provided with the information and services they need to utilise appropriate social and sexual behaviours to form the relationships they desire. MacKenzie (2018) adds that further harm may result as autistic individuals may internalise and accept these negative portrayals of sexual and emotional inadequacy, causing them to become anxious and disengage from social domains where they are likely to encounter these stereotypes. For example, social stigmatisation might cause an autistic adolescent to avoid situations, such as school dances, parties or clubs, which spark sexual feelings and provide opportunities for developing relationships that may lead to intimacy.

Parents are often a source of information and support about sex and intimate relationships. However, parents report feeling unprepared to share with their autistic children their insights about sex and intimate relationships (Nichols & Blakeley-Smith, 2009). Another impact of the asexuality myth is that denying the sexuality of autistic adolescents has inhibited the development of appropriate supports in this area for parents as well as their children. For most parents, the implications of imagining their child's sexual future is daunting, but for parents of autistic children, it can be overwhelming. Stokes and Kaur (2005) found that parents of both autistic and non-autistic children had similar concerns when their children were 10 years of age. As their children aged, the concerns of parents of non-autistic children decreased, while the concerns of parents of autistic children continued to increase. This finding may be related to a host of factors including anxiety about their child's future employment, ability to live independently and to have meaningful social relationships.

Researchers have found that the bulk of support provided to autistic children as they move into adulthood falls on the parents (Cheak-Zamora, Teti, & First, 2015). Without support to deal with their child's impending sexuality, a topic which is difficult for any parent, parents may focus on more manageable issues such as helping to prepare their child to live on their own or get a job. Nichols and Blakeley-Smith (2009) gathered data from parents about their concerns and then piloted an 8-week training program to support parents to address these concerns. This program covered topics such as sexuality issues, hopes and fears, communicating with their child, developing a sexual education plan, sexual behaviours, personal hygiene and abuse prevention. At the end of the training, parents felt they were much better equipped to support their child's future sexuality and needs in this area. This program illustrates the significant impact that can be achieved for parents, and hopefully for their children, with only a modest amount of support and information.

Researchers have stressed the importance of providing appropriate education and training to autistic adolescents and adults in the areas of sexuality and social relationships (Barnett & Maticka-Tyndale, 2015; Gougeon, 2010; Sullivan & Caterino, 2008). Unfortunately, teachers like parents, often report feeling uncomfortable and lacking knowledge related to providing appropriate sex and relationships education to their autistic students (Kalvya, 2010). Previously, educators and school personnel may have been persuaded that autistic individuals were not interested in sex or that it was the parent's place to deal with this topic. With information now demonstrating the key role that romantic and sexual relationships play in the quality of life of autistic adults (Tullis & Zangrillo, 2013), it has become apparent that this is an important area in which autistic adolescents and adults require support. As stated succinctly by one researcher, "sex matters" (Gougeon, 2010, p. 348). Not providing autistic adolescents with the information they need, while they are developing their sexuality, may inadvertently encourage inappropriate behaviours, such as stalking (Stokes et al., 2007) as they try to form intimate relationships. Education programs are essential to teach both sexual and social behaviours.

Research has shown that autistic students are less likely than their peers to be involved in sex education (MacKenzie, 2018), a finding that has been attributed to stereotypes about autism and sexuality (Koegel et al., 2014). Moreover, researchers have indicated that autistic students require sex education that is targeted at their particular needs (Stokes & Kaur, 2005) including knowledge of privacy rules, appropriate social behaviours and sexual responses. Barnett and Maticka-Tyndale (2015) add that autistic adolescents need education programs that help them to normalise the range of differences in sexual identity and experiences. Given the higher rates of autistic individuals who identify as homosexual, bisexual or gender non-conforming, this is particularly important. Sex education programs aimed at autistic students would need to take into consideration autistic communication styles and support needed for these individuals to understand sexual behaviours and their own sexuality (Goodall, 2016).

Autistic students may also need to have specific programs in addition to or even separate from the programs provided to their non-autistic peers. Hannah and Stagg (2016) compared the views of 20 non-autistic and 20 autistic students about their school's sex education program. They found that autistic students were dissatisfied with this program because they were not given an opportunity to learn the skills needed to form an intimate relationship. Hannah and Stagg concluded that school-based sexual education programs are typically based on non-autistic students' requirements. For instance, sex education programs do not include instruction on courtship behaviours, which is a need that is frequently mentioned by autistic individuals (Barnett & Maticka-Tyndale, 2015; Hannah & Stagg, 2016). This is illustrated by the statement of one student, "I feel like I've been given the tools, but I just didn't use them because they weren't clear enough" (Hannah & Stagg, 2016, p. 3682).

A final impact of the asexuality myth is that the denial of the sexuality of autistic adolescents and adults has left them vulnerable to victimisation and abuse. Brown-Lavoie et al. (2014) found that a lack of accurate sexual knowledge placed autistic individuals at two to three times greater risk of sexual victimisation. Other researchers have also confirmed that issues such as social naivete and difficulties with communication may cause autistic adolescents and adults to be victims of sexual crimes and may also inhibit their willingness to report these crimes (Koegel et al., 2014). Increased social and sexual knowledge has been found to at least partially mitigate the sexual vulnerability of autistic men and women.

The myth that autistic people are not interested in sex, or are sexual deviants, continues to impact the way that society views the capacity of these individuals to engage in romantic and sexual relationships. As a result, these individuals have not received the support and education they need to be successful. At the very least, this has prevented these individuals from experiencing a quality of life commensurate with their non-autistic peers. At worst, denying the sexuality of autistic individuals has placed them at risk of victimisation and social isolation. To mitigate the impact of this myth will require a shift in perspective starting with recognising the autistic view of sexuality and relationships.

10.4 The Future

To transform the asexuality myth, advocates argue that society must recognise "autistic sexuality" (Bertilsdotter-Rosqvist, 2014) and support autistic individuals to engage in intimate and sexual relationships in their own way. This will necessitate recognition that some autistic adolescents and adults engage in social and sexual relationships in unconventional ways and through unconventional behaviours. Instead of seeing these behaviours as problematic; however, they need to be recognised for the value they bring to the lives of the individuals involved. As one autistic individual describes:

> It is easy to think of different sexual expressions as problems—but whoever said that everything that is different has to be a problem? Medical staff and parents often try to get us with autism/AS to change our behaviour. Is this behaviour really a problem—and if so, whose problem is it? All sexual expressions must be accepted so long as they do not harm the person or others. You are to support and help us with our disabilities—not normalize us! (Bertilsdotter-Rosqvist, 2014, p. 357)

Hudak (2011) who identifies himself as a "philosophical advocate" (p. 57) and is the father of a young autistic man, suggests that society has to rethink its assumptions in engaging with autistic youth and adults regarding sexuality and intimacy. He identifies three presumptions that must be made for society to shift its current perceptions to embrace an alternative view of autistic youth and adults as able to and having the right to make decisions about their lives including their relationships and sexuality. Hudak reasons that without these presumptions, autistic individuals will continue to be limited in their capacity to seek the connections they desire and will be denied the rights afforded to others. Hudak's presumptions include:

- A presumption of competence in which all autistic adolescents and adults are perceived as capable beings with the capacity to think and reflect on their own lives;
- The presumption of imagination in which society is able to imagine the sexuality of autistic individuals as an essential and valued part of their growth and presume the capacity of these individuals to engage in conversations about their own sexuality; and

- The presumption of intimacy in which society views autistic individuals as desirous and able to form intimate and mutually beneficial relationships with others.

The essential element of these presumptions is changing from a focus on autistic sexuality, which is managed by others, to placing autistic individuals at the helm of deciding what types of relationships, if any, they want, and what they need to help them get there.

Similar to Hudak (2011), MacKenzie (2018), an autistic researcher, argues that until autistic individuals are viewed as "knowers of their own sexual experiences" (p. 1), their relationship and sexual needs will continue to be discounted. She adds that placing autistic individuals at the forefront of conversations about relationships and sexuality is necessary to shift the current power imbalance that perpetuates negative stereotypes about sexual deviance and inhibits the development of meaningful supports needed to enable autistic individuals to connect with others in ways that are safe and satisfying to both.

In an attempt to explore autistic discourse regarding sexuality and relationships, Bertilsdotter-Rosqvist (2014) examined articles published between 2002 and 2009 in the Swedish magazine, *Empowerment,* which is published by and for autistic adults. The most dominant theme across the articles was the recognition of an alternative storyline of autistic sexuality. Much of this discourse focused on the impact of sensory processing differences on sexuality and relationships. In particular, autism was presented as a difference in sexuality rather than as a deficit. This is explained by one individual who states:

> It is important to separate the sexuality's multiple and complex needs, which can be divided into three main areas: physical pleasure, relaxation, and the need for social contact and feeling appreciated. Problems with motor skills and perception can make the physical part of sex more difficult for people with autism/AS. Many are sensitive to touch, but with the right strategies this does not prevent one from having a functioning sex life. (p. 355)

Another common theme was the importance of recognising different forms of sexual expression (Bertilsdotter-Rosqvist, 2014). For example, some individuals discussed being sexually stimulated by the sight of items that others did not usually associate with sex, such as a particular type of cloth or a zipper. Other posts highlighted other ways in which they felt the autistic experience of sexuality differed. This included the observation that many autistic adults exhibit a degree of gender blindness and a decreased need to identify a person's sex, and greater degree of openness to non-heterosexuality and asexuality.

In contrast, other individuals felt that their sexuality was no different from that of non-autistic adults. These individuals stressed it was other barriers such as opportunities to find a partner that posed the biggest barrier for them. Some individuals did feel that they experienced deficits in sexuality or relationships as a result of their autistic symptomology. These posts particularly focused on the sexual vulnerability and victimisation experienced by many autistic individuals. Women were felt to be particularly susceptible to sexual abuse. Individuals stressed the importance of early education to help mitigate these risks by ensuring autistic individuals were aware of warning signs and had a repertoire of protective behaviours.

A last theme involved discourse around romantic relationships and steps in becoming a couple (Bertilsdotter-Rosqvist, 2014). Difficulties with reading signals and the expectations involved in being in love were recurrent. Others talked about needing information regarding how to meet someone or what to do on a date. This perspective has been echoed by autistic adults in other studies (MacKenzie, 2018) who have expressed the need for education and training to help them learn the social nuances and complexities involved in moving through the stages of courtship, dating and intimate relations. Martin, a 28-year-old autistic man, highlights some of the challenges he faces:

> As someone with ASD it's very hard for me to read hints about whether she's interested in me or just being friendly. And to know at what point she wants me to 'make a move' ... My ASD gives me a big disadvantage on the dating scene I feel. And I'm certain most male ASD's feel the same. When your social skills are limited, it's much harder to take the lead. ... (p. 110)

Other individuals discussed challenges such as being able to effectively convey their romantic intentions and being able to understand others' feelings (Bertilsdotter-Rosqvist, 2014). A number of individuals expressed anxiety about being able to fulfil the expectations involved in relationships. Of particular concern was being comfortable with the sensory aspects involved in intimate relationships and sex. Participants in another study (Barnett & Maticka-Tyndale, 2015) echoed these apprehensions, stating that their most common concerns were courtship difficulties and sensory dysregulation in the context of sexual relationships. Participants had developed strategies to address these challenges. Strategies included using sensory barriers (e.g., latex gloves); planning when and how to have sex; negotiating alternatives to sexual scripts developed by the non-autistic population; and practicing explicit and intentional communication with their partners. It should be noted that autistic adults, like researchers and parents, have stressed the need for early and comprehensive sexuality and relationship education, to help them manage their concerns about sexual and intimate relationships (Barnett & Maticka-Tyndale, 2015). Also emphasised is the need for these programs to incorporate specific details about what to do and what not to do in relationships, how to engage in safe and healthy sexual behaviours and relationships, and how to refrain from behaviours, which might offend or upset a partner. Providing direct instruction and chance for role play are two strategies that can help autistic adolescents and adults learn appropriate sexual-social etiquette (e.g., rules about when and how frequently to contact a potential partner, signs that a potential partner is or is not interested in having a sexual relationship, and coping strategies for when a potential partner terminates a romantic relationship) (Tullis & Zangrillo, 2013).

These examples illustrate the ways in which autistic individuals can create meaningful strategies that not only help them, but might offer solutions to others with similar needs. Transforming the asexuality myth in future will not just build on these insights, but will empower autistic adolescents and adults to take the lead in directing their own services and supports. In other words, providing meaningful strategies to support the differing perspectives inherent in autistic sexuality necessitates that these strategies are derived from the people who share this perspective.

10.5 Conclusion

Myths and stereotypes about autistic individuals' sexual and relationship preferences and behaviours have developed from a variety of factors, which include a tendency to infantilise autistic individuals, reported asexuality of autistic adults, and differences in social communication. Historically the romantic relationships and sexuality of autistic individuals has been under-researched and viewed as a problem to be managed and a general lack of acknowledgement of the sexual rights of autistic adults has resulted in a lack of information and support in this area. Parents and professionals also report they are uncertain and uncomfortable in approaching this topic with autistic adolescents as they develop their sexuality. Together, these factors have led to increased rates of sexual victimisation among the autistic community.

A recent increase in interest has led to a number of studies that indicate that the majority of autistic adolescents and adults do desire romantic and sexual relationships. Additionally, sexual preferences vary widely across the autistic population, with a higher than average number of individuals identifying as homosexual, bisexual and asexual. The need for targeted social and sexual education has been highlighted by parents, researchers, and autistic adults who often state that their biggest barrier is not lack of sexual knowledge, but uncertainty around the complexities of connecting with others to form more intimate relationships. Autistic advocates contend that current models do not support their needs and do not recognise the differences in autistic sexuality. Rather than models focusing on deficits of autistic individuals, a preferred future will transform current stereotypes into an alternative perspective that builds on presumptions of autistic individuals as competent sexual beings who deserve, and desire, the same quality of life as their non-autistic peers. At the same time, this view will recognise the rights of autistic individuals to express their sexuality in their own ways and the capability of these individuals to identify the information and support they need to engage with others in mutually beneficial relationships.

References

Baggs, A. (2009). Up in the clouds and down in the valley: My richness and yours. *Disability Studies Quarterly, 30*(1), 10.

Ballan, M. S. (2012). Parental perspectives of communication about sexuality in families of children with autism spectrum disorders. *Journal of Autism and Developmental Disorders, 42*(5), 676–684. https://doi.org/10.1007/s10803-011-1293-y.

Barnett, J. P., & Maticka-Tyndale, E. (2015). Qualitative exploration of sexual experiences among adults on the autism spectrum: Implications for sex education. *Perspect Sex Reprod Health, 47*(4), 171–179. https://doi.org/10.1363/47e5715.

Bertilsdotter-Rosqvist, H. (2014). Becoming an 'autistic couple': Narratives of sexuality and couplehood within the Swedish autistic self-advocacy movement. *Sexuality and Disability, 32*(3), 351–363. https://doi.org/10.1007/s11195-013-9336-2.

Brewer, R., Biotti, F., Catmur, C., Press, C., Happe, F., Cook, R., et al. (2016). Can neurotypical individuals read autistic facial expressions? A typical production of emotional facial expressions in autism spectrum disorders. *Autism Research, 9*(2), 262–271. https://doi.org/10.1002/aur.1508.

Brown-Lavoie, S. M., Viecili, M. A., & Weiss, J. A. (2014). Sexual knowledge and victimization in adults with autism spectrum disorders. *Journal of Autism and Developmental Disorders, 44*(9), 2185–2196. https://doi.org/10.1007/s10803-014-2093-y.

Byers, E. S., Nichols, S., & Voyer, S. D. (2013). Challenging stereotypes: Sexual functioning of single adults with high functioning autism spectrum disorder. *Journal of Autism and Developmental Disorders, 43*(11), 2617–2627. https://doi.org/10.1007/s10803-013-1813-z.

Byers, E. S., Nichols, S., Voyer, S. D., & Reilly, G. (2012). Sexual well-being of a community sample of high-functioning adults on the autism spectrum who have been in a romantic relationship. *Autism, 17*(4), 418–433. https://doi.org/10.1177/1362361311431950.

Causton-Theoharis, J., Ashby, C., & Cosier, M. (2009). Islands of loneliness: Exploring social interaction through the autobiographies of individuals with autism. *Journal of Intellectual and Developmental Disability, 47*(2), 84–96. https://doi.org/10.1352/1934-9556-47.2.84.

Cederlund, M., Hagberg, B., Billstedt, E., Gillberg, I. C., & Gillberg, C. (2008). Asperger syndrome and autism: A comparative longitudinal follow-up study more than 5 years after original diagnosis. *Journal of Autism and Developmental Disorders, 38*(1), 72–85. https://doi.org/10.1007/s10803-007-0364-6.

Cheak-Zamora, N. C., Teti, M., & First, J. (2015). 'Transitions are Scary for our kids, and they're Scary for us': Family member and youth perspectives on the challenges of transitioning to adulthood with autism. *Journal of Applied Research in Intellectual Disabilities, 28*(6), 548–560. https://doi.org/10.1111/jar.12150.

Corcoran, J., Berry, A., & Hill, S. (2015). The lived experience of US parents of children with autism spectrum disorders: A systematic review and meta-synthesis. *Journal of Intellectual Disabilities, 19*(4), 356–366. https://doi.org/10.1177/1744629515577876.

Costley, D., Baldwin, S., & Bruck, S. (2016). *Shining a light on the autism spectrum: Experiences and aspirations of adults*. New York: Taylor & Francis.

Dewinter, J., De Graaf, H., & Begeer, S. (2017). Sexual orientation, gender identity, and romantic relationships in adolescents and adults with autism spectrum disorder. *Journal of Autism and Developmental Disorders, 47*(9), 2927–2934. https://doi.org/10.1007/s10803-017-3199-9.

Dewinter, J., Vermeiren, R., Vanwesenbeeck, I., Lobbestael, J., & Van Nieuwenhuizen, C. (2015). Sexuality in adolescent boys with autism spectrum disorder: Self-reported behaviours and attitudes. *Journal of Autism and Developmental Disorders, 45*(3), 731–741. https://doi.org/10.1007/s10803-014-2226-3.

Gilmour, L., Schalomon, P. M., & Smith, V. (2012). Sexuality in a community based sample of adults with autism spectrum disorder. *Research in Autism Spectrum Disorders, 6*(1), 313–318. https://doi.org/10.1016/j.rasd.2011.06.003.

Goodall, E. (2016). *The autism spectrum guide to sexuality and relationships*. London: Jessica Kingsley.

Gougeon, N. A. (2010). Sexuality and autism: A critical review of selected literature using a social-relational model of disability. *American Journal of Sexuality Education, 5*(4), 328–361. https://doi.org/10.1080/15546128.2010.527237.

Hannah, L. A., & Stagg, S. D. (2016). Experiences of sex education and sexual awareness in young adults with autism spectrum disorder. *Journal of Autism and Developmental Disorders, 46*(12), 3678–3687. https://doi.org/10.1007/s10803-016-2906-2.

Hellemans, H., Colson, K., Verbraeken, C., Vermeiren, R., & Deboutte, D. (2007). Sexual behavior in high-functioning male adolescents and young adults with autism spectrum disorder. *Journal of Autism and Developmental Disorders, 37*(2), 260–269. https://doi.org/10.1007/s10803-006-0159-1.

Hofvander, B., Delorme, R., Chaste, P., Nyden, A., Wentz, E., Stahlberg, O., … Leboyer, M. (2009). Psychiatric and psychosocial problems in adults with normal-intelligence autism spectrum disorders. *BMC Psychiatry, 9*(35). http://doi.org/10.1186/1471-244X-9-35.

Hudak, G. M. (2011). Alone in the presence of others: Autistic sexuality and intimacy reconsidered. *Counterpoints, 392,* 57–70.

Jang, J., Matson, J. L., Adams, H. L., Konst, M. J., Cervantes, P. E., & Goldin, R. L. (2014). What are the ages of persons studied in autism research: A 20-year review. *Research in Autism Spectrum Disorders, 8*(12), 1756–1760. https://doi.org/10.1016/j.rasd.2014.08.008.

Kalvya, E. (2010). Teachers' perspectives of the sexuality of children with autism spectrum disorders. *Research in Autism Spectrum Disorders, 4*(3), 433–437. https://doi.org/10.1016/j.rasd.2009.10.014.

Kim, E. (2011). Asexuality in disability narratives. *Sexualities, 14*(4), 479–493. https://doi.org/10.1177/1363460711406463.

Koegel, L. K., Detar, W. J., Fox, A., & Koegel, R. L. (2014). Romantic relationships, sexuality, and autism spectrum disorders. *Adolescents and Adults with Autism Spectrum Disorders* (pp. 87–104).

Konstantareas, M. M., & Lunsky, Y. J. (1997). Sociosexual knowledge, experience, attitudes, and interests of individuals with autistic disorder and developmental delay. *Journal of Autism and Developmental Disorders, 27*(4), 397–413. https://doi.org/10.1023/A:1025805405188.

Locke, J., Ishijima, E. H., Kasari, C., & London, N. (2010). Loneliness, friendship quality and the social networks of adolescents with high-functioning autism in an inclusive school setting. *Journal of Research in Special Educational Needs, 10*(2), 74–81. https://doi.org/10.1111/j.1471-3802.2010.01148.x.

Loftis, S. F. (2015). *Imagining autism: Fiction and stereotypes on the spectrum*. Indiana: University Press.

MacKenzie, A. (2018). Prejudicial stereotypes and testimonial injustice: Autism, sexuality and sex education. *International Journal of Educational Research, 89,* 110–118. https://doi.org/10.1016/j.ijer.2017.10.007.

Mazurek, M. O. (2013). Social media use among adults with autism spectrum disorders. *Computers in Human Behavior, 29*(4), 1709–1714. https://doi.org/10.1016/j.chb.2013.02.004.

Mazurek, M. O. (2014). Loneliness, friendship, and well-being in adults with autism spectrum disorders. *Autism, 18*(3), 223–232. https://doi.org/10.1177/1362361312474121.

Mehzabin, P., & Stokes, M. A. (2011). Self-assessed sexuality in young adults with high-functioning autism. *Research in Autism Spectrum Disorders, 5*(1), 614–621. https://doi.org/10.1016/j.rasd.2010.07.006.

Müller, E., Schuler, A., & Yates, G. B. (2008). Social challenges and supports from the perspective of individuals with Asperger syndrome and other autism spectrum disabilities. *Autism, 12*(2), 173–190. https://doi.org/10.1177/1362361307086664.

Newport, J., & Newport, M. (2002). *Autism-Asperger's & sexuality: Puberty and beyond*. Arlington, TX: Future Horizons.

Nichols, S., & Blakeley-Smith, A. (2009). "I'm not sure we're ready for this …": Working with families toward facilitating healthy sexuality for individuals with autism spectrum disorders. *Social Work in Mental Health, 8*(1), 72–91. https://doi.org/10.1080/15332980902932383.

Nichols, S., & Byers, S. (2008, May 16). *Sexual well-being of high-functioning adults with autism spectrum disorders.* Paper presented at the International Meeting for Autism Research (IMFAR), London.

Orsmond, G. I., Shattuck, P. T., Cooper, B. P., Sterzing, P. R., & Anderson, K. A. (2013). Social participation among young adults with an autism spectrum disorder. *Journal of Autism and Developmental Disorders, 43*(11), 2710–2719. https://doi.org/10.1007/s10803-013-1833-8.

Pecora, L. A., Mesibov, G. B., & Stokes, M. A. (2016). Sexuality in high-functioning autism: A systematic review and meta-analysis. *Journal of Autism and Developmental Disorders, 46*(11), 3519–3556. https://doi.org/10.1007/s10803-016-2892-4.

Renty, J. O., & Roeyers, H. (2006). Quality of life in high-functioning adults with autism spectrum disorder: The predictive value of disability and support characteristics. *Autism, 10*(5), 511–524. https://doi.org/10.1177/1362361306066604.

Ruble, L. A., & Dalrymple, N. J. (1993). Social/sexual awareness of persons with autism: A parental perspective. *Archives of Sexual Behavior, 22*(3), 229–240. https://doi.org/10.1007/BF01541768.

Saxe, A., & Flanagan, T. (2013). Factors that impact support workers' perceptions of the sexuality of adults with developmental disabilities: A quantitative analysis. *Sexuality and Disability, 32*(1), 45–63. https://doi.org/10.1007/s11195-013-9314-8.

Stevenson, J. L., Harp, B., & Gernsbacher, M. A. (2011). *Infantilizing autism. Disability Studies Quarterly, 31*(3), 17–24.

Stokes, M., & Kaur, A. (2005). High-functioning autism and sexuality: A parental perspective. *Autism, 9*(3), 266–289. https://doi.org/10.1177/1362361305053258.

Stokes, M., Newton, N., & Kaur, A. (2007). Stalking, and social and romantic functioning among adolescents and adults with autism spectrum disorder. *Journal of Autism and Developmental Disorders, 37*(10), 1969–1986. https://doi.org/10.1007/s10803-006-0344-2.

Strunz, S., Schermuck, C., Ballerstein, S., Ahlers, C. J., Dziobek, I., & Roepke, S. (2016). Romantic relationships and relationship satisfaction among adults with Asperger syndrome and high-functioning autism. *Journal of Clinical Psychology, 73*(1), 113–125. https://doi.org/10.1002/jclp.22319.

Sullivan, A., & Caterino, L. C. (2008). Addressing the sexuality and sex education of individuals with autism spectrum disorders. *Education and Treatment of Children, 31*(3), 381–394.

Tammet, D. (2007). *Born on a blue day: Inside the extraordinary mind of an autistic savant*. London: Hodder & Soughton.

Taylor Gomez, M. (2012). The S words: Sexuality, sensuality, sexual expression and people with intellectual disability. *Sexuality and Disability, 30*(2), 237–245. https://doi.org/10.1007/s11195-011-9250-4.

Tullis, C. A., & Zangrillo, A. N. (2013). Sexuality education for adolescents and adults with autism spectrum disorders. *Psychology in the Schools, 50*(9), 866–875. https://doi.org/10.1002/pits.21713.

Wilson, C. E., Gillan, N., Spain, D., Robertson, D., Roberts, G., Murphy, C. M., … Murphy, D. G. (2013). Comparison of ICD-10R, DSM-IV-TR and DSM-5 in an adult autism spectrum disorder diagnostic clinic. *Journal of Autism and Developmental Disorders, 43*(11), 2515–2525. https://doi.org/10.1007/s10803-013-1799-6.

Chapter 11
Supporting Self-efficacy and Self-determination on the Autism Spectrum: Refuting the "Autism Can Be Outgrown" Myth

Abstract Over the past 50 years, there has been a great deal of debate about the defining characteristics and future trajectory of autistic children. Although many patterns have been suggested, no definitive biological traits have yet been definitively identified, and diagnosis currently relies on the observable manifestations of restricted and repetitive behaviours and interests, difficulties in social communication and sensory sensitivities. As autistic children grow, however, and particularly as they learn skills to help them cope in different settings, they may exhibit these behavioural characteristics to a much lesser degree than they did when they were young. This has resulted in the myth that autism can be outgrown. This chapter will examine the origins of this myth and will discuss the impact it has had on creating the misperception that autism is something to be overcome. The research on outcomes for autistic individuals at different stages of life will be explored, and an argument will be made for an alternative understanding of their competence. Theories of self-determination and self-efficacy will be examined, and recommendations will be made for supporting autistic people with a range of needs to self-advocate and create their own futures.

Keywords Autistic adults · Perception of competence
Self-advocacy and Self-determination · Self-efficacy

Since autism was first identified, researchers, professionals and families have debated the trajectory of development and future outcomes that can be expected for autistic children. Autism is a relatively new diagnosis included for the first time in the *Diagnostic and Statistical Manual of Mental Disorders—Third edition (DSM-III)* in 1980. In recent years, individuals originally diagnosed under the *DSM* have reached adulthood, which has led to a greater awareness of the experiences and needs of autistic adults. Although outcomes for this population are generally poor (Howlin & Moss, 2012), some individuals have achieved quite positive outcomes, despite early challenges. Claims have also been made that some of these individuals no longer meet the criteria for autism spectrum disorder (ASD) (Helt et al., 2008). These claims, as

M. Bennett et al., *Life on the Autism Spectrum*,
https://doi.org/10.1007/978-981-13-3359-0_11

well as lack of awareness of the experiences of autistic adults, have led to the myth that autism can be outgrown.

11.1 The Origins

The myth that autism can be outgrown has similar origins to the myth that autism can be cured. In both cases, the progress of autistic individuals through their lifespan is used as evidence that they have outgrown or been cured of autism. In addition, the myth that autism can be outgrown has developed from the continued association of autism with childhood. Kanner's (1943) original study of a group of autistic individuals focused solely on children he met in his clinic at Johns Hopkins. Although Kanner identified autism as a condition distinct from schizophrenia, many referred to autism as a form of childhood schizophrenia (Wolff, 2004) until 1980 when it was formally included as a distinct condition in the *DSM-III*. This helped to solidify the belief that autism was a condition primarily exhibited by children. In the years following the publication of Kanner's study, medical professionals began to identify similar characteristics in other children, while adults remained virtually absent in the autism literature. One explanation for this may be that as autism was thought to be a childhood condition, medical professionals and researchers working with adults may not have even been aware of autism and would likely attribute autistic-type symptoms to other disorders such as schizophrenia. Thus, the early association of autism with childhood would limit identification of autistic adults, providing further support for the conviction that autism only affected children.

The public invisibility of autistic adults throughout its early history is another factor that has contributed to the autism can be outgrown myth. After its original identification in the research literature, researchers and professionals viewed autism as a distinct disorder encompassing a specific set of characteristics, which resulted in a severe to profound disability for the autistic child. It was not until 1994 and the publication of the *DSM-IV* that autism was recognised as a spectrum condition. Before this change, many individuals diagnosed with autism would have also exhibited comorbid intellectual disabilities and significant language delays (Feinstein, 2011). As adults, these individuals would have been either kept at home or placed in segregated settings, excluding them from mainstream society. Thus, it could be argued that adults who had been diagnosed as being autistic were silent and invisible to the general public.

Prior to the disability rights movement of the 1970s and 80s, people diagnosed with autism and other significant disabilities were often segregated from society (D'Astous, Manthorpe, Lowton, & Glaser, 2014). Many of these individuals were placed into institutions for the "mentally deficient or mentally ill". Others remained at home with family members, where they lead a fairly sheltered life. As a result, people diagnosed with autism during this time were not likely to be included in community settings and would have often been placed in institutions, particularly if they exhibited more significant intellectual, language or behavioural needs. This theory is supported by the stories of two well-known autistic adults, Drs. Temple Grandin and Stephen Shore. Both these individuals have achieved a fair amount of success in their lives. They have both completed advanced study obtaining their PhDs and going on to become well-respected researchers, writers and speakers in their field. As young children both Dr. Grandin and Dr. Shore were not initially given a diagnosis of autism, as they were born before the publication of the *DSM-III.* Instead they were diagnosed with "brain damage" (Grandin, 2013) and as exhibiting "atypical development in addition to psychotic behaviours and autistic tendencies" (Shore, 2003a, b, p. 21). More significantly, both of their mothers were encouraged to institutionalise them, but refused, choosing instead to keep them at home and providing them with therapists and teachers who helped them learn new skills (Grandin, 2011; Shore, 2003a, b). Their narratives are two of the first that provided researchers and professionals with "insider" accounts of the lifespan experiences of autistic adults and greatly influenced the public's view of autistic people (Wolfe, 2013). Both Dr. Grandin and Dr. Shore have stressed the important role their parents played in shaping their future trajectory. However, if their parents had followed the traditional route at the time and followed suggestions to place them in institutions, it is highly probable that their stories would never have been heard.

Although some autistic adults would have been formally excluded or segregated from society, others may have been isolated from their communities in other ways. In his book *Neurotribes*, Silberman (2015) theorises that many adults who were previously thought of as quirky, eccentric or social misfits would today be diagnosed with autism spectrum disorder. These individuals were all able to function in their own way and make valuable contributions to humanity, although they often isolated themselves from mainstream society (James, 2006). Thus, it is probable that before the introduction of Asperger's syndrome and Pervasive Developmental Disorder-Not Otherwise Specified (PDD-NOS) in the *DSM-IV*, many autistic adults may have gone undiagnosed or would have been diagnosed with some other disorder. Recent studies (Bastiaansen et al., 2011; Ritvo et al., 2008) have worked to develop assessment instruments appropriate for this population. These studies demonstrate that many adults may meet the criteria for ASD, but were overlooked as children due to the expansion of diagnostic criteria or demonstrating milder symptomology. Women, in particular, have been found to be at risk for late diagnosis as they often exhibit different typology of symptomology (Head, McGillivray, & Stokes, 2014; Mandy et al., 2012) from autistic men. For example, in a recent study of successful autistic women, Webster and Garvis (2017) reported that all ten participants received their ASD diagnosis as adults. Many of these women were children before the introduction of Asperger's syndrome in 1994 and would not have met the criteria for a diagnosis of autistic disorder under the *DSM-III*. Although these women experienced a number of difficulties as children, they were identified as having unspecified behaviour problems or other conditions such as schizoid disorder or learning disabilities.

Given the early identification of autism as childhood schizophrenia, researchers have examined medical records to determine if adults previously diagnosed with schizophrenia would also meet the criteria for autism spectrum disorder. Roy and Balaratnasingam (2010) reviewed the medical records of Indigenous Australian adults who were diagnosed with schizophrenia but were suspected of having a developmental disability. They found that 13 of the 14 individuals satisfied the criteria for autistic disorder. Other researchers (Nylander & Gillberg, 2001; Vannucchi et al., 2014) have reported similar findings. Lai and Baron-Cohen (2015) contend that there is a lost generation of autistic adults due to factors such as misdiagnosis and lack of knowledge about the spectrum of autistic behaviours. They also suggest that some adults who would qualify for a diagnosis of Asperger's syndrome or PDD-NOS after 1994 might have been missed as almost most assessments were previously standardised for children, and not adults.

A final factor that has contributed to the myth that autism can be outgrown is what Stevenson, Harp and Gernsbacher (2011) refer to as the "infantilising of autism". This is linked to both the public perception of individuals with disabilities as childlike and the public face of autism as being that of a child. In a search of the photographs placed on websites for regional and state chapters of the Autism Society of America, Stevenson et al. found that 95% of the photographs depicting an autistic person were of children. They also found that after examining the language used in autism-related organisations, 75% of these organisations used only child-centric terminology to describe autism, while the other 25% used a combination of adult and child references. Evidence of this can be found in the autism prevalence reports provided by *Autism Speaks*, a prominent autism charity. These reports provide an overview of the number of children who have received a diagnosis of ASD, but do not include any figures on adult diagnoses. In their research, Stevenson et al. (2011) also found that 91% of autistic characters featured in books and 68% of autistic characters featured in films or television were children. Children were featured also four times more often than adults in news stories. Stevenson et al. (2011) concluded that the overwhelming depiction of autism as associated with childhood posed a barrier to services for autistic adults, who in order to access services, had to overcome the additional barrier of invisibility. Even researchers are not immune to the "child effect". Jang et al. (2014) conducted a systematic review of autism research over the past 20 years and determined that 94% of all studies focused on children or adolescents.

The historical segregation, misidentification and self-isolation of autistic adults have resulted in a public unawareness of their existence. This perception has no doubt been compounded by the absence of autistic adults in public images, forums and reports. It can be argued that these factors have combined to create the belief that autism is a childhood condition and, by association, lead some to believe that as children move into adulthood, they either recover or outgrow their issues. As more autistic adults, such as Dr. Temple Grandin and Dr. Stephen Shore, have begun to share their experiences, researchers have confirmed the intrinsic nature of autism as a lifelong condition (Eaves & Ho, 2008; Howlin & Moss, 2012; Seltzer et al., 2003; Volkmar, Reichow, McPartland, & Ebooks, 2014) that impacts people in different ways depending on a number of factors.

11.2 The Research

In recent years, researchers have begun to investigate the progression of autism across the lifespan. This research has found that although individuals do not outgrow autism, there is a wide variability in the trajectory and outcomes across autistic adults with some developing significant skills as they move through their lifespan. This has led some researchers to argue that a small proportion of autistic adults may develop enough skills that they no longer meet the diagnostic criteria for ASD (Fein et al., 2013; Orinstein et al., 2014). Seltzer et al. (2003) conducted an early study to describe how symptoms manifested in 405 individuals between 10 and 53 years of age, who were diagnosed with autistic disorder as children. They found that participants demonstrated unique trajectories across symptomology, with adolescents demonstrating increased social interactions, whereas adults demonstrated improved measures in restricted and repetitive behaviours and interests. Both age groups demonstrated fairly consistent difficulties in communication. These researchers concluded that many of the adults they studied would not meet the diagnostic criteria for autistic disorder if their current scores were used, although they did not state whether participants would have met the criteria for Asperger's syndrome or PDD-NOS.

Seltzer, Shattuck, Abbeduto and Greenberg (2004) conducted a systematic review to understand the phenotype of autism for adolescents and adults. They determined that across studies, most participants demonstrated a decrease in symptomology and improvement of skills and that they progressed at a fairly consistent rate. Despite this, most adults still exhibited many of the characteristics associated with autism and many required ongoing support in a number of areas. They also found that a small group (15%) of adults did demonstrate skills at a level consistent with that expected for non-autistic individuals. In a later study, Shattuck et al. (2007) examined whether 241 adolescents and autistic adults demonstrated a change in problematic behaviours across a 4.5-year period exhibiting fewer challenging behaviours and improved adaptive behaviours over time. Autistic adults with intellectual impairments were more likely to experience less improvement and more stability in symptomology. The researchers were unable to determine whether improvements were as a result of symptomology or related to developmental progression, although they suggested it was most likely a combination of the two. They also concluded that there was little evidence that autism could be outgrown, as most participants continued to need support and services and highlighted the importance of using a life course perspective in considering the need for support and services.

In other studies, researchers have explored the relationship between adult outcomes and factors such as intellectual ability, quality of life and family relationships. In Sweden, Billstedt, Gillberg and Gillberg (2011) conducted a follow-up study of 120 adults who were diagnosed with autism as children. They found that many still lived with their parents and experienced challenges in accessing appropriate employment or recreational opportunities. Despite this, measures indicated that they rated their quality of life to be fairly positive. Lord, Bishop and Anderson (2015) followed 85 individuals from their initial diagnosis of autism at 2 years of age into adulthood. They found that adults achieved a range of outcomes, with some demonstrating significant functional impairments, while others demonstrated social and adaptive behaviour skills at a level commensurate with their age. Woodman, Smith, Greenberg and Mailick (2015) conducted a longitudinal study of autistic adolescents and adults over a 8.5-year period. Their results indicated that a number of participants showed improvements in non-verbal (35%) and verbal communication skills (58%), social skills (40%), restricted and repetitive behaviours (61%) and problematic behaviours (42%) beyond levels which would be expected based on intellectual ability. Another small group of individuals (12%) demonstrated a decrease in skills over time. Maternal praise and the quality of the mother–child relationship were correlated with higher outcomes. In summary, while there is considerable variability, studies have found that most autistic individuals acquire new skills and show improvement, but still exhibit symptomology typically associated with ASD. However, a small proportion experience limited improvement in their overall level of functioning (Howlin & Magiati, 2017).

Although the research does indicate that the majority of individuals do not outgrow autism, a few researchers have attempted to determine the factors that enable some autistic individuals to achieve higher outcomes as adults than others. Howlin and Magiati (2017) conducted a review of the literature on outcomes for autistic adults and concluded that although studies varied considerably in their findings, some factors could be identified that consistently correlated to higher outcomes. Lord et al. (2015) found that adults who achieved more typical outcomes all had an intelligence quotient (IQ) over 70. Similarly, other studies (Magiati, Tay, & Howlin, 2014; Woodman, Smith, Greenberg, & Mailick, 2015) have found that IQ and particularly verbal IQ are predictive factors for higher outcomes for autistic adults, although individuals with higher IQs do not necessarily achieve good outcomes as adults. Other predictors include autism severity, family and environmental factors and the presence of comorbid mental health issues (Howlin & Magiati, 2017). It has also been speculated that on average women achieve higher outcomes than men, but the low number of women diagnosed with ASD makes it difficult to confirm this finding at the present time (Howlin & Magiati, 2017).

With the recent interest in autistic adults, research has also focused on examining the ways in which they compare to their non-autistic peers in participation in employment and other aspects of adult life (Howlin, Goode, Hutton, & Rutter, 2004; Howlin & Magiati, 2017; Levy & Perry, 2011; Volkmar, Reichow, McPartland, & Ebooks, 2014). In general, studies indicate that autistic adults demonstrate poorer outcomes in employment, community engagement and social relationships than either their non-autistic peers or peers diagnosed with other types of disabilities (Hendricks, 2010; Shattuck et al., 2012). Autistic adults tend to be underemployed relative to their education level and receive lower pay rates than their peers, both with and without disability (Baldwin, Costley, & Warren, 2014). In the USA, Roux et al. (2013) found that only 20.9% of autistic school leavers were employed on a full-time basis, whereas 39.7% of their peers with intellectual disabilities were employed full-time and 78% of peers with emotional, learning or speech impairments were in full-time employment. Additionally, autistic school leavers were paid less, earning an average of $8 an hour, compared to their peers with other disabilities, who earned an average of $9–$12 an hour. In an Australian study, Baldwin et al. (2014) surveyed 130 autistic adults to determine the types of jobs they held. This study revealed that most participants were employed in either clerical or administrative positions (22.8%), as labourers (22.8%) or in professional positions (22%). Although 28% of these participants were employed above their education level, a large proportion (46%) were employed below their level of education or training. Additionally, 32% of participants in this study were only employed on a casual basis and approximately half worked 30 hours a week or less.

The mental health status of autistic adults is another cause for concern. Croen et al. (2015) measured the proportion of psychiatric and medical conditions within a large sample (1507) of autistic adults in the USA. Autistic adults were much more likely than neurotypical peers to have comorbid anxiety disorder (29.13% versus 9.10%), attention deficit disorder (11.08% versus 1.95%), bipolar disorder (10.55% versus 1.67%), depression (25.75% versus 9.89%) and suicidal behaviours (1.79% versus 0.32%). Interestingly, neurotypical adults had higher rates of alcoholism and drug addiction. In addition, Croen and colleagues found that autistic adults also had higher rates of comorbid medical conditions such as diabetes (7.56% versus 4.33%), obesity (33.91% versus 27.01%), autoimmune diseases (13.87% versus 10.78%), cardiovascular diseases (36.96% versus 23.03%), neurological diseases (39.28% versus 22.05%), gastrointestinal disorders (34.70% versus 27.47%) and sleep disorders (17.58% versus 9.60%). Similarly, Fortuna et al. (2016) discovered that autistic adults had substantially more seizure disorders, constipation, depression, hypertension, allergies, diabetes and obesity than their neurotypical peers. These studies all indicate that in addition to employment-related needs, autistic adults continue to experience health issues as well as complex needs related to comorbidity with other conditions.

Researchers have also investigated the social outcomes of autistic adults. Many individuals have reported feeling lonely (Costley, Baldwin, & Bruck, 2016; Mazurek, 2014; Tobin, Drager, & Richardson, 2014), with loneliness linked to feelings of depression, anxiety and social isolation (Mazurek, 2014). Some studies indicate that autistic adults have less opportunities for socialisation (Costley et al., 2016; Tobin et al., 2014) and are more likely than their non-autistic peers or peers with other disabilities to be socially isolated (Müller, Schuler, & Yates, 2008; Orsmond, Shattuck, Cooper, Sterzing, & Anderson, 2013). Some autistic adults, however, have indicated that they have good friends (Eaves & Ho, 2008; Farley et al., 2009) and are happy with their social relationships (Costley et al., 2016). Other adults have made social connections via the internet and social media groups (Costley et al., 2016; Mazurek, 2013). Romantic relationships still pose a challenge for many autistic adults. Although some autistic individuals have stated they are not particularly interested in a romantic relationship (Farley et al., 2009; Strunz et al., 2017), many others have reported that they would like to be in a relationship, but have difficulty with navigating the social cues and expectations required (Autism Spectrum Australia (Aspect), 2012; Müller et al., 2008; Stokes, Newton, & Kaur, 2007; Strunz et al., 2017). Stokes et al. (2007) suggest this difficulty partially stems from a lack of opportunity to learn skills from friends or siblings. Although limited research has been conducted in this area, findings to date indicate that a minority of autistic adults are currently in a relationship (Costley et al., 2016; Howlin & Moss, 2012). In addition, there is some evidence that a number of autistic women, in particular, have experienced abusive romantic or sexual relationships (Bargiela, 2015; Webster & Garvis, 2017). These studies indicate that as well as continuing to need support in other areas, autistic adults often need support to help them to fully participate in social environments and to prevent them from becoming isolated from or taken advantage of by other members of their communities.

Some researchers have argued that the current outcome estimates do not necessarily fully reflect the experiences of autistic adults and recommend that alternative measures should be utilised to gain a comprehensive portrait of their perspectives and lives. For example, Burgess and Gutstein (2007) argue that current quality of life (QoL) measures may be inadequate to capture outcomes for autistic adults. They suggest that alternative measures of QoL need to encompass both subjective and objective measures. Such measures should consider the quality rather than the amount of support the individual receives, including social support. They also recommend that measures of QoL need to be developed that are autism-specific, multidimensional and relevant in developing meaningful interventions and supports. Other researchers have focused on assessing the resilience (Montgomery et al., 2008) or life satisfaction (Samson & Antonelli, 2013) of autistic individuals. Vermeulen (2014) contends that traditional outcome measures fail to consider whether the individual is happy, which is a more important indicator of quality of life than predetermined measures of employment or independent living status.

Damien Milton, a researcher and autistic adult, provides further insight, suggesting that ultimately researchers and professionals need to consider the perspective of autistic individuals and their families about whether they have achieved their own personal goals (2014). He argues that it is this measure that determines whether an outcome is positive or negative for the individuals most affected.

Researchers indicate that many of the barriers encountered by autistic adults are derived from either societal stigmatisation (Ashby & Causton-Theoharis, 2009) or from a lack of appropriate services that support them to navigate adult environments and enable them to develop the skills they need to participate and be successful in these environments (Baldwin & Costley, 2016; Müller et al., 2008). In contrast, a few studies have emphasised the factors that enable some adults to achieve despite the barriers. Ashby and Causton-Theoharis (2009) analysed seven autobiographical accounts of autistic adults to ascertain the factors that enabled them to feel competent and confident. Participants revealed a number of supportive factors many of which involved attitudes of other people and opportunities to participate and learn in different settings. These included the presumption of competence; building on their interests; making things less abstract and more concrete; provision of structure and inclusion in society. More recently, Webster and Garvis (2017) found that autistic women were able to develop self-efficacy as decision-makers and self-advocates as a result of decisions they had made and actions they had taken at critical points in their life. Other factors that build self-efficacy included understanding their diagnosis; the belief and support of people in their lives; reading about other autistic women and helping others. This study highlighted the important role that the attitudes and beliefs of others and the opportunity to make their own choices play in the outcomes of autistic adults.

The myth that autism can be outgrown is not supported by the prevailing research, which indicates that most autistic children still experience ongoing difficulties and at least some need for support as they move into adulthood. Moreover, adult life often presents these individuals with a new set of challenges and expectations as they navigate adult environments such as employment and social settings, which has led to less than satisfactory outcomes for autistic adults. Despite this, the majority of autistic individuals do progress in their ability to adapt and engage with others as they age, particularly if others believe in their ability to achieve and allow them to make their own choices along the way. Although some individuals do appear to increase their skills to the point that they no longer meet the diagnostic criteria for ASD, there is continuing debate about whether they are no longer autistic or whether diagnostic criteria and assessments are not sensitive enough for the variability in adult symptomology. However, the evidence clearly indicates that the majority of individuals do not outgrow autism and require supports that enable them to participate fully in their community as adults.

11.3 The Impact

The myth that autism can be outgrown has had a subtle but long-lasting impact for autistic individuals and their families. The most significant impact has been the continued focus on developing child-centred interventions, while creating appropriate services and supports for autistic adults has received limited attention (Krahn & Fenton, 2012; Pellicano, Dinsmore, & Charman, 2014). This imbalance has been based on the belief that if individuals receive intensive intervention in the early years, they will be able to achieve optimal outcomes (Orinstein et al., 2014). Researchers indicate, however, that improved skill development may be linked to a variety of factors, many of which are intrinsic to the individual, such as IQ, and language or motor skills (Sutera et al., 2007). Additionally, optimal outcome measures have focused primarily on the autistic adult's demonstration of skills within the "average" range and fail to consider the impact of environments on their ability to utilise these skills. For example, sensory issues or social demands can greatly reduce the ability of autistic individuals to communicate in different environments (Ashburner, Ziviani, & Rodger, 2008). Researchers have stressed the importance of a lifespan approach to services and supports for autistic individuals (Gotham et al., 2015; Michael, 2016).

Although there is no doubt that early intervention services and supports are beneficial (Ben Itzchak & Zachor, 2011), there is currently an inequity in funding between early intervention services and adult services. For example, in the USA, children are eligible for early intervention services as soon as they receive a diagnosis of autism, and education support ends when individuals are 21 years of age. In Australia, an initiative was passed in 2008 whereby children diagnosed with autism were eligible to receive $12,000 to access early intervention services, but these funds had to be utilised by the time the child turned 7 years of age (Valentine, Rajkovic, Dinning, & Thompson, 2010). Adults in Australia have only just been able to access funding through the passage of the National Disability Insurance Scheme, although this has not yet been implemented across the entire country, and it is still unclear how much this will enable autistic adults to access needed services or support. This inequity of support is particularly concerning as researchers stress that an overreliance on early intervention fails to consider the changing symptoms and needs of autistic children or to account for individuals who may receive their diagnosis after early childhood (Gotham et al., 2015).

A number of studies have found that due to the lack of services and supports for autistic adults, many autistic adults must rely on their families for financial assistance and support in obtaining employment (Billstedt et al., 2011; Costley et al., 2016; Gotham et al., 2015; Howlin & Moss, 2012). This is further aggravated by a limited amount of research that has focused on developing strategies and programs to support autistic adults (Howlin & Taylor, 2015). In contrast, a number of studies have trialled and evaluated early intervention strategies and programs (Boyd et al., 2014; Prior, Roberts, Rodger, Williams, & Sutherland, 2011) or identified evidence-based practices for children in schools (National Autism Center (NAC), 2015; Simpson, 2005; Wong et al., 2015). On a more positive note, there is some indication that more researchers are beginning to look at the needs of autistic adults. Recently, in the USA the *National Autism Center* published the first comprehensive evaluation of evidence-based strategies for autistic adults (NAC, 2015). In Australia, the Cooperative Research Centre for Living with Autism has launched a suite of research projects on the needs of autistic adults, which have obtained findings related to employment (Hedley, Uljarević, & Hedley, 2017), transition to work (Hedley et al., 2017) and the role of support in mediating anxiety and depression of autistic adults (Hedley, Uljarević, Wilmot, Richdale, & Dissanayake, 2017). This organisation has also worked closely with the autistic community to develop guidelines for engaging in inclusive research with autistic individuals and their families (Cooperative Research Centre for Living with Autism, 2016).

If research on adults is limited, research on older autistic adults is relatively non-existent. With the first individuals diagnosed with autism reaching their 50s and 60s, there has been a call for studies to investigate the needs of this population (Bennett, 2016; Piven & Rabins, 2011). Currently, little is known about the ways in which autism presents in the elderly or whether this group has needs that are unique from other age groups. For instance, it could be argued that this age group may be particularly vulnerable as they develop increasing comorbid health issues associated with aging, and their support network, such as parents, are no longer able to care for them (Bennett, 2016; Michael, 2016).

A final impact of the autism can be outgrown myth is the overemphasis on developing programs and interventions to eliminate the symptoms of autism. Parents are particularly susceptible to this belief. As Stevenson et al. (2011) states,

> They have, after all, like the rest of contemporary society, been inundated with rhetoric asserting that autistic children must either be cured or suffer a lifetime as unemployable burdens. Rarely has the alternative - a capable autistic adult needing appropriate workplace supports - been presented. Scarce resources will not be directed toward such an unidentified need. (p. 3)

In other words, when presented with a negative future, parents may feel pressured to obtain the right services and supports for their young children, in order to help them to be less autistic. Thus, instead of building skills, they focus on remediation of current deficits. It is this dynamic that must be changed in order to reconstruct the autism can be outgrown myth for a more positive future.

11.4 The Future

Altering the impact of the autism can be outgrown myth requires a new perspective in which autistic individuals are seen as competent of achieving positive futures (Ashby & Causton-Theoharis, 2009) even without eliminating their autistic symptomology. Instead of emphasising early intervention, a lifespan approach is needed, which focuses on capability development and supporting autistic children and adults to exercise self-determination and self-efficacy. This will enable them to become more effective self-advocates to ensure that services and research affecting them are meaningful to their lives and the lives of their family.

Self-determination involves the capacity to make your own choices and decisions, regarding QoL, without external pressure from others (Deci & Ryan, 1985). Self-determination is shaped by three psychological needs: competence, relatedness and autonomy (Deci & Ryan, 2008). Autonomy involves the ability to be the source of one's own actions in order to accomplish personal goals in keeping with personal interests and values. Relatedness is having a sense of connectedness and belonging with others in the community, whereas competence is achieved when an individual feels affective as they interact with their social environment. Deci and Ryan (2008) argue that these needs must be met if someone is to act as a self-determined individual. Wehmeyer, Kelchner and Richards (1996) state that for individuals with a disability, self-determination is defined as "acting as the primary causal agent in one's life and making choices and decisions regarding one's quality of life free from undue external influence or interference" (p. 632). An action is self-determined if it encompasses four essential characteristics: (1) an autonomous action; (2) self-regulated behaviours; (3) consciously empowered initiation and response to environmental stimulus or events and (4) a self-realising manner (Wehmeyer, 2013). For autistic individuals, this means they are able to act as causal agents in their own lives and to utilise skills such as choice-making, goal-setting, decision-making, problem-solving, self-awareness, self-management and self-advocacy.

Self-determination has been linked to higher outcomes and QoL as well as increased well-being and motivation (Chambers et al., 2007; McDougall, Evans, & Baldwin, 2010; Wehmeyer & Schwartz, 1997). To demonstrate self-determination, autistic individuals need both the support to develop their skills in areas such as problem solving and self-advocacy, and the environment and opportunity that support them to practise and utilise these skills. This involves not only seeing these individuals as having the potential to exercise agency and control over their lives, but also giving them the freedom to take risks, make their own decisions and deal with the consequences of these decisions even if it means experiencing failure. To address the basic needs of autonomy, relatedness and competence, autistic individuals need support to identify their own strengths and needs, to connect with others in different ways, to determine the ways that external factors combine with their internal solutions to create challenges in their lives and to identify and self-advocate for strategies that will enable them to succeed in different environments.

Unfortunately, researchers indicate that individuals who are viewed as being "disabled" are not provided with opportunities to engage in these skills until they are almost at the point of adulthood (Chambers et al., 2007). By this time, they have often experienced years of support and strategies that are based on presumption of incompetence or a deficit model and in which they are mostly passive recipients in their own learning. As a result, many have lost the ability to act as autonomous thinkers and decision-makers. This causes them to be more segregated from society and prevents them from developing connectedness to people, thereby denying them the opportunity to access naturalistic supports that come from having friends and support networks. To break this cycle, alternative strategies need to be employed in which autistic individuals are seen as the leaders of their own learning and advocates for their own needs. They also need many opportunities to engage with peers in a variety of ways in order to make meaningful connections, learn from others and build supportive networks in their lives.

Previous research has demonstrated that even individuals with significant communication and cognitive difficulties can develop self-determination and become causal agents and self-advocates in their own lives (Algozzine, Browder, Karvonen, & Test, 2001; Fullerton & Coyne, 1999; Wehmeyer, Palmer, Lee, Williams-Diehm, & Shogren, 2011). Chou, Wehmeyer, Palmer and Lee (2017) also reveal that autistic adolescents and adults may have lower levels of autonomy and empowerment than individuals with other disabilities. These researchers suggest that this may be the result of limited opportunities for social interaction. Held, Thoma and Thomas, (2004) present a case study of a teacher who utilised peer modelling and direct instruction to facilitate the self-determination of John, an adolescent autistic male with significant communication and intellectual challenges. After he was supported to develop alternative ways of engaging and communicating with the team, John successfully led his post-school transition planning process, working with his family and support team to identify future goals and actions to realise these goals. This process also enabled John to develop self-awareness of his particular strengths and needs in order to better self-advocate for future outcomes and supports that were most important to him.

Self-efficacy is related to self-determination. Self-efficacy involves an individual's belief that they have the knowledge, skills and power to effect change in their environment and to achieve desired outcomes (Bandura, 1997). Unlike self-determination, self-efficacy involves more than a set of skills. It requires a belief that you can enact these skills in different and often stressful situations to achieve your goals. Bandura (1997) explains that there are four sources of self-efficacy: (1) mastery experiences; (2) social persuasion; (3) vicarious experiences and (4) emotional and physiological factors. Mastery experiences involve gaining competence as a result of the success achieved from accomplishing a difficult task. Social persuasion is when others believe in someone and persuade them that they can be successful. Vicarious learning involves competence and emotional empowerment by watching or learning from others in a similar situation. Lastly, emotional and physiological factors are those inner characteristics, such as perseverance, that enable an individual to keep going when they encounter difficulty.

One recent study (Webster & Garvis, 2017) found that the most significant factor in the self-efficacy of autistic women who considered themselves successful was the sense of achievement and confidence they derived from succeeding at challenging tasks. Subsequently increased self-efficacy enabled these individuals to view themselves as successful in areas such as education, employment and self-advocating for themselves and for other autistic females. The women also highlighted the ways in which their unique characteristics and identity as autistic individuals helped them to define who they were and to feel free to succeed in their own way, instead of feeling that they had to meet other people's expectations. Webster and Garvis concluded that rather than being provided with programs to remediate their skill deficits, autistic adults should be given the security and support to set their own goals, face difficult tasks and challenges and engage in self-advocacy.

Vermeulen (2014) argues that happiness is not derived from a lack of difficulties, but from the feeling of accomplishment that comes when difficulties have been overcome. Thus, greater happiness equals increased mental, emotional and physiological well-being. A more positive future for autistic adults would involve not just accomplishments, but accomplishments that come as a result of succeeding in spite of their challenges. To enable autistic individuals to achieve their goals, professionals and researchers need to provide security and support that will enable them to face and manage challenges through their lifespan enabling them to become self-determined, self-efficacious adults. Focusing on the journey, rather than the destination, will allow autistic individuals in their own way to develop the skills they need in order to become fulfilled and successful adults.

11.5 Conclusion

The myth that autism can be outgrown has developed from several factors including the association of autism with childhood and the belief that with early intervention, some individuals can lose their autistic symptomology. Current research indicates that although the majority of autistic individuals do demonstrate progress as they move from childhood into adulthood, most experience high rates of unemployment, social isolation and physical and mental illness as well as stigmatisation and low expectations. A continued focus on developing interventions that will enable autistic children to develop skills in the "average range" has created an imbalance in funding and research aimed at adults. To counteract the myth that autism can be outgrown, outcomes for autistic individuals need to be reimagined. Rather than viewing these individuals as in need of support due to limitations, the focus should be on supporting their self-determination and self-efficacy, thereby providing them with the opportunity to develop needed skills, set their own goals and solve their own problems. Although it is a myth that autism can be outgrown, an alternative future would see that by becoming self-determined, autistic adults have in actuality outgrown the stigma and limitations that others place on them.

References

Algozzine, B., Browder, D., Karvonen, M., & Test, D. W. (2001). Effects of interventions to promote self-determination for individuals with disabilities. *Review of Educational Research, 71*(2), 219–277. https://doi.org/10.3102/00346543071002219.

Ashburner, J., Ziviani, J., & Rodger, S. (2008). Sensory processing and classroom emotional, behavioral and educational outcomes in children with autism spectrum disorder. *The American Journal of Occupational Therapy, 62*, 564–573. https://doi.org/10.5014/ajot.62.5.564.

Ashby, C. E., & Causton-Theoharis, J. N. (2009). Disqualified in the human race: A close reading of the autobiographies of individuals identified as autistic. *International Journal of Inclusive Education, 13*(5), 501–516. https://doi.org/10.1080/13603110801886673.

Autism Spectrum Australia (Aspect). (2012). *We belong: Investigating the experiences, aspirations and needs of adults with Asperger's disorder and high functioning autism*. Retrieved from http://www.autismspectrum.org.au/content/we-belong.

Baldwin, S., & Costley, D. (2016). The experiences and needs of female adults with high-functioning autism spectrum disorder. *Autism, 20*(4), 483–495. https://doi.org/10.1177/1362361315590805.

Baldwin, S., Costley, D., & Warren, A. (2014). Employment activities and experiences of adults with high-functioning autism and Asperger's Disorder. *Journal of Autism and Developmental Disorders, 44*(10), 2440–2449. https://doi.org/10.1007/s10803-014-2112-z.

Bandura, A. (1997). *Self-efficacy: The exercise of control*. New York: W.H. Freeman.

Bargiela, S. (2015). *Young women's experiences of having Autism Spectrum Disorder.* UCL (University College London).

Bastiaansen, J. A., Meffert, H., Hein, S., Huizinga, P., Ketelaars, C., Pijnenborg, M., … de Bildt, A. (2011). Diagnosing autism spectrum disorders in adults: The use of the Autism Diagnostic Observation Schedule (ADOS) module 4. *Journal of Autism and Developmental Disorders, 41*(9), 1256–1266. https://doi.org/10.1007/s10803-010-1157-x.

Ben Itzchak, E., & Zachor, D. A. (2011). Who benefits from early intervention in autism spectrum disorders? *Research in Autism Spectrum Disorders, 5*(1), 345–350. https://doi.org/10.1016/j.rasd.2010.04.018.

Bennett, M. (2016). "What is Life Like in the Twilight Years?" A letter about the scant amount of literature on the elderly with autism spectrum disorders. *Journal of Autism and Developmental Disorders, 46*(5), 1883–1884. https://doi.org/10.1007/s10803-016-2710-z.

Billstedt, E., Gillberg, I. C., & Gillberg, C. (2011). Aspects of quality of life in adults diagnosed with autism in childhood: A population-based study. *Autism, 15*(1), 7–20. https://doi.org/10.1177/1362361309346066.

Boyd, B. A., Hume, K., McBee, M. T., Alessandri, M., Gutierrez, A., Johnson, L., … Odom, S. L. (2014). Comparative efficacy of LEAP, TEACCH and non-model-specific special education programs for preschoolers with autism spectrum disorders. *Journal of Autism and Developmental Disorders, 44*(2), 366–380. https://doi.org/10.1007/s10803-013-1877-9.

Burgess, A. F., & Gutstein, S. E. (2007). Quality of life for people with autism: Raising the standard for evaluating successful outcomes. *Child and Adolescent Mental Health, 12*(2), 80–86. https://doi.org/10.1111/j.1475-3588.2006.00432.x.

Chambers, C. R., Wehmeyer, M. L., Saito, Y., Lida, K. M., Lee, Y., & Singh, V. (2007). Self-determination: What do we know? Where do we go? *Exceptionality, 15,* 3–15. https://doi.org/10.1080/09362830709336922.

Chou, Y.-C., Wehmeyer, M. L., Palmer, S. B., & Lee, J. (2017). Comparisons of self-determination among students with autism, intellectual disability, and learning disabilities: A multivariate analysis. *Focus on Autism and Other Developmental Disabilities, 32*(2), 124–132. https://doi.org/10.1177/1088357615625059.

Cooperative Research Centre for Living with Autism. (2016). *Inclusive research practice guides and checklists for autism research: Version 2*. Retrieved from https://www.autismcrc.com.au/sites/default/files/inline-files/Inclusive%20research%20practice%20guides%20and%20checklists%20-%20FInal%20report.pdf.

Costley, D., Baldwin, S., & Bruck, S. (2016). *Shining a light on the autism spectrum: Experiences and aspirations of adults*. New York: Taylor & Francis.

Croen, L. A., Zerbo, O., Qian, Y., Massolo, M. L., Rich, S., Sidney, S., et al. (2015). The health status of adults on the autism spectrum. *Autism, 19*(7), 814–823. https://doi.org/10.1177/1362361315577517.

D'Astous, V., Manthorpe, J., Lowton, K., & Glaser, K. (2014). Retracing the historical social care context of autism: A narrative overview. *The British Journal of Social Work, 46*(3), 789–807.

Deci, E. L., & Ryan, R. M. (1985). *Intrinsic motivation and self-determination in human behavior*. New York: Plenum.

Deci, E. L., & Ryan, R. M. (2008). Self-determination theory: A macrotheory of human motivation, development, and health. *Canadian Psychology, 49*(3), 182–185. https://doi.org/10.1037/a0012801.

Eaves, L. C., & Ho, H. H. (2008). Young adult outcomes of autism spectrum disorders. *Journal of Autism and Developmental Disorders, 38*(4), 739–747. https://doi.org/10.1007/s10803-007-0441-x.

Farley, M. A., McMahon, W. M., Fombonne, E., Jenson, W. R., Miller, J., Gardner, M., … Coon, H. (2009). Twenty-year outcome for individuals with autism and average or near-average cognitive abilities. *Autism Research, 2*(2), 109–118. https://doi.org/10.1002/aur.69.

Fein, D., Barton, M., Eigsti, I. M., Kelley, E., Naigles, L., Schultz, R. T., … Tyson, K. (2013). Optimal outcome in individuals with a history of autism. *Journal of Child Psychology and Psychiatry, 54*(2), 195–205. https://doi.org/10.1111/jcpp.12037.

Feinstein, A. (2011). *A history of autism: Conversations with the pioneers*. West Sussex, U.K.: Wiley.

Fortuna, R. J., Robinson, L., Smith, T. H., Meccarello, J., Bullen, B., Nobis, K., et al. (2016). Health conditions and functional status in adults with autism: A cross-sectional evaluation. *Journal of General Internal Medicine, 31*(1), 77–84. https://doi.org/10.1007/s11606-015-3509-x.

Fullerton, A., & Coyne, P. (1999). Developing skills and concepts for self-determination in young adults with autism. *Focus on Autism and Other Developmental Disabilities, 14*(1), 42–63. https://doi.org/10.1177/108835769901400106.

Gotham, K., Marvin, A. R., Taylor, J. L., Warren, Z., Anderson, C. M., Law, P. A., … Lipkin, P. H. (2015). Characterizing the daily life, needs, and priorities of adults with autism spectrum disorder from Interactive Autism Network data. *Autism, 19*(7), 794–804. https://doi.org/10.1177/1362361315583818.

Grandin, T. (2011). *The way I see it: A personal look at autism & Asperger's*. Arlington, TX: Future Horizons.

Grandin, T. (2013). *The autistic brain*. New York: Houghton Mifflin Harcourt.

Head, A. M., McGillivray, J. A., & Stokes, M. A. (2014). Gender differences in emotionality and sociability in children with autism spectrum disorders. *Molecular Autism, 5*(1), 19–27. https://doi.org/10.1186/2040-2392-5-19.

Hedley, D., Cai, R., Uljarevic, M., Wilmot, M., Spoor, J. R., Richdale, A., & Dissanayake, C. (2017). Transition to work: Perspectives from the autism spectrum. *Autism, Online First*, 1–14. https://doi.org/10.1177/1362361316687697.

Hedley, D., Uljarević, M., & Hedley, D. F. (2017). Employment and living with autism: Personal, social and economic impact. In *Inclusion, disability and culture* (pp. 295–311). Springer.

Hedley, D., Uljarević, M., Wilmot, M., Richdale, A., & Dissanayake, C. (2017). Brief report: Social support, depression and suicidal ideation in adults with autism spectrum disorder. *Journal of Autism and Developmental Disorders, 47*(11), 3669–3677. https://doi.org/10.1007/s10803-017-3274-2.

Held, M. F., Thoma, C. A., & Thomas, K. (2004). "The John Jones Show": How one teacher facilitated self-determined transition planning for a young man with autism. *Focus on Autism and Other Developmental Disabilities, 19*(3), 177–188. https://doi.org/10.1177/10883576040190030501.

Helt, M., Kelley, E., Kinsbourne, M., Pandey, J., Boorstein, H., Herbert, M., et al. (2008). Can children with autism recover? If so, how? *Neuropsychology Review, 18*(4), 339–366. https://doi.org/10.1007/s11065-008-9075-9.

Hendricks, D. (2010). Employment and adults with autism spectrum disorder: Challenges and strategies for success. *Journal of Vocational Rehabilitation, 32*(2), 125–134. https://doi.org/10.3233/jvr-2010-0502.

Howlin, P., Goode, S., Hutton, J., & Rutter, M. (2004). Adult outcome for children with autism. *Journal of Child Psychology and Psychiatry, 45*(2), 212–229. https://doi.org/10.1111/j.1469-7610.2004.00215.x.

Howlin, P., & Magiati, I. (2017). Autism spectrum disorder: Outcomes in adulthood. *Current Opinion in Psychiatry, 30*(2), 69–76. https://doi.org/10.1097/yco.0000000000000308.
Howlin, P., & Moss, P. (2012). Adults with autism spectrum disorders. *Canadian Journal of Psychiatry, 57*(5), 275–283. https://doi.org/10.1177/070674371205700502.
Howlin, P., & Taylor, J. L. (2015). Addressing the need for high quality research on autism in adulthood. *Autism, 19*(7), 771–773. https://doi.org/10.1177/1362361315595582.
James, I. M. (2006). *Asperger's syndrome and high achievement: Some very remarkable people*. London: Jessica Kingsley.
Jang, J., Matson, J. L., Adams, H. L., Konst, M. J., Cervantes, P. E., & Goldin, R. L. (2014). What are the ages of persons studied in autism research: A 20-year review. *Research in Autism Spectrum Disorders, 8*(12), 1756–1760. https://doi.org/10.1016/j.rasd.2014.08.008.
Krahn, T. M., & Fenton, A. (2012). Funding priorities: Autism and the need for a more balanced research agenda in Canada. *Public Health Ethics, 5*(3), 296–310. https://doi.org/10.1093/phe/phs027.
Lai, M.-C., & Baron-Cohen, S. (2015). Identifying the lost generation of adults with autism spectrum conditions. *The Lancet Psychiatry, 2*(11), 1013–1027. https://doi.org/10.1016/s2215-0366(15)00277-1.
Levy, A., & Perry, A. (2011). Outcomes in adolescents and adults with autism: A review of the literature. *Research in Autism Spectrum Disorders, 5*(4), 1271–1282. https://doi.org/10.1016/j.rasd.2011.01.023.
Lord, C., Bishop, S., & Anderson, D. (2015). Developmental trajectories as autism phenotypes. *American Journal of Medical Genetics Part C: Seminars in Medical Genetics, 169*(2), 198–208. https://doi.org/10.1002/ajmg.c.31440.
Magiati, I., Tay, X. W., & Howlin, P. (2014). Cognitive, language, social and behavioural outcomes in adults with autism spectrum disorders: A systematic review of longitudinal follow-up studies in adulthood. *Clinical Psychology Review, 34*(1), 73–86. https://doi.org/10.1016/j.cpr.2013.11.002.
Mandy, W., Chilvers, R., Chowdhury, U., Salter, G., Seigal, A., & Skuse, D. (2012). Sex differences in autism spectrum disorder: Evidence from a large sample of children and adolescents. *Journal of Autism and Developmental Disorders, 42*(7), 1304–1313. https://doi.org/10.1007/s10803-011-1356-0.
Mazurek, M. O. (2013). Social media use among adults with autism spectrum disorders. *Computers in Human Behavior, 29*(4), 1709–1714. https://doi.org/10.1016/j.chb.2013.02.004.
Mazurek, M. O. (2014). Loneliness, friendship, and well-being in adults with autism spectrum disorders. *Autism, 18*(3), 223–232. https://doi.org/10.1177/1362361312474121.
McDougall, J., Evans, J., & Baldwin, P. (2010). The importance of self-determination to perceived quality of life for youth and young adults with chronic conditions and disabilities. *Remedial and Special Education, 31*(4), 252–260. https://doi.org/10.1177/0741932509355989.
Michael, C. (2016). Why we need research about autism and ageing. *Autism, 20*(5), 515–516. https://doi.org/10.1177/1362361316647224.
Milton, D. (2014). So what exactly are autism interventions intervening with? *Good Autism Practice, 15*(w), 6–14.
Montgomery, J. M., Schwean, V. L., Burt, J.-A. G., Dyke, D. I., Thorne, K. J., Hindes, Y. L., … Kohut, C. S. (2008). Emotional intelligence and resiliency in young adults with Asperger's Disorder. *Canadian Journal of School Psychology, 23*(1), 70–93. https://doi.org/10.1177/0829573508316594.
Müller, E., Schuler, A., & Yates, G. B. (2008). Social challenges and supports from the perspective of individuals with Asperger syndrome and other autism spectrum disabilities. *Autism, 12*(2), 173–190. https://doi.org/10.1177/1362361307086664.
National Autism Center (NAC). (2015). *Findings and conclusions: National standards project Phase 2*. Retrieved from http://www.nationalautismcenter.org/national-standards-project/phase-2/.

Nylander, L., & Gillberg, C. (2001). Screening for autism spectrum disorders in adult psychiatric out-patients: A preliminary report. *Acta Psychiatrica Scandinavica, 103*(6), 428–434. https://doi.org/10.1034/j.1600-0447.2001.00175.x.

Orinstein, A. J., Helt, M., Troyb, E., Tyson, K. E., Barton, M. L., Eigsti, I. M., ... Fein, D. A. (2014). Intervention for optimal outcome in children and adolescents with a history of autism. *Journal of Developmental & Behavioral Pediatrics, 35*(4), 247–256. https://doi.org/10.1097/dbp.0000000000000037.

Orsmond, G. I., Shattuck, P. T., Cooper, B. P., Sterzing, P. R., & Anderson, K. A. (2013). Social participation among young adults with an autism spectrum disorder. *Journal of Autism and Developmental Disorders, 43*(11), 2710–2719. https://doi.org/10.1007/s10803-013-1833-8.

Pellicano, E., Dinsmore, A., & Charman, T. (2014). What should autism research focus upon? Community views and priorities from the United Kingdom. *Autism, 18*(7), 756–770. https://doi.org/10.1177/1362361314529627.

Piven, J., & Rabins, P. (2011). Autism spectrum disorders in older adults: Toward defining a research agenda. *Journal of the American Geriatrics Society, 59*(11), 2151–2155. https://doi.org/10.1111/j.1532-5415.2011.03632.x.

Prior, M., Roberts, J. M. A., Rodger, S., Williams, K., & Sutherland, R. (2011). *A review of the research to identify the most effective models of practice in early intervention of children with autism spectrum disorders*. Australia: Australian Government Department of Families, Housing, Community Services and Indigenous Affairs.

Ritvo, R. A., Ritvo, E. R., Guthrie, D., Yuwiler, A., Ritvo, M. J., & Weisbender, L. (2008). A scale to assist the diagnosis of autism and Asperger's disorder in adults (RAADS): A pilot study. *Journal of Autism and Developmental Disorders, 38*(2), 213–223. https://doi.org/10.1007/s10803-007-0380-6.

Roux, A. M., Shattuck, P. T., Cooper, B. P., Anderson, K. A., Wagner, M., & Narendorf, S. C. (2013). Postsecondary employment experiences among young adults with an autism spectrum disorder. *Journal of the American Academy of Child and Adolescent Psychiatry, 52*(9), 931–939. https://doi.org/10.1016/j.jaac.2013.05.019.

Roy, M., & Balaratnasingam, S. (2010). Missed diagnosis of autism in an Australian indigenous psychiatric population. *Australas Psychiatry, 18*(6), 534–537. https://doi.org/10.3109/10398562.2010.498048.

Samson, A. C., & Antonelli, Y. (2013). Humor as character strength and its relation to life satisfaction and happiness in Autism Spectrum Disorders. *Humor, 26*(3). https://doi.org/10.1515/humor-2013-0031.

Seltzer, M. M., Krauss, M. W., Shattuck, P. T., Orsmond, G. I., Swe, A., & Lord, C. (2003). The symptoms of autism spectrum disorders in adolescence and adulthood. *Journal of Autism and Developmental Disorders, 33*(6), 565–581. https://doi.org/10.1023/b:jadd.0000005995.02453.0b.

Seltzer, M. M., Shattuck, P., Abbeduto, L., & Greenberg, J. S. (2004). Trajectory of development in adolescents and adults with autism. *Mental Retardation and Developmental Disabilities Research Reviews, 10*(4), 234–247. https://doi.org/10.1002/mrdd.20038.

Shattuck, P. T., Narendorf, S. C., Cooper, B., Sterzing, P. R., Wagner, M., & Taylor, J. L. (2012). Postsecondary education and employment among youth with an autism spectrum disorder. *Pediatrics*, 2011–2864. https://doi.org/10.1542/peds.2011-2864.

Shattuck, P. T., Seltzer, M. M., Greenberg, J. S., Orsmond, G. I., Bolt, D., Kring, S., ... Lord, C. (2007). Change in autism symptoms and maladaptive behaviors in adolescents and adults with an autism spectrum disorder. *Journal of Autism and Developmental Disorders, 37*(9), 1735–1747. https://doi.org/10.1007/s10803-006-0307-7.

Shore, S. (2003a). My life with Asperger syndrome. In R. W. DuCharme & T. P. Gulotta (Eds.), *Asperger syndrome a guide for professionals and families* (pp. 189–209). Boston, MA: Springer.

Shore, S. M. (2003b). *Beyond the wall: Personal experiences with autism and Asperger syndrome*. Shawnee Mission, KS: AAPC Publishing.

Silberman, S. (2015). *Neurotribes: The legacy of autism and the future of neurodiversity*. New York: Avery, an imprint of Penguin Random House.

Simpson, R. L. (2005). Evidence-based practices and students with autism spectrum disorders. *Focus on Autism and Other Developmental Disabilities, 20*(3), 140–149. https://doi.org/10.1177/10883576050200030201.

Stevenson, J. L., Harp, B., & Gernsbacher, M. A. (2011). Infantilizing autism. *Disability Studies Quarterly, 31*(3), 17–24.

Stokes, M., Newton, N., & Kaur, A. (2007). Stalking, and social and romantic functioning among adolescents and adults with autism spectrum disorder. *Journal of Autism and Developmental Disorders, 37*(10), 1969–1986. https://doi.org/10.1007/s10803-006-0344-2.

Strunz, S., Schermuck, C., Ballerstein, S., Ahlers, C. J., Dziobek, I., & Roepke, S. (2017). Romantic relationships and relationship satisfaction among adults with Asperger syndrome and high-functioning autism. *Journal of Clinical Psychology, 73*(1), 113–125. https://doi.org/10.1002/jclp.22319.

Sutera, S., Pandey, J., Esser, E. L., Rosenthal, M. A., Wilson, L. B., Barton, M., … Fein, D. (2007). Predictors of optimal outcome in toddlers diagnosed with autism spectrum disorders. *Journal of Autism and Developmental Disorders, 37*(1), 98–107. https://doi.org/10.1007/s10803-006-0340-6.

Tobin, M. C., Drager, K. D. R., & Richardson, L. F. (2014). A systematic review of social participation for adults with autism spectrum disorders: Support, social functioning, and quality of life. *Research in Autism Spectrum Disorders, 8*(3), 214–229. https://doi.org/10.1016/j.rasd.2013.12.002.

Valentine, K., Rajkovic, M., Dinning, B., & Thompson, D. (2010). *Occasional paper no. 35: Post-diagnosis support for children with autism spectrum disorder, their families and carers*. Canberra: Research Publications Unit.

Vannucchi, G., Masi, G., Toni, C., Dell'Osso, L., Marazziti, D., & Perugi, G. (2014). Clinical features, developmental course, and psychiatric comorbidity of adult autism spectrum disorders. *CNS Spectrums, 19*(2), 157–164.

Vermeulen, P. (2014). The practice of promoting happiness in autism. In E. Hurley & G. Jones (Eds.), *Good autism practice: Autism, happiness and wellbeing* (pp. 8–17). Birmingham: British Institute of Learning Difficulties.

Volkmar, F. R., Reichow, B., McPartland, J. C., & Ebooks, C. (2014). *Adolescents and adults with autism spectrum disorders* (Vol. 1). New York, NY: Springer.

Webster, A. A., & Garvis, S. (2017). The importance of critical life moments: An explorative study of successful women with autism spectrum disorder. *Autism, 21*(6), 670–677. https://doi.org/10.1177/1362361316677719.

Wehmeyer, M. L. (2013). *The Oxford handbook of positive psychology and disability*. New York: Oxford University Press.

Wehmeyer, M. L., Kelchner, K., & Richards, S. (1996). Essential characteristics of self-determined behavior of individuals with mental retardation. *American Journal of Mental Retardation, 100*(6), 632–642.

Wehmeyer, M. L., Palmer, S. B., Lee, Y., Williams-Diehm, K., & Shogren, K. A. (2011). A randomized-trial evaluation of the effect of whose future is it anyway? on self-determination. *Career Development for Exceptional Individuals, 34*(1), 45–56. https://doi.org/10.1177/0885728810383559.

Wehmeyer, M. L., & Schwartz, M. (1997). Self-determination and positive adult outcomes: A follow-up study of youth with mental retardation or learning disabilities. *Exceptional Children, 63*(2), 245–255. https://doi.org/10.1177/001440299706300207.

Wolfe, C. (2013). *Learning from Temple Grandin, or, animal studies, disability studies, and who comes after the subject* (pp. 91–106). Lewisburg: Bucknell University Press.

Wolff, S. (2004). The history of Autism. *European Child & Adolescent Psychiatry, 13*, 201–208. https://doi.org/10.1007/s00787-004-0363-5.

Wong, C., Odom, S. L., Hume, K. A., Cox, A. W., Fettig, A., Kucharczyk, S., … Schultz, T. R. (2015). Evidence-based practices for children, youth, and young adults with autism spectrum disorder: A comprehensive review. *Journal of Autism and Developmental Disorders, 45*(7), 1951–1966. https://doi.org/10.1007/s10803-014-2351-z.

Woodman, A. C., Smith, L. E., Greenberg, J. S., & Mailick, M. R. (2015). Change in autism symptoms and maladaptive behaviors in adolescence and adulthood: The role of positive family processes. *Journal of Autism and Developmental Disorders, 45*(1), 111–126. https://doi.org/10.1007/s10803-014-2199-2.